Communications and Networking

edited by
Jun Peng

Communications and Networking

Edited by Boris Lembrikov

CBS, Edition 2016

Published by InTech

Janeza Trdine 9, 51000 Rijeka, Croatia

Publishing Process Manager Iva Lipovic

Technical Editor Goran Bajac

Cover Designer Martina Sirotic

Image Copyright Alex Staroseltsev, 2010. Used under license from Shutterstock.com

Additional hard copies can be obtained from orders@intechopen.com

Communications and Networking, Edited by Jun Peng
p. cm.
ISBN 978-953-307-114-5

Contents

Preface

This book "Communications and Networking" focuses on the issues at the lowest two layers of communications and networking and provides recent research results on some of these issues. In particular, it first introduces recent research results on many important issues at the physical layer and data link layer of communications and networking and then briefly shows some results on some other important topics such as security and the application of wireless networks.

This book has twenty one chapters that are authored by researchers across the world. Each chapter introduces not only a basic problem in communications and networking but also describes approaches to the problem. The data in most chapters are based on published research results and provide insights on the problems of the relevant chapters. Most chapters in this book also provide references for the relevant topics and interested readers might find these references useful if they would like to explore more on these topics.

Several chapters of this book focus on issues related to Orthogonal Frequency-Division Multiplexing (OFDM). For example, chapter 1 and chapter 2 are on channel estimation for OFDM-related systems. Chapter 3 is on cooperative relays in OFDM systems. Chapter 4 introduces some recent results on packet separation in OFDM based random access wireless networks. Chapter 4 is on sub-carrier matching and power allocation in oFDM-based multihop systems. Chapter 6 presents some results on performance evaluation of OFDM related systems.

Multiple chapters of this book are on coding, link capacity, throughput, and optimisation. For example, chapter 7 and chapter 9 are about source and channel coding in communications and networking. Chapter 8 is on link capacity in distributed antenna systems. Chapter 10 introduces throughput optimisation for UWB-based ad hoc networks. Chapter 12 presents some results on optimising radio networks.

This book also contains several chapter on forwarding, scheduling, and medium access control in communications and networking. In particular, chapter 13 introduces packet scheduling algorithms for communication networks. Chapter 14 is about reliable data forwarding in wireless sensor networks. Chapter 15 introduces cross-layer connection admission control in packetized systems. Chapter 16 presents advanced access schemes for future broadband wireless networks. Chapter 17 introduces medium access control in distributed wireless networks. Finally, chapter 18 is about cognitive radio networks.

In addition, this book has several chapters on some other issues of communications and networking. For example, chapter 19 is about security of wireless LANs and wireless multihop networks, chapter 20 is on localisation and tracking and chapter 21 introduces the use of mesh networks in tectonic monitoring.

In summary, this book covers a wide range of interesting topics of communications and networking. The introductions, data, and references in this book would help the readers know more about communications and networking and help them explore this exciting and fact-evolving field.

Editor

Jun Peng
University of Texas - Pan American,
Edinburg, Texas,
United States of America

1

Transform Domain based Channel Estimation for 3GPP/LTE Systems

Moussa Diallo[1], Rodrigue Rabineau[1], Laurent Cariou[1] and Maryline Hélard[2]
[1]Orange Labs, 4 rue du Clos Courtel, 35512 Cesson-Sévigné Cedex,
[2]INSA Rennes, 20 Avenue des Buttes de Coesmes, 35700 Rennes Cedex
France

1. Introduction

Orthogonal frequency division multiplexing (OFDM) is now well known as a powefull modulation scheme for high data rate wireless communications owing to its many advantages, notably its high spectral efficiency, mitigation of intersymbol interference (ISI), robustness to frequency selective fading environment, as well as the feasibility of low cost transceivers [1].

On the other hand multiple input multiple output (MIMO) systems can also be efficiently used in order to increase diversity and improve performance of wireless systems [2] [3] [4]. Moreover, as OFDM allows a frequency selective channel to be considered as flat on each subcarrier, MIMO and OFDM techniques can be well combined. Therefore, MIMO-ODFM systems are now largely considered in the new generation of standards for wireless transmissions, such as 3GPP/LTE [5] [6].

In most MIMO-OFDM systems, channel estimation is required at the receiver side for all sub-carriers between each antenna link. Moreover, since radio channels are frequency selective and time-dependent channels, a dynamic channel estimation becomes necessary. For coherent MIMO-OFDM systems, channel estimation relies on training sequences adapted to the MIMO configuration and the channel characteristics [7] and based on OFDM channel estimation with pilot insertion, for which different techniques can be applied: preamble method and comb-type pilot method.

In order to estimate the channel of an OFDM systems, one's first apply least square (LS) algorithm to estimate the channel on the pilot tones in the frequency domain. A second step can be performed to improve the quality of the estimation and provide interpolation to find estimates on all subcarriers. In a classical way, this second step is performed in the frequency domain. An alternative is to perform this second step by applying treatment in a transform domain, that can be reached after a discrete Fourier transform (DFT) or a discrete cosine transform (DCT), and called transform domain channel estimation (TD-CE). The DFT based method is considered as a promising method because it can provide very good results by significantly reducing the noise on the estimated channel coefficients [8]. However, some performance degradations may occur when the number of OFDM inverse fast fourier transform (IFFT) size is different from the number of modulated subcarriers [8]. This problem called "border effect" phenomenon is due to the insertion of null carriers at the spectrum extremities (virtual carriers) to limit interference with the adjacent channels, and can be encountered in most of multicarrier systems.

To cope for this problem, DCT has been proposed instead of DFT, for its capacity to reduce the high frequency components in the transform domain [9]. Its improvements are however not sufficient in systems designed with a great amount of virtual subcarriers, which suffer from a huge border effect [10]. This is the case of a 3GPP/LTE system.

The aim of the paper is to study, for a 3GPP/LTE system, two improved DCT based channel estimations, designed to correctly solve the problem of null carriers at the border of the spectrum. These two TD-CE will also be compared in terms of performance and complexity. In the first approach, a truncated singular value decomposition (TSVD) of pilots matrix is used to mitigate the impact of the "border effect". The second approach is based on the division of the whole DCT window into 2 overlapping blocks.

The paper is organized as follows. Section II introduces the mobile wireless channel and briefly describes the MIMO-OFDM system with channel estimation component. Section III is dedicated to transform domain channel estimations (TD-CE), with description of the classical Least Square algorithm in III-A, and presents the conventional DFT and DCT based channel estimation in III-B and III-C, respectively. Next, the two proposed DCT based channel estimation are described in the sections IV and V. Finally, a performance evaluation and comparison is shown in section VI.

2. MIMO-OFDM system description

In this paper we consider a coherent MIMO-OFDM system, with N_t transmit antennas and N_r receive antennas. As shown in Fig.1, the MIMO scheme is first applied on data modulation symbols (e.g. PSK or QAM), then an OFDM modulation is performed per transmit antenna. Channel estimation is then required at receive side for both the one tap per sub-carrier equalization and the MIMO detection.

The OFDM signal transmitted from the i-th antenna after performing IFFT (OFDM modulation) to the frequency domain signal $X_i \in C^{N \times 1}$ can be given by:

$$x_i(n) = \sqrt{\frac{1}{N}} \sum_{k=0}^{N-1} X_i(k) e^{j\frac{2\pi kn}{N}}, \qquad 0 \leq (n,k) \leq N \tag{1}$$

where N is the number of FFT points.

The time domain channel response between the transmitting antenna i and the receiving antenna j under the multipath fading environments can be expressed by the following equation:

$$h_{ij}(n) = \sum_{l=0}^{L-1} h_{ij,l} \delta(n - \tau_{ij,l}) \tag{2}$$

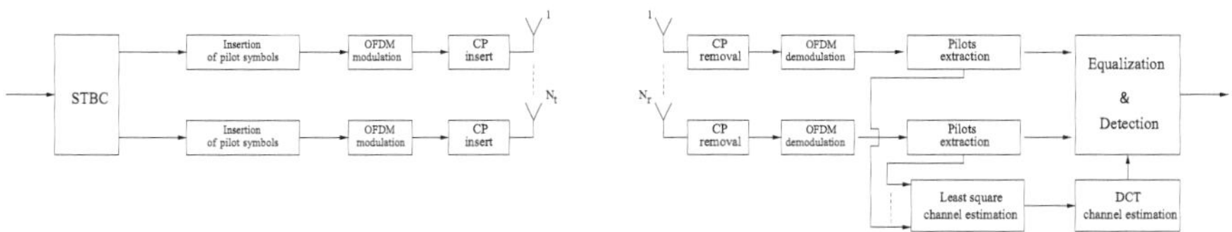

Fig. 1. MIMO-OFDM block diagram.

with L the number of paths, $h_{ij,l}$ and $\tau_{ij,l}$ the complex time varying channel coefficient and delay of the l-th path.

The use of a guard interval allows both the preservation of the orthogonality between the tones and the elimination of the inter symbol interference (ISI) between consecutive OFDM symbols. Thus by using (1) and (2), the received frequency domain signal is given by:

$$R_j(k) = \sum_{i=0}^{N_t-1} X_i(k)H_{ij}(k) + \Xi(k) \tag{3}$$

where $H_{ij}(k)$ is the discrete response of the channel on subcarrier k between the i-th transmit antenna and the j-th receive antenna and Ξ_k the zero-mean complex Gaussian noise after the FFT (OFDM demodulation) process.

3. Transform Domain Channel Estimation (TD-CE)

In a classical coherent SISO-OFDM system, channel estimation is required for OFDM demodulation. When no knowledge of the statistics on the channel is available, a least square (LS) algorithm can be used in order to estimate the frequency response on the known pilots that had been inserted in the transmit frame. An interpolation process allows then the estimation of the frequency response of the channel, i.e. for each sub-carrier. In a MIMO-OFDM system, since the received signal is a superposition of the transmitted signals, orthogonally between pilots is mandatory to get the channel estimation without co-antenna interference (CAI).

We choose to apply TD-CE to a 3GPP/LTE system where the orthogonality between training sequences is based on the simultaneous transmission on each subcarrier of pilot symbols on one antenna and null symbols on the other antennas as depicted in Fig.2.

A. Least Square channel estimation (LS)

Assuming orthogonality between pilots dedicated to each transmit antenna, the LS estimates can be expressed as follows:

$$H_{ij,LS} = H_{ij} + (diag(X))^{-1}\Xi. \tag{4}$$

Therefore LS estimates can be only calculated for $\frac{M}{N_t}$ subcarriers where M is the number of modulated subcarriers. Then interpolation has to be performed to obtain an estimation for all the subcarriers.

B. DFT based channel estimation

From (4), it can be observed that LS estimates can be strongly affected by a noise component. To improve the accuracy of the channel estimation, the DFT-based method has been proposed in order to reduce the noise component in the time domain [8]. Fig.3 illustrates the transform domain channel estimation process using DFT. After removing the unused subcarriers, the LS estimates are first converted into the time domain by the IDFT algorithm and a smoothing filter (as described in Fig.3) is applied in the time domain assuming that the maximum multi-path delay is within the cyclic prefix of the OFDM symbols. After the smoothing, the DFT is applied to return in the frequency domain.

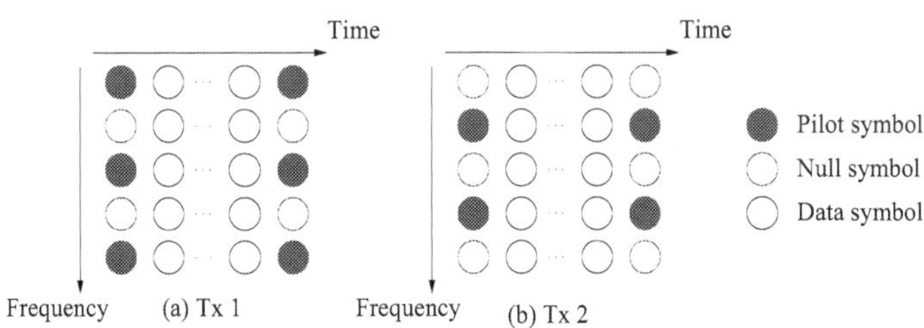

Fig. 2. Pilot insertion structure in 3GPP with $N_t = 2$.

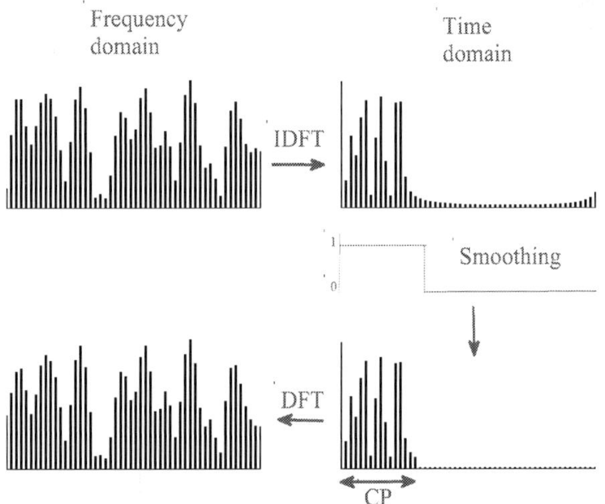

Fig. 3. Transform domain channel estimation process using DFT.

The time domain channel response of the LS estimated channel can be expressed by (5). From (4), it is possible to divide $h_{n,LS}^{IDFT}$ into two parts.

$$h_{n,LS}^{IDFT} = \sqrt{\frac{1}{M-1}} \sum_{k=0}^{M} H_{k,LS} e^{j\frac{2\pi nk}{M}}$$

$$= h_n^{IDFT} + \xi_n^{IDFT} \tag{5}$$

where ξ_n^{IDFT} is the noise component in the time domain and h_n^{IDFT} is the IDFT of the LS estimated channel without noise which is developed as:

$$h_n^{IDFT} = \sqrt{\frac{1}{M}} \sum_{l=0}^{L-1} h_l e^{-j\pi\tau_l(1-\frac{M}{N})} \sum_{k=0}^{M-1} e^{-j\frac{2\pi k}{M}(\frac{M}{N}\tau_l - n)} \tag{6}$$

It can be easily seen from (6) that if the number of FFT points N is equal to the number of modulated subcarriers M, the impulse response h_n^{IDFT} will exist only from $n = 0$ to $L - 1$, with the same form as (2), i.e the true channel.

Nevertheless when $N > M$, the last term of (6) $\sum_{k=0}^{M-1} e^{-j\frac{2\pi k}{M}(\frac{M}{N}\tau_l - n)}$ can be expressed as.

$$
\begin{cases}
M & \dfrac{M / hcf(M,N)}{N / hcf(M,N)}\tau_l : \le L \ \ and \in \mathbb{N} \\[2em]
\dfrac{1 - e^{-j2\pi(\frac{M}{N}\tau_l - n)}}{1 - e^{-j\frac{2\pi}{M}(\frac{M}{N}\tau_l - n)}} & otherwise
\end{cases}
\tag{7}
$$

where hcf is the <u>highest</u> common factor and $\mathbb{N}$ natural integer.
From (7) it is important to note that:
- On the one hand, the channel taps are not all completely retrieved in the first CP samples of the channel impulse response.
- On the other hand, the impulse channel response obviously exceeds the Guard Interval (CP). This phenomenon is called Inter-Taps Interference (ITI). Removing the ITI by the smoothing filter generates the "border effect" phenomenon.

C. DCT based channel estimation

The DCT based channel estimator can be realized by replacing IDFT and DFT (as shown in Fig.3) by DCT and IDCT, respectively. DCT conceptually extends the original M points sequence to $2M$ points sequence by a mirror extension of the M points sequence [12]. As illustrated by Fig. 4, the waveform will be smoother and more continuous in the boundary between consecutive periods.

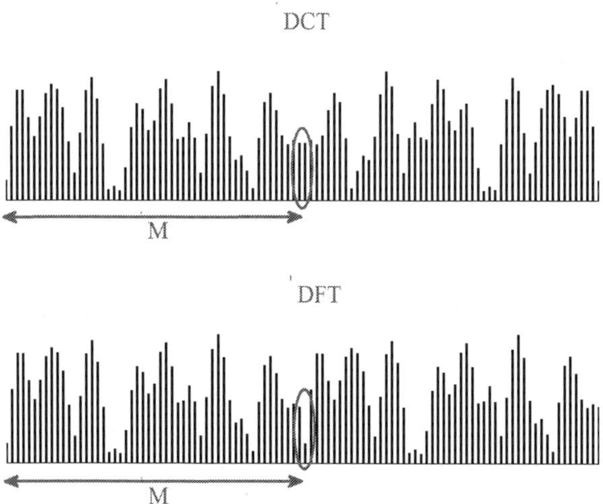

Fig. 4. DCT and DFT principle.

The channel impulse response in the transform domain is given by:

$$h_{n,LS}^{DCT} = V_n^M \sum_{k=0}^{M-1} H_{k,LS}.cos\frac{\pi(2k+1)n}{2M} \tag{8}$$

where V_n^M is the coefficient of DCT which can take two different values, depending on the value of n.

$$V_n^M = \begin{cases} \sqrt{1/M} & n=0 \\ \sqrt{2/M} & n \neq 0 \end{cases} \tag{9}$$

From the DCT calculation and the multi-path channel characteristics, the impulse response given by (8) is concentrated at lower order components in the transform domain. It is important to note that the level of impulse response at the order higher than N_{max} is not null, but can be considered as negligible; this constitutes the great interest of the DCT. The channel response in the transform domain can be expressed by:

$$h_n^{DCT} = \begin{cases} h_{n,LS}^{DCT} & 0 \leq n \leq N_{max} - 1 \\ 0 & N_{max} \leq n \leq M-1 \end{cases} \tag{10}$$

The frequency channel response is then given by:

$$H_k^{DCT} = \sum_{n=0}^{M-1} V_n^M.h_n^{DCT}.cos\frac{\pi(2k+1)n}{2M} \tag{11}$$

As a summary of this conventional DCT based estimation, it is important to note this following remark:
In the conventional DCT based method, the ITI is less important than in DFT one but a residual "border effect" is still present.

4. DCT with TSVD based channel estimation

In the classical DCT approach, it is shown that all the channel paths are retrieved. Nevertheless, the residual ITI will cause the "border effect". The following approach is a mixture of Zero Forcing (ZF) and a truncated singular value decomposition in order to reduce the impact of null subcarriers in the spectrum [13]. The DCT transfer matrix C of size $N \times N$ can be defined with the following expression:

$$C = \begin{bmatrix} 1 & 1 & \dots & 1 \\ 1 & D_N & \dots & D_N(2N+1) \\ \vdots & \vdots & \dots & \vdots \\ 1 & D_N(N-1) & \dots & D_N((2N+1)(N-1)) \end{bmatrix} \tag{12}$$

where $D_N(kn) = V_n^N.cos(\frac{\pi}{2N}(2k+1)(n))$.

To accommodate the non-modulated carriers, it is necessary to remove the rows of the matrix C corresponding to the position of null subcarriers (see Fig.2). From (10), we can just use the first N_{max} columns of C. Hence the DCT transfer matrix becomes: $\tilde{C}'_i = C(\frac{N-M}{2}+i:N_t:\frac{N+M}{2}-1,1:N_{max})$ where $0 \le i \le N_t$ is the transmit antenna index.

Let us rewrite (8) in a matrix form:

$$h_{LS}^{DCT} = \tilde{C}'.H_{LS} \tag{13}$$

To mitigate the ITI, the first step of this new approach is to apply the ZF criterion [14]:

$$h_{LS}^{IDCT-ZF} = (\tilde{C}'^H\tilde{C}')^{-1}\tilde{C}'^H H_{LS} = \tilde{C}'^\dagger H_{LS} \tag{14}$$

The main problem arises when the condition number (CN) of $\tilde{C}'^H\tilde{C}'$, defined by the ratio between the greater and the lower singular value, becomes high. Fig.5 shows the behavior of the singular value of $\tilde{C}'^H\tilde{C}'$ whether null carriers are placed at the edge of the spectrum or not. When all the subcarriers are modulated, the singular values are all the same and the CN is equal to 1. However, when null carriers are placed at the edges of the spectrum, the CN becomes very high. For instance, as we can see in Fig.5, if $N = 1024$, $N_{max} = 84$ and $M = 600$ as in 3GPP, the CN is 2.66×10^{16}.

To reduce the "border effect", i.e the impact of ITI, it is necessary to have a small condition number. The second step of this new approach is to consider the truncated singular value decomposition (TSVD) of the matrix $\tilde{C}'^H\tilde{C}'$ of rank N_{max}.

Fig.6 shows the block diagram of the DCT based channel estimation and the proposed scheme. In the proposed scheme (Fig.6(b)), after performing the SVD of the matrix $\tilde{C}'^H\tilde{C}'$, we propose to only consider the T_h most important singular values among the N_{max} in order to reduce the CN. The TSVD solution is defined by:

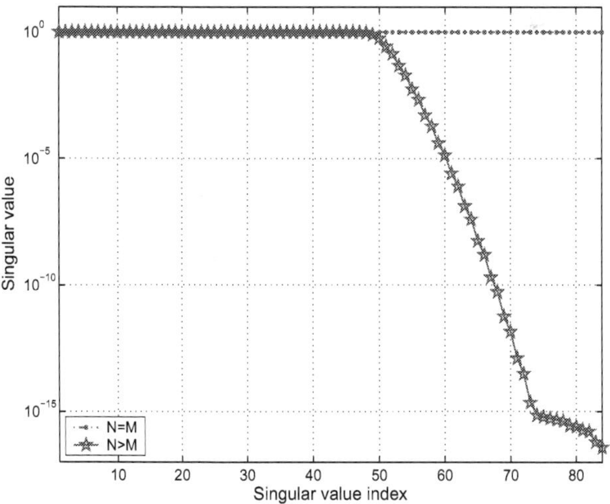

Fig. 5. Singular value of $\tilde{C}'^H\tilde{C}'$ with $N_{max} = 84$, $CP = 72$ and $N = M = 1024$ or $N = 1024$, $M = 600$

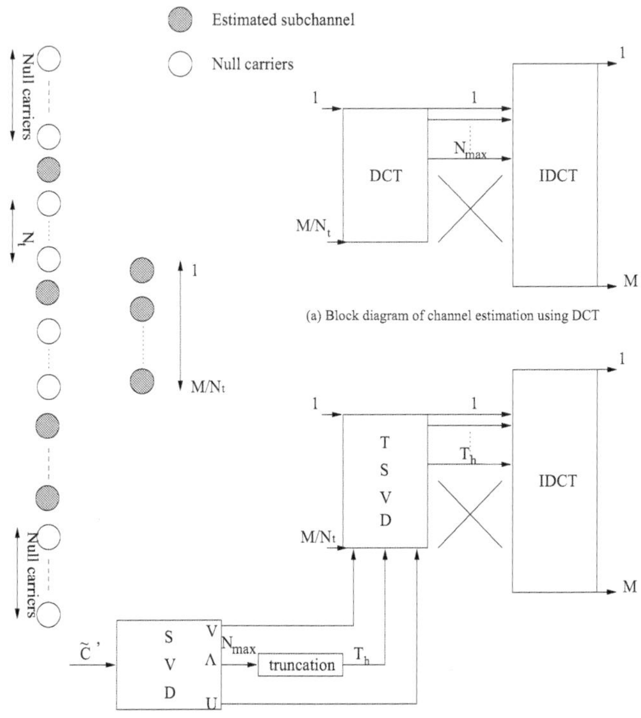

Fig. 6. Block diagram of channel estimation using DCT and the proposed scheme.

$$h_{n,LS}^{DCT-ZF-TSVD} = \sum_{s=1}^{T_h} \frac{u_s^H H_{n,LS}}{\sigma_s} v_s \tag{15}$$

where T_h is the threshold, u_s, v_s and σ_s are the left singular vector, the right singular vector and the singular values of $\tilde{C}'$.
An IDCT ($\tilde{C}'^H$) is then used to get back to the frequency domain.

$$H_k^{DCT-ZF-TSVD} = C^{global} = \tilde{C}'^H \tilde{C}'^\dagger \tag{16}$$

T_h ($\in 1, 2, ...,N_{max}$) can be viewed as a compromise between the accuracy on pseudo-inverse calculation and the CN reduction. The adjustment of T_h is primarily to enhance the channel estimation quality. Its value depends only on the system parameters (position of the null carriers), which is predefined and known at the receiver side. T_h can be in consequence calculated in advance for any MIMO-OFDM system. To find a good value of T_h, is important to master its effect on the channel estimation i.e on the matrix $C^{global} \in \mathbb{C}^{M/N_t \times M}$. As an example, Fig.7 shows the behavior of the M/N_t singular values of C^{global} for different T_h where CP = 72, N = 1024, M = 600 and N_t = 4.

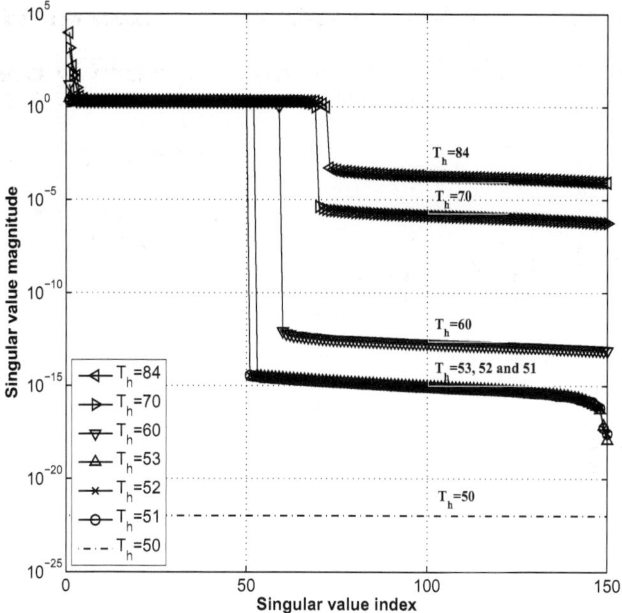

Fig. 7. Singular values of $\tilde{C}'^{H}\tilde{C}'^{t}$ with $CP = 72$, $N = 1024$ and $M = 600$ for different values of T_h

For $T_h = 51, 52, 53$ the singular values of C^{global} are the same on the first T_h samples and almost zero for others samples. We can consider that the rank of the matrix C^{global} becomes T_h instead of N_{max}. Therefore the noise effect is minimized and CN is equal to 1.

However, all the singular values become null when $T_h = 50$ due to a very large loss of energy. As illustrated by the Fig.8 which is a zoom of Fig.7 on the first singular values, their behavior can not be considered as a constant for $T_h = 60, 70, 84$ and then the CN becomes higher.

5. DCT with 2 overlapping blocks

The principle of this approach is to divide the whole DCT window into R blocks as proposed in [18]. In this paper we consider $R = 2$, that was demonstrated to reach same bit error rate (BER) performance that higher R values.

As illustrated in Fig.9, the concatenation of the 2 overlapping blocks cannot exceed N.

The classical DCT smoothing process described in the section III-C is applied to each 2 blocks of size $N/2$ by keeping only the energy of the channel in the first $Nmax/2$ samples. However, the residual ITI causes "border effect" on the edge of each block. Then, to recover the channel coefficients, we average the values in the overlapping windows between the different blocks except some subcarriers at the right and the left edge of block 1 and block 2 respectively as described in Fig.10.

The noise power is averaged on N samples instead of M in this approach. Thereby it presents a gain ($10log_{10}(\frac{N}{M})$) in comparison to the classical DCT based channel estimation.

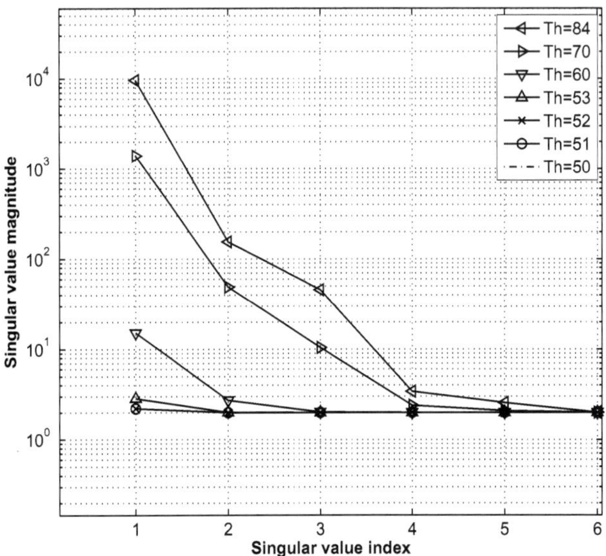

Fig. 8. Singular values of $\tilde{C}'^H\tilde{C}'^\dagger$ with $CP = 72$, $N = 1024$, $M = 600$ and $Nt = 4$ for different values of T_h

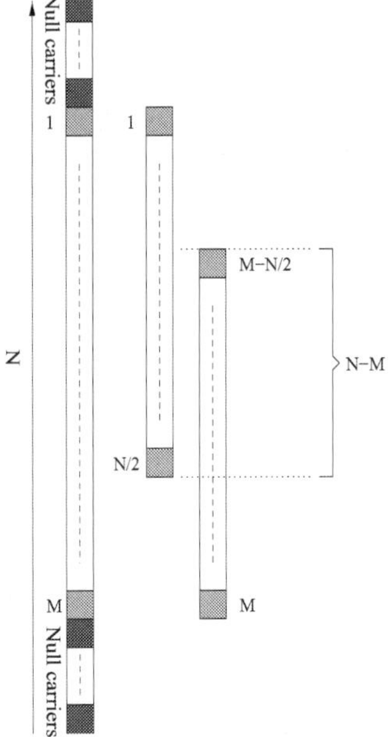

Fig. 9. Principle of the DCT with 2 overlapping blocks

2

Channel Estimation for Wireless OFDM Communications

Jia-Chin Lin
National Central University
Taiwan

1. Introduction

1.1 Preliminary

Orthogonal frequency-division multiplexing (OFDM) communication techniques have recently received significant research attention because of their ability to maintain effective transmission and highly efficient bandwidth utilization in the presence of various channel impairments, such as severely frequency-selective channel fades caused by long multipath delay spreads and impulsive noise (Bingham, 1990; Zou & Wu, 1995). In an OFDM system, a high-rate serial information-bearing symbol stream is split into many low-rate parallel streams; each of these streams individually modulates a mutually orthogonal sub-carrier. The spectrum of an individual sub-channel overlaps with those expanded from the adjacent sub-channels. However, the OFDM sub-carriers are orthogonal as long as they are synthesized such that the frequency separation between any two adjacent sub-carriers is exactly equal to the reciprocal of an OFDM block duration. A discrete Fourier transform (DFT) operation can perfectly produce this sub-carrier arrangement and its relevant modulations (Darlington, 1970; Weinstein & Ebert, 1971). Because of the advanced technologies incorporated into integrated circuit (IC) chips and digital signal processors (DSPs), OFDM has become a practical way to implement very effective modulation techniques for various applications. As a result, OFDM technologies have recently been chosen as candidates for 4th-generation (4G) mobile communications in a variety of standards, such as IEEE 802.16 (Marks, 2008) and IEEE 802.20 (Klerer, 2005) in the United States, and international research projects, such as EU-IST-MATRICE (MATRICE, 2005) and EU-IST-4MORE (4MORE, 2005) for 4G mobile communication standardization in Europe.

Regarding the history of OFDM, recall that Chang published a paper on the synthesis of band-limited signals for parallel multi-channel transmission in the 1960s (Chang, 1966). The author investigated a technique for transmitting and receiving (transceiving) parallel information through a linear band-limited channel without inter-channel interference (ICI) or inter-symbol interference (ISI). Saltzberg then conducted relevant performance evaluations and analyses (Saltzberg, 1967).

1.2 IFFT and FFT utilization: A/D realization of OFDM

A significant breakthrough in OFDM applicability was presented by Weinstein and Ebert in 1971 (Weinstein & Ebert, 1971). First, DFT and inverse DFT (IDFT) techniques were applied to OFDM implementation to perform base-band parallel sub-channel modulations and demodulations (or multiplexing and demultiplexing) (Weinstein & Ebert, 1971). This study provided an effective discrete-time signal processing method to simultaneously modulate (and demodulate) signals transmitted (and received) on various sub-channels without requiring the implementation of a bank of sub-carrier modulators with many analog multipliers and oscillators. Meanwhile, ISI can be significantly reduced by inserting a guard time-interval (GI) in between any two consecutive OFDM symbols and by applying a raised-cosine windowing method to the time-domain (TD) signals (Weinstein & Ebert, 1971). Although the system studied in this work cannot always maintain orthogonality among sub-carriers when operated over a time-dispersive channel, the application of IDFT and DFT to OFDM communication is not only a crucial contribution but also a critical driving force for commercial applicability of recent wireless OFDM communication because the fast algorithms of IDFT and DFT, i.e., inverse fast Fourier transform (IFFT) and fast Fourier transform (FFT), have been commercialized and popularly implemented with ASICs or sub-functions on DSPs.

1.3 Cyclic prefix

Orthogonality among sub-carriers cannot be maintained when an OFDM system operates over a time-dispersive channel. This problem was first addressed by Peled and Ruiz in 1980 (Peled & Ruiz, 1980). Rather than inserting a blank GI between any two consecutive OFDM symbols, which was the method employed in the previous study (Weinstein & Ebert, 1971), a cyclic extension of an OFDM block is inserted into the original GI as a prefix to an information-bearing OFDM block. The adopted cyclic prefix (CP) effectively converts the linear convolution of the transmitted symbol and the channel impulse response (CIR) into the cyclic convolution; thus, orthogonality among sub-carriers can be maintained with channel time-dispersion if the CP is sufficiently longer than the CIR. However, energy efficiency is inevitably sacrificed, as the CPs convey no desired information.

1.4 Applications

OFDM technology is currently employed in the European digital audio broadcasting (DAB) standard (DAB, 1995). In addition, digital TV broadcasting applications based on OFDM technology have been under comprehensive investigation (DVB, 1996; Couasnon et al., 1994; Marti et al., 1993; Moeneclaey & Bladel, 1993; Tourtier et al., 1993). Furthermore, OFDM technology in conjunction with other multiple-access techniques, in particular code-division multiple-access (CDMA) techniques, for mobile communications has also been the focus of a variety of research efforts (Hara & Prasad, 1997; Sourour & Nakagawa, 1996; Kondo & Milstein, 1996; Reiners & Rohling, 1994; Fazel, 1994). For those employed in wireline environments, OFDM communication systems are often called "Discrete Multi-Tone" (DMT) communications, which have also attracted a great deal of research attention as a technology that effectively achieves high-rate transmission on currently existing telephone networks (Bingham, 1990; Young et al., 1996; Chow, 1993; Tu, 1991). One of the major advantages of the OFDM technique is its robustness with multipath reception. OFDM applications often are expected to operate in a severely frequency-selective environment. Therefore, OFDM communication has recently been selected for various broadband mobile communications, e.g., 4G mobile communications. This chapter will focus on such applications.

1.5 System description and signal modelling

The primary idea behind OFDM communication is dividing an occupied frequency band into many parallel sub-channels to deliver information simultaneously. By maintaining sufficiently narrow sub-channel bandwidths, the signal propagating through an individual sub-channel experiences roughly frequency-flat (i.e., frequency-nonselective) channel fades. This arrangement can significantly reduce the complexity of the subsequent equalization sub-system. In particular, current broadband wireless communications are expected to be able to operate in severe multipath fading environments in which long delay spreads inherently exist because the signature/chip duration has become increasingly shorter. To enhance spectral (or bandwidth) efficiency, the spectra of adjacent sub-channels are set to overlap with one another. Meanwhile, the orthogonality among sub-carriers is maintained by setting the sub-carrier spacing (i.e., the frequency separation between two consecutive sub-carriers) to the reciprocal of an OFDM block duration.

By taking advantage of a CP, the orthogonality can be prevented from experiencing ICI even for transmission over a multipath channel (Peled & Ruiz, 1980). Although several variants of OFDM communication systems exist (Bingham, 1990; Weinstein & Ebert, 1971; Floch et al., 1995), CP-OFDM (Peled & Ruiz, 1980) is primarily considered in this section due to its popularity. A CP is obtained from the tail portion of an OFDM block and then prefixed into a transmitted block, as shown in Fig. 1.

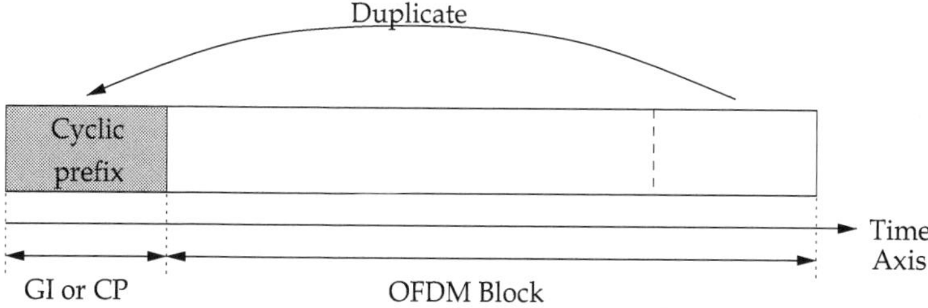

Fig. 1. An OFDM symbol consisting of a CP and an information-bearing OFDM block.

A portion of the transmitted OFDM symbol becomes periodic. The CP insertion converts the linear convolution of the CIR and the transmitted symbol into the circular convolution of the two. Therefore, CPs can avoid both ISI and ICI (Bingham, 1990). In this fundamental section, the following assumptions are made for simplicity: (1) a cyclic prefix is used; (2) the CIR length does not exceed the CP length; (3) the received signal can be perfectly synchronized; (4) noise is complex-valued, additive, white Gaussian noise (AWGN); and (5) channel time-variation is slow, so the channel can be considered to be constant or static within a few OFDM symbols.

1.5.1 Continuous-time model

A continuous-time base-band equivalent representation of an OFDM transceiver is depicted in Fig. 2. The OFDM communication system under study consists of N sub-carriers that occupy a total bandwidth of $B = \frac{1}{T_s}$ Hz. The length of an OFDM symbol is set to T_{sym} seconds; moreover, an OFDM symbol is composed of an OFDM block of length $T = NT_s$ and a CP of length T_g. The transmitting filter on the kth sub-carrier can be written as

$$p_k(t) = \begin{cases} \dfrac{1}{\sqrt{T}} e^{j2\pi \frac{B}{N} k(t - T_g)} & 0 \le t \le T_{sym} \\[2ex] 0 & \text{otherwise,} \end{cases} \tag{1}$$

where $T_{sym} = T + T_g$. Note that $p_k(t) = p_k(t + T)$ when t is within the guard interval $[0, T_g]$. It can be seen from Equation 1 that $p_k(t)$ is a rectangular pulse modulated by a sub-carrier with frequency $k \cdot \frac{B}{N}$. The transmitted signal $s_i(t)$ for the ith OFDM symbol can thus be obtained by summing over all modulated signals, i.e.,

$$s_i(t) = \sum_{k=0}^{N-1} X_{k,i} p_k \left(t - i T_{sym} \right), \tag{2}$$

where $X_{0,i}, X_{1,i}, \cdots, X_{N-1,i}$ are complex-valued information-bearing symbols, whose values are often mapped according to quaternary phase-shift keying (QPSK) or quadrature amplitude modulation (QAM). Therefore, the transmitted signal $s(t)$ can be considered to be a sequence of OFDM symbols, i.e.,

$$\begin{aligned} s(t) &= \sum_{i=-\infty}^{\infty} s_i(t) \\ &= \sum_{i=-\infty}^{\infty} \sum_{k=0}^{N-1} X_{k,i} p_k \left(t - i T_{sym} \right). \end{aligned} \tag{3}$$

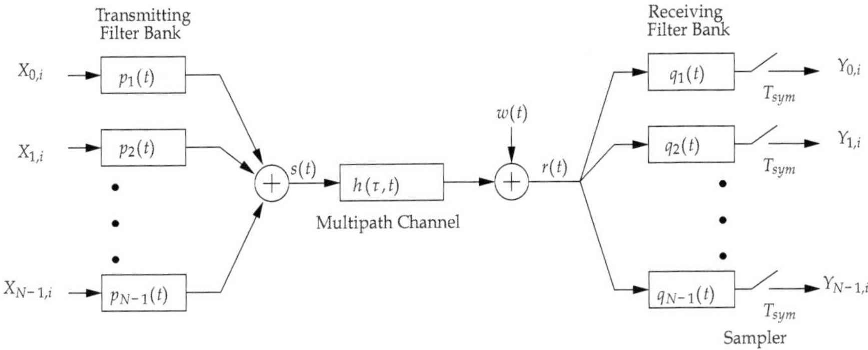

Fig. 2. Continuous-time base-band equivalent representation of an OFDM transceiver.

If the length of the CIR $h(\tau, t)$ does not exceed the CP length T_g, the received signal $r(t)$ can be written as

$$\begin{aligned} r(t) &= \left(h * s \right)(t) + w(t) \\ &= \int_0^{T_g} h(\tau, t) s(t - \tau) d\tau + w(t), \end{aligned} \tag{4}$$

where the operator "$*$" represents the linear convolution and $w(t)$ is an AWGN.

At the receiving end, a bank of filters is employed to match the last part $[T_g, T_{sym}]$ of the transmitted waveforms $p_k(t)$ on a subchannel-by-subchannel basis. By taking advantage of matched filter (MF) theory, the receiving filter on the kth sub-channel can be designed to have the following impulse response:

$$q_k(t) = \begin{cases} p_k^*\left(T_{sym} - t\right), & 0 \le t < T = T_{sym} - T_g \\ 0, & \text{otherwise.} \end{cases} \qquad (5)$$

Because the CP can effectively separate symbol dispersion from preceding or succeeding symbols, the sampled outputs of the receiving filter bank convey negligible ISI. The time index i can be dropped for simplicity because the following derivations address the received signals on a symbol-by-symbol basis and the ISI is considered to be negligible. Using Equations 3, 4 and 5, the sampled output of the kth receiving MF can be written as

$$
\begin{aligned}
Y_k &= \left(r * q_k\right)(t)\Big|_{t=T_{sym}} \\[2mm]
&= \int_{-\infty}^{\infty} r(\varsigma)q_k\left(T_{sym} - \varsigma\right)d\varsigma \\[2mm]
&= \int_{T_g}^{T_{sym}} \left(\int_0^{T_g} h(\tau,t)s(\varsigma - \tau)d\tau + w(\varsigma) \right) p_k^*(\varsigma)d\varsigma \\[2mm]
&= \int_{T_g}^{T_{sym}} \left(\int_0^{T_g} h(\tau,t)\left[\sum_{l=0}^{N-1} X_l p_l(\varsigma - \tau) \right] d\tau \right) p_k^*(\varsigma)d\varsigma + \int_{T_g}^{T_{sym}} w(\varsigma)p_k^*(\varsigma)d\varsigma.
\end{aligned}
\qquad (6)
$$

It is assumed that although the CIR is time-varying, it does not significantly change within a few OFDM symbols. Therefore, the CIR can be further represented as $h(\tau)$. Equation 6 can thus be rewritten as

$$
Y_k = \sum_{l=0}^{N-1} X_l \int_{T_g}^{T_{sym}} \left(\int_0^{T_g} h(\tau)p_l(\varsigma - \tau)d\tau \right) p_k^*(\varsigma)d\varsigma + \int_{T_g}^{T_{sym}} w(\varsigma)p_k^*(\varsigma)d\varsigma.
\qquad (7)
$$

From Equation 7, if $T_g < \varsigma < T_{sym}$ and $0 < \tau < T_g$, then $0 < \varsigma - \tau < T_{sym}$. Therefore, by substituting Equation 1 into Equation 7, the inner-most integral of Equation 7 can be reformulated as

$$
\begin{aligned}
\int_0^{T_g} h(\tau)p_l(\varsigma - \tau)d\tau &= \int_0^{T_g} h(\tau)\frac{e^{j2\pi l(\varsigma-\tau-T_g)B/N}}{\sqrt{T}}d\tau \\[2mm]
&= \frac{e^{j2\pi l(\varsigma-T_g)B/N}}{\sqrt{T}} \int_0^{T_g} h(\tau)e^{-j2\pi l\tau B/N}d\tau, \quad T_g < \varsigma < T_{sym}.
\end{aligned}
\qquad (8)
$$

Furthermore, the integration in Equation 8 can be considered to be the channel weight of the lth sub-channel, whose sub-carrier frequency is $f = lB/N$, i.e.,

$$
H_l = H\left(l\frac{B}{N}\right) = \int_0^{T_g} h(\tau)e^{-j2\pi l\tau B/N}d\tau,
\qquad (9)
$$

where $H(f)$ denotes the channel transfer function (CTF) and is thus the Fourier transform of $h(\tau)$. The output of the kth receiving MF can therefore be rewritten as

$$
\begin{aligned}
Y_k &= \sum_{l=0}^{N-1} X_l \int_{T_g}^{T_{sym}} \frac{e^{j2\pi l(\varsigma - T_g)B/N}}{\sqrt{T}} H_l p_k^*(\varsigma)d\varsigma + \int_{T_g}^{T_{sym}} w(\varsigma)p_k^*(\varsigma)d\varsigma \\
&= \sum_{l=0}^{N-1} X_l H_l \int_{T_g}^{T_{sym}} p_l(\varsigma)p_k^*(\varsigma)d\varsigma + W_k,
\end{aligned}
\tag{10}
$$

where

$$
W_k = \int_{T_g}^{T_{sym}} w(\varsigma)p_k^*(\varsigma)d\varsigma.
$$

The transmitting filters $p_k(t)$, $k = 0,1, \cdots, N-1$ employed here are mutually orthogonal, i.e.,

$$
\begin{aligned}
\int_{T_g}^{T_{sym}} p_l(t)p_k^*(t)dt &= \int_{T_g}^{T_{sym}} \frac{e^{j2\pi l(t-T_g)B/N}}{\sqrt{T}} \frac{e^{-j2\pi k(t-T_g)B/N}}{\sqrt{T}} dt \\
&= \delta[k-l],
\end{aligned}
\tag{11}
$$

where

$$
\delta[k-l] = \begin{cases} 1 & k = l \\ 0 & \text{otherwise} \end{cases}
$$

is the Kronecker delta function. Therefore, Equation 10 can be reformulated as

$$
Y_k = H_k X_k + W_k, \qquad k = 0,1,\cdots,N-1,
\tag{12}
$$

where W_k is the AWGN of the kth sub-channel. As a result, the OFDM communication system can be considered to be a set of parallel frequency-flat (frequency-nonselective) fading sub-channels with uncorrelated noise, as depicted in Fig. 3.

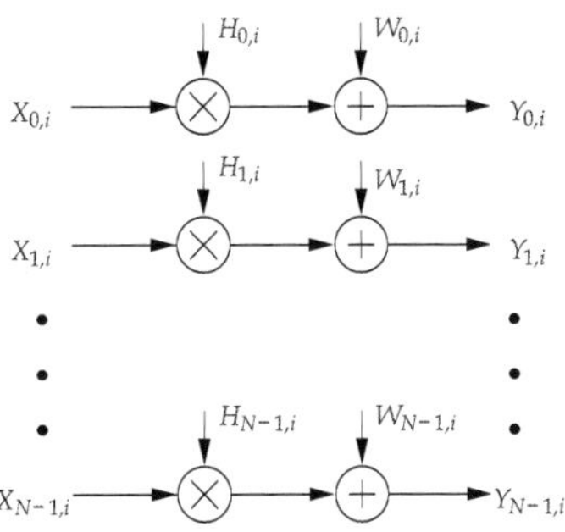

Fig. 3. OFDM communication is converted to transmission over parallel frequency-flat sub-channels.

1.5.2 Discrete-time model

A fully discrete-time representation of the OFDM communication system studied here is depicted in Fig. 4. The modulation and demodulation operations in the continuous-time model have been replaced by IDFT and DFT operations, respectively, and the channel has been replaced by a discrete-time channel.

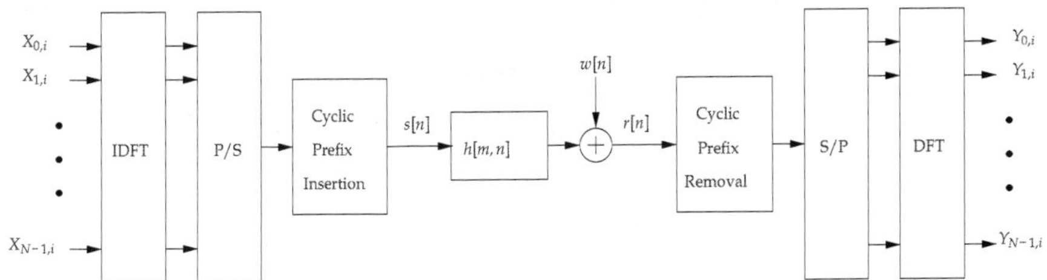

Fig. 4. Discrete-time representation of a base-band equivalent OFDM communication system.

If the CP is longer than the CIR, then the linear convolution operation can be converted to a cyclic convolution. The cyclic convolution is denoted as '$\otimes$' in this chapter. The ith block of the received signals can be written as

$$\begin{aligned}
\mathbf{Y}_i &= \mathrm{DFT}_N\left\{\mathrm{IDFT}_N\left\{\mathbf{X}_i\right\}\otimes\mathbf{h}_i+\mathbf{w}_i\right\}\\
&= \mathrm{DFT}_N\left\{\mathrm{IDFT}_N\left\{\mathbf{X}_i\right\}\otimes\mathbf{h}_i\right\}+\mathbf{W}_i,
\end{aligned} \tag{13}$$

where $\mathbf{Y}_i = [Y_{0,i}\ Y_{1,i}\ \cdots\ Y_{N-1,i}]^T$ is an $N \times 1$ vector, and its elements represent N demodulated symbols; $\mathbf{X}_i = [X_{0,i}\ X_{1,i}\ \cdots\ X_{N-1,i}]^T$ is an $N \times 1$ vector, and its elements represent N transmitted information-bearing symbols; $\mathbf{h}_i = [h_{0,i}\ h_{1,i}\ \cdots\ h_{N-1,i}]^T$ is an $N \times 1$ vector, and its elements represent the CIR padded with sufficient zeros to have N dimensions; and $\mathbf{w}_i = [w_{0,i}\ w_{1,i}\ \cdots\ w_{N-1,i}]^T$ is an $N \times 1$ vector representing noise. Because the noise is assumed to be white, Gaussian and circularly symmetric, the noise term

$$\mathbf{W}_i = \mathrm{DFT}_N(\mathbf{w}_i) \tag{14}$$

represents uncorrelated Gaussian noise, and $W_{k,i}$ and $w_{n,i}$ can be proven to have the same variance according to the Central Limit Theorem (CLT). Furthermore, if a new operator $"\odot"$ is defined to be element-by-element multiplication, Equation 13 can be rewritten as

$$\begin{aligned}
\mathbf{Y}_i &= \mathbf{X}_i\odot\mathrm{DFT}_N\left\{\mathbf{h}_i\right\}+\mathbf{W}_i\\
&= \mathbf{X}_i\odot\mathbf{H}_i+\mathbf{W}_i,
\end{aligned} \tag{15}$$

where $\mathbf{H}_i = \mathrm{DFT}_N\{\mathbf{h}_i\}$ is the CTF. As a result, the same set of parallel frequency-flat sub-channels with noise as presented in the continuous-time model can be obtained.

Both the aforementioned continuous-time and discrete-time representations provide insight and serve the purpose of providing a friendly first step or entrance point for beginning readers. In my personal opinion, researchers that have more experience in communication fields may be more comfortable with the continuous-time model because summations, integrations and convolutions are employed in the modulation, demodulation and (CIR) filtering processes. Meanwhile, researchers that have more experience in signal processing fields may be more comfortable with the discrete-time model because vector and matrix operations are employed in the modulation, demodulation and (CIR) filtering processes. Although the discrete-time model may look neat, clear and reader-friendly, several presumptions should be noted and kept in mind. It is assumed that the symbol shaping is rectangular and that the frequency offset, ISI and ICI are negligible. The primary goal of this chapter is to highlight concepts and provide insight to beginning researchers and practical engineers rather than covering theories or theorems. As a result, the derivations shown in Sections 3 and 4 are close to the continuous-time representation, and those in Sections 5 and 6 are derived from the discrete-time representation.

2. Introduction to channel estimation on wireless OFDM communications

2.1 Preliminary

In practice, effective channel estimation (CE) techniques for coherent OFDM communications are highly desired for demodulating or detecting received signals, improving system performance and tracking time-varying multipath channels, especially for mobile OFDM because these techniques often operate in environments where signal reception is inevitably accompanied by wide Doppler spreads caused by dynamic surroundings and long multipath delay spreads caused by time-dispersion. Significant research efforts have focused on addressing various CE and subsequent equalization problems by estimating sub-channel gains or the CIR. CE techniques in OFDM systems often exploit several pilot symbols transceived at given locations on the frequency-time grid to determine the relevant channel parameters. Several previous studies have investigated the performance of CE techniques assisted by various allocation patterns of the pilot/training symbols (Coleri et al., 2002; Li et al., 2002; Yeh & Lin, 1999; Negi & Cioffi, 1998). Meanwhile, several prior CEs have simultaneously exploited both time-directional and frequency-directional correlations in the channel under investigation (Hoeher et al., 1997; Wilson et al., 1994; Hoeher, 1991). In practice, these two-dimensional (2D) estimators require 2D Wiener filters and are often too complicated to be implemented. Moreover, it is difficult to achieve any improvements by using a 2D estimator, while significant computational complexity is added (Sandell & Edfors, 1996). As a result, serially exploiting the correlation properties in the time and frequency directions may be preferred (Hoeher, 1991) for reduced complexity and good estimation performance. In mobile environments, channel tap-weighting coefficients often change rapidly. Thus, the comb-type pilot pattern, in which pilot symbols are inserted and continuously transmitted over specific pilot sub-channels in all OFDM blocks, is naturally preferred and highly desirable for effectively and accurately tracking channel time-variations (Negi & Cioffi, 1998; Wilson et al., 1994; Hoeher, 1991; Hsieh & Wei, 1998).

Several methods for allocating pilots on the time-frequency grid have been studied (Tufvesson & Maseng, 1997). Two primary pilot assignments are depicted in Fig. 5: the block-type pilot arrangement (BTPA), shown in Fig. 5(a), and the comb-type pilot arrangement (CTPA), shown in Fig. 5(b). In the BTPA, pilot signals are assigned in specific OFDM blocks to occupy all sub-channels and are transmitted periodically. Both in general and in theory, BTPA is more suitable in a slowly time-varying, but severely frequency-selective fading environment. No interpolation method in the FD is required because the pilot block occupies the whole band. As a result, the BTPA is relatively insensitive to severe

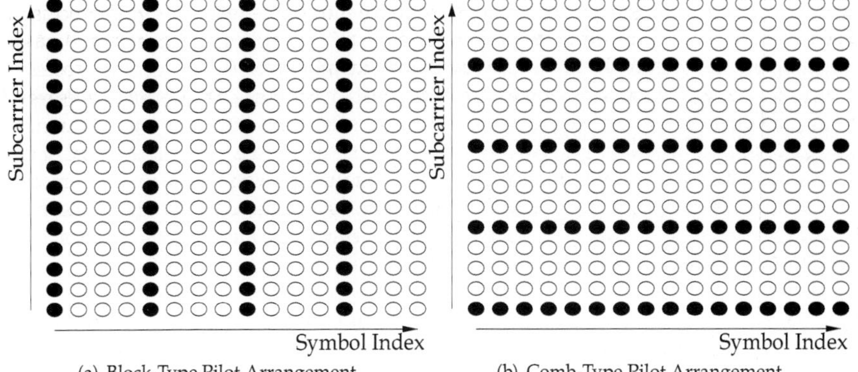

Fig. 5. Two primary pilot assignment methods

frequency selectivity in a multipath fading channel. Estimates of the CIR can usually be obtained by least-squares (LS) or minimum-mean-square-error (MMSE) estimations conducted with assistance from the pilot symbols (Edfors et al., 1996; Van de Beek et al., 1995).

In the CTPA, pilot symbols are often uniformly distributed over all sub-channels in each OFDM symbol. Therefore, the CTPA can provide better resistance to channel time-variations. Channel weights on non-pilot (data) sub-channels have to be estimated by interpolating or smoothing the estimates of the channel weights obtained on the pilot sub-channels (Zhao & Huang, 1997; Rinne & Renfors, 1996). Therefore, the CTPA is, both in general and in theory, sensitive to the frequency-selectivity of a multipath fading channel. The CTPA is adopted to assist the CE conducted in each OFDM block in Sections 3 and 4, while the BTPA is discussed in Section 5.

2.2 CTPA-based CE

Conventional CEs assisted by comb-type pilot sub-channels are often performed completely in the frequency domain (FD) and include two steps: jointly estimating the channel gains on all pilot sub-channels and smoothing the obtained estimates to interpolate the channel gains on data (non-pilot) sub-channels. The CTPA CE technique (Hsieh & Wei, 1998) and the pilot-symbol-assisted modulation (PSAM) CE technique (Edfors et al., 1998) have been shown to be practical and applicable methods for mobile OFDM communication because their ability to track rapidly time-varying channels is much better than that of a BTPA CE technique. Several modified variants for further improvements and for complexity or rank reduction by means of singular-value-decomposition (SVD) techniques have been investigated previously (Hsieh & Wei, 1998; Edfors et al., 1998; Seller, 2004; Edfors et al., 1996; Van de Beek et al., 1995; Park et al., 2004). In addition, a more recent study has proposed improving CE performance by taking advantage of presumed slowly varying properties in the delay subspace (Simeone et al., 2004). This technique employs an intermediate step between the LS pilot sub-channel estimation step and the data sub-channel interpolation step in conventional CE approaches (Hsieh & Wei, 1998; Edfors et al., 1998; Seller, 2004; Edfors et al., 1996; Van de Beek et al., 1995; Park et al., 2004) to track the delay subspace to improve the accuracy of the pilot sub-channel estimation. However, this technique is based on the strong assumption that the multipath delays are slowly time-varying and can easily be estimated separately from the channel gain estimation. A prior channel estimation study (Minn & Bhargava, 2000) also exploited CTPA and TD CE. The proposed technique (Minn & Bhargava, 2000) was called the Frequency-Pilot-Time-Average (FPTA) method. However, time-averaging over a period that may be longer than the coherence time of wireless channels to suppress interference not only cannot work for wireless applications with real-time requirements but may also be impractical in a mobile channel with a short coherence time. A very successful technique that takes advantage of TD CE has been proposed (Minn & Bhargava, 1999). However, this technique focused on parameter estimation to transmit diversity using space-time coding in OFDM systems, and the parameter settings were not obtained from any recent mobile communication standards. To make fair comparisons of the CE performance and to avoid various diversity or space-time coding methods, only uncoded OFDM with no diversity is addressed in this chapter.

The CTPA is also employed as the framework of the technique studied in Sections 3 and 4 because of its effectiveness in mobile OFDM communications with rapidly time-varying, frequency-selective fading channels. A least-squares estimation (LSE) approach is performed serially on a block-by-block basis in the TD, not only to accurately estimate the CIR but also to effectively track rapid CIR variations. In fact, a generic estimator is thus executed on each OFDM block without assistance from a priori channel information (e.g., correlation functions in the frequency and/or in the time directions) and without increasing computational complexity.

Many previous studies (Edfors et al., 1998; Seller, 2004; Edfors et al., 1996; Van de Beek et al., 1995; Simeone et al., 2004) based on CTPA were derived under the assumption of perfect timing synchronization. In practice, some residual timing error within several sampling durations inevitably occurs during DFT demodulation, and this timing error leads to extra phase errors that phase-rotate demodulated symbols. Although a method that solves this problem in conventional CTPA OFDM CEs has been studied (Hsieh & Wei, 1998; Park et al., 2004), this method can work only under some special conditions (Hsieh & Wei, 1998). Compared with previous studies (Edfors et al., 1998; Seller, 2004; Edfors et al., 1996; Van de Beek et al., 1995; Simeone et al., 2004), the studied technique can be shown to achieve better resistance to residual timing errors because it does not employ a priori channel information and thus avoids the model mismatch and extra phase rotation problems that result from residual timing errors. Also, because the studied technique performs ideal data sub-channel interpolation with a domain-transformation approach, it can effectively track extra phase rotations with no phase lag.

2.3 BTPA-based CE

Single-carrier frequency-division multiple-access (SC-FDMA) communication was selected for the long-term evolution (LTE) specification in the third-generation partnership project (3GPP). SC-FDMA has been the focus of research and development because of its ability to maintain a low peak-to-average power ratio (PAPR), particularly in the uplink transmission, which is one of a few problems in recent 4G mobile communication standardization. Meanwhile, SC-FDMA can maintain high throughput and low equalization complexity like orthogonal frequency-division multiple access (OFDMA) (Myung et al., 2006). Moreover, SC-FDMA can be thought of as an OFDMA with DFT pre-coded or pre-spread inputs. In a SC-FDMA uplink scenario, information-bearing symbols in the TD from any individual user terminal are pre-coded (or pre-spread) with a DFT. The DFT-spread resultant symbols can be transformed into the FD. Finally, the DFT-spread symbols are fed into an IDFT multiplexer to accomplish FDM.

Although the CTPA is commonly adopted in wireless communication applications, such as IEEE 802.11a, IEEE 802.11g, IEEE 802.16e and the EU-IST-4MORE project, the BTPA is employed in the LTE. As shown in the LTE specification, 7 symbols form a slot, and 20 slots form a frame that spans 10 ms in the LTE uplink transmission. In each slot, the 4th symbol is used to transmit a pilot symbol. Section 5 employs BTPA as the framework to completely follow the LTE specifications. A modified Kalman filter- (MKF-) based TD CE approach with fast fading channels has been proposed previously (Han et al., 2004). The MKF-based TD CE tracks channel variations by taking advantage of MKF and TD MMSE equalizers. A CE technique that also employs a Kalman filter has been proposed (Li et al., 2008). Both methods successfully address the CE with high Doppler spreads.

The demodulation reference signal adopted for CE in LTE uplink communication is generated from Zadoff-Chu (ZC) sequences. ZC sequences, which are generalized chirp-like poly-phase sequences, have some beneficial properties according to previous studies (Ng et al., 1998; Popovic, 1992). ZC sequences are also commonly used in radar applications and as synchronization signals in LTE, e.g., random access and cell search (Levanon & Mozeson, 2004; LTE, 2009). A BTPA-based CE technique is discussed in great detail in Section 5.

2.4 TD-redundancy-based CE

Although the mobile communication applications mentioned above are all based on cyclic-prefix OFDM (CP-OFDM) modulation techniques, several encouraging contributions have investigated some alternatives, e.g., zero-padded OFDM (ZP-OFDM) (Muquest et al., 2002; Muquet et al., 2000) and pseudo-random-postfix OFDM (PRP-OFDM) (Muck et al., 2006; 2005; 2003) to replace the TD redundancy with null samples or known/pre-determined sequences. It has been found that significant improvements over CP-OFDM can be realized with either ZP-OFDM or PRP-OFDM (Muquest et al., 2002; Muquet et al., 2000; Muck et al., 2006; 2005; 2003). In previous works, ZP-OFDM has been shown to maintain symbol recovery irrespective of null locations on a multipath channel (Muquest et al., 2002; Muquet et al., 2000). Meanwhile, PRP-OFDM replaces the null samples originally inserted between any two OFDM blocks in ZP-OFDM by a known sequence. Thus, the receiver can use the a priori knowledge of a fraction of transmitted blocks to accurately estimate the CIR and effectively reduce the loss of transmission rate with frequent, periodic training sequences (Muck et al., 2006; 2005; 2003). A more recent OFDM variant, called Time-Domain Synchronous OFDM (TDS-OFDM) was investigated in terrestrial broadcasting applications (Gui et al., 2009; Yang et al., 2008; Zheng & Sun, 2008; Liu & Zhang, 2007; Song et al., 2005). TDS-OFDM works similarly to the PRP-OFDM and also belongs to this category of CEs assisted by TD redundancy.

Several research efforts that address various PRP-OFDM CE and/or subsequent equalization problems have been undertaken (Muck et al., 2006; 2005; 2003; Ma et al., 2006). However, these studies were performed only in the context of a wireless local area network (WLAN), in which multipath fading and Doppler effects are not as severe as in mobile communication. In addition, the techniques studied in previous works (Muck et al., 2006; 2005; 2003; Ma et al., 2006) take advantage of a time-averaging method to replace statistical expectation operations and to suppress various kinds of interference, including inter-block interference (IBI) and ISI. However, these moving-average-based interference suppression methods investigated in the previous studies (Muck et al., 2006; 2005; 2003; Ma et al., 2006) cannot function in the mobile environment because of rapid channel variation and real-time requirements. In fact, it is difficult to design an effective moving-average filter (or an integrate-and-dump (I/D) filter) for the previous studies (Muck et al., 2006; 2005; 2003; Ma et al., 2006) because the moving-average filter must have a sufficiently short time-averaging duration (i.e., sufficiently short I/D filter impulse response) to accommodate both the time-variant behaviors of channel tap-weighting coefficients and to keep the a priori statistics of the PRP unchanged for effective CE and must also have a sufficiently long time-averaging duration (i.e., sufficiently long I/D filter impulse response) to effectively suppress various kinds of interference and reduce AWGN.

A previous work (Ohno & Giannakis, 2002) investigated an optimum training pattern for generic block transmission over time-frequency selective channels. It has been proven that the TD training sequences must be placed with equal spacing to minimize mean-square errors. However, the work (Ohno & Giannakis, 2002) was still in the context of WLAN and broadcasting applications, and no symbol recovery method was studied. As shown in Section 6, the self-interference that occurs with symbol recovery and signal detection must be further eliminated by means of the SIC method.

3. Frequency-domain channel estimation based on comb-type pilot arrangement

3.1 System description

The block diagram of the OFDM transceiver under study is depicted in Fig. 6. Information-bearing bits are grouped and mapped according to Gray encoding to become multi-amplitude-multi-phase symbols. After pilot symbol insertion, the block of data $\{X_k,\ k = 0, 1,\ \cdots,\ N-1\}$ is then fed into the IDFT (or IFFT) modulator. Thus, the modulated symbols $\{x_n,\ n = 0, 1,\ \cdots,\ N-1\}$ can be expressed as

$$x_n = \frac{1}{\sqrt{N}} \sum_{k=0}^{N-1} X_k e^{j2\pi kn/N},\quad n = 0,1,\cdots,N-1,\tag{16}$$

where N is the number of sub-channels. In the above equation, it is assumed that there are no virtual sub-carriers, which provide guard bands, in the studied OFDM system. A CP is arranged in front of an OFDM symbol to avoid ISI and ICI, and the resultant symbol $\{x_{cp,n},\ n = -L,-L+1,\ \cdots,N-1\}$ can thus be expressed as

$$x_{cp,n} = \begin{cases} x_{N+n} & n = -L,-L+1,\cdots,-1 \\ x_n & n = 0,1,\cdots,N-1, \end{cases}\tag{17}$$

where L denotes the number of CP samples. The transmitted signal is then fed into a multipath fading channel with CIR $h[m,n]$. The received signal can thus be represented as

$$y_{cp}[n] = x_{cp}[n] \otimes h[m,n] + w[n],\tag{18}$$

where $w[n]$ denotes the AWGN. The CIR $h[m,n]$ can be expressed as (Steele, 1999)

$$h[m,n] = \sum_{i=0}^{M-1} \alpha_i e^{j2\pi v_i nT_s} \delta[mT_s - \tau_i],\tag{19}$$

where M denotes the number of resolvable propagation paths, α_i represents the ith complex channel weight of the CIR, v_i denotes the maximum Doppler frequency on the ith resolvable propagation path, m is the index in the delay domain, n is the time index, and τ_i denotes the delay of the ith resolvable path.

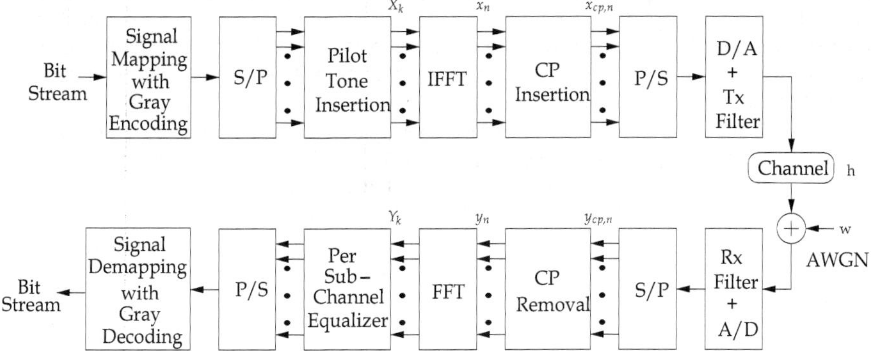

Fig. 6. A base-band equivalent block diagram of the studied OFDM transceiver.

After the CP portion is effectively removed from $y_{cp,n}$, the received samples y_n are sifted and fed into the DFT demodulator to simultaneously demodulate the signals propagating through the multiple sub-channels. The demodulated symbol obtained on the kth sub-channel can thus be written as

$$Y_k = \frac{1}{\sqrt{N}} \sum_{n=0}^{N-1} y_n e^{-j2\pi kn/N}, \qquad k = 0,1,\cdots,N-1. \tag{20}$$

If the CP is sufficiently longer than the CIR, then the ISI among OFDM symbols can be neglected. Therefore, Y_k can be reformulated as (Zhao & Huang, 1997; Hsieh & Wei, 1998)

$$Y_k = X_k H_k + I_k + W_k, \qquad k = 0,1,\cdots,N-1, \tag{21}$$

where

$$H_k = \sqrt{N} \sum_{i=0}^{M-1} \alpha_i e^{j\pi v_i T} \frac{\sin(\pi v_i T)}{\pi v_i T} e^{-j\frac{2\pi \tau_i}{N}k},$$

$$I_k = \frac{1}{\sqrt{N}} \sum_{i=0}^{M-1} \alpha_i \sum_{\substack{k'=0 \\ k'\neq k}}^{N-1} X(k') \frac{1-e^{j2\pi(v_i T+k'-k)}}{1-e^{j\frac{2\pi}{N}(v_i T+k'-k)}} e^{-j\frac{2\pi \tau_i}{N}k'}, \qquad k = 0,1,\cdots,N-1 \tag{22}$$

and $\{W_k, k = 0,1, \cdots, N-1\}$ is the Fourier transform of $\{w_n, n = 0,1, \cdots, N-1\}$.

The symbols $\{Y_{p,k}\}$ received on the pilot sub-channels can be obtained from $\{Y_k, k = 0, 1, \cdots, N-1\}$, the channel weights on the pilot sub-channels $\{H_{p,k}\}$ can be estimated, and then the channel weights on the data (non-pilot) sub-channels can be obtained by interpolating or smoothing the obtained estimates of the pilot sub-channel weights $H_{p,k}$. The transmitted information-bearing symbols $\{X_k, k=0, 1, \cdots, N-1\}$ can be recovered by simply dividing the received symbols by the corresponding channel weights, i.e.,

$$\hat{X}_k = \frac{Y_k}{\hat{H}_k}, \qquad k = 0,1,\cdots,N-1, \tag{22}$$

where $\hat{H}_k$ is an estimate of H_k. Eventually, the source binary data may be reconstructed by means of signal demapping.

3.2 Pilot sub-channel estimation

In the CTPA, the N_p pilot signals $X_{p,m}$, $m = 0,1, \cdots, N_p - 1$ are inserted into the FD transmitted symbols X_k, $k = 0,1, \cdots, N - 1$ with equal separation. In other words, the total N sub-carriers are divided into N_p groups, each of which contains $Q = N/N_p$ contiguous sub-carriers. Within any group of sub-carriers, the first sub-carrier, with the lowest central frequency, is adopted to transmit pilot signals. The value of $\rho = Q^{-1}$ denotes the pilot density employed in the OFDM communication studied here. The pilot density ρ represents the portion of the entire bandwidth that is employed to transmit the pilots, and it must be as low as possible to maintain sufficiently high bandwidth efficiency. However, the Nyquist sampling criterion sets a lower bound on the pilot density ρ that allows the CTF to be effectively reconstructed with a subcarrier-domain (i.e., FD) interpolation approach. The OFDM symbol transmitted over the kth sub-channel can thus be expressed as

$$X_k = X_{mQ+l}$$
$$= \begin{cases} X_{p,m}, & l = 0, \\ \text{information}, & l = 1,2,\cdots,Q-1. \end{cases} \tag{23}$$

The pilot signals $\{X_{p,m}, m = 0, 1, \cdots, N_p - 1\}$ can either be a common complex value or sifted from a pseudo-random sequence.

The channel weights on the pilot sub-channels can be written in vector form, i.e.,

$$\begin{aligned} \mathbf{H}_p &= \left[H_p(0) \; H_p(1) \; \cdots \; H_p(N_p-1) \right]^T \\ &= \left[H(0) \; H(Q) \; \cdots \; H\big((N_p-1)Q\big) \right]^T. \end{aligned} \tag{24}$$

The received symbols on the pilot sub-channels obtained after the FFT demodulation can be expressed as

$$\mathbf{Y}_p = \left[Y_{p,0} \; Y_{p,1} \; \cdots \; Y_{p,N_p-1} \right]^T. \tag{25}$$

Moreover, $\mathbf{Y}_p$ can be rewritten as

$$\mathbf{Y}_p = \mathbf{X}_p \cdot \mathbf{H}_p + \mathbf{I}_p + \mathbf{W}_p, \tag{26}$$

where

$$\mathbf{X}_p = \begin{bmatrix} X_p(0) & & 0 \\ & \ddots & \\ 0 & & X_p(N_p-1) \end{bmatrix},$$

$\mathbf{I}_p$ denotes the ICI vector and $\mathbf{W}_p$ denotes the AWGN of the pilot sub-channels.

In conventional CTPA-based CE methods, the estimates of the channel weights of the pilot sub-channels can be obtained by means of the LS CE, i.e.,

$$\widehat{\mathbf{H}}_{LS} = \left[H_{p,LS}(0) \ H_{p,LS}(1) \ \cdots \ H_{p,LS}(N_p-1) \right]^T$$
$$= \left(\mathbf{X}_p^H \mathbf{X}_p \right)^{-1} \mathbf{X}_p^H \mathbf{Y}_p = \mathbf{X}_p^{-1} \mathbf{Y}_p \qquad (27)$$
$$= \left[\frac{Y_p(0)}{X_p(0)} \ \frac{Y_p(1)}{X_p(1)} \ \cdots \ \frac{Y_p(N_p-1)}{X_p(N_p-1)} \right]^T .$$

Although the aforementioned LS CE $\widehat{\mathbf{H}}_{LS}$ enjoys low computational complexity, it suffers from noise enhancement problems, like the zero-forcing equalizer discussed in textbooks. The MMSE criterion is adopted in CE and equalization techniques, and it exhibits better CE performance than the LS CE in OFDM communications assisted by block pilots (Van de Beek et al., 1995). The main drawback of the MMSE CE is its high complexity, which grows exponentially with the size of the observation samples. In a previous study (Edfors et al., 1996), a low-rank approximation was applied to a linear minimum-mean-square-error (LMMSE) CE assisted by FD correlation. The key idea to reduce the complexity is using the singular-value-decomposition (SVD) technique to derive an optimal low-rank estimation, the performance of which remains essentially unchanged. The MMSE CE performed on the pilot sub-channels is formulated as follows (Edfors et al., 1996):

$$\widehat{\mathbf{H}}_{LMMSE} = \mathbf{R}_{\hat{H}_{LS}\hat{H}_{LS}} \mathbf{R}_{H_p\hat{H}_{LS}}^{-1} \widehat{\mathbf{H}}_{LS}$$
$$= \mathbf{R}_{H_pH_p} \left(\mathbf{R}_{H_pH_p} + \sigma_w^2 \left(\mathbf{X}_p \mathbf{X}_p^H \right)^{-1} \right)^{-1} \widehat{\mathbf{H}}_{LS} , \qquad (28)$$

where $\widehat{\mathbf{H}}_{LS}$ is the LS estimate of $\mathbf{H}_p$ derived in Equation 27, σ_w^2 is the common variance of W_k and w_n, and the covariance matrices are defined as follows:

$$\mathbf{R}_{H_pH_p} = E\left\{ \mathbf{H}_p \mathbf{H}_p^H \right\} ,$$
$$\mathbf{R}_{H_p\hat{H}_{LS}} = E\left\{ \mathbf{H}_p \widehat{\mathbf{H}}_{LS}^H \right\} ,$$
$$\mathbf{R}_{\hat{H}_{LS}\hat{H}_{LS}} = E\left\{ \widehat{\mathbf{H}}_{LS} \widehat{\mathbf{H}}_{LS}^H \right\} .$$

It is observed from Equation 28 that a matrix inversion operation is involved in the MMSE estimator, and it must be calculated symbol by symbol. This problem can be solved by using a constant pilot, e.g., $X_{p,m} = c$, $m = 0,1, \cdots, N_p - 1$. A generic CE can be obtained by averaging over a sufficiently long duration of transmitted symbols (Edfors et al., 1996), i.e.,

$$\widehat{\mathbf{H}}_{LMMSE} = \mathbf{R}_{H_pH_p} \left(\mathbf{R}_{H_pH_p} + \frac{\beta}{\Gamma}\mathbf{I} \right)^{-1} \widehat{\mathbf{H}}_{LS} , \qquad (29)$$

where $\Gamma = \dfrac{E\{|X_{p,k}|^2\}}{\sigma_w^2}$ is the average signal-to-noise ratio (SNR) and $\beta = E\{|X_{p,k}|^2\}E\{1/|X_{p,k}|^2\}$ is a constant determined by the signal mapping method employed in the pilot symbols. For example, $\beta = 17/9$ if 16-QAM is employed in the pilot symbols. If the auto-correlation matrix $\mathbf{R}_{H_pH_p}$ and the value of the SNR are known in advance, $\mathbf{R}_{H_pH_p}\left(\mathbf{R}_{H_pH_p} + \frac{\beta}{\Gamma}\mathbf{I}\right)^{-1}$ only needs to be calculated once. As shown in Equation 29, the CE requires N_p complex multiplications per pilot sub-carrier. To further reduce the number of multiplication operations, a low-rank approximation method based on singular-value decomposition (SVD) was adopted in the previous study (Edfors et al., 1996). Initially, the channel correlation matrix can be decomposed as

$$\mathbf{R}_{H_pH_p} = \mathbf{U}\Lambda\mathbf{U}^H, \tag{30}$$

where $\mathbf{U}$ is a matrix with orthonormal columns $\mathbf{u}_0, \mathbf{u}_1, \cdots, \mathbf{u}_{N_p-1}$, and Λ is a diagonal matrix with singular values $\lambda_0, \lambda_1, \cdots, \lambda_{N_p-1}$ as its diagonal elements. The rank-ϱ approximation of the LMMSE CE derived in Equation 29 can thus be formulated as

$$\widehat{\mathbf{H}}_{SVD} = \mathbf{U}\begin{bmatrix} \Delta_\varrho & 0 \\ 0 & 0 \end{bmatrix}\mathbf{U}^H\widehat{\mathbf{H}}_{LS}, \tag{31}$$

where Δ_ϱ denotes a diagonal matrix with terms that can be expressed as

$$\delta_k = \frac{\lambda_k}{\lambda_k + \frac{\beta}{\Gamma}}, \qquad k = 0, 1, \cdots, \varrho. \tag{32}$$

After some manipulation, the CE in Equation 31 requires $2\varrho N_p$ complex multiplications, and the total number of multiplications per pilot tone becomes 2ϱ. In general, the number of essential singular values, ϱ, is much smaller than the number of pilot sub-channels, N_p, and the computational complexity is therefore considerably reduced when the low-rank SVD-based CE is compared with the full-rank LMMSE-based CE derived in Equation 29. Incidentally, low-rank SVD-based CE can combat parameter mismatch problems, as shown in previous studies (Edfors et al., 1996).

3.3 Data sub-channel interpolation

After joint estimation of the FD channel weights from the pilot sub-channels is complete, the channel weight estimation on the data (non-pilot) sub-channels must be interpolated from the pilot sub-channel estimates. A piecewise-linear interpolation method has been studied (Rinne & Renfors, 1996) that exhibits better CE performance than piecewise-constant interpolation. A piecewise-linear interpolation (LI) method, a piecewise second-order polynomial interpolation (SOPI) method and a transform-domain interpolation method are studied in this sub-section.

3.3.1 Linear interpolation

In the linear interpolation method, the channel weight estimates on any two adjacent pilot sub-channels are employed to determine the channel weight estimates of the data sub-channel located between the two pilot sub-channels (Rinne & Renfors, 1996). The channel estimate of the kth data sub-channel can be obtained by the LI method, i.e.,

$$\hat{H}_{LI,x,k} = \hat{H}_{LI,x,mQ+l} = \left(1 - \frac{l}{Q}\right)\hat{H}_{x,m} + \frac{l}{Q}\hat{H}_{x,m+1}, \quad \begin{array}{l} x = LS, LMMSE, SVD, \\ m = 0,1,\cdots,N_p - 2, \\ 1 \le l \le (Q-1), \end{array} \tag{33}$$

where $mQ < k = mQ + l < (m+1)Q$, $m = \lfloor \frac{k}{Q} \rfloor$, $\lfloor \cdot \rfloor$ denotes the greatest integer less than or equal to the argument and l is the value of k modulo Q.

3.3.2 Second-order polynomial interpolation

Intuitively, a higher-order polynomial interpolation may fit the CTF better than the aforementioned first-order polynomial interpolation (LI). The SOPI can be implemented with a linear, time-invariant FIR filter (Liu & Wei, 1992), and the interpolation can be written as

$$\begin{aligned} \hat{H}_{SOPI,k} &= \hat{H}_{SOPI,x,mQ+l} \\ &= c_1\hat{H}_{x,m-1} + c_0\hat{H}_{x,m} + c_{-1}\hat{H}_{x,m+1}, \end{aligned} \tag{34}$$

where

$$x = LS, LMMSE, SVD, \qquad m = 1,2\cdots,N_p - 2, \qquad 1 \le l \le (Q-1),$$

$$c_1 = \frac{\psi(\psi+1)}{2}, \qquad c_0 = -(\psi-1)(\psi+1), \qquad c_{-1} = \frac{\psi(\psi-1)}{2},$$

$$\psi = \frac{l}{N}.$$

3.3.3 Transform-domain-processing-based interpolation (TFDI)

An ideal low-pass filtering method based on transform-domain processing was adopted for the data sub-channel interpolation (Zhao & Huang, 1997). In accordance with the CTPA, the pilot sub-channels are equally spaced every Q sub-channels. This implies that the coherence bandwidth of the multipath fading channel under consideration is sufficiently wider than the bandwidth occupied by Q sub-channels. After the pilot sub-channel estimation was completed, the interpolation methods mentioned in 3.3.2 and 3.3.3 were used to search for some low-order-polynomial-based estimations (say, LI and SOPI) of the channel weights of the data sub-channels. A transform-domain-processing-based interpolation (TFDI) method proposed in a previous study was used to jointly smooth/filter out the sub-channel weight estimates of the data sub-channels (Zhao & Huang, 1997). The TFDI method consists of the following steps: (1) first, it transforms the sub-channel weight estimates obtained from the pilot sub-channels into the transform domain, which can be thought of as the TD here; (2) it keeps the essential elements unchanged, which include at most the leading N_p (multipath) components because the coherence bandwidth is as wide as N/N_p sub-channels; (3) it sets the tail $(N - N_p)$ components to zero; and (4) finally, it performs the inverse transformation back to the sub-carrier domain, which may be called the FD in other publications. In this approach, a high-resolution interpolation method based on zero-padding and DFT/IDFT (Elliott, 1988) is employed. The TFDI technique can be thought of as ideal interpolation using an ideal lowpass filter in the transform domain.

3.4 Remarks

In this section, FD CE techniques based on CTPA were studied. Pilot sub-channel estimation techniques based on LS, LMMSE and SVD methods were studied along with data sub-channel interpolation techniques based on LI, SOPI and TFDI. The material provided in this section may also be found in greater detail in many prior publications (cited in this section) for interested readers. Of course, this author strongly encourages potential readers to delve into relevant research.

Many previous studies, e.g., (Zhao & Huang, 1997; Hsieh & Wei, 1998), prefer to adopt the IDFT as $\sum_{k=0}^{N-1} X_k e^{j2\pi kn/N}$ and the DFT as $\frac{1}{N}\sum_{k=0}^{N-1} x_n e^{j2\pi kn/N}$, rather than adopt those written in Equations 16 and 20. Although these representations are equivalent from the viewpoint of signal power, the formulations in Equations 16 and 20 are definitely more effective and convenient because they can keep the post-DFT-demodulation noise variance the same as the pre-DFT-demodulation noise variance. While performance analysis or comparison is conducted in terms of SNR, readers should be noted to take much care on this issue.

4. Time-domain channel estimation based on least-squares technique

4.1 Preliminary

A LS CE technique for mobile OFDM communication over a rapidly time-varying frequency-selective fading channel is demonstrated in this section. The studied technique, which uses CTPA, achieves low error probabilities by accurately estimating the CIR and effectively tracking rapid CIR time-variations. Unlike the technique studied in Section 3, the LS CE technique studied in this section is conducted in the TD, and several virtual sub-carriers are used. A generic estimator is performed serially block by block without assistance from a priori channel information and without increasing the computational complexity. The technique investigated in this section is also resistant to residual timing errors that occur during DFT demodulation. The material studied in this section has been thoroughly documented in a previous study and its references (Lin, 2008c). The author strongly encourages interested readers to look at these previous publications to achieve a deeper and more complete understanding of the material.

4.2 System description

The base-band signal $\{x_n\}$ consists of $2K$ complex sinusoids, which are individually modulated by $2K$ complex information-bearing QPSK symbols $\{X_k\}$, i.e.,

$$x_n = \frac{1}{\sqrt{N}} \sum_{k=-K}^{K-1} X_{|k|_N} e^{j2\pi nk/N}, \qquad n = 0,1,\cdots,N-1, \qquad N \geq 2K, \tag{35}$$

where $X_{|k|_N}$ denotes the complex symbol transmitted on the $|k|_N$th sub-channel, N is the IDFT size, n is the TD symbol index, k is the FD subcarrier index, $2K$ is the total number of sub-channels used to transmit information and $|k|_N$ denotes the value of k modulo N. In Equation 35, $N_v = N - 2K$ sub-carriers are appended in the high-frequency bands as virtual sub-carriers and can be considered to be guard bands that avoid interference from other applications in adjacent bands and are not employed to deliver any information. It should be noted that x_n and X_k form an N-point DFT pair, i.e., $\text{DFT}_N\{x_n, n = 0,1, \cdots, N - 1\} = \{X_0, X_1, \cdots, X_{K-1}, 0, 0, \cdots, 0, X_{N-K}, X_{N-K+1}, \cdots, X_{N-1}\}$, where the 0s denote the symbols transmitted via the virtual sub-channels. In a CTPA OFDM system, the symbols transmitted on the sub-channels can be expressed in vector form for simplicity:

$$\mathbf{X} = \{X_k\} \in \mathbf{C}^{N \times 1}, \tag{36}$$

where

$$X_k = \begin{cases} 0, & k \in \zeta_v = \{K, K+1, \cdots, N-K-1\} \\ P_l, & k \in \zeta_p = \{|(N-K)+(Q+1)/2+l\cdot Q|_N | l = 0,1,\cdots, N_p - 1\} \\ D_{k'}, & k \in \zeta \setminus \zeta_v \setminus \zeta_p; \end{cases}$$

$\zeta = \{0,1, \cdots, N - 1\}$; $K = (N - N_v)/2$; P_l denotes the lth pilot symbol; N_p denotes the number of pilot sub-channels; Q denotes the pilot sub-channel separation, which is an odd number in the case under study; $D_{k'}$ represents the k'th information-bearing data symbol; ζ_v stands for the set of indices of the virtual sub-channels; and ζ_p stands for the set of indices of the pilot sub-channels. The OFDM block modulation can be reformulated as the following matrix operation:

$$\mathbf{x} = \mathbf{F_I} \cdot \mathbf{X}, \tag{37}$$

where

$$\mathbf{x} = \{x_n\} \in \mathbf{C}^{N \times 1};$$
$$\mathbf{F_I} = \{f_{n,k}\} \in \mathbf{C}^{N \times N},$$
$$f_{n,k} = \frac{1}{\sqrt{N}} \exp\left(j \frac{2\pi kn}{N}\right), \quad 0 \le k \le N-1, \quad 0 \le n \le N-1.$$

$\mathbf{x}$ in Equation 37 can be rewritten as follows:

$$\mathbf{x} = \bar{\mathbf{x}} + \tilde{\mathbf{x}}, \tag{38}$$

where

$$\bar{\mathbf{x}} = \{\bar{x}_n\} \in \mathbf{C}^{N \times 1},$$
$$\bar{x}_n = \frac{1}{\sqrt{N}} \sum_{l=0}^{N_p-1} P_l \cdot \exp\left(j2\pi n |(N-K)+(Q+1)/2+l\cdot Q|_N / N\right),$$
$$n = 0,1,\cdots, N-1,$$

which is the TD sequence obtained from the pilot symbols modulated on the pilot sub-channels; and

$$\tilde{\mathbf{x}} = \{\tilde{x}_n\} \in \mathbf{C}^{N\times 1},$$

$$\tilde{x}_n = \frac{1}{\sqrt{N}} \sum_{\substack{k=0 \\ k \notin \zeta_v \\ k \notin \zeta_p}}^{N-1} X_k \cdot \exp(j2\pi nk/N), \qquad n = 0,1,\cdots,N-1,$$

which is the TD sequence that results from the information-bearing QPSK symbols modulated on the data (non-pilot) sub-channels. In accordance with the CLT, $\tilde{x}_n$, $n = 0,1, \cdots,$ $N-1$ are independent, identically distributed (IID) zero-mean Gaussian random variables with variance $\frac{N-N_v-N_p}{N}\sigma_{X_k}^2$, where $\sigma_{X_k}^2$ is the transmitted signal power.

After the TD signal $\mathbf{x}$ is obtained by conducting the IDFT modulation, a CP with length L is inserted, and the resulting complex base-band transmitted signal $\mathbf{s}$ can be expressed as

$$\mathbf{s} = \mathbf{G_I} \cdot \mathbf{x} = \mathbf{G_I} \cdot \mathbf{F_I} \cdot \mathbf{X} \in \mathbf{C}^{(N+L)\times 1}, \tag{39}$$

where

$$\mathbf{G_I} = \begin{bmatrix} \mathbf{0}_{L\times(N-L)} & \mathbf{I}_L \\ & \mathbf{I}_N \end{bmatrix} \in N^{(N+L)\times N},$$

$\mathbf{G_I}$ is the matrix for CP insertion, $\mathbf{I}$ is an identity matrix of the size noted in the subscript and $\mathbf{0}$ is a matrix of the size noted in the subscript whose entries are all zeros. The transmitted signal $\mathbf{s}$ is fed into a parallel-to-serial (P/S) operator, a digital-to-analog converter (DAC), a symbol shaping filter and finally an RF modulator for transmission. For complex base-band signals, the equivalent base-band representation of a multipath channel can be expressed as $\tilde{h}(\tau,t) = \Sigma_{m'} h_{m'}(t) \delta(\tau - \tau_{m'})$, where t denotes the time parameter, $h_{m'}(t)$ represents the m'th tap-weighting coefficient and τ is the delay parameter. The above 2-parameter channel model obeys the wide-sense stationary uncorrelated scattering (WSSUS) assumption. Based on the WSSUS and quasi-stationary assumptions, the channel tap-weighting coefficients are time-varying but do not change significantly within a single OFDM block duration of length NT_s, where T_s is the sampling period. Because the fractional durations (i.e., in a fraction of T_s) of delays are not taken into consideration, for a given time instant the above-mentioned tapped-delay-line channel model can be thought of as a CIR. Therefore, the channel model can be rewritten in a discrete-time representation for simplicity as $\mathbf{h} = \{h_m\} \in \mathbf{C}^{M\times 1}$, where M depends on the multipath delay spread. MT_s is thus the longest path delay; M varies according to the operating environment and cannot be known a priori at the receiving end. The received OFDM symbols can then be written in the following vector representation: $\mathbf{r}' = \mathbf{s} * \mathbf{h} + \mathbf{w}'$, where $*$ denotes the convolution operation, $\mathbf{r}' \in \mathbf{C}^{(N+L+M-1)\times 1}$ and $\mathbf{w}'$ is an AWGN vector whose elements are IID zero-mean Gaussian random variables with variance σ_w^2. While in practice a residual timing error ϑ may occur with the employed symbol timing synchronization mechanism, the steady-state-response portion of $\mathbf{r}'$ can hopefully be obtained from

$$\mathbf{r}_\vartheta = \mathbf{G_{R,\vartheta}} \cdot \mathbf{r}', \qquad \mathbf{G_{R,\vartheta}} = \begin{bmatrix} \mathbf{0}_{N\times(L-\vartheta)} & \mathbf{I}_N & \mathbf{0}_{N\times(M+\vartheta-1)} \end{bmatrix}. \tag{40}$$

If the residual timing error ϑ in the above equation falls within $[0, L - M]$, there is no ISI in the received signal. In practice, ϑ may be only a few samples long and may be less than M, and $\vartheta = 0$ represents perfect synchronization. The demodulation process at the receiving end can be performed by means of a DFT operation, and the received signal vector should thus be transformed back into the sub-carrier space, i.e.,

$$\mathbf{R}_{\vartheta} = \mathbf{F_T} \cdot \mathbf{r}_{\vartheta} \in \mathbf{C}^{N \times 1}, \tag{41}$$

where

$$\mathbf{F_T} = \{f'_{k,n}\} \in \mathbf{C}^{N \times N},$$

$$f'_{k,n} = \frac{1}{\sqrt{N}} \exp\left(-j2\pi kn / N\right), \quad n = 0,1,\cdots,N-1; \quad k = 0,1,\cdots,N-1.$$

Moreover, $\mathbf{F_T}$ is the complex conjugate of $\mathbf{F_I}$ defined below Equation 37 and denotes the DFT matrix. Thus, the demodulated signals $\mathbf{R}_{\vartheta}$ on the sub-channels are obtained by the DFT operation, as shown in Equation 41. In addition, some specific components of $\mathbf{R}_{\vartheta}$ represent the outputs of the transmitted pilot symbols that pass through the corresponding pilot sub-channels. These entries of $\mathbf{R}_{\vartheta}$, i.e., R_k^{ϑ}, $k \in \zeta_p$, are exploited to estimate the pilot sub-channel by FDLS estimation, LMMSE or a complexity-reduced LMMSE via SVD, as shown in the previous section. After the pilot sub-channel gains have been estimated by FDLS, LMMSE or SVD, smoothing or interpolation/extrapolation methods are used to filter out the estimates of the data sub-channel gains from inter-path interference (IPI), ICI and noise. The previously mentioned pilot sub-channel estimation and data sub-channel interpolation/extrapolation can often be considered to be an up-sampling process conducted in the FD and can therefore be performed fully on the sub-channel space studied in Section 3.

As a matter of fact, the studied technique exploits a TD LS (TDLS) method to estimate the leading channel tap-weighting coefficients in the CIR, performs zero-padding to form an N-element vector and finally conducts the DFT operation on the resultant vector to effectively smooth in the FD. The studied technique accomplishes ideal interpolation with the domain transformation method used previously (Zhao & Huang, 1997). The whole CTF, including all of the channel gains on the pilot, data and virtual sub-channels over the entire occupied frequency band, can therefore be estimated simultaneously. The multipath delay spread of the transmission channel is typically dynamic and cannot be determined a priori at the receiving end. Therefore, the number of channel tap-weighting coefficients is often assumed to be less than L to account for the worst ISI-free case. The training sequence $\bar{\mathbf{x}}$ in the time direction, which is actually IDFT-transformed from the N_p in-band pilot symbols, has a period of approximately $\frac{N}{Q}$ because the pilot sub-channels are equally spaced by Q sub-channels. Therefore, the studied technique based on CTPA can effectively estimate at most the leading $\frac{N}{Q}$ channel tap-weighting coefficients. Meanwhile, in accordance with the Karhunen-Loève (KL) expansion theorem (Stark & Woods, 2001), the training sequence $\bar{\mathbf{x}}$ can be considered to be a random sequence with N_p degrees of freedom. Therefore, the order of the TDLS technique studied in this section can be conservatively determined to be at most N_p because $\bar{\mathbf{x}}$ can be exploited to sound a channel with an order less than or equal to N_p. Based on the above reasoning, the number of channel tap-weighting coefficients is assumed to be less than or equal to N_p, and the longest excess delay is thus assumed to be less than $N_p T_s$. Therefore, the received signals $\mathbf{r}_{\vartheta}$ can be reformulated as

$$\mathbf{r}_\vartheta = \mathbf{c}_\vartheta \cdot \mathbf{g} + \mathbf{w}_\vartheta = \overline{\mathbf{c}}_\vartheta \cdot \mathbf{g} + \tilde{\mathbf{w}}_\vartheta, \tag{42}$$

where $\mathbf{c}_\vartheta = \overline{\mathbf{c}}_\vartheta + \tilde{\mathbf{c}}_\vartheta;\ \tilde{\mathbf{w}}_\vartheta = \tilde{\mathbf{c}}_\vartheta \mathbf{g} + \mathbf{w}_\vartheta;$

$$\mathbf{c}_\vartheta = \left\{ c_{p,q}^\vartheta \right\} \in \mathbf{C}^{N \times N_p}, \qquad c_{p,q}^\vartheta = x_{|p-\vartheta-q|_N} = \overline{x}_{|p-\vartheta-q|_N} + \tilde{x}_{|p-\vartheta-q|_N},$$

$$\overline{\mathbf{c}}_\vartheta = \left\{ \overline{c}_{p,q}^\vartheta \right\} \in \mathbf{C}^{N \times N_p}, \qquad \overline{c}_{p,q}^\vartheta = \overline{x}_{|p-\vartheta-q|_N},$$

$$\tilde{\mathbf{c}}_\vartheta = \left\{ \tilde{c}_{p,q}^\vartheta \right\} \in \mathbf{C}^{N \times N_p}, \qquad \tilde{c}_{p,q}^\vartheta = \tilde{x}_{|p-\vartheta-q|_N},$$

$$0 \le p \le N - 1, \qquad 0 \le q \le N_p - 1;$$

$\mathbf{c}_\vartheta$ is an $N \times N_p$ circulant matrix, and its left-most column is represented by

$$\mathrm{column}_0 \left(\mathbf{c}_\vartheta \right) = \left[x_{|N-\vartheta|_N} \quad x_{|N+1-\vartheta|_N} \quad \cdots \quad x_{|N-1-\vartheta|_N} \right]^T;$$

$\mathbf{w}_\vartheta = \{ w_{k-\vartheta} \} \in \mathbf{C}^{N \times 1}$ is an AWGN vector whose N elements, $w_{k-\vartheta}$, $k = L, L+1, \cdots, L+N-1$, are IID zero-mean Gaussian random variables with variance σ_w^2; and $\mathbf{g} = \{ g_m \} \in \mathbf{C}^{N_p \times 1}$ contains the effective components that represent the channel tap-weighting coefficients. If no residual timing error exists, i.e., $\vartheta = 0$, then $g_m = h_m$, $m = 0,1, \cdots, M-1$ and $g_m = 0$, $M \le m < N_p$. Here $M \le N_p$, and at least $(N_p - M)$ components in $\mathbf{g}$ must be zeros due to the lack of precise information about M at the receiving end, especially given that mobile OFDM communication systems often operate on a rapidly time-varying channel. As a result, the CIR can be estimated by means of a standard over-determined LS method, i.e.,

$$\hat{\mathbf{g}}^{\mathrm{TDLS}} = \left\{ \hat{g}_m^{\mathrm{TDLS}} \right\} = \left(\overline{\mathbf{c}}_0^H \overline{\mathbf{c}}_0 \right)^{-1} \overline{\mathbf{c}}_0^H \cdot \mathbf{r}_\vartheta \in \mathbf{C}^{N_p \times 1}, \tag{43}$$

where the superscript $(\cdot)^H$ denotes a Hermitian operator, and

$$\overline{\mathbf{c}}_0 = \left\{ \overline{c}_{p,q}^0 \right\} \in \mathbf{C}^{N \times N_p}, \quad \overline{c}_{p,q}^0 = \overline{x}_{|p-q|_N}, \quad 0 \le p \le N - 1, \quad 0 \le q \le N_p - 1.$$

In practice, a residual timing error that occurs in the DFT demodulation process inherently leads to phase errors in rotating the demodulated symbols. The phase errors caused by a timing error ϑ are linearly dependent on both the timing error ϑ and the sub-channel index k. Any small residual timing error can severely degrade the transmission performance in all of the previous studies that exploit two-stage CTPA CEs (Hsieh & Wei, 1998; Edfors et al., 1998; Seller, 2004; Edfors et al., 1996; Van de Beek et al., 1995; Park et al., 2004; Zhao & Huang, 1997). On the other hand, the studied technique has a higher level of tolerance to timing errors. Because the timing error ϑ that occurs with the received training sequence (i.e., delayed replica of $\overline{x}$) is the same as the error that occurs with the received data sequence (i.e., delayed replica of $\tilde{x}$), the extra phase errors inserted into the demodulated symbols on individual sub-channels are the same as those that occur in the estimates of the sub-channel gains. Therefore, the extra phase rotations in the studied technique can be completely removed in the succeeding single-tap equalization process conducted on individual sub-channels. As a result, the studied technique can effectively deal with the problems caused by a residual timing error.

4.3 Remarks

The TD LS CE technique for OFDM communications has been studied in practical mobile environments. The studied TDLS technique based on the CTPA can accurately estimate the CIR and effectively track rapid CIR variations and can therefore achieve low error probabilities. A generic estimator is also performed sequentially on all OFDM blocks without assistance from a priori channel information and without increasing the computational complexity. Furthermore, the studied technique also exhibits better robustness to residual timing errors that occur in the DFT demodulation.

Whether OFDM communication should employ FD CE or TD CE has become an endless debate, because FD CE and equalization have attracted significant attention in recent years. While the LS method is not new, the TD CE may also not be considered novel. Although authors of some other publications thought that TDLS CE was not important, this must be a misunderstanding, and this section provides a very practical study. The material studied in this section has been deeply investigated in a previous study and its references (Lin, 2008c). This author strongly encourages interested readers, especially practical engineers and potential researchers, to examine the study and references closely to gain a deeper understanding of the applicability and practical value of the OFDM TD LS CE.

5. Channel estimation based on block pilot arrangement

5.1 Preliminary

The preceding two sections describe CE techniques based on the CTPA and taking advantage of either FD estimation or TD estimation methods. A CE technique based on the BTPA is discussed in this section. SC-FDMA has been chosen in the LTE specifications as a promising uplink transmission technique because of its low PAPR. Moreover, SC-FDM systems can be considered to be pre-coded OFDM communication systems, whose information symbols are pre-coded by the DFT before being fed into a conventional OFDMA (Myung et al., 2006).

In practice, pilot signals or reference signals for CE in SC-FDMA systems are inserted to occupy whole sub-channels periodically in the time direction, which can be considered to be BTPA. In this section, the signal model and system description of a BTPA-based CE technique is studied. The material discussed in this section can be found, in part, in a previous study (Huang & Lin, 2010).

5.2 System description

The information-bearing Gray-encoded symbols $\chi_u[n]$, $n = 0,1, \cdots, N_u - 1$ are pre-spread by an N_u-point DFT to generate the FD symbols $X_u[\kappa]$, $\kappa = 0,1, \cdots, N_u - 1$, i.e.,

$$X_u[\kappa] = \frac{1}{\sqrt{N_u}} \sum_{n=0}^{N_u-1} \chi_u[n] e^{-j2\pi n\kappa/N_u}, \qquad \begin{array}{l} \kappa = 0,1,\cdots,N_u-1, \\ u = 0,1,\cdots,U-1, \end{array} \tag{44}$$

where U denotes the number of the users transmitting information toward the base-station, u denotes the user index, N_u denotes the sub-channel number which the uth user occupies, n denotes the time index and κ denotes the sub-carrier index. For a localized chunk arrangement used in the LTE specification, $X_u[\kappa]$, $\kappa = 0,1, \cdots, N_u - 1$ are allocated onto N_u sub-channels, i.e.,

$$S_u[k] = \begin{cases} X_u[\kappa], & k = \Gamma_u(\kappa) = \sum_{i=0}^{u-1} N_i + \kappa \\ 0, & k \neq \Gamma_u(\kappa), \quad \kappa = 0,1,\cdots,N_u - 1. \end{cases} \tag{45}$$

The transmitted signal of the uth user is given by

$$s_u[n] = \frac{1}{\sqrt{N}} \sum_{k=0}^{N-1} S_u[k]e^{j2\pi kn/N}, \quad \begin{array}{l} n = 0,1,\cdots,N-1; \\ u = 0,1,\cdots,U-1. \end{array} \tag{46}$$

The signal received at the base-station can be expressed as

$$r[n] = \sum_{u=0}^{U-1}\sum_{m=0}^{M-1} h_u[m,n]s_u[n-m] + w[n], \quad n = 0,1,\cdots,N-1, \tag{47}$$

where $h_u[m,n]$ is the sample-spaced channel impulse response of the mth resolvable path on the time index n for the uth user, M denotes the total number of resolvable paths on the frequency-selective fading channel and $w[n]$ is AWGN with zero mean and a variance of σ_w^2. The time-varying multipath fading channel considered here meets the WSSUS assumption. Therefore, the channel-weighting coefficient $h_u[m,n]$ is modelled as a zero-mean complex Gaussian random variable, with an autocorrelation function that is written as

$$E\{h_u[m,n]h_u^*[k,l]\} = \sigma_u^2[m]J_0\left(2\pi v_u|n-l|T_s\right)\delta[m-k], \tag{48}$$

where $\delta[\cdot]$ denotes the Dirac delta function, $J_0(\cdot)$ denotes the zeroth-order Bessel function of the first kind, v_u denotes the maximum Doppler frequency of the uth user and $\sigma_u^2[m]$ denotes the power of the mth resolvable path on the channel that the uth user experiences. In addition, it is assumed in the above equation that the channel tap-weighting coefficients on different resolvable paths are uncorrelated and that the channel tap-weighting coefficients on an individual resolvable path have the Clarke's Doppler power spectral density derived by Jakes (Jakes & Cox, 1994). To simplify the formulation of Equation 47, it is assumed that timing synchronization is perfect, ISI can be avoided and CP can be removed. At the receiving end, the FFT demodulation is conducted, and the received TD signal $r[n]$ is thus transformed into the FD for demultiplexing, i.e.,

$$\begin{aligned} R[k] &= \frac{1}{\sqrt{N}} \sum_{n=0}^{N-1} r[n]e^{-j2\pi nk/N} \\ &= \sum_{u=0}^{U-1} \bar{H}_{u,N/2}[k]S_u[k] + W[k], \quad k = 0,1,\cdots,N-1, \end{aligned} \tag{49}$$

where

$$\bar{H}_{u,N/2}[k] \doteq H_u[k,n], \qquad\qquad n = 0,1,\cdots,N-1,$$

$$H_u[k,n] = \frac{1}{\sqrt{N}} \sum_{m=0}^{N-1} h_u[m,n]e^{-j2\pi mk/N}, \qquad \forall k = \Gamma_u(\kappa),$$

$$W[k] = \frac{1}{\sqrt{N}} \sum_{n=0}^{N-1} w[n]e^{-j2\pi nk/N}, \qquad\qquad k = 0,1,\cdots,N-1.$$

In conventional FD CE, the weighting coefficient on the kth sub-channel $\bar{H}_{u,N/2}[k]$ is estimated by the FD LS CE, i.e.,

$$\hat{H}_{\text{FDLS}}[k] = \frac{R[k]S_p^*[k]}{\left|S_p[k]\right|^2}, \quad k = \Gamma_u(\kappa), \tag{50}$$

where $S_p[k]$ represents the pilot symbols in the FD, which are known a priori at the receiving end. In the LTE uplink, $S_p[k]$, $\forall k$ are obtained by transforming a Zadoff-Chu sequence onto the sub-carrier domain. Several CE techniques have been discussed in greater detail in a previous study (Huang & Lin, 2010). When the CE conducted by taking advantage of the pilot block is complete, several interpolation (or extrapolation) methods are conducted in the time direction to effectively smooth (or predict) the CTF or CIR upon transmission of the information-bearing symbols.

6. Channel estimation assisted from time-domain redundancy

6.1 Preliminary

To illustrate CE assisted by TD redundancy, a LS CE technique is studied in this section. The studied technique can apply pseudo-random-postfix orthogonal-frequency-division multiplexing (PRP-OFDM) communications to mobile applications, which often operate on a rapidly time-varying frequency-selective fading channel. Because conventional techniques that exploit a moving-average filter cannot function on a rapid time-varying channel, the studied technique takes advantage of several self-interference cancellation (SIC) methods to reduce IPI, ISI and IBI effectively and in a timely manner. The studied technique can thus overcome frequency selectivity caused by multipath fading and time selectivity caused by mobility; in particular, OFDM communication is often anticipated to operate in environments where both wide Doppler spreads and long delay spreads exist. Because conventional techniques based on MMSE CE usually require a priori channel information or significant training data, the studied method exploits a generic estimator assisted by LS CE that can be performed serially, block by block, to reduce computational complexity.

6.2 System description

The ith $N \times 1$ digital input vector $\mathbf{X}_N[i]$ is first modulated at the transmitting end with an IDFT operation. Thus, the TD information-bearing signal block can be expressed as

$$\mathbf{x}'_N[i] = \mathbf{F}_N^H \mathbf{X}_N[i], \tag{51}$$

where $\mathbf{X}_N[i]$ contains $2K \leq N$ QPSK-mapping information-bearing symbols;

$$\mathbf{F}_N = \frac{1}{\sqrt{N}}\left\{W_N^{kl}\right\}, \quad W_N = e^{-j2\pi/N}, \quad 0 \leq k < N, \quad 0 \leq l < N.$$

Immediately after the IDFT modulation process, a postfix vector $\mathbf{c}'_L = [c_0 \; c_1 \; \cdots \; c_{L-1}]^T$ is appended to the IDFT modulation output vector $\mathbf{x}'_N[i]$. In this section, $\mathbf{c}'_L$ is sifted from a partial period of a long pseudo-random sequence, and $\mathbf{c}'_L$ is phase-updated at every frame that contains several TD OFDM signal blocks, rather than using a deterministic postfix vector with a pseudo-random weight as in the conventional PRP-OFDM (Muck et al., 2006;

2005; 2003). This change is desirable when considering that previous works did not suggest long PRP sequences (Muck et al., 2006; 2005; 2003) and that pseudo-random sequences, e.g., the m-sequences or Gold sequences, are actually more general in various communication applications. Therefore, the ith transmitted block, with a length of $\Xi = N + L$, can be expressed as

$$\mathbf{x}_\Xi[i] = \mathbf{F}_{zp}^H \mathbf{X}_N[i] + \mathbf{c}_\Xi,$$
(52)

where

$$\mathbf{F}_{zp}^H = \begin{bmatrix} \mathbf{I}_N \\ \mathbf{0}_{L \times N} \end{bmatrix} \mathbf{F}_N^H, \quad \mathbf{c}_\Xi = \begin{bmatrix} \mathbf{0}_{N \times 1} \\ \mathbf{c}'_{L \times 1} \end{bmatrix}_{\Xi \times 1},$$

$\mathbf{I}_N$ denotes an $N \times N$ identity matrix and $\mathbf{0}_{L \times N}$ denotes a zero matrix of the size indicated in the subscript. The elements of $\mathbf{x}_\Xi[i]$ are then transmitted sequentially one by one (probably with transmit filtering or symbol shaping).

The channel studied here is modelled with a tapped-delay line of order $v - 1$, i.e., the impulse response of the investigated channel can be written as $\mathbf{h} = [h_0 \; h_1 \; \cdots \; h_{v-1}]^T$. It is commonly assumed that the length of the postfix (or prefix) L is larger than the length of the channel impulse response v. Typically, the multipath delay spread of the transmission channel is dynamic and cannot be determined a priori at the receiving end. Therefore, the number of channel tap-weighting coefficients is often assumed to be up to L to consider the worst ISI-free case, i.e., $v = L$. Thus, the longest excess delay is vT_s, where T_s denotes the sample duration.

At the receiving end, the ith OFDM symbol block can be formulated as

$$\mathbf{r}_\Xi[i] = \left(\mathbf{h}_{IBI,\Xi} + \mathbf{h}_{ISI,\Xi} \right) \mathbf{x}_\Xi[i] + \mathbf{w}_\Xi[i],$$
(53)

where $\mathbf{h}_{IBI,\Xi}$ is an $\Xi \times \Xi$ Toeplitz upper-triangular matrix in which the upper-most row is represented by

$$\text{row}_0 \left(\mathbf{h}_{IBI,\Xi} \right) = \left[0 \cdots 0 \, h_{v-1} \, h_{v-2} \cdots h_1 \right],$$

$\mathbf{h}_{ISI,\Xi}$ is an $\Xi \times \Xi$ Toeplitz lower-triangular matrix in which the left-most column is represented by

$$\text{column}_0 \left(\mathbf{h}_{ISI,\Xi} \right) = \left[h_0 \, h_1 \cdots h_{v-1} \, 0 \cdots 0 \right]^T ;$$

and $\mathbf{w}_\Xi[i]$ is the ith AWGN vector of elements with variance σ_w^2.

6.2.1 Channel estimation

In this section, the CIR is considered to be time-varying, but not significantly changing within one or two OFDM blocks. The symbols employed here in the CE can be written as follows:

$$\mathbf{r}_{CE, L+v-1}[i] = \begin{bmatrix} \langle \mathbf{r}_\Xi[i-1]_{N:\Xi-1} \rangle \\ \langle \mathbf{r}_\Xi[i]_{0:v-2} \rangle \end{bmatrix}_{(L+v-1) \times 1},$$
(54)

where $\langle \mathbf{A} \rangle_{p:q}$ denotes either a column vector with elements arranged as $[A_p \, A_{p+1} \, \cdots \, A_q]^T$, sifted from a column vector $\mathbf{A}$, or a row vector with elements arranged as $[A_p \, A_{p+1} \, \cdots \, A_q]$, sifted from a row vector $\mathbf{A}$. In fact, $\mathbf{r}_{CE,L+v-1}[i]$ can be reformulated in detail as follows:

$$\mathbf{r}_{CE,L+v-1}[i] = \mathbf{C}[i]\mathbf{h} + \mathbf{w}''[i] = \mathbf{C}_o \mathbf{h} + \mathbf{w}'[i], \tag{55}$$

where $\mathbf{w}''[i]$ is an $(L + v - 1) \times 1$ AWGN vector of elements whose variances are σ_w^2;

$$\mathbf{C}[i] = \left(\mathbf{C}_L[i] + \mathbf{C}_o + \mathbf{C}_U[i] \right),$$

$\mathbf{C}_o$ is an $(L + v - 1) \times v$ Toeplitz matrix in which the left-most column is represented by

$$\mathrm{column}_0\left(\mathbf{C}_o \right) = \begin{bmatrix} c_0 & c_1 & \cdots & c_{L-1} & 0 & \cdots & 0 \end{bmatrix}^T ;$$

$\mathbf{C}_U[i]$ is an $(L + v - 1) \times v$ upper-triangular Toeplitz matrix in which the upper-most row is represented by

$$\mathrm{row}_0\left(\mathbf{C}_U[i] \right) = [0 \ \langle \mathbf{x}_\Xi[i-1] \rangle_{N-1:N-(v-1)}];$$

$\mathbf{C}_L[i]$ is an $(L + v - 1) \times v$ lower-triangular Toeplitz matrix in which the left-most column is represented by

$$\mathrm{column}_0\left(\mathbf{C}_L[i] \right) = [\mathbf{0}_{1 \times L} \ \langle \mathbf{x}_\Xi[i] \rangle_{0:v-2}^T]^T ;$$

and

$$\mathbf{w}'[i] = \mathbf{w}''[i] + \mathbf{C}_L[i]\mathbf{h} + \mathbf{C}_U[i]\mathbf{h}.$$

In the above equation, $\mathbf{C}_L[i]\mathbf{h}$ results in ISI extending from on-time symbols onto the CE. Meanwhile, $\mathbf{C}_U[i]\mathbf{h}$ leads to IBI extending from preceding symbols onto the CE. In accordance with the LS philosophy (Stark & Woods, 2001; Kay, 1993), the CE studied here can thus be formulated as

$$\hat{\mathbf{h}}_0[i] = \left(\mathbf{C}_o^H \mathbf{C}_o \right)^{-1} \mathbf{C}_o^H \bar{\mathbf{r}}_{CE,L+v-1}[i], \tag{56}$$

where

$$\bar{\mathbf{r}}_{CE,L+v-1}[i] = \frac{1}{2}\left(\mathbf{r}_{CE,L+v-1}[i] + \mathbf{r}_{CE,L+v-1}[i+1] \right).$$

In fact, the CE performed using $\bar{\mathbf{r}}_{CE,L+v-1}[i]$ forces the channel estimator $\hat{\mathbf{h}}_0[i]$, derived in Equation 56, to effectively exploit the first-order statistics to conduct the TD LI as employed in a previous work (Ma et al., 2006). Because of the LS philosophy, the statistics of $\mathbf{w}'[i]$ need not be completely known prior to performing the CE and $(\mathbf{C}_o^H \mathbf{C}_o)^{-1} \mathbf{C}_o^H$ can be pre-calculated and pre-stored as a generic LS CE to reduce complexity. Furthermore, by taking advantage of decision-directed (DD) SIC, estimates of the CIR can be iteratively obtained by

$$\hat{\mathbf{h}}_1[i] = \{(\mathbf{C}_o^H \mathbf{C}_o)^{-1} \mathbf{C}_o^H\} \check{\mathbf{r}}_{CE,L+v-1}[i], \tag{57}$$

where

$$\tilde{r}_{CE,L+v-1}[i] = \frac{1}{2}\left(r_{CE,L+v-1}[i] - \hat{C}_U[i-1]\hat{h}_1[i-1] + r_{CE,L+v-1}[i+1]\right), \quad i \geq 1;$$

$$\hat{h}_1[0] = \hat{h}_0[0]; \qquad \hat{C}_U[0]\hat{h}_1[0] = 0_{(L+v-1)\times 1} \text{ (initialization)};$$

and $\hat{C}_U[i-1]$ denotes an $(L+v-1)\times L$ upper-triangular Toeplitz matrix in which the upper-most row is $[0 \ \langle \hat{x}_\Xi[i-1]\rangle_{N-1:N-(v-1)}]$, which results from the DD symbols. Eventually, the estimates of sub-channel gains in individual frequency bins can be obtained by performing the DFT on the zero-padded replicas of either $\hat{h}_0[i]$ or $\hat{h}_1[i]$, i.e.,

$$\hat{H}_k[i] = F_N \begin{bmatrix} I_v & 0_{v\times(N-v)} \\ 0_{(N-v)\times v} & 0_{(N-v)\times(N-v)} \end{bmatrix} \hat{h}_k[i], \quad k = 0,1. \tag{58}$$

6.2.2 Symbol recovery

For information detection at the receiving end, the ith information symbol within the DFT window can be obtained as

$$r_{SD,N}[i] = \langle r_\Xi[i]\rangle_{0:N-1}, \tag{59}$$

and thus, its corresponding FD symbol is

$$R_{SD,0,N}[i] = F_N r_{SD,N}[i]. \tag{60}$$

OLA: Based on the signal formatting in the PRP-OFDM communication under investigation, the ICI caused by various excess delays can be taken into account by modifying the signal symbol for signal detection to be

$$R_{SD,1,N}[i] = F_N\left(r_{SD,N}[i] + r_{ICIc,N}[i]\right), \tag{61}$$

where

$$r_{ICIc,N}[i] = \begin{bmatrix} \langle r_\Xi[i]\rangle_{N:N+v-2} \\ 0_{(N-v+1)\times 1} \end{bmatrix}$$

is exploited here for the purpose of ICI compensation. In fact, $R_{SD,1,N}[i]$ in Equation 61 can be considered to be a complexity-reduced variant modified from the method that was called the overlap-add (OLA) approach in previous studies (Muquest et al., 2002; Muck et al., 2003). It has been proven in previous studies (Muquet et al., 2000) that the OLA helps the ZP-OFDM achieve the same performance as the CP-OFDM because the OLA can reduce ICI by compensating for IPI and timing errors to maintain the orthogonality among sub-carriers, as in the CP-OFDM.

OLA with SIC: The conventional OLA mentioned above introduces some self-interference to the PRP-OFDM. Therefore, the self-interference occurring in the PRP-OFDM signal detection has to be eliminated. As a result, the signals fed into the detection can be formulated as

Popovic, B. M. (1992). Generalized chirp-like polyphase sequences with optimum correlation properties, *IEEE Transactions on Information Theory* Vol. 38(No. 4): 1406–1409.

Reiners, C. & Rohling, H. (1994). Multicarrier transmission technique in cellular mobile communication systems, *Proceedings of 1994 IEEE 44th Vehicular Technology Conference*, IEEE Vehicular Technology Society, Stockholm, pp. 1645–1649.

Rinne, J. & Renfors, M. (1996). Optimal training and redundant precoding for block transmissions with application to wireless ofdm, *IEEE Transactions Consumer Electronics* Vol. 42(No. 4): 959–962.

Saltzberg, B. (1967). Performance of an efficient parallel data transmission system, *IEEE Transactions on Communication Technology* Vol. 15(No. 6): 805–811.

Sandell, M. & Edfors, O. (1996). A comparative study of pilot-based channel estimators for wireless ofdm, *Research Report / 1996:19. Div. Signal Processing, Lulea Univ. Technology, Lulea, Sweden* Vol.(No.).

Seller, O. (2004). Low complexity 2d projection-based channel estimators for mc-cdma, *Proceedings of 15th IEEE International Symposium on Personal, Indoor and Mobile Radio Communications, 2004 (PIMRC 2004)*, IEEE Communications Society, Barselona, pp. 2283 – 2288.

Simeone, O., Bar-Ness, Y. & Spagnolini, U. (2004). Pilot-based channel estimation for ofdm systems by tracking the delay-subspace, *IEEE Transactions on Wireless Communications* Vol. 3(No. 1): 315–325.

Song, B., Gui, L., Guan, Y. & Zhang, W. (2005). On channel estimation and equalization in tds-ofdm based terrestrial hdtv broadcasting system, *IEEE Transactions Consumer Electronics* Vol. 51(No. 3): 790–797.

Sourour, E. A. & Nakagawa, M. (1996). Performance of orthogonal multicarrier cdma in a multipath fading channel, *IEEE Transactions on Communications* Vol. 44(No. 3): 356 – 367.

Stark, H. & Woods, J. W. (2001). *Probability and Random Processes with Applications to Signal Processing*, Prentice Hall, 3rd ed.

Steele, R. (1999). *Mobile Radio Communications*, John Wiley & Sons, Inc.

Tourtier, P. J., Monnier, R. & Lopez, P. (1993). Multicarrier model for digital hdtv terrestrial broadcasting, *Signal processing: Image communication* Vol. 5(No. 5-6): 379–403.

Tu, J. C. (1991). *Theory, Design and Application of Multi-Channel Modulation for Digital Communications*, Ph. D. Dissertation, Stanford University, CA.

Tufvesson, F. & Maseng, T. (1997). Pilot assisted channel estimation for ofdm in mobile cellular systems, *Proceedings of 1997 IEEE 47th Vehicular Technology Conference*, IEEE Vehicular Technology Society, Phoenix, AZ, pp. 1639–1643.

Van de Beek, J.-J., Edfors, O., Sandell, M., Wilson, S. K. & Borjesson, P. O. (1995). On channel estimation in ofdm systems, *Proceedings of 1995 IEEE 45th Vehicular Technology Conference*, IEEE Vehicular Technology Society, Chicago, IL, pp. 815–819.

Weinstein, S. B. & Ebert, P. M. (1971). Data transmission by frequency-division multiplexing using the discrete fourier transform, *IEEE Transactions on Communication Technology* Vol. 19(No. 5): 628–634.

Wilson, S. K., Khayata, R. E. & Cioffi, J. M. (1994). 16-qam modulation with orthogonal frequency-division multiplexing in a rayleigh-fading environment, *Proceedings of*

1994 IEEE 44th Vehicular Technology Conference, IEEE Vehicular Technology Society, Stockholm, pp. 1660–1664.

Yang, F., Wang, J., Wang, J., Song, J. & Yang, Z. (2008). Novel channel estimation method based on pn sequence reconstruction for chinese dttb system, *IEEE Transactions Consumer Electronics* Vol. 54(No. 4): 1583–1589.

Yeh, C.-S. & Lin, Y. (1999). Channel estimation techniques based on pilot arrangement in ofdm systems, *IEEE Transactions on Broadcasting* Vol. 45(No. 4): 400–409.

Young, G., Foster, K. T. & Cook, J. W. (1996). Broadband multimedia delivery over copper, *Electronics & Communication Engineering Journal* Vol. 8(No. 1): 25.

Zhao, Y. & Huang, A. (1997). A novel channel estimation method for ofdm mobile communication systems based on pilot signals and transform-domain processing, *Proceedings of 1997 IEEE 47th Vehicular Technology Conference*, IEEE Vehicular Technology Society, Phoenix, AZ, pp. 2089–2093.

Zheng, Z.-W. & Sun, Z.-G. (2008). Robust channel estimation scheme for the tds-ofdm based digital television terrestrial broadcasting system, *IEEE Transactions Consumer Electronics* Vol. 54(No. 4): 1576–1582.

Zou,W. Y. &Wu, Y. (1995). Cofdm: an overview, *IEEE Transactions on Broadcasting* Vol. 41(No. 1): 1–8.

3

OFDM Communications with Cooperative Relays

H. Lu[1], H. Nikookar[1] and T. Xu[2]
[1]International Research Centre for Telecommunications and Radar (IRCTR)
[2]Circuits and Systems Group (CAS)
Dept. EEMCS, Delft University of Technology
Mekelweg 4, 2628 CD, Delft,
The Netherlands

1. Introduction

1.1 Cooperative relay communications

Signal fading due to multi-path propagation is one of the major impairments to meet the demands of next generation wireless networks for high data rate services. To mitigate the fading effects, time, frequency, and spatial diversity techniques or their hybrid can be used. Among different types of diversity techniques, spatial diversity is of special interest as is does not incur system losses in terms of delay and bandwidth efficiency.

Recently, cooperative diversity in wireless network has received great interest and is regarded as a promising technique to mitigate multi-path fading, which results in a fluctuation in the amplitude of the received signal. The cooperative communications is a new communication paradigm which generates independent paths between the user and the base station by introducing a relay channel. The relay channel can be thought of as an auxiliary channel to the direct channel between the source and destination. The basic idea behind cooperation is that several users in a network pool their resources in order to form a virtual antenna array which creates spatial diversity (Laneman et al., 2004; Sendonaris et al., Part I, 2003; Sendonaris et al., Part II, 2003). Since the relay node is usually several wavelengths distant from the source, the relay channel is guaranteed to fade independently from the direct channel, which introduces a full-rank Multiple-input-multiple-output (MIMO) channel between the source and the destination. This cooperative spatial diversity leads to an increased exponential decay rate in the error probability with increasing signal-to-noise ratio (SNR) (Liu et al., 2009).

Before discussing cooperative OFDM, let us first review some fundamental knowledge of OFDM and MIMO, which is associated with the cooperative OFDM study in this chapter.

1.2 Physical layer of cooperative wireless networks (OFDM & MIMO)
1.2.1 OFDM basics

In the modern wireless communication, OFDM technology has been widely used due to its spectral efficiency and inherent flexibility in allocating power and bit rate over distinct subcarriers which are orthogonal to each other. Different from a serial transmission, OFDM is a multi-carrier block transmission, where, as the name suggests, information-bearing symbols are processed in blocks at both the transmitter and the receiver.

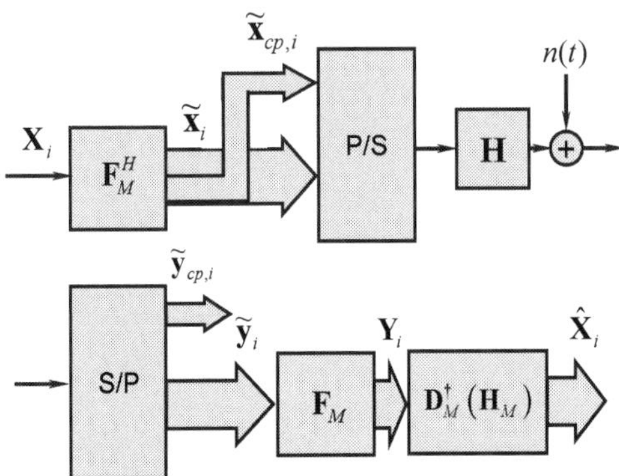

Fig. 1. Discrete-time block equivalent models of CP-OFDM, top: transmitter & channel, bottom: receiver.

A number of benefits the OFDM brings to cooperative relay systems originate from the basic features that OFDM possesses. To appreciate those, we first outline Cyclic Prefix (CP)-OFDM's operation using the discrete-time baseband equivalent block model of a single-transceiver system depicted in Fig.1, where $\mathbf{X}_i$ is the so-called frequency signal at the i-th time symbol duration in one OFDM frame, then it will be transferred as $\tilde{\mathbf{x}}_i$ in the time domain by the M-point inverse fast Fourier transform (IFFT) matrix $\mathbf{F}_M^{-1} = \mathbf{F}_M^H$ with (m, k)-th entry $\exp(j2\pi mk / M)/\sqrt{M}$, i.e., $\tilde{\mathbf{x}}_i = \mathbf{F}_M^H \mathbf{X}_i$, $\mathbf{F}_M$ is the M-point fast Fourier transform (FFT) matrix. where $(\cdot)^H$ denotes conjugate transposition, $(\cdot)^\dagger$ denotes matrix pseudoinverse, and $(\cdot)^{-1}$ denotes matrix inversion and m, k denote the index in frequency and time domain, respectively. Applying the triangle inequality to the M-point IFFT definition shows that the entries of $\mathbf{F}_M^H \mathbf{X}_i$ have magnitudes that can exceed those of $\mathbf{X}_i$ by a factor as high as M. In other words, IFFT processing can increase the peak to average power ratio (PAPR) by a factor as high as the number of subcarriers (which in certain applications can exceed 1000). Then a CP of length D is inserted between each $\tilde{\mathbf{x}}_i$ to form the redundant OFDM symbols $\tilde{\mathbf{x}}_{cp,i}$, which are sequentially transmitted through the channel. The total number of the time domain signals in each OFDM symbol is, thus, $C = M + D$. If we define $\mathbf{F}_{cp} := [\mathbf{F}_D, \mathbf{F}_M]^H$ as the $C \times M$ expanded IFFT matrix, where $\mathbf{F}_D$ is the last D columns of $\mathbf{F}_M$, that way, the redundant OFDM symbol to be transmitted can also be expressed as $\tilde{\mathbf{x}}_{cp,i} = \mathbf{F}_{cp} \mathbf{X}_i$. With $(\cdot)^T$ denotes transposition, and assuming no channel state information (CSI) to be available at the transmitter, then the received symbol $\tilde{\mathbf{y}}_{cp,i}$ at the i-th time symbol duration can be written as:

$$\tilde{\mathbf{y}}_{cp,i} = \mathbf{H}\mathbf{F}_{cp}\mathbf{X}_i + \mathbf{H}_{ISI}\mathbf{F}_{cp}\mathbf{X}_{i-1} + \tilde{\mathbf{n}}_{C,i} \tag{1}$$

where $\mathbf{H}$ is the $C \times C$ lower triangular Toeplitz filtering matrix with first column $[h_1 \cdots h_L \quad 0 \cdots 0]^T$, where L is the channel order (i.e., $h_i = 0, \ \forall i > L$), $\mathbf{H}_{ISI}$ is the $C \times C$ upper triangular Toeplitz filtering matrix with first row $[0 \cdots 0 \quad h_L \cdots h_2]$, which captures intersymbol interference (ISI), $\tilde{\mathbf{n}}_{C,i}$ denotes the additive white Gaussian noise (AWGN) vector with variance N_0 and Length C. After removing the CP at the receiver, ISI is also discarded, and (1) can be rewritten as:

$$\tilde{\mathbf{y}}_i = \mathbf{C}_M(\mathbf{h})\mathbf{F}_M^H \mathbf{X}_i + \tilde{\mathbf{n}}_{M,i} \tag{2}$$

where $\mathbf{C}_M(\mathbf{h})$ is $M \times M$ circulant matrix with first row $[h_1 \quad 0\cdots 0 \quad h_L \cdots h_2]$, and $\tilde{\mathbf{n}}_{M,i}$ is a vector formed by the last M elements of $\tilde{\mathbf{n}}_{C,i}$.

The procedure of adding and removing CP forces the linear convolution with the channel impulse response to resemble a circular convolution. Equalization of CP-OFDM transmissions ties to the well known property that a circular convolution in the time domain, is equivalent to a multiplication operation in the frequency domain. Hence, the circulant matrix can be diagonalized by post- (pre-) multiplication by (I)FFT matrices, and only a single-tap frequency domain equalizer is sufficient to resolve the multipath effect on the transmitted signal. After demodulation with the FFT matrix, the received signal is given by:

$$\mathbf{Y}_i = \mathbf{F}_M \mathbf{C}_M(\mathbf{h})\mathbf{F}_M^H \mathbf{X}_i + \mathbf{F}_M \tilde{\mathbf{n}}_{M,i}$$

$$= \mathrm{diag}(H_1 \cdots H_M)\mathbf{X}_i + \mathbf{F}_M \tilde{\mathbf{n}}_{M,i}$$

$$= \mathbf{D}_M(\mathbf{H}_M)\mathbf{X}_i + \mathbf{n}_{M,i} \tag{3}$$

where $\mathbf{H}_M = [H_1 \cdots H_M]^T = \sqrt{M}\mathbf{F}_M \mathbf{h}$, with

$$H_k \equiv H(2\pi k / M) := \sum_{l=1}^{L} h_l e^{-j2\pi kl/M} \tag{4}$$

denoting the channel's transfer function on the k-th subcarrier, $\mathbf{D}_M(\mathbf{H}_M)$ stands for the $M \times M$ diagonal matrix with $\mathbf{H}_M$ on its diagonal, $\mathbf{n}_{M,i} := \mathbf{F}_M \tilde{\mathbf{n}}_{M,i}$.

Equations (3) and (4) show that an OFDM system which relies on M subcarriers to transmit the symbols of each block $\mathbf{X}_i$, converts an FIR frequency-selective channel to an equivalent set of M flat fading subchannels. This is intuitively reasonable since each narrowband subcarrier that is used to convey each information-bearing symbol per OFDM block "sees" a narrow portion of the broadband frequency-selective channel which can be considered frequency flat. This scalar model enables simple equalization of the FIR channel (by dividing (3) with the corresponding scalar subchannel $\mathbf{H}_M$) as well as low-complexity decoding across subchannels using (Muquet et al., 2009; Wang & Giannakis, 2000). Transmission of symbols over subcarriers also allows for a flexible allocation of the available bandwidth to multiple users operating with possibly different rate requirements imposed by multimedia applications, which may include communication of data, audio, or video. When CSI is available at the transmitter side, power and bits can be adaptively loaded per OFDM subcarrier, depending on the strength of the intended subchannel. Because of orthogonality of ODFM subcarriers, OFDM system exhibits robustness to the narrow band interference.

The price paid for OFDM's attractive features in equalization, decoding, and possibly adaptive power and bandwidth allocation is its sensitivity to subcarrier drifts and the high PAPR that IFFT processing introduces to the entries of each block transmitted. Subcarrier drifts come either from the carrier-frequency and phase offsets between transmit-receive oscillators or from mobility-induced Doppler effects, with the latter causing a spectrum of frequency drifts. Subcarrier drifts cause inter-carrier interference (ICI), which renders (3) invalid. On the other hand, high PAPR necessitates backing-off transmit-power amplifiers to avoid nonlinear distortion effects (Batra et al., 2004).

However, the same multipath robustness can be obtained by adopting ZP instead of CP (Lu et al., 2009). If the length of the zero-padding equals the length of CP, then the ZP-OFDM will achieve the same spectrum efficiency as CP-OFDM.

The only difference between the transmission part of the ZP-OFDM and CP-OFDM, as shown in Fig. 2, is the CP replaced by D appending zeros at the end of the symbol. If we define $\mathbf{F}_{zp} := [\mathbf{F}_M, \mathbf{0}]^H$, and $Z = C = M + D$, the transmitted OFDM symbol can be denoted as $\tilde{\mathbf{x}}_{zp,i} = \mathbf{F}_{zp}\mathbf{X}_i$. The received symbol is now expressed as:

$$\tilde{\mathbf{y}}_{zp,i} = \mathbf{HF}_{zp}\mathbf{X}_i + \mathbf{H}_{ISI}\mathbf{F}_{zp}\mathbf{X}_{i-1} + \tilde{\mathbf{n}}_{Z,i}. \tag{5}$$

The key advantage of ZP-OFDM relies on two aspects: first, the all-zero $D \times M$ matrix $\mathbf{0}$ is able to take good care of the ISI, when the length of the padded zeros is not less than the maximum channel delay. Second, according to the Eq. (4), multipath channel will introduce 3 impact factors, h_l, k and l to the received signal, which stand for the amplitude, subcarriers (in frequency domain) and delay (in time domain), respectively. Therefore, different CP copies from multipath certainly pose stronger interference than ZP copies. Thus, without equalization or some pre-modulation schemes, like Differential-PSK, the ZP-OFDM has a natural better bit error rate (BER) performance than the CP-OFDM. Furthermore, the linear structure of the channel matrix in ZP-OFDM ensures the symbol recovery regardless of the channel zeros locations.

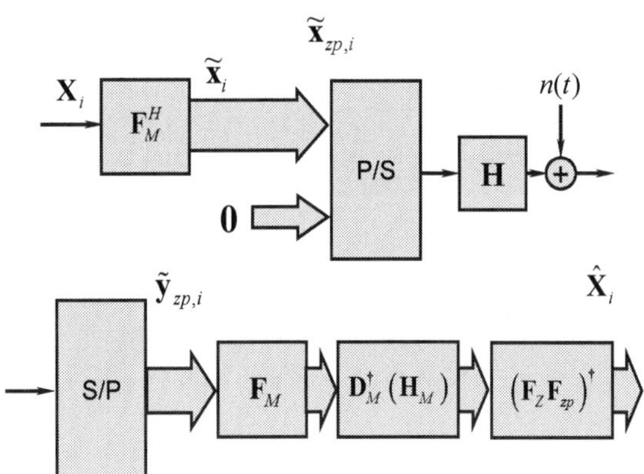

Fig. 2. Discrete-time block equivalent models of ZP-OFDM, top: transmitter & channel, bottom: receiver.

Nevertheless, because of the zero-padding and linear structure of ZP-OFDM, it outperforms CP-OFDM in terms of the lower PAPR (Batra et al., 2004; Lu et al., 2009). Similar to silent periods in TDMA, trailing zeros will not pose problems to high-power amplifiers (HPA). By adopting the proper filter, they will not give rise to out-of-band spectral leakage, either. The circulant channel convolution matrix $\mathbf{C}_M$ (**h**) in the CP-OFDM is invertible if and only if the channel transfer function has no zeros on the FFT grid, i.e., $H_k \neq 0$, $\forall k \in [1, M]$, therefore, when channel nulls hit the transmitted symbols, the signal recovery becomes impossible. However, in the ZP-OFDM, the tall Toeplitz structure of equivalent channel matrix always guarantees its full rank (it only becomes rank deficient when the channel impulse response is identically zero, which is impossible in practice) (Muquet et al., 2009). In other words, the full rank property guarantees the detection of transmitted symbols.

In the blind channel estimation and blind symbol synchronization, ZP-OFDM also has its advantage in reducing the system complexity. Therefore, for more efficient utilization of the spectrum and low power transmission, a fast-equalized ZP-OFDM seems more promising than the CP-OFDM.

The above reviewed advantages and limitations of single-transceiver CP-OFDM and ZP-OFDM systems are basically present in the cooperative scenario which we present later under the name of cooperative OFDM.

1.2.2 From MIMO to cooperative communications

MIMO systems have been constructed comprising multiple antennas at both the transmitter and receiver to offer significant increases in data throughput and link range without additional expenditure in frequency and time domain. The spatial diversity has been studied intensively in the context of MIMO systems (Barbarossa, 2005). It has been shown that utilizing MIMO systems can significantly improve the system throughput and reliability (Foschini & Gans, 1998).

In the fourth generation wireless networks to be deployed in the next couple of years, namely, mobile broadband wireless access (MBWA) or IEEE 802.20, peak date rates of 260 Mbps can be achieved on the downlink, and 60 Mbps on the uplink (Hwang et al., 2007). These data rates can, however, only be achieved for full-rank MIMO users. More specifically, full-rank MIMO users must have multiple antennas at the mobile terminal, and these antennas must see independent channel fades to the multiple antennas located at the base station. In practice, not all users can guarantee such high rates because they either do not have multiple antennas installed on their small-size devices, or the propagation environment cannot support MIMO because, for example, there is not enough scattering. In the latter case, even if the user has multiple antennas installed full-rank MIMO is not achieved because the paths between several antenna elements are highly correlated.

To overcome the above limitations of achieving MIMO gains in future wireless networks, we must think of new techniques beyond traditional point-to-point communications. The traditional view of a wireless system is that it is a set of nodes trying to communicate with each other. From another point of view, however, because of the broadcast nature of the wireless channel, we can think of those nodes as a set of antennas distributed in the wireless system. Adopting this point of view, nodes in the network can cooperate together for a distributed transmission and processing of information. The cooperating node acts as a relay node for the source node. Since the relay node is usually several wavelengths distant from the source, the relay channels are guaranteed to fade independently from the direct channels, as well as each other which introduces a full-rank MIMO channel between the source and the destination. In the cooperative communications setup, there is a-priori few constraints to different nodes receiving useful energy that has been emitted by another transmitting node. The new paradigm in user cooperation is that, by implementing the appropriate signal processing algorithms at the nodes, multiple terminals can process the transmissions overheard from other nodes and be made to collaborate by relaying information for each other. The relayed information is subsequently combined at a destination node so as to create spatial diversity. This creates a network that can be regarded as a system implementing a distributed multiple antenna where collaborating nodes create diverse signal paths for each other (Liu et al., 2009). Therefore, we study the cooperative relay communication system, and consequently, a cooperative ZP-OFDM to achieve the full diversity is investigated.

The rest of the chapter is organized as follows. In Section II, we first provide and discuss the basic models of AF, DF and their hybrid scheme. The performance analysis of the hybrid DF-AF is presented in Section III. The cooperative ZP-OFDM scheme, which will be very promising for the future cooperative Ultra Wide Band (UWB) system, is addressed in Section IV, the space time frequency coding (STFC) scheme for the full diversity cooperation is proposed as well. The conclusions of the chapter appear in Section VI.

2. System model

Cooperative communications is a new paradigm shift for the fourth generation wireless system that will guarantee high data rates to all users in the network, and we anticipate that it will be the key technology aspect in the fifth generation wireless networks (Liu et al., 2009).

In terms of research ascendance, cooperative communications can be seen as related to research on relay channel and MIMO systems. The concept of user cooperation itself was introduced in two-part series of papers (Sendonaris et al., Part I, 2003; Sendonaris et al., Part II, 2003). In these works, Sendonaris *et al.* proposed a two-user cooperation system, in which pairs of terminals in the wireless network are coupled to help each other forming a distributed two-antenna system. Cooperative communications allows different users or nodes in a wireless network to share resources and to create collaboration through distributed transmission/processing, in which each user's information is sent out not only by the user but also by the collaborating users (Nosratinia et al., 2004). Cooperative communications promises significant capacity and multiplexing gain increase in the wireless system (Kramer et al., 2005). It also realizes a new form of space diversity to combat the detrimental effects of severe fading. There are mainly two relaying protocols: AF and DF.

2.1 Amplify and forward protocol

In AF, the received signal is amplified and retransmitted to the destination. The advantage of this protocol is its simplicity and low cost implementation. But the noise is also amplified at the relay. The AF relay channel can be modeled as follows. The signal transmitted from the source x is received at both the relay and destination as

$$y_{s,r} = \sqrt{E_s}h_{s,r}x + n_{s,r}, \text{ and } y_{s,D} = \sqrt{E_s}h_{s,D}x + n_{s,D} \tag{6}$$

where $h_{s,r}$ and $h_{s,D}$ are the channel gains between the source and the relay and destination, respectively, and are modeled as Rayleigh flat fading channels. The terms $n_{s,r}$ and $n_{s,D}$ denote the additive white Gaussian noise with zero-mean and variance N_0, E_s is the average transmission energy at the source node. In this protocol, the relay amplifies the signal from the source and forwards it to the destination ideally to equalize the effect of the channel fading between the source and the relay. The relay does that by simply scaling the received signal by a factor A_r that is inversely proportional to the received power, which is denoted by

$$A_r = \sqrt{\frac{E_s}{E_s h_{s,r} + N_0}} \tag{7}$$

The destination receives two copies from the signal x through the source link and relay link. There are different techniques to combine the two signals at the destination. The optimal technique that maximizes the overall SNR is the maximal ratio combiner (MRC). Note that the MRC combining requires a coherent detector that has knowledge of all channel coefficients, and the SNR at the output of the MRC is equal to the sum of the received signal-to-noise ratios from all branches.

2.2 Decode and forward protocol

Another protocol is termed as a decode-and-forward scheme, which is often simply called a DF protocol. In the DF, the relay attempts to decode the received signals. If successful, it re-encodes the information and retransmits it. Although DF protocol has the advantage over AF protocol in reducing the effects of channel interferences and additive noise at the relay, the system complexity will be increased to guarantee the correct signal detection.

Note that the decoded signal at the relay may be incorrect. If an incorrect signal is forwarded to the destination, the decoding at the destination is meaningless. It is clear that for such a scheme the diversity achieved is only one, because the performance of the system is limited by the worst link from the source–relay and source-destination (Laneman et al., 2004).

Although DF relaying has the advantage over AF relaying in reducing the effects of noise and interference at the relay, it entails the possibility of forwarding erroneously detected signals to the destination, causing error propagation that can diminish the performance of the system. The mutual information between the source and the destination is limited by the mutual information of the weakest link between the source–relay and the combined channel from the source-destination and relay-destination.

Since the reliable decoding is not always available, which also means DF protocol is not always suitable for all relaying situations. The tradeoff between the time-consuming decoding, and a better cooperative transmission, finding the optimum hybrid cooperative schemes, that include both DF and AF for different situations, is an important issue for the cooperative wireless networks design.

2.3 Hybrid DF-AF protocol

In this chapter, we consider a hybrid cooperative OFDM strategy as shown in Fig. 3, where we transmit data from source node S to destination node D through R relays, without the direct link between S and D. This relay structure is called 2-hop relay system, i.e., first hop from source node to relay, and second hop from relay to destination. The channel fading for different links are assumed to be identical and statistically independent, quasi-statistic, i.e., channels are constant within several OFDM symbol durations. This is a reasonable assumption as the relays are usually spatially well separated and in a slow changing environment. We assume that the channels are well known at the corresponding receiver sides, and a one bit feedback channel from destination to relay is used for removing the unsuitable AF relays. All the AWGN terms have equal variance N_0. Relays are re-ordered according to the descending order of the SNR between S and Q, i.e., $\mathrm{SNR}_{SQ_1} > \cdots > \mathrm{SNR}_{SQ_R}$, where SNR_{SQ_r} denotes the r-th largest SNR between S and Q.

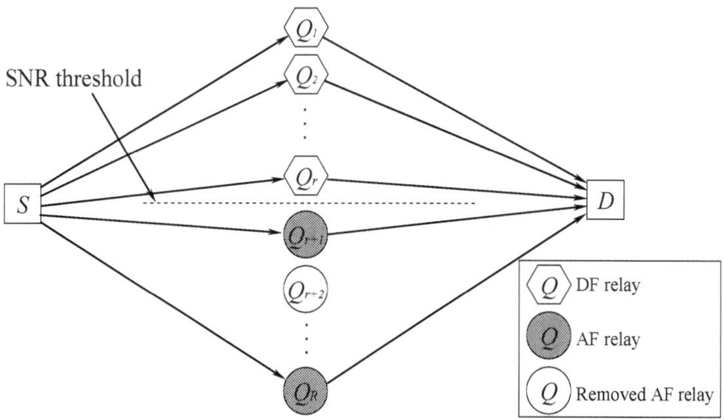

Fig. 3. Hybrid relay cooperation with dynamic optimal combination of DF-AF relays (S: Source, D: Destination, Q_r: r-th Relay)

In this model, relays can determine whether the received signals are decoded correctly or not, just simply by comparing the SNR to the threshold, which will be elaborated in Section 3.1. Therefore, the relays with SNR above the threshold will be chosen to decode and forward the data to the destination, as shown with the white hexagons in Fig.3. The white circle is the removed AF relay according to the dynamic optimal combination strategy which will be proposed in Section 3.2. The rest of the relays follow the AF protocol, as shown with the white hexagons in Fig. 3 (Lu & Nikookar, 2009; Lu et al., 2010).

The received SNR at the destination in the hybrid cooperative network can be denoted as

$$\gamma_h = \sum_{Q_i \in DF} \frac{E_Q h_{Q_i,D}}{N_0} + \sum_{Q_j \in AF} \frac{\dfrac{E_S h_{S,Q_j}}{N_0} \dfrac{E_Q h_{Q_j,D}}{N_0}}{\dfrac{E_S h_{S,Q_j}}{N_0} + \dfrac{E_Q h_{Q_j,D}}{N_0} + 1} \tag{8}$$

where $h_{Q_i,D}$, h_{S,Q_j} and $h_{Q_j,D}$ denote the power gains of the channel from the i-th relay to the destination in DF protocol, source node to the j-th relay in AF protocol and j-th relay to the destination in AF protocol, respectively. E_S and E_Q in (8) are the average transmission energy at the source node and at the relays, respectively. By choosing the amplification factor A_{Q_j} in the AF protocol as:

$$A_{Q_j}^2 = \frac{E_S}{E_S h_{S,Q_j} + N_0} \tag{9}$$

and forcing the E_Q in DF equal to E_S, it will be convenient to maintain constant average transmission energy at relays, equal to the original transmitted energy at the source node.

In this chapter, OFDM is used as a modulation technique in the cooperative system to gain from its inherent advantages and combat frequency selective fading of each cooperative link, with W_r, $r = 1,2,\cdots,R$ independent paths. Later, we also show that, by utilizing the space-frequency coding, hybrid DF-AF cooperative OFDM can also gain from the frequency selective fading and achieve the multi-path diversity with a diversity gain of W_{min} = min (W_r). As shown in the Fig.4, the r-th relay first decides to adopt DF or AF protocol according to the SNR threshold. For the DF-protocol, the symbols are decoded at the relays, and then an IFFT operation is applied on these blocks to produce the OFDM symbol. Before transmission, a prefix (CP or ZP) is added to each OFDM symbol. For the AF-protocol, relays which undergo the deep fading will be removed by using the dynamic optimal combination strategy discussed later in this section. Other AF relays are proper relays, amplify and forward the data to the destination. At the destination node, after the prefix removal, the received OFDM symbols are fast-Fourier-transformed, and the resulting symbols at the destination are used for the combination and detection.

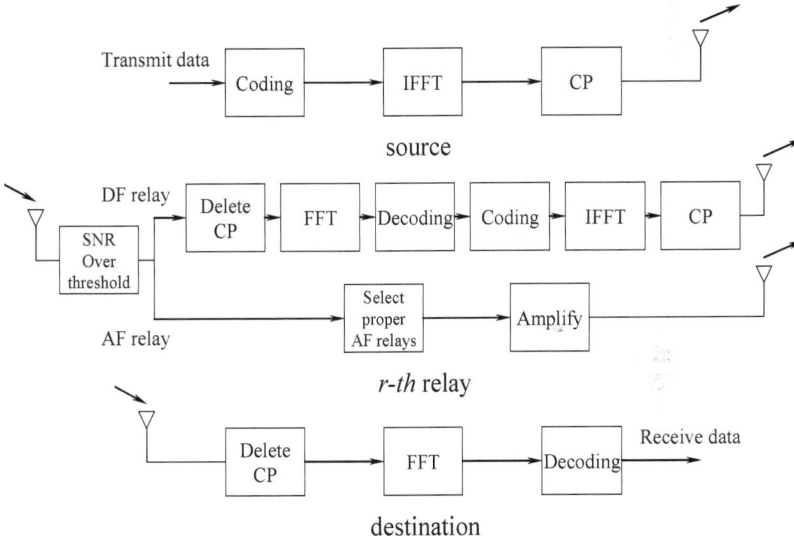

Fig. 4. Relay selection in the hybrid DF-AF cooperative OFDM wireless transmission strategy (top: source, middle: relay, bottom: destination)

The receiver at the destination collects the data from DF and AF relays with a MRC. Because of the amplification in the intermediate stage in the AF protocol, the overall channel gain of the AF protocol should include the source to relay, relay to destination channels gains and amplification factor. The decision variable u at the MRC output is given by

$$u = \sum_{Q_i \in DF} \frac{\left(H_{Q_i,D}\right)^* Y_{Q_i}}{\left(H_{Q_i,D}\right)^* H_{Q_i,D}} + \sum_{Q_j \in AF} \frac{\left(H_{S,Q_j} A_{Q_j} H_{Q_j,D}\right)^* Y_{Q_j}}{\left(H_{S,Q_j} A_{Q_j} H_{Q_j,D}\right)^* \left(H_{S,Q_j} A_{Q_j} H_{Q_j,D}\right)} \tag{10}$$

where Y_{Q_i} and Y_{Q_j} are the received signal from DF i-th relay and AF j-th relays, respectively, and $(\cdot)^*$ denotes the conjugate operation. $H_{Q_i,D}$, H_{S,Q_i} and $H_{Q_j,D}$ are frequency response of the channel power gains, respectively.

In the proposed hybrid DF-AF cooperative network, DF plays a dominant role in the whole system. However, switching to AF scheme for the relay nodes with SNR below the threshold often improves the total transmission performance, and accordingly AF plays a positive compensating role.

3. Performance analysis of Hybrid DF-AF protocol

3.1 Threshold for DF and AF relays

In general, mutual information I is the upper bound of the target rate B bit/s/Hz, i.e., the spectral efficiency attempted by the transmitting terminal. Normally, $B \leq I$, and the case $B > I$ is known as the outage event. Meanwhile, channel capacity, C, is also regarded as the maximum achievable spectral efficiency, i.e., $B \leq C$.

Conventionally, the maximum average mutual information of the direct transmission between source and destination, i.e., I_D, achieved by independent and identically distributed (i.i.d) zero-mean, circularly symmetric complex Gaussian inputs, is given by

$$I_D = \log_2\left(1 + \text{SNR}\, h_{S,D}\right) \tag{11}$$

as a function of the power gain over source and destination, $h_{S,D}$. According to the inequality $B \leq I$, we can derive the SNR threshold for the full decoding as

$$\text{SNR} \geq \frac{2^B - 1}{h_{S,D}} \tag{12}$$

Then, we suppose all of the X relays adopt the DF cooperative transmission without direct transmission. The maximum average mutual information for DF cooperation I_{DF_co} is shown (Laneman et al., 2004) to be

$$I_{DF\_co} = \frac{1}{X}\min\left\{\log_2\left(1 + \sum_{r=1}^{R}\text{SNR}\, h_{S,Q_r}\right), \log_2\left(1 + \sum_{r=1}^{R}\text{SNR}\, h_{Q_r,D}\right)\right\} \tag{13}$$

which is a function of the channel power gains. Here, R denotes the number of the relays. For the r-th DF link, requiring both the relay and destination to decode perfectly, the maximum average mutual information I_{DF_li} can be shown as

$$I_{DF\_li} = \min\left\{\log_2\left(1 + \text{SNR}\, h_{S,Q_r}\right), \log_2\left(1 + \text{SNR}\, h_{Q_r,D}\right)\right\} \tag{14}$$

The first term in (14) represents the maximum rate at which the relay can reliably decode the source message, while the second term in (14) represents the maximum rate at which the destination can reliably decode the message forwarded from relay. We note that such mutual information forms are typical of relay channel with full decoding at the relay (Cover & El Gamal, 1979). The SNR threshold of this DF link for target rate B is given by $I_{DF\_li} \geq B$ which is derived as

$$\mathrm{SNR} \geq \frac{2^B - 1}{\min\left(h_{S,Q_r}, h_{Q_r,D}\right)} \tag{15}$$

In the proposed hybrid DF-AF cooperative transmission, we only consider that a relay can fully decode the signal transmitted over the source-relay link, but not the whole DF link. Thus, the SNR threshold for the full decoding at the r-th relay reaches its lower bound as

$$\gamma_{th} \geq \frac{2^B - 1}{h_{S,Q_r}} \tag{16}$$

For the DF protocol, let R denote the number of the total relays, M denote the set of participating relays, whose SNRs are above the SNR threshold, and the reliable decoding is available. The achievable channel capacity, C_{DF}, with SNR threshold is calculated as

$$C_{DF} = \sum_M \frac{1}{R} \mathrm{E}\left(\log_2\left(1 + y|M\right)\right) \Pr(M) \tag{17}$$

where $\mathrm{E}(\cdot)$ denotes the expectation operator, $y|M = (R-K)\gamma_{S,D} + \sum_{Q \in M}\gamma_{Q,D}$ denotes the instantaneous received SNR at the destination given set M with K participating relays, where $\gamma_{n,m}$ denotes the instantaneous received SNR at node m, which is directly transmitted from n to m. Since $y|M$ is the weighted sum of independent exponential random variables (Farhadi & Beaulieu, 2008), the probability density function (PDF) of $y|M$ can be obtained using its moment generating function (MGF) and partial fraction technique for evaluation of the inverse Laplace transform, see Eq. (8d) and Eq. (8e) in (Farhadi & Beaulieu, 2008). $\Pr(M)$ in (17) is the probability of a particular set of participating relays which are obtained as

$$\Pr(M) = \prod_{Q \in M} \exp\left(-\frac{R\gamma_{th}}{\Gamma_{S,Q \in M}}\right) \prod_{Q \notin M}\left(1 - \exp\left(-\frac{R\gamma_{th}}{\Gamma_{S,Q \notin M}}\right)\right) \tag{18}$$

where $\Gamma_{u,v}$ denotes the average SNR over the link between nodes u and v.

Combining (13), (17) and (18) with the inequality $I_{DF\_co} \leq C_{DF}$, since the maximum average mutual information, I, is upper bound by the achievable channel capacity, C, we can calculate the upper bound of SNR threshold γ_{th} for fully decoding in the DF protocol.

Now, we can obtain the upper bound and the lower bound of the SNR threshold γ_{th} for the hybrid DF-AF cooperation. However, compared to the upper bound, the lower bound as shown in the (16) is more crucial for improving the transmission performance. This is because the DF protocol plays a dominant role in the hybrid cooperation strategy, and accordingly we want to find the lower bound which provides as much as possible DF relays. We will elaborate this issue later. Fully decoding check can also be guaranteed by employing the error detection code, such as cyclic redundancy check. However, it will increase the system complexity (Lin & Constello, 1983).

3.2 Dynamic optimal combination scheme

In the maximum ratio combining the transmitted signal from R cooperative relays nodes, which underwent independent identically distributed Rayleigh fading, and forwarded to the destination node are combined. In this case the SNR per bit per relay link γ_r has an exponential probability density function (PDF) with average SNR per bit $\bar{\gamma}$:

$$p_{\gamma_r}\left(\gamma_r\right) = \frac{1}{\bar{\gamma}} e^{-\gamma_r/\bar{\gamma}} \tag{19}$$

Since the fading on the R paths is identical and mutually statistically independent, the SNR per bit of the combined SNR γ_c will have a Chi-square distribution with $2R$ degrees of freedom. The PDF $p_{\gamma_c}\left(\gamma_c\right)$ is

$$p_{\gamma_c}\left(\gamma_c\right) = \frac{1}{(R-1)!\bar{\gamma}_c^{\,R}} \gamma_c^{\,R-1} e^{-\gamma_c/\bar{\gamma}_c} \tag{20}$$

where $\bar{\gamma}_c$ is the average SNR per channel, then by integrating the conditional error probability over $\bar{\gamma}_c$, the average probability of error P_e can be obtained as

$$P_e = \int_0^\infty \mathbb{Q}\left(\sqrt{2g\gamma_c}\right) p_{\gamma_c}\left(\gamma_c\right) d\gamma_c \tag{21}$$

where $g = 1$ for coherent BPSK, $g = \frac{1}{2}$ for coherent orthogonal BFSK, $g = 0.715$ for coherent BFSK with minimum correlation, and $\mathbb{Q}(\cdot)$ is the Gaussian Q-function, i.e., $\mathbb{Q}(x) = 1/\sqrt{2\pi} \int_x^\infty \exp\left(-t^2/2\right) dt$. For the BPSK case, the average probability of error can be found in the closed form by successive integration by parts (Proakis, 2001), i.e.,

$$P_e = \left(\frac{1-\mu}{2}\right)^R \sum_{k=0}^{R-1} \binom{R-1+k}{k} \left(\frac{1+\mu}{2}\right)^R \tag{22}$$

where

$$\mu = \sqrt{\frac{\bar{\gamma}_c}{1+\bar{\gamma}_c}} \tag{23}$$

In the hybrid DF-AF cooperative network with two hops in each AF relay, the average SNR per channel $\bar{\gamma}_c$ can be derived as

$$\bar{\gamma}_c = \frac{\gamma_h}{K + 2 \times J} \tag{24}$$

where K and J are the numbers of the DF relays and AF relays, respectively. γ_h can be obtained from (8). In the DF protocol, due to the reliable detection, we only need to consider the last hops, or the channels between the relay nodes and destination node.

As the average probability of error P_e is a precise indication for the transmission performance, we consequently propose a dynamic optimal combination strategy for the hybrid DF-AF cooperative transmission. In this algorithm the proper AF relays are selected to make P_e reach maximum.

First of all, like aforementioned procedure, relays are reordered according to the descending order of the SNR between source and relays, as shown in the Fig.3. According to the proposed SNR threshold, we pick up the DF relays having SNR greater than threshold. Then, we proceed with the AF relay selection scheme, where the inappropriate AF relays are removed. The whole dynamic optimal combination strategy for the hybrid DF-AF cooperation is shown in the flow chart of Fig. 5.

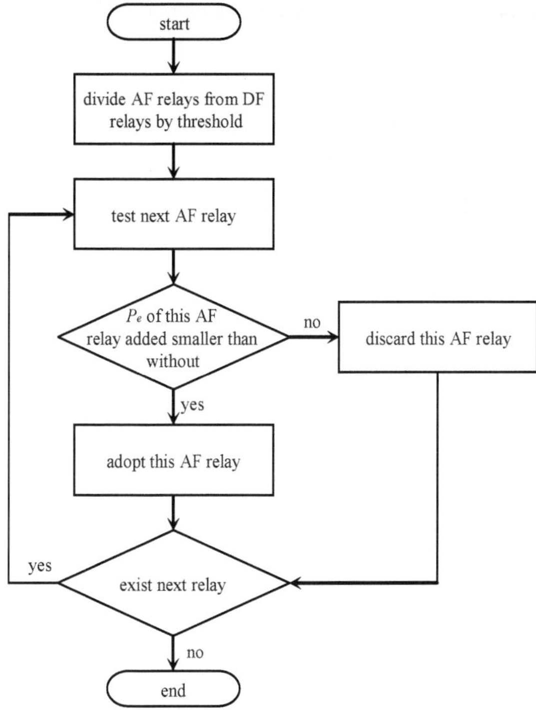

Fig. 5. Flow chart of the dynamic optimal combination strategy for the hybrid DF-AF cooperation

By exploiting the space-frequency coding proposed in (Li et al., 2009), we can further gain from the hybrid DF-AF cooperative OFDM in the frequency selective channel by coding across relays and OFDM tones, and obtain the multi-path diversity. According to the Eq. (14) in (Li et al., 2009), the multi-path diversity of the hybrid DF-AF cooperative OFDM can be shown by the upper bound of the error probability as:

$$P_e < G_c^{-RW_{min}} \left(\frac{\log \gamma_h}{\gamma_h} \right)^{RW_{min}}$$

$$\approx \left(G_c \gamma_h \right)^{-RW_{min}} \text{ as } \gamma_h \to \infty \tag{25}$$

where G_c is a constant, which can be shown as Eq. (35) in (Li et al., 2009), γ_h is the average SNR at the destination in the hybrid cooperative network, and can be calculated by (8) in this chapter.

It can be seen from (25) that the achievable diversity gain is RW_{min}, i.e., the product of the cooperative (relay) diversity R and the multi-path diversity W_{min}. Here $W_{min} = \min(W_r)$, where W_r, $r = 1, 2, \cdots, R$ is the number of independent paths in each relay-destination link.

3.3 Simulation results

First, we simulated BPSK modulation, Rayleigh channel, flat fading, without OFDM, and supposed the SNR threshold for correct decoding is $4E_b/N_0$, then we assumed $h_{Q_i,D} = h_{S,Q_j} = h_{Q_j,D} = 1$, for all branches, to verify proposed analytical BER expression. The resulting average BERs were plotted against the transmit SNR defined as SNR $= E_b/N_0$. As shown in the Fig. 6, the theoretical curves of multi-DF cooperation derived from our analytical closed-form BER expression clearly agree with the Monte Carlo simulated curves, while the theoretical curves of 2-AF and 3-AF cooperation match the simulation result only at the low SNR region.

Fig. 7 shows the BER performance for hybrid DF-AF cooperation. For the DF-dominant hybrid cooperation, the theoretical curves exhibit a good match with the Monte Carlo simulation results curves. The slight gap between theoretical and simulation BER results for the hybrid case of 1-DF + multi-AF can be explained by the AF relay fading which was considered as a double Gaussian channel, a product of two complex Gaussian channel (Patel et al., 2006). Obviously, the distribution of combined SNR (i.e., γ_c) will no longer follow the chi-square distribution giving rise to this slight difference.

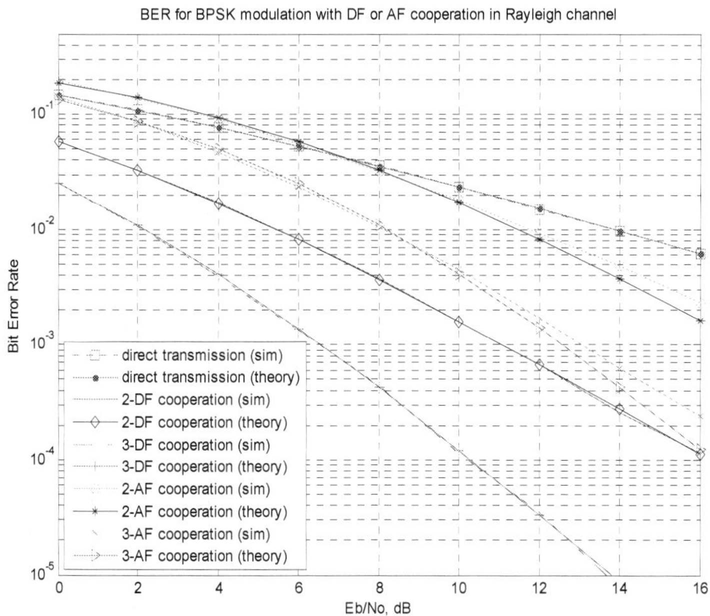

Fig. 6. BER performance for DF or AF cooperation.

In this proposed hybrid cooperation protocol, DF is dominant. We show this characteristic of the hybrid DF-AF cooperation by the following theorem:

Theorem 1: For the F-hop relay link, and the full decoding in DF protocol, as long as the SNR of the last hop is larger than $1/F$ times of the arithmetic mean of the whole link SNR, DF always plays a more important role than AF in improving the BER performance.

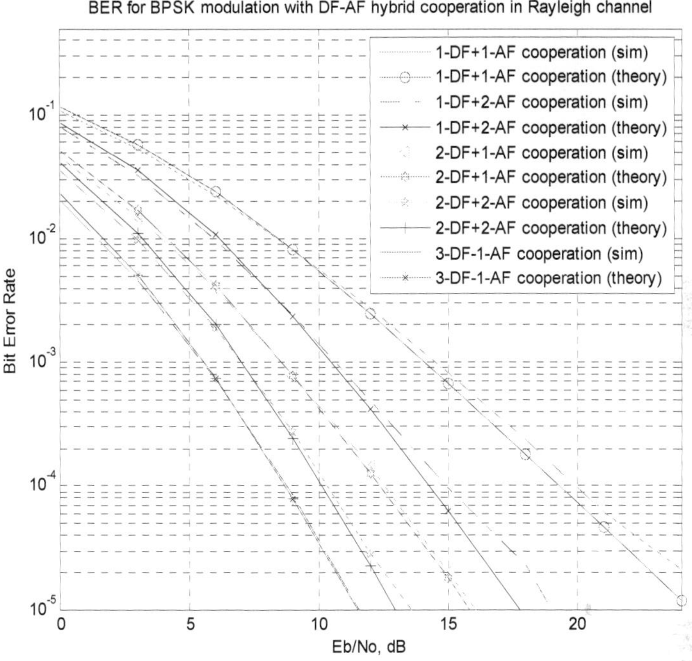

Fig. 7. BER performance for hybrid DF+AF cooperation.

Proof: According to the (22) and (23), the average probability of error P_e is a decreasing function w.r.t. combined SNR, γ_c. The SNR of the F-hop AF relay link, γ_{AF}, is the $1/F$ times of the harmonic mean of γ_i, $\forall\ i \in [1, F]$, i.e. (Hasna & Alouini, 2002),

$$\gamma_{\text{AF}} = \frac{\gamma_1\gamma_2,\ldots,\gamma_L}{\sum_{i=1}^{L}\gamma_1\gamma_2,\ldots,\gamma_{i-1}\gamma_{i+1},\ldots,\gamma_L} \tag{26}$$

Using Pythagorean means theorem, the harmonic mean is always smaller than the arithmetic mean. ∎

For instance, in the high SNR region, the second term of (8) can be approximated as the ½ times the harmonic mean of the 2-hop SNR in AF relay link (i.e., 1 is negligible in the denominator). As in practice, it is very easy for the last hop relay to achieve a SNR larger than $1/L$ times of the arithmetic mean of the whole link SNR, we can only consider the last hop of the reliably decoded DF protocol. Therefore, under the condition of the correct decoding, DF can enhance the error probability performance better than AF in the cooperative relay network.

This DF dominant hybrid cooperative networks strategy can be verified by the above simulation results as well. Comparing 2-DF to 2-AF in Fig. 6, or 2-DF plus 1-AF to 1-DF plus 2-AF in Fig. 7, or other hybrid DF-AF protocols with the same R, we can see that the fully decoded DF protocols always show a better BER performance than AF protocols. Therefore, DF protocols with a reliable decoding play a more important role in hybrid cooperative networks than AF protocols. Meanwhile, we can see from the figure that, changing to the AF scheme for the relay nodes with SNR below the threshold also improves the BER performance, as well as the diversity gain of the whole network. In fact, this is a better way than just discarding these relay nodes.

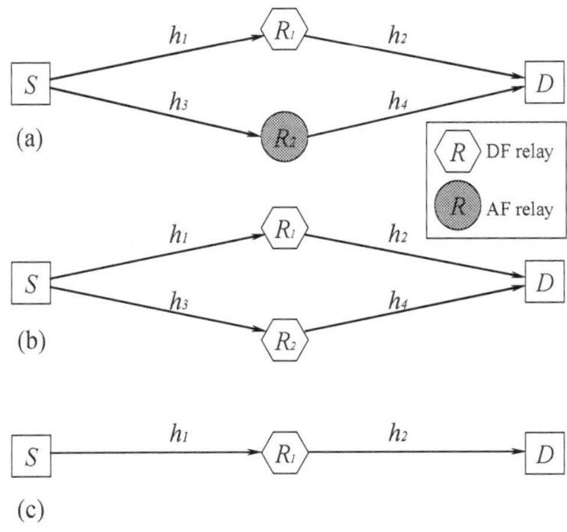

Fig. 8. hybrid DF-AF cooperation and DF cooperation architectures with different average power gains. (a) hybrid DF-AF cooperation, (b) dual DF cooperation, (c) single DF cooperation. (S: Source, D: Destination, h: average power gain between two nodes).

Reference (Louie et al., 2009) proposes a closed-form BER expression for two-hop AF protocol, which includes Gauss' hypergeometric and Gamma functions. This closed-form BER expression needs more computational burden to derive the cooperative analytical expression. In (Sadek et al., 2007), the analytical expression for multi-node DF protocol is provided with a complicated form as well. Instead, the compact closed-form BER expression for hybrid DF-AF cooperation proposed in this chapter allows us to achieve insight into the results with relatively low computations. The simple expressions can also help understanding the factors affecting the system performance. It can also be used for designing different network functions such as power allocation, scheduling, routing, and node selection.

In order to study the effect of the channel gains between source, relay and destination, we compare the hybrid DF-AF with the dual DF as well as the single DF cooperation in Fig. 8. In this figure, h_1, h_2, h_3 and h_4 stand for the average power gain between corresponding two nodes. In this simulation, the SNR threshold for correct decoding is assumed to be $4E_b/N_0$, and we set the first hop average power gain in DF protocol, i.e., h_1 in Fig. 8 (a) and Fig. 8 (c), and h_1, h_3 in Fig. 8 (b) as 4, which means that the relay in DF protocol can fully decode the signal. The average power gains of the first hop in AF protocol, i.e., h_3 in Fig. 8 (a) increases from 0.25 to 20. It can be seen from the Fig. 9 that the dual DF cooperation with reliable decoding outperforms the hybrid DF-AF cooperation, when corresponding average power gains are the same, i.e., diamond marked curve is better than square marked curve in Fig. 9. Meanwhile, the comparison of the curves shows that, the AF relay which undergoes the deep fading deteriorates the BER performance of hybrid DF-AF cooperation in the low SNR region. Thus, this AF relay should be removed according to the proposed dynamic optimal combination strategy to improve the transmission performance. Sum up the above discussion, due to power control, long transmission range, serious attenuation, etc., high SNR at relay and full decoding for DF protocol is not always available. In this case, relays can change to AF protocol with enough SNR to gain from the cooperative diversity.

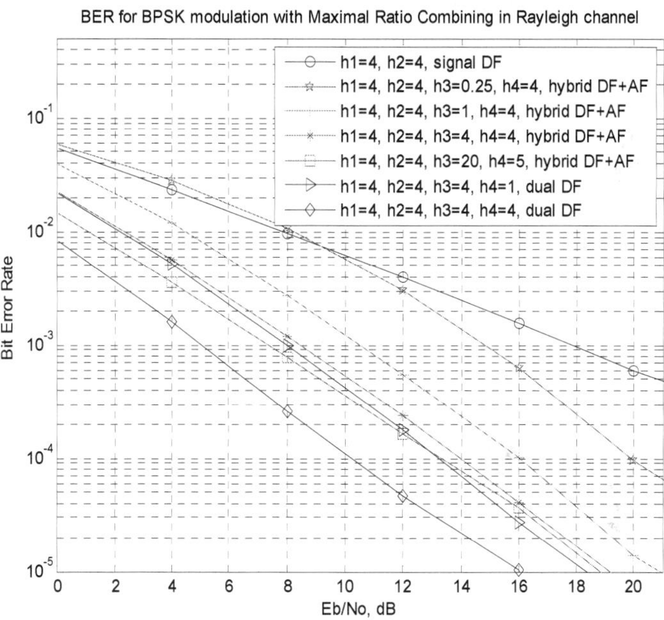

Fig. 9. BER performance for hybrid DF-AF cooperation and DF cooperation with different path gains.

Finally, we illustrate the validity of the theoretical results for the OFDM cooperation via simulations. An OFDM system with 64-point FFT and a CP length of 16 samples, which accounts for 25% of the OFDM symbol was considered. In the simulation, a more practical scenario was considered with a 3-path Rayleigh fading between each source node and relay node or relay node and destination node, i.e., $W_r = 3$. The 3-path delays were assumed at 0, 1, 2 samples, respectively. As illustrated in the Fig. 10, OFDM with CP can nicely cope with the multi-path, and the theoretical curves derived from (22) clearly agree with the Monte Carlo simulation curves. The simulation results indicate that under the condition of ISI resolved by OFDM and reliable decoding, the cooperative diversity gains from the increasing R, which is also shown by (8).

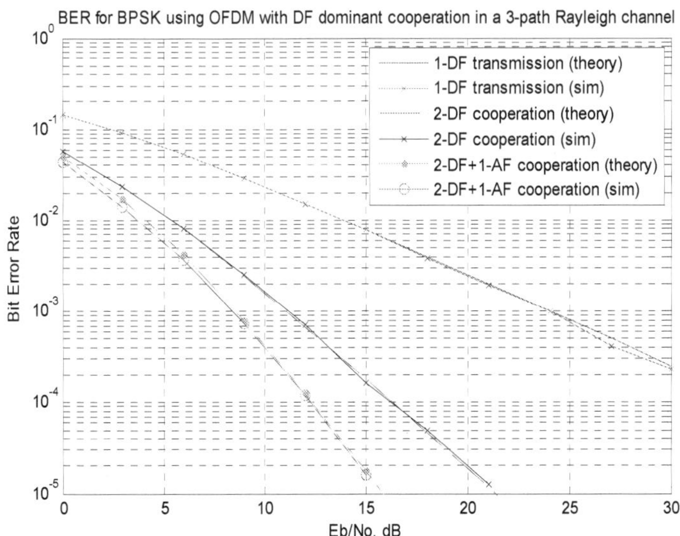

Fig. 10. BER performance for DF dominant OFDM cooperation.

4. ZP-OFDM with cooperative relays

4.1 CP and ZP for cooperative OFDM

Among the many possible multicarrier modulation techniques, OFDM is the one that has gained more acceptance as the modulation technique for high-speed wireless networks and 4G mobile broadband standards. Conventionally, CP is exploited to eliminate inter-symbol-interference (ISI) due to multipath. With a cyclic extension, the linear convolution channel is transformed into a circular convolution channel, and the ISI can be easily resolved. However, the cyclic prefix is not the only solution to combat the multipath. ZP has been recently proposed as an alternative to the CP in OFDM transmissions and Cognitive Radio (Lu et al., 2009). One of the advantages of using a ZP is that the transmitter requires less power back-off at the analog amplifier. Since the correlation caused by the cyclic prefix creates discrete spectral lines (ripples) into the average power spectral density of the transmitted signal and the radio emission power levels are limited by the Federal Communications Commission (FCC), the presence of any ripples in the power spectrum density (PSD) requires additional power back-off at the transmitter. In fact, the amount of power back-off that is required is equal to the peak-to-average ratio of the PSD.

A multiband (MB) ZP OFDM-based approach to design UWB transceivers has been recently proposed in (Batra et al., 2004) and (Batra, 2004) for the IEEE Standard. In Dec. 2008, the European Computer Manufacturers Association (ECMA) adopted ZP-OFDM for the latest version of High rate UWB Standard (Standard ECMA-368, 2008). Because of its advantage in the low power transmission, ZP-OFDM will have the potential to be used in other low power wireless communications systems.

We know that the multiple transmissions in the cooperative system may not be either time or frequency synchronized, i.e., signals transmitted from different transmitters arrive at the receiver as different time instances, and multiple carrier frequency offsets (CFOs) also exist due to the oscillator mismatching. Different from the conventional MIMO system, the existence of multiple CFOs in the cooperative systems makes the direct CFOs compensation hard if not impossible. Therefore, in this section, we will investigate the cooperative ZP-OFDM system with multipath channel and CFOs, a subject that has not been addressed before. We propose a STFC, to hold the linear structure of the ZP-OFDM, and achieve the full cooperative spatial diversity, i.e., full multi-relay diversity. Furthermore, we show that, with only *linear receivers*, such as zero forcing (ZF) and minimum mean square error (MMSE) receivers, the proposed code achieves full diversity.

4.2 Full cooperative diversity with linear equalizer
4.2.1 Fundamental limits of diversity with linear equalizer

To quantify the performance of different communication systems, two important criteria are the average bit-error rates (BERs) and capacity. The BER performance of wireless transmissions over fading channels is usually quantified by two parameters: diversity order and coding gain (Liu et al., 2003; Tse & Viswanath, 2005). The diversity order is defined as the asymptotic slope of the BER versus signal-to-noise ratio (SNR) curve plotted in log-log scale. It describes how fast the error probability decays with SNR, while the coding gain measures the performance gap among different schemes when they have the same diversity. The higher the diversity, the smaller the error probability at high-SNR regimes. To cope with the deleterious effects of fading on the system performance, diversity-enriched transmitters and receivers have well-appreciated merits. Reference (Ma & Zhang, 2008) reveals the relationship between the channel orthogonality deficiency (*od*) and system full diversity. The orthogonality deficiency (*od*) indicates the degree of difficulty for the signal detection in the certain transceiver and channel condition (the smaller *od*, the easier signal detection). References (Shang & Xia, 2007; Shang & Xia, 2008) provide the two conditions for linear equalizer to achieve the full diversity. We will illustrate in this Section how to design the STFC to achieve full diversity for ZP-OFDM system.

In addition to focusing on diversity performance, practical systems also give high priority to reducing receiver complexity. Although maximum likelihood equalizer (MLE) enjoys the maximum diversity performance, its exponential decoding complexity makes it infeasible for certain practical systems. Some near-ML schemes (e.g., sphere decoding) can be used to reduce the decoding complexity. However, at low SNR or when large decoding blocks are sent/or high signal constellations are employed, the complexity of near-ML schemes is still high. In addition, these near-ML schemes adopt linear equalizers as preprocessing steps. To further reduce the complexity, when the system model is linear, one may apply linear equalizers (LEs) (Ma & Zhang, 2008).

4.2.2 System model and Linear ZP-OFDM

We consider a cooperative ZP-OFDM system as shown in the Fig. 11. Here the DF protocol is adopted in the cooperative communication model. Relays can fully decode the information, and participate in the cooperation, and occupy different frequency bands to transmit data to the destination. Each relay-destination link undergoes multipath Rayleigh fading. For the relay r, $r \in [1,2,...,R]$, R is the number of relays, the received signal $\mathbf{y}_r$ can be formulated as

$$\mathbf{y}_r = \mathbf{F}_{P,r}\mathbf{D}_{P,r}\mathbf{H}_r\mathbf{T}_{ZP}\mathbf{F}_{N,r}^{H}\mathbf{x}_r + \mathbf{n} \qquad (27)$$

where $\mathbf{x}_r \triangleq [x_0, \cdots, x_{N-1}]^T$ is the vector of the so called frequency transmitted information signal, and N is the signal length. The subscript r here indicates the variables or operators related to the r-th relay. To simplify the exposition, we only consider the effect of CFOs on signal. The noise term is denoted as $\mathbf{n}$, which stands for i.i.d. complex white Gaussian noise with zero mean. $\mathbf{F}_{N,r}$ stands for the N-point FFT matrix with (m, k)-th entry $\exp(j2\pi mk / N)/\sqrt{N}$, while $\mathbf{F}_{P,r}$ stands for the P-point FFT matrix.

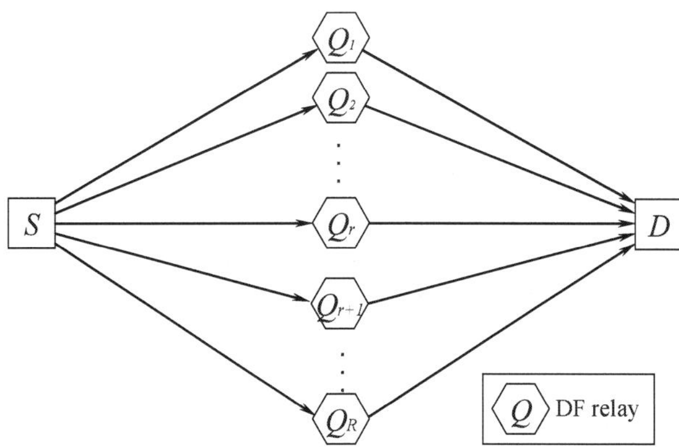

Fig. 11. Cooperative ZP-OFDM system architecture, (S: Source, D: Destination, Q_r: r-th Relay).

The matrix

$$\mathbf{T}_{ZP} = \begin{bmatrix} \mathbf{I}_N \\ 0 \end{bmatrix}_{P \times N} \tag{28}$$

performs the zero-padding on the transmitted signal with V zeros, where $\mathbf{I}_N$ is $N \times N$ identity matrix, and $P = N + V$.

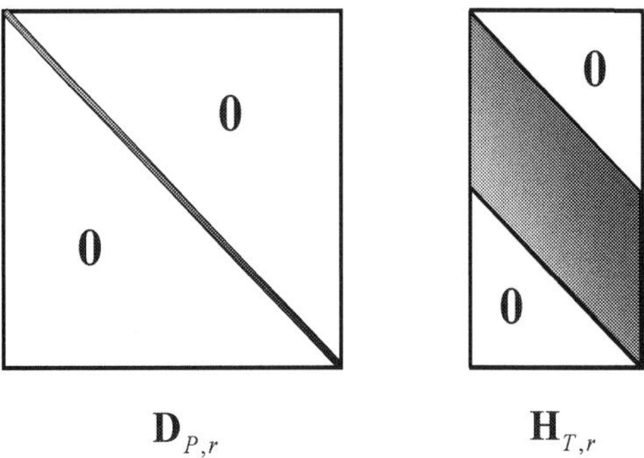

Fig. 12. Structure of (left) $\mathbf{D}_{P,r}$ and (right) $\mathbf{H}_{T,r}$ matrix. Blank parts are all 0's.

The matrix $\mathbf{H}_r$ is a $P \times P$ lower triangular matrix with its first column vector is $\left[h_{1,r},\cdots,h_{L,r},0\cdots0\right]^{T}$, and its first row vector is $\left[h_{1,r},0\cdots0\right]$, and this matrix denotes the multipath channel over the r-th relay and destination link, L is the length of channel. Without loss of generality, we assumed that the channel lengths of different relay-destination links are all L. To avoid ISI, we should have $L \le V$, and we assume $L = V$. The $\mathbf{D}_{P,r}$ is a diagonal matrix representing the residual carrier frequency error over the r-th relay and destination link and is defined in terms of its diagonal elements as $\mathbf{D}_{P,r} = \mathrm{diag}\left(1,\alpha_r,\cdots,\alpha_r^{P-1}\right)$, with $\alpha_r = \exp\left(j2\pi\Delta q_r / N\right)$, $\mathrm{diag}(\cdot)$ is diagonal matrix with main diagonal $(\cdot)$, and Δq_r is the normalized carrier frequency offset of r-th relay with the symbol duration of ZP-OFDM. Here, we notice that $\mathbf{H}_{T,r} = \mathbf{H}_r\mathbf{T}_{ZP}$ is a full column rank tall Toeplitz matrix, and its correlation matrix always guaranteed to be invertible. The structures of $\mathbf{D}_{P,r}$ and $\mathbf{H}_{T,r}$ can be shown as Fig. 12.

Since $\mathbf{H}_{T,r}$ relates to the linear convolution, we refer to this tall Toeplitz structure as linear structure, which assures symbol recovery (perfect detectability in the absence of noise) regardless of the channel zeros locations. The linear structure of ZP-OFDM provides a better BER performance and an easier blind channel estimation and blind symbol synchronization as well, while this is not the case for the CP-OFDM. In fact, the channel-irrespective symbol detectable property of ZP-OFDM is equivalent to claiming that ZP-OFDM enjoys maximum diversity gain. Intuitively, this can be understood as the ZP-OFDM retains the entire linear convolution of each transmitted symbol with the channel. Then, we will show how to use the linear property of $\mathbf{H}_{T,r}$ to achieve full spatial diversity in the cooperative system. Consequently, (27) can be rewritten as

$$\mathbf{y}_r = \mathbf{F}_{P,r}\mathbf{D}_{P,r}\mathbf{H}_{T,r}\mathbf{F}_{N,r}^{H}\mathbf{x}_r + \mathbf{n} \tag{29}$$

In this section, we consider a simple frequency division space frequency system for each relay $\mathbf{x}_r$, i.e., arranging transmitted symbols in different frequency bands according to the corresponding relay, as shown in the Fig. 13. By doing so, we can exploit the linear structure of ZP-OFDM to achieve the full cooperative diversity with linear receiver regardless of the existence of CFOs.

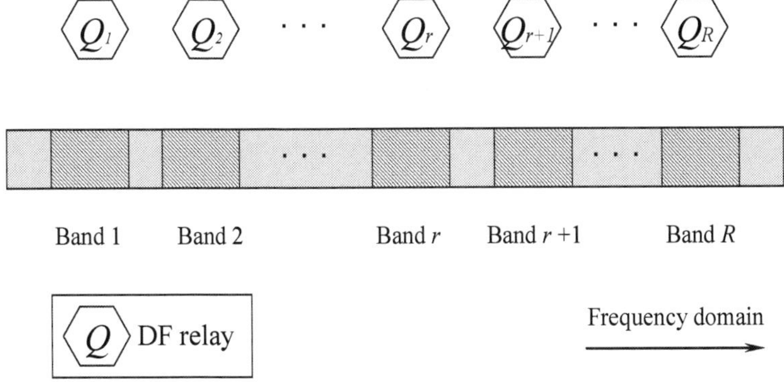

Fig. 13. Frequency division cooperative ZP-OFDM system.

We take $\mathbf{x}_r$ as the information symbols correctly received at the r-th relay nodes involved in the DF-cooperative scheme. After full decoding, $\mathbf{x}_r$ is assigned to the corresponding r-th frequency band as shown in the Fig. 13, and forwarded to the destination.

Considering the frequency division system, the received signal at the destination of all R relay nodes yields

$$\mathbf{y} = \mathbf{F}_P \mathbf{D} \mathbf{H} \mathbf{F}_N^H \mathbf{x} + \mathbf{n} \qquad (30)$$

where $\mathbf{F}_P = \mathrm{diag}\left(\mathbf{F}_{P,1}, \mathbf{F}_{P,2}, \cdots, \mathbf{F}_{P,R}\right)$, $\mathbf{D} = \mathrm{diag}\left(\mathbf{D}_{P,1}, \mathbf{D}_{P,2}, \cdots, \mathbf{D}_{P,R}\right)$, $\mathbf{H} = \mathrm{diag}\left(\mathbf{H}_{T,1}, \mathbf{H}_{T,2}, \cdots, \mathbf{H}_{T,R}\right)$, $\mathbf{F}_N^H = \mathrm{diag}\left(\mathbf{F}_{N,1}^H, \mathbf{F}_{N,2}^H, \cdots, \mathbf{F}_{N,R}^H\right)$ are all diagonal matrices with each relay's components on their diagonals. For instance, we consider a 2-relay cooperation system, i.e., $R = 2$, the structures of $\mathbf{F}_P$, $\mathbf{D}$, $\mathbf{H}$ and $\mathbf{F}_N^H$ can be illustrated as Fig. 14. In (30), $\mathbf{x} = \left[\mathbf{x}_1^T, \mathbf{x}_2^T, \cdots, \mathbf{x}_R^T\right]^T$ denotes the forwarded signal from all relays occupying different frequency bands.

If we denote $\mathbb{H} = \mathbf{F}_P \mathbf{D} \mathbf{H} \mathbf{F}_N^H$, then (30) becomes

$$\mathbf{y} = \mathbb{H} \mathbf{x} + \mathbf{n} \qquad (31)$$

On the other hand, let us go back to (27), right multiplying $\mathbf{T}_{ZP}$ changes $\mathbf{H}_r$ from a $P \times P$ lower triangular matrix into a $P \times N$ tall Toeplitz matrix $\mathbf{H}_{T,r}$ with its first column vector as $\left[h_{1,r}, \cdots, h_{L,r}, 0 \cdots 0\right]^T$, and we denote $\mathbf{x}_{t,r} = \mathbf{F}_{N,r}^H \mathbf{x}_r$, which is well known as time domain signal in OFDM system, then (27) can be represented as

$$\mathbf{y}_r = \mathbf{F}_{P,r} \mathbf{D}_{P,r} \mathbf{H}_{T,r} \mathbf{x}_{t,r} + \mathbf{n} \qquad (32)$$

where $\mathbf{H}_{T,r} \mathbf{x}_{t,r}$ stands for the linear convolution of the multipath channel with the time domain transmitted signal, this is a special property possessed by the ZP-OFDM system. According to the commutativity of the linear convolution, we have $\mathbf{H}_{T,r} \mathbf{x}_{t,r} = \mathbf{X}_{T,r} \mathbf{h}_r$, where $\mathbf{X}_{T,r}$ is a $P \times L$ tall Toeplitz matrix with $\left[\mathbf{x}_{t,r}^T, \mathbf{0}^T\right]^T$ as its first column, and $\mathbf{h}_r = \left[h_{1,r}, \cdots, h_{L,r}\right]^T$. Consequently, (32) can be transformed into another form as

$$\mathbf{y}_r = \mathbf{F}_{P,r} \mathbf{D}_{P,r} \mathbf{X}_{T,r} \mathbf{h}_r + \mathbf{n} \qquad (33)$$

We denote $\mathbf{h}_c = \left[\mathbf{h}_1^T, \mathbf{h}_2^T, \cdots, \mathbf{h}_R^T\right]^T$, $\mathbf{S}_r = \mathbf{F}_{P,r} \mathbf{D}_{P,r} \mathbf{X}_{T,r}$, $\mathbb{S} = \mathrm{diag}\left(\mathbf{S}_1, \mathbf{S}_2, \cdots, \mathbf{S}_R\right)$, and consider the received signal of all R relay nodes, then we get the received signal as

$$\mathbf{y} = \mathbb{S} \mathbf{h}_c + \mathbf{n} \qquad (34)$$

Equations (31) and (34) are two equivalent received data models of this frequency division cooperative ZP-OFDM system. $\mathbb{H}$ in (31) is regarded as the overall equivalent channel, while $\mathbb{S}$ in (34) is the equivalent signal matrix of this frequency division cooperative ZP-OFDM system. In the following section, we will exploit $\mathbb{H}$ and $\mathbf{h}_c$ from (31) and (34) to show the verification of the full cooperative spatial diversity.

	

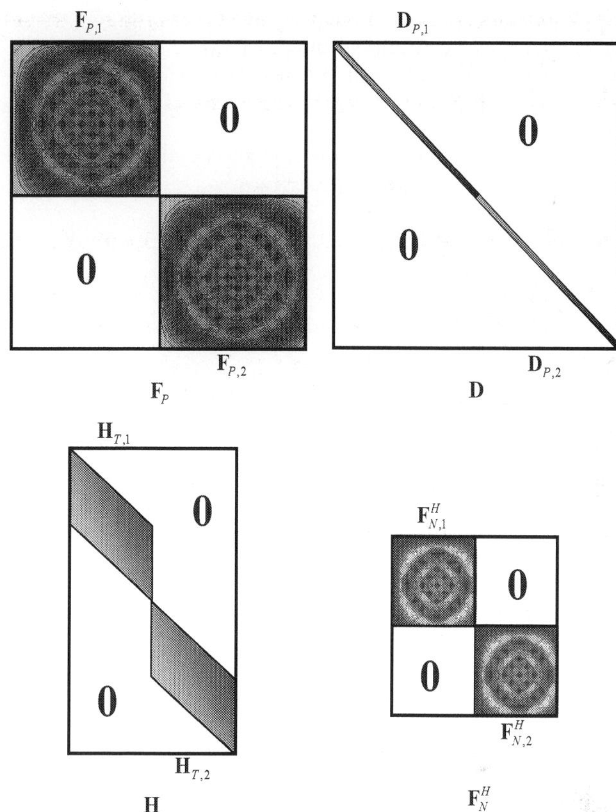

Fig. 14. Structures of the FFT matrices, CFOs matrix and channel matrix for 2-relay cooperative system, top left: FFT matrix $\mathbf{F}_P$, top right: CFOs matrix $\mathbf{D}$, bottom left: channel matrix: $\mathbf{H}$, bottom right: FFT matrix $\mathbf{F}_N^H$. Blank parts are all 0's.

4.3 Space time frequency coding design
4.3.1 Conditions of the full diversity with linear equalizer

In this section, we will show how linear receiver is the only required to achieve full cooperative diversity order RL. We first cite the following theorem from (Shang & Xia, 2007; Shang & Xia, 2008):

Theorem 2 (Shang & Xia, 2007; Shang & Xia, 2008): For PAM, PSK and square QAM constellations, if the following condition holds

$$\|\mathbb{H}\| \leq \alpha \|\mathbf{h}_c\| \quad \text{and} \quad \det\left(\mathbb{H}^H \mathbb{H}\right) \geq \beta \|\mathbf{h}_c\|^{2N}$$

where α and β are positive constants independent of $\mathbf{h}_c$, $\|\cdot\|$ is the Frobenius norm of a vector/matrix, and N is the number of symbols in the transmitted signal, i.e., the length of

$\mathbf{x}_r$ in (29). Then, for any realization of $\mathbb{H}$, with ZF or MMSE receiver, full diversity can be achieved, i.e., the symbol error probability (SEP) P_e satisfies:

$$P_e\left(\hat{s}_l \to s_l\right) \le \bar{c} \cdot \rho^{-RL}, \quad l=1,2,\cdots,L$$

where $\bar{c} \triangleq \dfrac{\eta-1}{\eta}(a\hat{c})^{-2}$, η is the cardinality of the constellation, and $a = \dfrac{3}{2\left(\eta^2-1\right)}$, $\dfrac{\sin^2\left(\pi/\eta\right)}{2}$ and $\dfrac{3}{4(\eta-1)}$ for PAM, PSK, and square QAM, respectively. $\hat{c} = \beta\left(\dfrac{L-1}{\alpha^2}\right)^{L-1}$, and ρ is the symbol SNR.

In what follows, we will show that, with the STFC, the frequency division cooperative ZP-OFDM system satisfies the conditions in Theorem 2. In other words, the proposed frequency division system can achieve full diversity with linear receivers. Note that here the full diversity order is RL.

4.3.2 Space time frequency coding design and verification

According to the above mentioned conditions, we design a linear structure STFC, which guarantees the full cooperative spatial diversity and without redundant power gains. By right multiplying a matrix on $\overline{\mathbf{F}}_N^H\mathbf{x}$, where $\mathbf{I}_r$ is an $N \times N$ identity matrix, $r \in [1,2,\cdots,R]$, $\overline{\mathbf{F}}_N^H = \mathbf{F}_{N,r}^H$ is an N-point IFFT matrix, and $\overline{\mathbf{x}} = \mathbf{x}_r \triangleq [x_0,\cdots,x_{N-1}]^T$ stands for the frequency transmitted information signal, the received signal at the destination from all R relay nodes yields

$$\mathbf{y} = \mathbf{F}_P\mathbf{DHG}\overline{\mathbf{F}}_N^H\overline{\mathbf{x}} + \mathbf{n} \tag{35}$$

where $\mathbf{F}_P$, $\mathbf{D}$ and $\mathbf{H}$ are the same as (30). We denote $\mathbf{HG}=\hat{\mathbf{H}}_T$ and $\overline{\mathbf{x}}_t = \overline{\mathbf{F}}_N^H\overline{\mathbf{x}}$, where $\hat{\mathbf{H}}_T = \left[\mathbf{H}_{T,1}^T,\mathbf{H}_{T,2}^T,\cdots,\mathbf{H}_{T,R}^T\right]^T$, $\overline{\mathbf{x}}_t$ is the time domain signal. We notice that matrix $\mathbf{G}$ spreads $\overline{\mathbf{x}}_t$ according to the corresponding relays, and forms a frequency division system, since the relays perform the forwarding in the different bands, as shown clearly in the Fig.13. Therefore, the Matrix $\mathbf{G}$ can be regarded as a coding scheme on the time domain signal, for different relays and different bands, and so called space time frequency code. Then, (35) becomes

$$\mathbf{y} = \mathbf{F}_P\mathbf{D}\hat{\mathbf{H}}_T\overline{\mathbf{F}}_N^H\overline{\mathbf{x}} + \mathbf{n} \tag{36}$$

If we denote $\mathbb{H} = \mathbf{F}_P\mathbf{D}\hat{\mathbf{H}}_T\overline{\mathbf{F}}_N^H$ as the equivalent channel matrix, we get

$$\mathbf{y} = \mathbb{H}\overline{\mathbf{x}} + \mathbf{n} \tag{37}$$

We notice that $\hat{\mathbf{H}}_T$ is a linear Toeplitz matrix. Similar to (32) and (33), we have $\hat{\mathbf{H}}_T\overline{\mathbf{x}}_t = \hat{\mathbf{X}}_T\hat{\mathbf{h}}$, where $\hat{\mathbf{X}}_T$ is a $[P \times R] \times [P \times (R-1)+L]$ tall Toeplitz matrix with $\left[\overline{\mathbf{x}}_t^T,\mathbf{0}^T\right]^T$ as its first

Lin, S. & Constello, D. J. Jr. (1983). *Error Control Coding: Fundamentals and Applications.*, NJ: Prentice-Hall, *ISBN*: 013283796X, Englewood Cliffs

Liu, Z.; Xin, Y. & Giannakis, G. B. (2003). Linear constellation precoded OFDM with maximum multipath diversity and coding gains, *IEEE Trans. Commun.*, Vol. 51, No. 3, pp. 416–427, *ISSN: 0090-6778*

Liu, K. J. R.; Sadek, A. K.; Su W. & Kwasinski, A. (2009). *Cooperative communications and networks*, Cambridge University Press, ISBN-13 978-0-521-89513-2, Cambridge

Louie, R.; Li, Y.; Suraweera, H. A. & Vucetic, B. (2009). Performance analysis of beamforming in two hop amplify and forward relay network with antenna correlation, *IEEE Trans. Wireless Communications*, Vol. 8, No. 6, pp. 3132-3141, *ISSN: 1536-1276*

Lu, H.; Nikookar, H. & Lian, X. (2010). Performance evaluation of hybrid DF-AF OFDM cooperation in Rayleigh Channel, to appear in European Wireless Technology Conference, 2010

Lu, H. & Nikookar, H. (2009). A thresholding strategy for DF-AF hybrid cooperative wireless networks and its performance, Proceedings of IEEE SCVT '09, UCL, Louvain. Nov. 2009

Lu, H.; Nikookar, H. & Chen, H. (2009). On the potential of ZP-OFDM for cognitive radio, Proceedings of WPMC'09, pp. 7-10, Sendai, Japan. Sep. 2009

Ma, X. & Zhang, W. (2008). Fundamental limits of linear equalizers: diversity, capacity, and complexity, *IEEE Trans. Inform. Theory*, Vol. 54, No. 8, pp. 3442-3456, *ISSN*: 0018-9448

Muquet, B.; Wang, Z.; Giannakis, G. B.; Courville, M. & Duhamel, P. (2002). Cyclic prefixing or zero padding for wireless multicarrier transmissions, *IEEE Transaction on Communications*, Vol. 50, No. 12, pp. 2136–2148, *ISSN: 0090-6778*

Nosratinia, A.; Hunter,T. E. & Hedayat, A. (2004). Cooperative communciation in wireless networks, *IEEE Commun. Mag.*, Vol. 42, pp. 74–80, *ISSN*: 0163-6804

Patel, C.; Stüber, G. & Pratt, T. (2006). Statistical properties of amplify and forward relay fading channels, *IEEE Trans. Veh. Technol.*, Vol. 55, No. 1, pp. 1-9, *ISSN*: 0018-9545

Proakis, J. G. (2001). *Digital Communications*, 4th ed., McGraw Hill, *ISBN*-13: 978-0072321111, New York

Sadek, A. K.; Su, W. & Liu, K. J. R. (2007). Multi-node cooperative communications in wireless networks, *IEEE Trans. Signal Processing*, Vol. 55, No. 1, pp. 341-355, *ISSN*: 1053-587X

Sendonaris, A.; Erkip, E. & Aazhang, B. (2003). User cooperation diversity—Part I: System description, *IEEE Trans. Commun.*, Vol. 51, No. 11, pp. 1927–1938, *ISSN: 0090-6778*

Sendonaris, A.; Erkip, E. & Aazhang, B. (2003). User cooperation diversity—Part Part II: Implementation aspects and performance analysis, *IEEE Trans. Commun.*, Vol. 51, No. 11, pp. 1939–1948, *ISSN: 0090-6778*

Shang, Y. & Xia, X.-G. (2007). A criterion and design for space-time block codes achieving full diversity with linear receivers, Proceedings of IEEE ISIT'07, Nice, France, pp. 2906–2910, June 2007

Shang, Y. & Xia, X.-G. (2008). On space-time block codes achieving full diversity with linear receivers, *IEEE Trans. Inform. Theory*, Vol. 54, pp. 4528–4547, *ISSN*: 0018-9448

Standard ECMA-368 High Rate Ultra Wideband PHY and MAC Standard, 3rd edition, Dec. 2008

Tse, D. N. C. & Viswanath, P. (2005). *Fundamentals of Wireless Communications.*, U.K.: Cambridge Univ. Press, *ISBN*-13: 9780521845274, Cambridge

Wang, Z. & Giannakis, G. B. (2000). Wireless multicarrier communications: Where Fourier meets Shannon, *IEEE Signal Processing Mag.*, Vol. 17, No. 3, pp. 1–17, *ISSN*: 1053-5888

Zhang, J.-K.; Liu, J. & Wong, K. M. (2005). Linear Toeplitz space time block codes, Proceedings of IEEE ISIT'05, Adelaide, Australia, Sept. 2005

$$R_{k,l}^{r} = \sum_{p=1}^{N_p} S_{k,l}^{p} H_{k,l}^{p,r} + N_{k,l}^{r} \tag{1}$$

with $H_{k,l}^{p,r}$ denoting the overall channel frequency response in the kth frequency of the lth OFDM block for user p during transmission attempt r. $N_{k,l}^{p}$ denotes the corresponding channel noise and $S_{k,l}^{p}$ is the data symbol selected from a given constellation, transmitted on the kth ($k=1,...,N$) subcarrier of the lth OFDM block by user p ($p=1,...,N_p$). Since we are applying interleaving to the retransmissions, to simplify the mathematical representation we will just assume that it is the sequence of channel coefficients $H_{k,l}^{p,r}$ that are interleaved instead of the symbols (therefore we do not use the index r in $S_{k,l}^{p}$).

After the symbol de-interleavers the sequences of samples associated to all retransmissions are used for detecting all the packets inside the Multipacket Detector with the help of a channel estimator block. After the Multipacket Detector, the demultiplexed symbols sequences pass through the demodulator, de-interleaver and channel decoder. This channel decoder has two outputs: one is the estimated information sequence and the other is the sequence of log-likelihood ratio (LLR) estimates of the code symbols. These LLRs are passed through the Decision Device which outputs soft-decision estimates of the code symbols. These estimates enter the Transmitted Signal Rebuilder which performs the same operations of the transmitters (interleaving, modulation). The reconstructed symbol sequences are then used for a refinement of the channel estimates and also for possible improvement of the multipacket detection task for the subsequent iteration. This can be accomplished using an IC in the Multipacket Detector block.

4.2 Multipacket Detector

The objective of the Multipacket Detector is to separate multiple colliding packets. It can accomplish this with several different methods. In the first receiver iterations it can apply either the MMSE criterion (Minimum Mean Squared Error), the ZF criterion (Zero Forcing) or a Maximum Likelihood Soft Output criterion (MLSO) (Souto et al., 2008). Using matrix notation the MMSE estimates of the transmitted symbols in subcarrier k and OFDM block l is given by

$$\hat{\mathbf{S}}_{k,l} = \hat{\mathbf{H}}_{k,l}^{H} \cdot \left(\hat{\mathbf{H}}_{k,l} \hat{\mathbf{H}}_{k,l}^{H} + \sigma^2 \mathbf{I} \right)^{-1} \mathbf{R}_{k,l} \tag{2}$$

where $\hat{\mathbf{S}}_{k,l}$ is the $N_p \times 1$ estimated transmitted signal vector with one user in each position, $\hat{\mathbf{H}}_{k,l}$ is the $N_p \times N_p$ channel matrix estimate with each column representing a different user and each line representing a different transmission attempt, $\mathbf{R}_{k,l}$ is the $N_p \times 1$ received signal vector with one received transmission attempt in each position and σ^2 is the noise variance. The ZF estimate can be simply obtained by setting σ to 0 in (2). In the MLSO criterion we use the following estimate for each symbol

$$\hat{S}_{k,l}^{p} = E\left[S_{k,l}^{p} \middle| \mathbf{R}_{k,l} \right] = \sum_{s_i \in \Lambda} s_i \cdot \frac{P\left(S_{k,l}^{p} = s_i \right)}{p\left(\mathbf{R}_{k,l} \right)} p\left(\mathbf{R}_{k,l} \middle| S_{k,l}^{p} = s_i \right) \tag{3}$$

where s_i corresponds to a constellation symbol from the modulation alphabet Λ, $E[\cdot]$ is the expected value, $P(\cdot)$ represents a probability and $p(\cdot)$ a probability density function (PDF). Considering equiprobable symbols $P\left(S_{k,l}^{p}=s_i\right)=1/M$, where M is the constellation size. The PDF values required in (3) can be computed as:

$$p\left(\mathbf{R}_{k,l}\middle|S_{k,l}^{p}=s_i\right)=\frac{1}{M^{N_p-1}}\sum_{\mathbf{S}_{k,l}^{\text{interf}}\in\Lambda^{N_p-1}}p\left(\mathbf{R}_{k,l}\middle|S_{k,l}^{p}=s_i,\mathbf{S}_{k,l}^{\text{interf}}\right)$$

$$=\frac{1}{M^{N_p-1}}\sum_{\mathbf{S}_{k,l}^{\text{interf}}\in\Lambda^{N_p-1}}\frac{1}{\left(2\pi\sigma^2\right)^{N_p}}\exp\sum_{r=1}^{N_p}-\frac{\left|R_{k,l}^{r}-\sum_{m=1}^{N_p}S_{k,l}^{m}\hat{H}_{k,l}^{m,r}\right|^2}{2\sigma^2} \tag{4}$$

Where $\mathbf{S}_{k,l}^{\text{interf}}$ is a $(N_p-1)\times 1$ vector representing a possible combination of colliding symbols except the one belonging to packet p. An interference canceller (IC) can also be used inside the Multipacket Detector, but usually is only recommendable after the first receiver iteration (Souto et al., 2008). In iteration q, for each packet p in each transmission attempt r, the IC subtracts the interference caused by all the other packets in that attempt. This can be represented as:

$$\left(R_{k,l}^{r,p}\right)^{(q)}=R_{k,l}^{r}-\sum_{\substack{m=1\\m\neq p}}^{N_p}\left(\hat{S}_{k,l}^{m}\right)^{(q-1)}\hat{H}_{k,l}^{m,r} \tag{5}$$

Where $\left(\hat{S}_{k,l}^{m}\right)^{(q-1)}$ is the transmitted symbol estimate obtained in the previous iteration for packet m, subcarrier k and OFDM block l.

4.3 Channel estimation

To achieve coherent detection at the receiver known pilot symbols are periodically inserted into the data stream. The proposed frame structure is shown in Fig. 4. For an OFDM system with N carriers, pilot symbols are multiplexed with data symbols using a spacing of ΔN_T OFDM blocks in the time domain and ΔN_F subcarriers in the frequency domain. To avoid interference between pilots of different users, FDM (Frequency Division Multiplexing) is employed for the pilots, which means that pilot symbols cannot be transmitted over the same subcarrier by different users. No user can transmit data symbols on subcarriers reserved for pilots, therefore, the minimum allowed spacing in the frequency domain is $\left(\Delta N_F\right)_{\min}=N_{p,\max}$, where $N_{p,\max}$ is the maximum number of users that can try to transmit simultaneously.

To obtain the frequency channel response estimates for each transmitting/receiving antenna pair the receiver applies the following steps in each iteration:

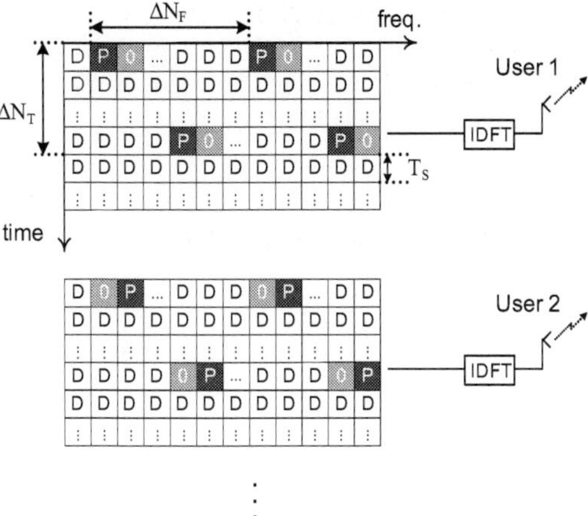

Fig. 4. Proposed frame structure for MIMO-OFDM transmission with implicit pilots (P – pilot symbol, D – data symbol, 0 – empty subcarrier).

1. The channel estimate between transmit antenna m and receive antenna n for each pilot symbol position, is simply computed as:

$$\tilde{H}_{k,l}^{p,r} = \frac{\left(S_{k,l}^{p,Pilot}\right)^{*}}{\left|S_{k,l}^{p,Pilot}\right|^{2}} R_{k,l}^{r} \tag{6}$$

where $S_{k,l}^{p,Pilot}$ corresponds to a pilot symbol transmitted in the kth subcarrier of the lth OFDM block by user p. Obviously, not all indexes k an l will correspond to a pilot symbol since $\Delta N_T > 1$ or $\Delta N_F > 1$.

2. Channel estimates for the same subcarrier k, user p and transmission attempt r but in time domain positions (index l) that do not carry a pilot symbol can be obtained through interpolation using a finite impulse response (FIR) filter with length W as follows:

$$\tilde{H}_{k,l+t}^{p,r} = \sum_{j=-\lfloor(W-1)/2\rfloor}^{\lfloor W/2 \rfloor} h_t^j \tilde{H}_{k,l+j\cdot\Delta N_T}^{p,r} \tag{7}$$

where t is the OFDM block index relative to the last one carrying a pilot (which is block with index l) and h_t^j are the interpolation coefficients of the estimation filter which depend on the channel estimation algorithm employed. There are several proposed algorithms in the literature like the optimal Wiener filter interpolator (Cavers, 1991) or the low pass sinc interpolator (Kim et al., 1997).

3. After the first iteration the data estimates can also be used as pilots for channel estimation refinement (Valenti, 2001). The respective channel estimates are computed as

$$\left(\tilde{H}_{k,l}^{p,r}\right)^{(q)} = \frac{R_{k,l}^{r}\left(\hat{S}_{k,l}^{p}\right)^{(q-1)*}}{\left|\left(\hat{S}_{k,l}^{p}\right)^{(q-1)}\right|^{2}} \qquad (8)$$

4.   The channel estimates are enhanced by ensuring that the corresponding impulse response has a duration N_G (number of samples at the cyclic prefix). This is accomplished by computing the time domain impulse response through $\{\left(\tilde{h}_{i,l}^{p,r}\right)^{(q)}$; i=0,1,...,N-1}= DFT$\{\left(\tilde{H}_{k,l}^{p,r}\right)^{(q)}$; k=0,1, ...,N-1}, followed by the truncation of this sequence according to $\{\left(\hat{h}_{i,l}^{p,r}\right)^{(q)} = w_i\left(\tilde{h}_{i,l}^{p,r}\right)^{(q)}$; i=0,1,...,N-1 with $w_i = 1$ if the ith time domain sample is inside the cyclic prefix duration and $w_i = 0$ otherwise. The final frequency response estimates are then obtained as $\{\left(\hat{H}_{k,l}^{p,r}\right)^{(q)}$; k=0,1,...,N-1}= IDFT$\{\left(\hat{h}_{i,l}^{p,r}\right)^{(q)}$; i=0,1,...,N-1}.

4.4 Detection of users involved in a collision

One of the difficulties of employing multipacket detector schemes, namely the ones proposed in this chapter, lies in finding out which users have packets involved in the collision. Missing a user will result in an insufficient number of retransmissions to reliably extract the others while assuming a non-transmitting user as being active will also degrade the packet separation and waste resources by requesting an excessive number of retransmissions. In the following we propose a simple detection method that can be combined with the multipacket detection approach described previously. This method considers the use of OFDM blocks with pilots multiplexed with conventional data blocks, as described in the previous subsection. We assume that the maximum number of users that can attempt to transmit their packets in a given physical channel is $N_{p,max}$. Since each user p has a specific subset of subcarriers reserved for its pilot symbols the receiver can use those subcarriers to estimate whether the user is transmitting a packet or not. To accomplish that objective it starts by computing the decision variable:

$$Y_p = \sum_{k',l'}^{N_{pilots}} \left|R_{k',l'}^{1}\right|^{2}, \quad p = 1,...,N_{p,max} \qquad (9)$$

for all users, with (k',l') representing all positions (subcarriers and OFDM blocks) containing a pilot symbol of user p and N_{pilots} being the total number of pilots used inside the sum. The decision variable, Y_p, can then be compared with a threshold y^{th} to decide if a user is active or not.

The threshold should be chosen so as to maximize the overall system throughput. Assuming a worst-case scenario where any incorrect detection of the number of users results in the loss of all packets then, from (Tsatsanis et al., 2000), the gross simplified system throughput (not taking into account bit errors in decoded packets) is given by:

$$R = \frac{N_{p,max}\left(1-P_e\right)}{N_{p,max}\left(1-P_e\right)+P_e^{N_{p,max}}}\left(1-P_M\right)\left[\left(1-P_e\right)\left(1-P_M\right)+P_e\left(1-P_F\right)\right]^{N_{p,max}-1} \qquad (10)$$

where P_e is the probability of a user's buffer being empty at the beginning of a transmission slot, P_M is the probability of a missed detection and P_F is the false alarm probability. The threshold, y^{th}, that maximizes (10) can be found through:

$$\frac{\partial R}{\partial y} = 0 \tag{11}$$

resulting

$$\frac{\partial P_M}{\partial y}\Big[(1-P_e)(1-P_M)N_{p,\max} + P_e(1-P_F)\Big] = (N_{p,\max}-1)(1-P_M)P_e\frac{\partial(1-P_F)}{\partial y} \tag{12}$$

Assuming low false alarm and missed detection probabilities, i.e.,

$$\begin{cases} 1-P_M \approx 1 \\ 1-P_F \approx 1 \end{cases} \tag{13}$$

and noting that:

$$\begin{cases} p_1(y) = \dfrac{\partial(1-P_F)}{\partial y} \\[2mm] p_2(y) = \dfrac{\partial P_M}{\partial y} \end{cases} \tag{14}$$

where $p_1(y)$ is the probability density function (PDF) of $\sum_{k',l'}^{N_{pilots}}\left|N^1_{k',l'}\right|^2$ and $p_2(y)$ is the PDF

of $\sum_{k',l'}^{N_{pilots}}\left|S^{p,pilot}_{k',l'}H^{p,1}_{k',l'} + N^1_{k',l'}\right|^2$, (12) can be rewritten as

$$p_1(y) = p_2(y)\frac{N_{p,\max} - P_e(N_{p,\max}-1)}{(N_{p,\max}-1)P_e} \tag{15}$$

Therefore we can compute the threshold from the weighted intersection of the two PDFs, $p_1(y)$ and $p_2(y)$. Regarding the first PDF, since $N^1_{k,l}$ are zero mean independent complex Gaussian variables with variance $E\left[\left|N^1_{k,l}\right|^2\right] = N_0$ ($N_0/2$ is the noise power spectral density), $\left|N^1_{k,l}\right|^2$ will have an exponential distribution with average $\mu_1 = E\left[\left|N^1_{k,l}\right|^2\right]$. Therefore the decision variable corresponds to a sum of independent exponential random variables and, as a result, follows an Erlang distribution expressed as

$$p_1(y) = \frac{y^{N_{pilots}-1}\exp\left(-\dfrac{y}{\mu_1}\right)}{\mu_1^{N_{pilots}}(N_{pilots}-1)!} \tag{16}$$

Regarding the second PDF, $R^1_{k,l} = S^{p,pilot}_{k,l} H^{p,1}_{k,l} + N^1_{k,l}$ and $\left| R^1_{k,l} \right|^2$ are also zero mean complex Gaussian and exponential variables with average given by $\mu_2 = \left| S^{p,pilot}_{k,l} \right|^2 E\left[\left| H^{p,1}_{k,l} \right|^2 \right] + N_0$, respectively. However they are not necessarily uncorrelated for different k and l. Since the receiver does not have a priori knowledge about the PDP (Power Delay Profile) of each user while it is still detecting them it does not know the correlation between different channel frequency response coefficients. For that reason, we opted to employ a threshold located in the middle of those obtained assuming two extreme cases: uncorrelated channel frequency response coefficients and constant channel frequency response coefficients.

4.5 Uncorrelated channel frequency response

If the different channel frequency response coefficients, $H^{p,1}_{k,l}$, can be assumed uncorrelated for different k and l (for example a severe time-dispersive channel) then the decision variable Y_p will correspond to a sum of uncorrelated exponential variables resulting again in an Erlang random variable described by the following PDF

$$p_2(y) = \frac{y^{N_{pilots}-1} \exp\left(-\dfrac{y}{\mu_2}\right)}{\mu_2^{N_{pilots}}\left(N_{pilots}-1\right)!} \tag{17}$$

Therefore, the intersection of PDFs (16) and (17) results in the threshold given by

$$y^{th} = \frac{N_{pilots} \ln\left(\dfrac{\mu_2}{\mu_1}\right)}{\dfrac{1}{\mu_1} - \dfrac{1}{\mu_2}} \tag{18}$$

4.6 Constant channel frequency response

If the channel is basically non time dispersive then the channel frequency response coefficients, $H^{p,1}_{k,l}$, will be almost constant for different k and l and, thus, the decision variable Y_p will correspond to a sum of correlated exponential variables. To obtain the PDF for this case it is necessary to remind the fact that the exponential distribution is a special case of the gamma distribution. Consequently, we can employ the expression derived in (Aalo, 1995) for the sum of correlated gamma variables which, for this case, becomes

$$p_2(y) = \frac{\left(\dfrac{y}{\mu_2}\right)^{N_{pilots}-1} \exp\left(-\dfrac{y}{\left(1-\sqrt{\rho}\right)\mu_2}\right) {}_1F_1\left(1, N_{pilots}; \dfrac{\sqrt{\rho}N_{pilots}y}{\left(1-\sqrt{\rho}\right)\left(1-\sqrt{\rho}+\sqrt{\rho}N_{pilots}\right)\mu_2}\right)}{\left(N_{pilots}-1\right)!\left(1-\sqrt{\rho}\right)^{N_{pilots}-1}\left(1-\sqrt{\rho}+\sqrt{\rho}N_{pilots}\right)\mu_2} u(y) \tag{19}$$

where ρ is the correlation coefficient between different received samples which is constant and is defined as

$$\rho = \rho_{(k,l),(k',l')} = \frac{Cov\left(\left|R_{k,l}^1\right|^2, \left|R_{k',l'}^1\right|^2\right)}{\sqrt{Var\left(\left|R_{k,l}^1\right|^2\right)Var\left(\left|R_{k',l'}^1\right|^2\right)}}, \ (k,l) \neq (k',l') \tag{20}$$

with

$$Cov\left(\left|R_{k,l}^1\right|^2, \left|R_{k',l'}^1\right|^2\right) = 2\left|S_{k,l}^{p,pilot}\right|^4 \left(E\left[\left|H_{k,l}^{p,1}\right|^2\right]\right)^2 + 2\left|S_{k,l}^{p,pilot}\right|^2 E\left[\left|H_{k,l}^{p,1}\right|^2\right]N_0 + N_0^2 - \mu_2^2 \tag{21}$$

and

$$Var\left(\left|R_{k,l}^1\right|^2\right) = 2\left|S_{k,l}^{p,pilot}\right|^4 \left(E\left[\left|H_{k,l}^{p,1}\right|^2\right]\right)^2 + 4\left|S_{k,l}^{p,pilot}\right|^2 E\left[\left|H_{k,l}^{p,1}\right|^2\right]N_0 + 2N_0^2 - \mu_2^2 \tag{22}$$

Alternatively, from (Alouini et al., 2001), we can also represent (19) as a single gamma-series

$$p_2(y) = \frac{\lambda_1}{\lambda_{N_{pilots}}} \sum_{t=0}^{\infty} \frac{\delta_t \, y^{N_{pilots}+t-1} \exp\left(-\frac{y}{\lambda_1}\right)}{\lambda_1^{N_{pilots}+t}\left(N_{pilots}+t-1\right)!} \tag{23}$$

with

$$\delta_t = \begin{cases} 1, & t = 0 \\ \dfrac{1}{t}\displaystyle\sum_{i=1}^{t}\left(1 - \dfrac{\lambda_1}{\lambda_{N_{pilots}}}\right)^i \delta_{t-i}, & t > 0 \end{cases} \tag{24}$$

and

$$\lambda_1 = \mu_2\left(1 - \sqrt{\rho}\right); \quad \lambda_{N_{pilots}} = \mu_2\left[1 + \sqrt{\rho}\left(N_{pilots} - 1\right)\right] \tag{25}$$

$_1F_1(\cdot,\cdot;\cdot)$ is the confluent hypergeometric function (Milton & Stegun, 1964). The weighted intersection of PDFs (16) and (19) or (23) (threshold y^{th}) can be easily found numerically.

5. Medium access control

To evaluate the detection technique presented above we will use the analysis presented in (3GPP TR101 102 v3.2.0, 1998) for the network-assisted diversity multiple access (NDMA) MAC protocol. It is assumed that the users transmit packets to a BS, which is responsible for running most of the calculations and to handle transmission collisions. The BS detects collisions and uses a broadcast control channel to send a collision signal, requesting the users to resend the collided packets the required number of times (p-1 for a collision of p packets). The remaining section studies how the throughput is influenced by the block/packet error rate (BLER), and compares the results with the performance of a contention-free scenario, based on TDMA.

5.1 Throughput analysis

Following the NDMA throughput analysis of (3GPP TR101 102 v3.2.0, 1998), we consider a sequence of epochs where epoch is an empty slot or a set of slots where users send the same packet due to a BS request. Denoting P_e as the probability of a user's buffer being empty at the beginning of an epoch, the binomial expressions for the probability of the epoch length for J users are

$$P_{busy}(p) = \binom{J}{p}(1 - P_e)^p P_e^{J-p}, p = 1, 2, \ldots, J \tag{26}$$

for a busy epoch and

$$P_{idle}(p) = \begin{cases} P_e^J, & p = 1 \\ 0, & p \neq 1 \end{cases} \tag{27}$$

for an idle epoch. The probability of having a useful epoch is

$$P_{usefull}(p) = \binom{J}{p}(1 - P_e)^p P_e^{J-p} P_D(p)^p \tag{28}$$

where $P_D(p)$ is the frame's correct detection probability (equal to $1 - BLER$) when p users are transmitting. We assume that no detection errors occur in the determination of the number of senders colliding. Finally, the throughput can be defined as

$$R_{NDMA} = \frac{\text{average length of useful epoch}}{\text{average length of busy or idle epoch}} \tag{29}$$

By using (26) and (29), and after some simplifications, we can write

$$R_{NDMA} = \frac{\sum_{p=1}^{J} p \binom{J-1}{p-1}(1 - P_e)^p P_e^{J-p} P_D(p)^p}{J(1 - P_e) + P_e^J} \tag{30}$$

5.2 Queue analysis

If there are no detection errors at the receiver (i.e., the BS), then the busy and idle epochs have the distributions described by

$$P_{busy}(p) = \binom{J-1}{p-1}(1 - P_e)^{J-1} P_e^{J-p}, 1 \leq p \leq J \tag{31}$$

and

$$P_{idle}(p) = \begin{cases} P_e^{J-1} + (J-1)(1 - P_e) P_e^{J-2}, p = 1 \\ \binom{J-1}{p}(1 - P_e)^{p-1} P_e^{J-p-1}, 1 \leq p \leq J-1 \end{cases} \tag{32}$$

Curves representing the false DER (false detection of users) and missed DER (users not detected) are shown. It is visible that for E_b/N_0=2dB that the DER is mostly caused by undetected users (the receiver cannot distinguish them from noise) with an error rate between 0.2-0.3% while false alarms are virtually inexistent.

Next we compare NDMA and TDMA throughputs for the scenario simulated previously. Throughput is calculated as described in Section 5, using BLER obtained above (it should be emphasized that our throughput model does not take into account invalid detection of the number of senders on a collision).

In Fig. 9, Fig. 10 and Fig. 11 show how R_{NDMA} and R_{TDMA} depend on the offered load, for E_b/N_0 values of 2dB, 4dB and 6dB, respectively. The offered load (λJ) varies from very light load (10%) until the saturation value (100%), where all bandwidth is required to satisfy the offered load. Results show that NDMA clearly outperforms TDMA for the conditions tested, especially for loads above 60%, with higher differences for lower E_b/N_0. The reason for this behavior is that our receiver can take full advantage of the overall energy spent to transmit the packet (i.e., the energy for all retransmission attempts). Therefore, the performance of transmitting with success a given packet when we have a collision of several packets is higher than without collisions (as in the TDMA case) due to the BLER performance improvement with larger N_P (as shown in Fig. 7). The only case where our technique is worse than conventional TDMA schemes is for slow-varying channels without symbol interleaving, especially for large system loads, since the correlation between different retransmissions can be very high, precluding an efficient packet separation.

The throughput obtained in fixed or variable channels combined with interleaving is only slightly worse than that obtained in uncorrelated channels.

We would like to point out that although the throughput for high system load can be close to 100%, the corresponding packet delay grows fast for large system loads, since the number of retransmission increases with the number of collisions, and the number of collisions is higher for higher system loads.

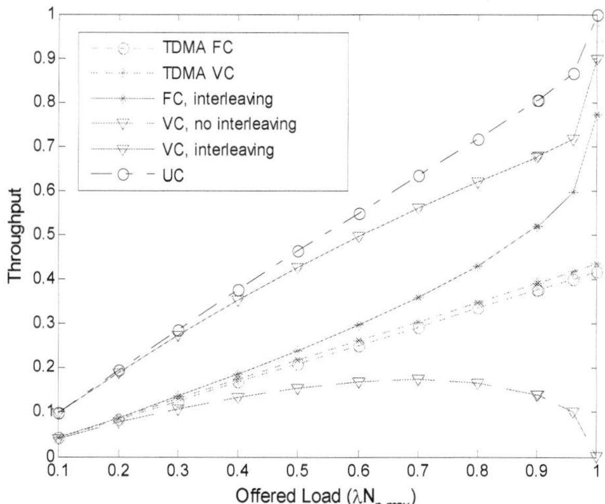

Fig. 9. Throughput when Eb/N0=2dB.

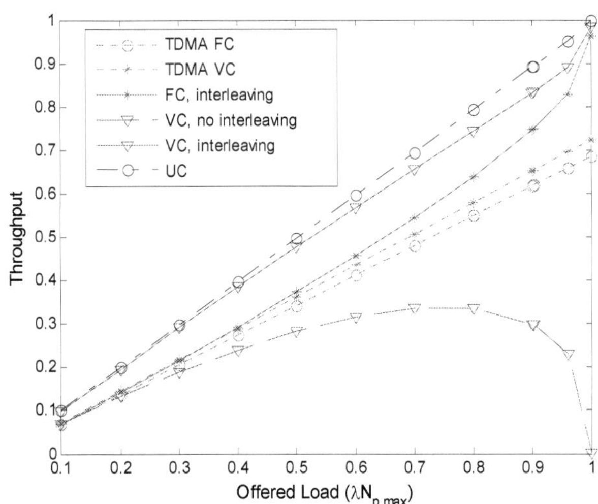

Fig. 10. Throughput when Eb/N0=4dB.

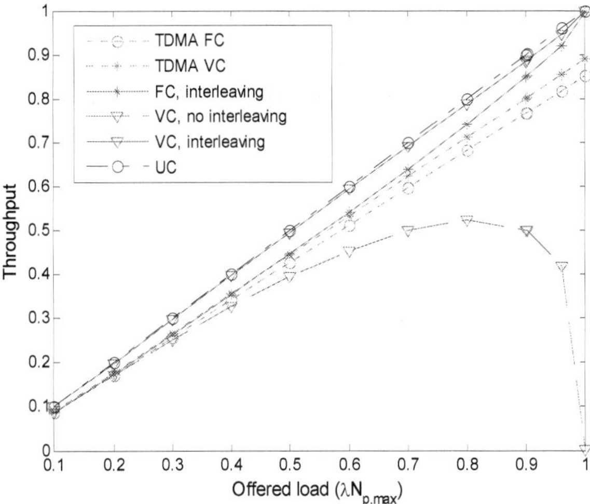

Fig. 11. Throughput when Eb/N0=6dB.

7. Conclusions

In this chapter we considered a multipacket detection technique to cope with MAC collisions in OFDM-based systems. This technique allows high throughputs, since the total number of transmissions can be equal to the number of packets involved in the collision.
Since our packet separation technique requires different channels for different retransmissions we proposed the use of different interleavers for different retransmissions. This allows good performances even slow-varying channels. In fact, we can an efficient packet separation even when the channel remains fixed for all retransmissions. We also included a method to estimate the number of users involved in a collision, as well as the corresponding channel characteristics.

8. Acknowledgments

This work was partially supported by the FCT - Fundação para a Ciência e Tecnologia (pluriannual funding and U-BOAT project PTDC/EEA-TEL/67066/2006), and the C-MOBILE project IST-2005-27423.

9. References

3GPP. 25.212-v6.2.0 (2004) "Multiplexing and Channel Coding (FDD),2004 , 3rd Generation Partnership Project, Sophia- Antipolis, France.

3GPP. TR25.814 (2006). "Physical Layers Aspects for Evolved UTRA".,2006 ,3rd Generation Partnership Project, Sophia- Antipolis, France.

3GPP TR101 112 v3.2.0 (1998). 'Selection procedures for the choice of radio transmission technologies of UMTS'., 1998 , 3rd Generation Partnership Project, Sophia-Antipolis, France.

Aalo, V. A. (1995). "Performance of maximal-ratio diversity systems in a correlated Nakagami-fading environment". *IEEE Trans. Commun.*, vol. 43, pp. 2360–2369, 0090-6778.

Abramowitz, M., & Stegun, I. A. (1964). *Handbook of Mathematical Functions with Formulas, Graphs, and Mathematical Tables*. Dover Publications, 0-486-61272-4, New York, USA

Alouini, M. -S.; Abdi, A. & Kaveh, M. (2001). "Sum of Gamma Variates and Performance of Wireless Communication Systems Over Nakagami-Fading Channels". *IEEE Trans. On Veh. Tech.*, pp. vol. 50, no. 6, pp.1471-1480, 2001, 1751-8628.

Cavers, J. K. (1991). "An analysis of Pilot Symbol Assisted Modulation for Rayleigh Fading Channels". *IEEE Trans. On Veh. Tech.*, vol. 40, no. 4, pp.686-693, November, 1991, 0018-9545.

Cimini, L. (1985). "Analysis and Simulation of a Digital Mobile Channel using Orthogonal Frequency Division Multiplexing". *IEEE Trans. on Comm*, Vol. 33, No. 7, pp.665-675 ,July , 1985.

Dinis, R.; Carvalho; P., Bernardo; L., Oliveira; R., Serrazina, M. & Pinto, P. (2007). " Frequency-Domain Multipacket Detection: A High Throughput Technique for SC-FDE Systems ". *IEEE GLOBECOM'07.*, pp.4619–4624, 978-1-4244-1043-9, Washington DC., USA, December 2007.

Dinis, R.; Serrazina, M., & Carvalho, P. (2007). "An Efficient Detection Technique for SC-FDE Systems with Multiple Packet Collisions", *IEEE ICCCN'07*, pp.402-407 , ,Turtle Bay, USA, September 2007.

Kay, M. S. (1993). *Fundamentals of Statistical Signal Processing: Estimation Theory*, Prentice-Hall, 0-13-3457117, Englewood Cliffs.

Kim, Y. -S.; Kim, C. -J.; Jeong, G. -Y.; Bang, Y. -S.; Park, H. -K. & Choi, S. S. (1997). "New Rayleigh fading channel estimator based on PSAM channel sounding technique". *IEEE International Conf. on Comm.* ,Vol. 3 , pp.1518-1520., 0-7803-3925-8 Montreal, Canada , June 1997.

Nee, R. van & Prasad, R. (2000). *"OFDM for Wireless Multimedia Communications"*. Artech House, 978-0890065303, Norwood, MA, USA.

Souto, N.; Correia, A.; Dinis, R.; Silva, J. C. & Abreu, L. (2008). "Multiresolution MBMS transmissions for MIMO UTRA LTE systems". *IEEE International Symposium on Broadband Multimedia Systems and Broadcasting.*, pp.1-6, 978-1-4244-1648-6, Las Vegas, USA, June 2008.

Tsatsanis, M.; Zhang, R. & Banerjee, S. (2000). Network-Assisted Diversity for Random Access Wireless Networks, *IEEE* ,48, 3,Mar. 2000, pp.702-708, 1053-587X

Valenti, M. C. (2001). "Iterative Channel Estimation and Decoding of Pilot Symbol Assisted Turbo Codes Over Flat-Fading Channels". *IEEE Journal on Selected Areas in Communications*,Vol. 19 ,No. 9 ,Setember 2001 , pp. 1697-1705.

Wang, X.; Yu, Y. & Giannakis, G. (2005). "A Robust High-Throughput Three Algorithm Using Successive Interference Cancellation". *IEEE GLOBECOM'05.*,Vol.6, pp. – 3601, St. Louis, USA, 0-7803-9414-3.

Yu, Y. & Giannakis, G. (2005). "SICTA: A 0.693 Contention Tree Algorithm Using Successive Interference Cancellation". *IEEE INFOCOM'05.* ,Vol. 3 , 1908 – 1916,March, 2005, 0743-166X

Zhang, R. & Tsatsanis, M. (2002). "Network-Assisted Diversity Multiple Access in Time-Dispersive Channels". *IEEE Trans. On Comm.*, Vol. 50, No. 4, pp. 623-632.,April 2002, 0090-6778

Joint Subcarrier Matching and Power Allocation for OFDM Multihop System

Wenyi Wang and Renbiao Wu
Tianjin Key Lab for Advanced Signal Processing, Civil Aviation University of China
China

1. Introduction

Relay networks have recently attracted extensive attention due to its potential to increase coverage area and channel capacity. In a relay network, a source node communicates with a destination node with the help of the relay node. The performances of improving the channel capacity and coverage area have been explored and evaluated in the literature (Sendonaris et al., 2003)-(Laneman et al., 2004). There are two main forwarding strategies for relay node: amplify-and-forward (AF) and decode-and-forward (DF) (Laneman et al., 2004). The AF cooperative relay scheme was developed and analyzed in (Shastry & Adve, 2005), where a significant gain in the network lifetime due to node cooperation was shown. Power allocation is studied and compared for AF and DF relaying strategies for relay networks, which improves the channel capacity (Serbetli & Yener, 2006). However, DF means that the signal is decoded at the relay and recoded for retransmission. It is different from AF, where the signal is magnified to satisfy the power constraint and forwarded at the relay. This has the main advantage that the transmission can be optimized for different links, separately. In this chapter, the relay strategy DF is used.

In wideband systems, orthogonal frequency division multiplexing (OFDM) is a mature technique to mitigate the problems of frequency selectivity and intersymbol interference. The optimization of power allocation for different subcarriers offers substantial gain to the system performance. Therefore, the combination of relay network and OFDM modulation is an even more promising way to improve capacity and coverage area. However, as the fading gains for different channels are mutually independent, the subcarriers which experience deep fading over the source-relay channel may not be in deep fading over the relay-destination channel. This motivates us to consider adaptive subcarrier matching and power allocation schemes, where the bits on the subcarriers from the source to the relay are reassigned to the subcarriers from the relay to the destination. The system architecture of OFDM two-hop relay system is demonstrated in the Fig.1.

A fundamental analysis of cooperative relay systems was done by Kramer (Kramer et al., 2006), who has given channel capacity of several schemes. Relaying for OFDM systems was considered theoretically in (Shastry & Adve, 2005). Multi-user OFDM relay networks were studied by Zhu (Zhu et al., 2005), where the subcarrier was allocated to transmit own information and forward other nodes' information. Relay selection in OFDM relay networks was studied by Dai (Dai et al., 2007), which indicated the maximum diversity by selecting different relay for the different subcarrier. Radio resource allocation algorithm for relay

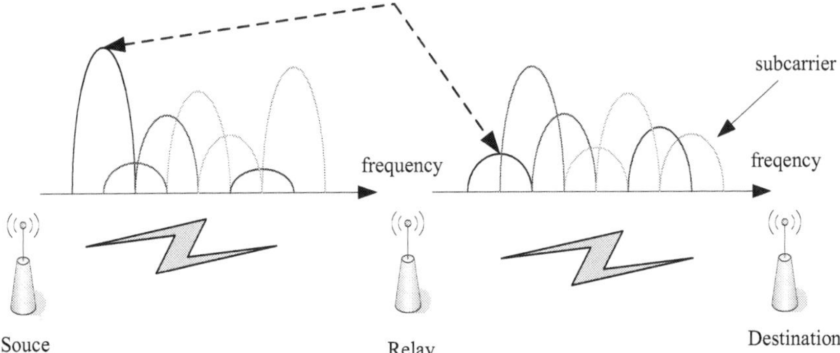

Fig. 1. System architecture of OFDM two-hop relay system

aided cellular OFDMA system was done in (Kaneko & Popovski, 2007). Adaptive relaying scheme for OFDM that taking channel state information into account has been proposed in (Herdin, 2006), where subcarrier matching was considered for OFDM amplify-and-forward scheme but the power allocation was not considered. Performances of OFDM dual-hop system with and without subcarrier matching were studied in (Suraweera & Armstrong, 2007) and (Athaudage et al., 2008), separately. The problems of resource allocation were considered in OFDMA cellular and OFDMA multihop system (Pischella & Belfiore, 2008) and (Kim et al., 2008). Bit loading algorithms were studied in (Ma et al., 2008) and (Gui et al., 2008). The subcarrier matching was also utilized to improve capacity in cognitive radio system (Pandharipande & Ho, 2007)-(Pandharipande & Ho, 2008).

In this chapter, the resource allocation problem is studied to maximize the system capacity by joint subcarrier matching and power allocation for the system with system-wide and separate power constraints. The schemes of optimal joint subcarrier matching and power allocation are proposed. All the proposed schemes perform better than the several other schemes, where there is no subcarrier matching or no power allocation.

The rest of this chapter is organized as follows. Section 2 discusses the optimal subcarrier matching and power allocation for the system with system-wide power constraint. Section 3 discusses the optimal subcarrier matching and power allocation for the system with separate power constraints. Section 6 compares the capacities of optimal schemes with that of several other schemes. Conclusions are drawn in section 5.

2. The system with system-wide power constraint

2.1 System architecture and problem formulation

An OFDM multihop system is considered where the source communicates with the destination using a single relay. The relay strategy is decode-and-forward. All nodes hold one antenna. It is assumed that the destination receives signal only from the relay but not from the source because of distance or obstacle. A two-stage transmission protocol is adopted. This means that the communication between the source and the destination covers two equal time slots. Fig.2 shows the block diagram of joint subcarrier matching and power allocation. The source transmits an OFDM symbol over the source-relay channel during the first time slot. At the same time, the relay receives and decodes the symbol. During the

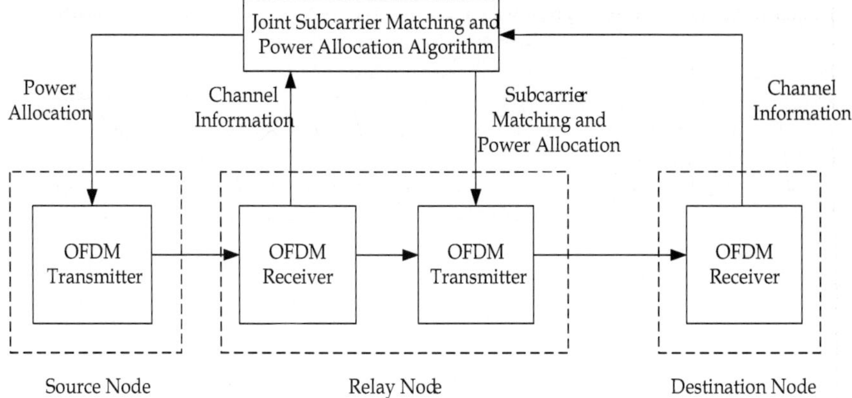

Fig. 2. Block diagram of joint subcarrier matching and power allocation

second time slot, the relay reencodes the signal with the same codebook as the one used at the source, and transmits it towards the destination over the relay-destination channel. The destination decodes the signal based on the received signal only from the relay. Furthermore, full channel state information (CSI) is assumed. The source transmits the signal to the relay with power allocation among the subcarriers based on the algorithm of joint subcarrier matching and power allocation. The relay receives the signal and decodes the signal. Then, the relay reorders the subcarrier to match subcarrier, and allocates power among the subcarriers according to the algorithm of joint subcarrier matching and power allocation. At last, the destination decodes the signal.

In this chapter, it is assumed that the different channels experience independent fading. The system consists of N subcarriers with total system power constraint. The power spectral densities of additive white Gaussian noise (AWGN) are equal at the relay and the destination. The channel capacity of the subcarrier i over the source-relay channel is given as follows

$$R_{s,i}\left(P_{s,i}\right) = \frac{1}{2}\log_2\left(1 + \frac{P_{s,i}h_{s,i}}{N_0}\right) \tag{1}$$

where $P_{s,i}$ is the power allocated to the subcarrier i ($1 \leq i \leq N$) at the source, $h_{s,i}$ is the corresponding channel power gain, and N_0 is the power spectral density of AWGN. Similarly, the channel capacity of the subcarrier j over the relay-destination channel is given as follows

$$R_{r,j}\left(P_{r,j}\right) = \frac{1}{2}\log_2\left(1 + \frac{P_{r,j}h_{r,j}}{N_0}\right) \tag{2}$$

where $P_{r,j}$ is the power allocated to the subcarrier j ($1 \leq j \leq N$) at the relay, and $h_{r,j}$ is the corresponding channel power gain.

Consequently, when the subcarrier i over the source-relay channel is matched to the subcarrier j over the relay-destination channel, the channel capacity of this subcarrier pair is given as follows

$$R_{ij} = \min\{R_{s,i}(P_{s,i}), R_{r,j}(P_{r,j})\} \tag{3}$$

Theoretically, the bits transmitted at the source can be reallocated to the subcarriers at the relay in arbitrary way. But for simplification, an additional constraint is that the bits transported on a subcarrier over the source-relay channel can be reallocated to only one subcarrier over the relay-destination channel, i.e., only one-to-one subcarrier matching is permitted. This means that the bits on different subcarriers over the source-relay channel will not be reallocated to the same subcarrier at the relay.

For the optimal joint subcarrier matching and power allocation problem, we can formulate it as an optimization problem. The optimization problem is given as

$$\max_{P_{s,i},P_{r,j},\rho_{ij}} \sum_{i=1}^{N} \min\left\{ R_{s,i}\left(P_{s,i}\right), \sum_{j=1}^{N} \rho_{ij} R_{r,j}\left(P_{r,j}\right) \right\}$$

$$\text{subject to} \ \sum_{i=1}^{N} P_{s,i} + \sum_{j=1}^{N} P_{r,j} \leq P_{tot}$$

$$P_{s,i}, P_{r,j} \geq 0, \forall i,j$$

$$\sum_{j=1}^{N} \rho_{ij} = 1, \rho_{ij} = \{0,1\}, \forall i,j$$

where P_{tot} is the total system power constraint, and ρ_{ij} can only be either 1 or 0, indicating whether the bits transmitted on the subcarrier i at the source are retransmitted on the subcarrier j at the relay. The last constraint shows that only one-to-one subcarrier matching is permitted. By introducing the parameter C_i, the optimization problem can be transformed into

$$\max_{P_{s,i},P_{r,j},\rho_{ij},C_i} \sum_{i=1}^{N} C_i$$

$$\text{subject to} \ R_{s,i}\left(P_{s,i}\right) \geq C_i$$

$$\sum_{j=1}^{N} \rho_{ij} R_{r,j}\left(P_{r,j}\right) \geq C_i$$

$$\sum_{i=1}^{N} P_{s,i} + \sum_{j=1}^{N} P_{r,j} \leq P_{tot}$$

$$P_{s,i}, P_{r,j} \geq 0, \forall i,j$$

$$\sum_{j=1}^{N} \rho_{ij} = 1, \rho_{ij} = \{0,1\}, \forall i,j$$

Consequently the original maximization problem is transformed into a mixed binary integer programming problem. It is prohibitive to find the global optimum in terms of computational complexity. However, when ρ_{ij} is given, the objective function and all constraint functions are convex, so the optimization problem is a convex optimization problem. Then the optimal power allocation can be achieved by interior-point algorithm. Therefore, the optimal joint subcarrier matching and power allocation can be found by finding the largest objective function among all subcarrier matching possibilities, and the corresponding subcarrier matching as well as power allocation is jointly optimal. But, it has been proved to be NP-hard and is fundamentally difficult (Korte & Vygen, 2002). In next subsection, with analytical argument, a low complexity and optimal joint subcarrier matching and power allocation scheme is given, where the optimal subcarrier matching is to match subcarriers by the order of the channel power gains and the optimal power allocation among the subcarrier pairs is based on water-filling.

2.2 Optimal joint subcarrier matching and power allocation for the system including two subcarriers

Supposing that the system includes only two subcarriers ($N = 2$): the channel power gains over the source-relay channel are $h_{s,1}$ and $h_{s,2}$, and the channel power gains over the relay-destination channel are $h_{r,1}$ and $h_{r,2}$. Without loss of generality, we assume that $h_{s,1} \leq h_{s,2}$ and $h_{r,1} \leq h_{r,2}$. The total system power constraint is also P_{tot}. As discussed in the subsection 2.1, the optimal joint subcarrier matching and power allocation can be found by two steps: (1) for every matching possibility (i.e., ρ_{ij} is given), find the optimal power allocation and the total channel capacity; (2) compare the all the total channel capacities, the largest one is the largest total channel capacity, whose subcarrier matching and power allocation are jointly optimal. But this process is prohibitive in terms of complexity. In this subsection, an analytical argument is given to prove that the optimal subcarrier matching is to match subcarrier by the order of the channel power gains and the optimal power allocation between the matched subcarrier pairs is based on water-filling. The more important is that they are jointly optimal.

Before giving the scheme, the equivalent channel power gain is given for any matched subcarrier pair. For any given matched subcarrier pair, with the total power constraint, an equivalent channel power gain can be obtained by the following proposition, whose channel capacity is equivalent to the channel capacity of this subcarrier pair.

Proposition 1: For any given matched subcarrier pair, with total power constraint, an equivalent subcarrier channel power gain (e.g., h_i') can be obtained, which is related to the channel power gains (e.g., $h_{s,i}$ and $h_{r,j}$) of the subcarrier pair as follows

$$\frac{1}{h_i'} = \frac{1}{h_{s,i}} + \frac{1}{h_{r,j}} \tag{4}$$

Proof: With the total power constraint P_i', the channel capacity of this subcarrier pair is

$$R_i' = \max_{P_{s,i}} \min\left\{ \frac{1}{2}\log_2\left(1 + \frac{P_{s,i}h_{s,i}}{N_0}\right), \frac{1}{2}\log_2\left(1 + \frac{(P_i' - P_{s,i})h_{r,i}}{N_0}\right) \right\} \tag{5}$$

where $P_{s,i}$ is the power allocated to the subcarrier i at the source, $P_i' - P_{s,i}$ is the remainder power allocated to the subcarrier j at the relay.

The first term is a monotonically increasing function of $P_{s,i}$ and the second term is a monotonically decreasing function of $P_{s,i}$. Therefore, the optimal power allocation between the corresponding subcarriers can be obtained easily

$$\frac{1}{2}\log_2\left(1 + \frac{P_{s,i}h_{s,i}}{N_0}\right) = \frac{1}{2}\log_2\left(1 + \frac{(P_i' - P_{s,i})h_{r,j}}{N_0}\right) \tag{6}$$

which means that $h_{s,i}P_{s,i} = h_{r,j}(P_i' - P_{s,i})$. As a result, the channel capacity of the subcarrier pair is

$$R_i' = \frac{1}{2}\log_2\left(1 + \frac{h_{s,i}h_{r,j}P_i'}{\left(h_{s,i} + h_{r,j}\right)N_0}\right) \tag{7}$$

It can be seen that the subcarrier pair is equivalent to a single subcarrier channel with the same total power constraint. The equivalent channel power gain h_i' can be expressed

$$h_i' = \frac{h_{s,i}h_{r,j}}{h_{s,i} + h_{r,j}} \tag{8}$$

or

$$\frac{1}{h_i'} = \frac{1}{h_{s,i}} + \frac{1}{h_{r,j}} \tag{9}$$

Here, there are two ways to match the subcarriers: (i) the subcarrier 1 over the source-relay channel is matched to the subcarrier 1 over the relay-destination channel, and the subcarrier 2 over the source-relay channel is matched to the subcarrier 2 over the relay-destination channel (i.e., $h_{s,1} \sim h_{r,1}$ and $h_{s,2} \sim h_{r,2}$); (ii) the subcarrier 1 over the source-relay channel is matched to the subcarrier 2 over the relay-destination channel, and the subcarrier 2 over the source-relay channel is matched to the subcarrier 1 over the relay-destination channel (i.e., $h_{s,1} \sim h_{r,2}$ and $h_{s,2} \sim h_{r,1}$).

For the two ways of matching subcarriers, the equivalent channel power gains are denoted as $h_{k,i}'$ which can be obtained easily based on the proposition 1. Here, k implies the method of matching subcarrier and i is the equivalent subcarrier index. Then, the power allocation between the subcarrier pairs can be reformed as follow

$$\max_{P_i'} \quad \sum_{i=1}^{2}\frac{1}{2}\log_2\left(1 + \frac{h_{k,i}'P_i'}{N_0}\right)$$

$$\text{subject to} \sum_{i=1}^{2}P_i' \leq P_{tot}$$

where P_i' is the power allocated to the equivalent subcarrier i.

It's clear that the optimal power allocation is based on water-filling (Cover & Thomas, 1991). Therefore, once the subcarrier matching is provided, the optimal power allocation is easily obtained. The remainder task is to decide which way of subcarrier matching is better. The better method can be found by getting the channel capacities of the two ways and comparing them. But, here, we give an analytical argument to prove that the optimal subcarrier matching way is the first way.

Before giving the optimal subcarrier matching way, based on the proposition 1, we can get following lemma.

Lemma 1: For the two ways of matching subcarrier, the relationship between the equivalent channel power gains can be expressed

$$\frac{1}{h'_{1,1}} + \frac{1}{h'_{1,2}} = \frac{1}{h'_{2,1}} + \frac{1}{h'_{2,2}} \tag{10}$$

Proof: Based on the proposition 1, the equivalent channel power gains of the two ways can be expressed $\frac{1}{h'_{1,1}} = \frac{1}{h_{s,1}} + \frac{1}{h_{r,1}}$, $\frac{1}{h'_{1,2}} = \frac{1}{h_{s,2}} + \frac{1}{h_{r,2}}$ and $\frac{1}{h'_{2,1}} = \frac{1}{h_{s,1}} + \frac{1}{h_{r,2}}$, $\frac{1}{h'_{2,2}} = \frac{1}{h_{s,2}} + \frac{1}{h_{r,1}}$. By summing up the corresponding terms, it is clearly that the relationship can be derived.

By making use of the lemma 1, the following proposition can be proved, which states the optimal subcarrier matching way.

Proposition 2: For the system including two subcarriers, the optimal subcarrier matching is to match the subcarriers by the order of channel power gains. Together with the optimal power allocation for this subcarrier matching, they are optimal joint subcarrier matching and power allocation. In this case, the optimal subcarrier matching is as $h_{s,1} \sim h_{r,1}$ and $h_{s,2} \sim h_{r,2}$.

Proof: For the two ways of matching subcarrier, based on the lemma 1, the equivalent channel power gains satisfy the following constraint, $\frac{1}{h'_{k,1}} + \frac{1}{h'_{k,2}} = H(H \geq 0)$, where the parameter H is a constant. For the the first way, we can get $\frac{1}{h'_{1,1}} - \frac{1}{h'_{1,2}} = x_1 (H \geq x_1 \geq 0)$. For the second way, without loss of generality, it is assumed that $\frac{1}{h'_{2,1}} - \frac{1}{h'_{2,2}} = x_2 (H \geq x_2 \geq 0)$.

Therefore, the $h'_{k,i}$ can be expressed as $h'_{k,1} = \frac{2}{H+x_k}$ and $h'_{k,2} = \frac{2}{H-x_k}$. The corresponding total channel capacity is

$$R_{tot,k}(P'_1, P'_2) = \frac{1}{2}\log_2\left(1 + \frac{P'_1}{(H+x_k)\frac{N_0}{2}}\right) + \frac{1}{2}\log_2\left(1 + \frac{P'_2}{(H-x_k)\frac{N_0}{2}}\right) \tag{11}$$

For denotation simplicity, we denote $\frac{N_0}{2}$ as σ_2^2. The partial derivative of the channel capacity with respect to x_k can be gotten by making use of $P'_2 = P_{tot} - P'_1$

$$\frac{\partial R_{tot,k}(P'_1, P'_2)}{\partial x_k} = \frac{1}{2\ln 2} \frac{2P'_1 x_k (P_{tot} - P'_1) + (H^2\sigma_2^2 - x_k^2\sigma_2^2)(P_{tot} - 2P'_1) + 2P_{tot}Hx_k\sigma_2^2}{(H^2 - x_k^2)\left[(H+x_k)\sigma_2^2 + P'_1\right]\left[(H-x_k)\sigma_2^2 + (P_{tot} - P'_1)\right]} \tag{12}$$

It is noted that, because of $h'_{k,1} \leq h'_{k,2}$, $P'_1 \leq \frac{1}{2}P_{tot}$. Therefore, it is clear that $\dfrac{\partial R_{tot,k}(P'_1, P'_2)}{\partial x_k}$ is greater than 0. Therefore, the total channel capacity is a monotonically increasing function of x_k. This means that, the larger is the difference between the equivalent channel power gains, the larger is the total channel capacity. At the same time, it is clearly that the difference between the equivalent channel power gains of the first way is larger than the one of the second way. Therefore, the relationship of the total channel capacities of the two ways can be expressed

$$R_{tot,2}(P'_1, P'_2) \leq R_{tot,1}(P'_1, P'_2) \tag{13}$$

Therefore, we can get the following relationship

$$\max_{P_i'} R_{tot,2}\left(P_1', P_2'\right) = R_{tot,2}\left(\overline{P}_1', \overline{P}_2'\right) \le R_{tot,1}\left(\overline{P}_1', \overline{P}_2'\right) = \max_{P_i'} R_{tot,1}\left(P_1', P_2'\right) \tag{14}$$

where $\overline{P}_1'$ and $\overline{P}_2'$ are the optimal power allocation for the first term. Note that the first term is the total channel capacity of the first way and the last term is the one of the second way. It proves that the first way, whose difference between the equivalent channel power gains is larger, is optimal subcarrier matching way. The more important is that, as the total channel capacity of the fisrt way is the larger one, this subcarrier matching and the corresponding power allocation are the optimal joint subcarrier matching and power allocation. Specially, the optimal subcarrier matching is to match subcarriers by the order of the channel power gains.

The optimal joint subcarrier matching and power allocation scheme has been given by now. Specially, the optimal subcarrier matching is to match the subcarriers by the order of the channel power gains and the optimal power allocation between the matched subcarrier pairs is according to the water-filling. The power allocation between the matched subcarrier pair is to make the channel capacities of the two subcarriers equivalent.

2.3 Optimal joint subcarrier matching and power allocation for the system including unlimited number of subcarriers

This subsection extends the method in the subsection 2.2 to the system including unlimited number of the subcarriers. The number of the subcarriers is finite, where the subcarrier channel power gains are $h_{s,i}(i \ge 2)$ and $h_{r,j}(j \ge 2)$. First, the optimal power allocation among the matched subcarrier pair is proposed for given subcarrier matching. Second, we prove that the subcarrier matching by the order of the channel power gains is optimal.

When the subcarrier matching is given, the equivalent channel gains of the subcarrier pairs can be gotten based on the proposition 1, e.g., h_i' ($1 \le i \le N$). The power allocation can be formulated as

$$\max_{P_i'} \quad \sum_{i=1}^{N} \frac{1}{2}\log_2\left(1 + \frac{h_i' P_i'}{\sigma_N^2}\right)$$

$$\text{subject to} \sum_{i=1}^{N} P_i' \le P_{tot} \tag{15}$$

where the $\sigma_N^2 = N_0$. It is clearly that the power allocation is also based on water-filling. Therefore, the optimal power allocation among the matched subcarrier pairs is according to the water-filling.

Here, without loss of generality, the channel power gains are assumed $h_{s,i} \le h_{s,i+1}$ and $h_{r,j} \le h_{r,j+1}$. The following proposition gives the optimal subcarrier matching.

Proposition 3: For the system including unlimited number of the subcarriers, the optimal subcarrier matching is

$$h_{s,i} \sim h_{r,i} \tag{16}$$

Together the optimal power allocation for this subcarrier matching, they are optimal joint subcarrier matching and power allocation

Proof: This proposition will be proved in the contrapositive form. Assuming that there is a subcarrier matching method whose matching result including two matched subcarrier pairs $h_{s,i} \sim h_{r,i+n}$ and $h_{s,i+n} \sim h_{r,i}$ ($n > 0$), which means that $h_{s,i} \le h_{s,i+n}$, $h_{r,i} \le h_{r,i+n}$, and the total capacity is larger than that of the matching method in proposition 3.

given), find the optimal power allocation and the total channel capacity; (2) compare the all channel capacities, the largest one is the ultimate system capacity, whose subcarrier matching and power allocation are jointly optimal. But, this process is prohibitive to find global optimum in terms of complexity. In this subsection, an analytical argument is given to prove that the optimal subcarrier matching is to match subcarrier by the order of the channel power gains.

Here, we assume that the system includes only two subcarriers, i.e, $N = 2$. The channel power gains over the source-relay channel are denoted as $h_{s,1}$ and $h_{s,2}$, and the channel power gains over the relay-destination channel are denoted as $h_{r,1}$ and $h_{r,2}$. Without loss of generality, we assume that $h_{s,1} \geq h_{s,2}$ and $h_{r,1} \geq h_{r,2}$, i.e., the subcarriers are sorted according to the channel power gains. The system power constraints are P_s and P_r at the source and the relay, separately.

In this case, the mixed binary integer programming problem can be reduced to the following optimization problem.

$$\max_{P_{s,i},P_{r,j},\rho_{ij},C_i} \sum_{i=1}^{2} C_i$$

$$\text{subject to } \frac{1}{2}\log_2\left(1+\frac{P_{s,i}h_{s,i}}{N_0}\right) \geq C_i$$

$$\sum_{j=1}^{2}\rho_{ij}\frac{1}{2}\log_2\left(1+\frac{P_{r,j}h_{r,j}}{N_0}\right) \geq C_i$$

$$\sum_{i=1}^{2}P_{s,i} \leq P_s, \sum_{j=1}^{2}P_{r,j} \leq P_r$$

$$P_{s,i},P_{r,j} \geq 0, \forall i,j$$

$$\sum_{j=1}^{2}\rho_{ij} = 1, \rho_{ij} = \{0,1\}, \forall i,j$$

Here, there are two possibilities to match the subcarriers: (1) the subcarrier 1 over the sourcerelay channel is matched to the subcarrier 1 over the relay-destination channel, and the subcarrier 2 over the source-relay channel is matched to the subcarrier 2 over the relay-destination channel (i.e., $h_{s,1} \sim h_{r,1}$ and $h_{s,2} \sim h_{r,2}$); (2) the subcarrier 1 over the source-relay channel is matched to the subcarrier 2 over the relay-destination channel, and the subcarrier 2 over the source-relay channel is matched to the subcarrier 1 over the relay-destination channel (i.e., $h_{s,1} \sim h_{r,2}$ and $h_{s,2} \sim h_{r,1}$). As there are only two possibilities, the optimal subcarrier matching can be obtained by comparing the capacities of two possibilities. However, the process has to be repeated when the channel power gains are changed. Next, optimal subcarrier matching way will be given without computing the capacities of all subcarrier matching possibilities, after Lemma 2 is proposed and proved.

Lemma 2: For global optimum of the upper optimization problem, the capacity of the better subcarrier is greater than that of the worse subcarrier, where better and worse are according to the channel power gain at the source and the relay.

Proof: We will prove this *Lemma* in the contrapositive form. First, for the global optimum, we assume the power allocations at the source are $P'_{s,1}$ and $P_s - P'_{s,1}$, and assume $R'_{s,1} \leq R'_{s,2}$, i.e., the capacity of better subcarrier is less than that of worse subcarrier, which means

$$\log_2\left(1+\frac{h_{s,1}P'_{s,1}}{N_0}\right) \leq \log_2\left(1+\frac{h_{s,2}\left(P_s - P'_{s,1}\right)}{N_0}\right) \qquad (27)$$

As the capacity of optimum is the greatest one, the capacity is greater than any other power allocation. When the subcarrier matching is constant, there are no other power allocations to the two subcarriers denoted as $P^*_{s,1}$ and $P_s - P^*_{s,1}$, which make the capacities of two subcarrier satisfied with following relations

$$R^*_{s,1} \geq R'_{s,2} \qquad (28)$$

$$R^*_{s,2} \geq R'_{s,1} \qquad (29)$$

If the power allocation $P^*_{s,1}$ and $P_s - P^*_{s,1}$ exist, we can rematch the subcarriers to improve system capacity by exchanging the subcarrier 1 and subcarrier 2, i.e., changing the subcarrier matching. According to the new subcarrier matching and power allocation, it is clear that the system capacity can be improved.

Here, we will prove that there exist the power allocations which are satisfied with the equations (28) and (29).

$$\log_2\left(1+\frac{h_{s,1}P^*_{s,1}}{N_0}\right) \geq \log_2\left(1+\frac{h_{s,2}\left(P_s - P'_{s,1}\right)}{N_0}\right) \qquad (30)$$

$$\log_2\left(1+\frac{h_{s,2}\left(P_s - P^*_{s,1}\right)}{N_0}\right) \geq \log_2\left(1+\frac{h_{s,1}P'_{s,1}}{N_0}\right) \qquad (31)$$

By solving the above inequalities, we can get the following inequation

$$\frac{h_{s,2}}{h_{s,1}}\left(P_s - P'_{s,1}\right) \leq P^*_{s,1} \leq P_s - \frac{h_{s,1}}{h_{s,2}}P'_{s,1} \qquad (32)$$

At the same time, to satisfy the inequality (27), the following relation has to be satisfied

$$P'_{s,1} \leq \frac{h_{s,2}P_s}{h_{s,1} + h_{s,2}} \qquad (33)$$

By making use of the above inequality, we can get

$$
\begin{aligned}
\frac{h_{s,2}}{h_{s,1}}\left(P_s - P'_{s,1}\right) - \left(P_s - \frac{h_{s,1}}{h_{s,2}}P'_{s,1}\right) &= \frac{h_{s,2}}{h_{s,1}}P_s - P_s + \frac{\left(h_{s,1}+h_{s,2}\right)\left(h_{s,1}-h_{s,2}\right)}{h_{s,1}h_{s,2}}P'_{s,1} \\
&\leq \frac{h_{s,2}}{h_{s,1}}P_s - P_s + \frac{\left(h_{s,1}+h_{s,2}\right)\left(h_{s,1}-h_{s,2}\right)}{h_{s,1}h_{s,2}}\frac{h_{s,2}P_s}{h_{s,1}+h_{s,2}} \\
&= \frac{h_{s,2}}{h_{s,1}}P_s - P_s - \frac{h_{s,2}}{h_{s,1}}P_s + P_s \\
&= 0
\end{aligned}
$$

Therefore, the following inequality is proved

$$\frac{h_{s,2}}{h_{s,1}}\left(P_s - P'_{s,1}\right) \le P_s - \frac{h_{s,1}}{h_{s,2}} P'_{s,1} \tag{34}$$

This means that we can always find $P^*_{s,1}$ which satisfies the inequality (32). The new power allocation $P^*_{s,1}$ makes the inequalities (28) and (29) satisfied.

Then, we can rematch the subcarriers by exchanging the subcarrier 1 and subcarrier 2 at the source to improve the system capacity. This means that the system capacity of the new subcarrier matching and power allocation is greater than that of the original power allocation.

Therefore, for any power allocations which make the subcarrier capacity of worse subcarrier is greater than that of the better subcarrier, we always can find new power allocation to improve system capacity and make the subcarrier capacity of better subcarrier greater than that of worse subcarrier.

At the relay, for the global optimum, the similar process can be used to prove that the capacity of better subcarrier is greater than that of the worse subcarrier.

Therefore, for the global optimum at the source and the relay, we can conclude that the subcarrier capacity of better subcarrier is greater than that of the worse subcarrier with any channel power gains.

By making use of *Lemma 2*, the following proposition can be proved, which states the optimal subcarrier matching way for the global optimum.

Proposition 4: For the global optimum in the system including only two subcarriers, the optimal subcarrier matching is that the better subcarrier is matched to the better subcarrier and the worse subcarrier is matched to the worse subcarrier, i.e., $h_{s,1} \sim h_{r,1}$ and $h_{s,2} \sim h_{r,2}$.

Proof: Following *Lemma 2*, we know that the capacity of the better subcarrier is greater than the capacity of the worse subcarrier for the global optimum, i.e., $R^*_{s,1} \ge R^*_{s,2}$, $R^*_{r,1} \ge R^*_{r,2}$. There are two ways to match subcarrier: first, the better subcarrier is matched to the better subcarrier, i.e., $h_{s,1} \sim h_{r,1}$ and $h_{s,2} \sim h_{r,2}$; second, the better subcarrier is matched to the worse subcarrier, i.e., . $h_{s,1} \sim h_{r,2}$ and $h_{s,2} \sim h_{r,1}$.

We can prove the optimal subcarrier matching is the first way by proving the following inequality

$$\min\left(R^*_{s,1},R^*_{r,1}\right) + \min\left(R^*_{s,2},R^*_{r,2}\right) \ge \min\left(R^*_{s,1},R^*_{r,2}\right) + \min\left(R^*_{s,2},R^*_{r,1}\right) \tag{35}$$

where the left is the system capacity of the first subcarrier matching and the right is that of the second subcarrier matching.

To prove the upper inequality, we can list all possible relations of $R^*_{s,1}$, $R^*_{r,1}$, $R^*_{s,2}$ and $R^*_{r,2}$. Restricted to the relations $R^*_{s,1} \ge R^*_{s,2}$ and $R^*_{r,1} \ge R^*_{r,2}$, there are six possibilities (1) $R^*_{s,1} \ge R^*_{s,2} \ge R^*_{r,1} \ge R^*_{r,2}$; (2) $R^*_{s,1} \ge R^*_{r,1} \ge R^*_{s,2} \ge R^*_{r,2}$; (3) $R^*_{s,1} \ge R^*_{r,1} \ge R^*_{r,2} \ge R^*_{s,2}$; (4) $R^*_{r,1} \ge R^*_{r,2} \ge R^*_{s,1} \ge R^*_{s,2}$; (5) $R^*_{r,1} \ge R^*_{s,1} \ge R^*_{r,2} \ge R^*_{s,2}$; (6) $R^*_{r,1} \ge R^*_{s,1} \ge R^*_{s,2} \ge R^*_{r,2}$. For the every possibility, it is easy to prove the inequality (35) satisfied. Details are omitted for sake of the length.

So far, for the system including two subcarriers, the optimal joint subcarrier matching has been given. Specially, the optimal subcarrier matching is to match the subcarriers by the order of the channel power gains.

3.2.2 Optimal subcarrier matching for the system including unlimited number of subcarriers

This subsection extends the method in the previous subsection to the system including unlimited number of the subcarriers. The number of the subcarriers is finite (e.g., $2 \leq N \leq \infty$), where the subcarrier channel power gains are $h_{s,i}$ and $h_{r,j}$.

As before the channel power gains are assumed $h_{s,i} \geq h_{s,i+1}(1 \leq i \leq N-1)$ and $h_{r,j} \geq h_{r,j+1}(1 \leq j \leq N-1)$. For the global optimum, the following proposition gives the optimal subcarrier matching.

Proposition 5: For the global optimum in the system including unlimited number of the subcarriers, the optimal subcarrier matching is

$$h_{s,i} \sim h_{r,i} \tag{36}$$

Together with the optimal power allocation for this subcarrier matching, they are optimal joint subcarrier matching and power allocation

Proof: This proposition will be proved in the contrapositive form. For the global optimum, assuming that there is a subcarrier matching method whose matching result including two matched subcarrier pairs $h_{s,i} \sim h_{r,i+n}$ and $h_{s,i+n} \sim h_{r,i}$ ($n > 0$), and the total capacity is greater than that of the matching method in *Proposition 4*.

When the power allocated to other subcarriers and the other subcarrier matching are constant, the total channel capacity of the two subcarrier pairs can be improved based on *Proposition 4*, which implies the channel capacity can be improved by rematching the subcarriers to $h_{s,i} \sim h_{r,i}$ and $h_{s,i+n} \sim h_{r,i+n}$. It is contrary to the assumption. Therefore, there is no subcarrier matching way better than the way in *Proposition 4*. At the same time, as the total capacity of this subcarrier matching and the corresponding optimal power allocation scheme is the largest one, this subcarrier matching together with the corresponding optimal power allocations is the optimal joint subcarrier matching and power allocation.

Therefore, for the system including unlimited number of the subcarriers, the optimal subcarrier matching is to match the subcarrier according to the order of channel power gains, i.e., $h_{s,i} \sim h_{r,i}$. As it is optimal subcarrier matching for the global optimum, together with the optimal power allocation for this subcarrier matching, they are optimal joint subcarrier matching and power allocation.

3.3 Optimal power allocation for optimal subcarrier matching

When the subcarrier matching is given, the parameters ρ_{ij} in optimization problem (9) is constant, e.g., $\rho_{ii} = 1$ and $\rho_{ij} = 0 (i \neq j)$. Therefore, the optimization problem can be reduced to as follows

$$\max_{P_{s,i}, P_{r,i}, C_i} \quad \sum_{i=1}^{N} C_i$$

$$\text{subject to} \quad \frac{1}{2}\log_2\left(1 + \frac{P_{s,i}h_{s,i}}{N_0}\right) \geq C_i$$

$$\frac{1}{2}\log_2\left(1 + \frac{P_{r,i}h_{r,i}}{N_0}\right) \geq C_i$$

$$\sum_{i=1}^{N} P_{s,i} \leq P_s, \sum_{i=1}^{N} P_{r,i} \leq P_r$$

$$P_{s,i}, P_{r,i} \geq 0, \forall i, j$$

Hadamard (W-H) codes for a synchronous system (e.g., the downlink of a cellular system) guarantees the absence of MAI in an ideal channel and a minimum MAI in real channels.[1]

2.1 Linear equalization

Within linear combining techniques, various schemes based on the channel state information (CSI) are known in the literature, where signals coming from different sub-carriers are weighted by suitable coefficients G_m (m being the sub-carrier index).

The equal gain combining (EGC) consists in equal weighting of each sub-carrier contribution and compensating only the phases as in (1)

$$G_m = \frac{H_m^*}{|H_m|} \qquad (1)$$

where G_m indicates the $m^{\underline{th}}$ complex channel gain and H_m is the $m^{\underline{th}}$ channel coefficient (operation * stands for complex conjugate).

If the number of active users is negligible with respect to the number of sub-carriers, that is the system is noise-limited, the best choice is represented by a combination in which the sub-carrier with higher signal-to-noise ratio (SNR) has the higher weight, as in the maximal ratio combining (MRC)

$$G_m = H_m^*. \qquad (2)$$

The MRC destroys the orthogonality between the codes. For this reason, when the number of active user is high (the system is interference-limited) a good choice is given by restoring at the receiver the orthogonality between the sequences. This means to cancel the effects of the channel on the sequences as in the orthogonality restoring combining (ORC), also known as zero forcing, where

$$G_m = \frac{1}{H_m}. \qquad (3)$$

This implies a total cancellation of the multiuser interference, but, on the other hand, this method enhances the noise, because the sub-carriers with low SNR have higher weights. Consequently, a correction on G_m is introduced with threshold orthogonality restoring combining (TORC)

$$G_m = u\left(|H_m| - \rho_{\text{TH}}\right)\frac{1}{H_m} \qquad (4)$$

where $u(\cdot)$ is the unitary-step function and the threshold ρ_{TH} is introduced to cancel the contributions of sub-carriers highly corrupted by the noise.

However, exception made for the two extreme cases of one active user (giving MRC) and negligible noise (giving ORC) the presented methods do not represent the optimum solution for real cases of interest.

---

[1] In the uplink a set of spreading codes, such as Gold codes, with good auto- and cross-correlation properties, should be employed. However in this case a multi-user detection scheme in the receiver is essential because the asynchronous arrival times destroy orthogonality among the sub-carriers.

The optimum choice for linear equalization is the minimum mean square error (MMSE) technique, whose coefficient can be written as

$$G_m = \frac{H_m^*}{\left|H_m\right|^2 + \dfrac{1}{N\bar{\gamma}}} \tag{5}$$

where N_u is the number of active users and $\bar{\gamma}$ is the mean SNR averaged over small-scale fading. Hence, in addition to the CSI, MMSE requires the knowledge of the signal power, the noise power, and the number of active users, thus representing a more complex linear technique to be implemented, especially in the downlink, where the combination is typically performed at the mobile unit.

To overcome the additional complexity due to estimation of these quantities, a low-complex suboptimum MMSE equalization can be realized (K. Fazel, 2003). With suboptimum MMSE, the equalization coefficients are designed such that they perform optimally only in the most critical cases for which successful transmission should be guaranteed

$$G_m = \frac{H_m^*}{\left|H_m\right|^2 + \lambda} \tag{6}$$

where λ is the threshold at which the optimal MMSE equalization guarantees the maximum acceptable bit error probability (BEP) and requires only information about H_m. However, the value of λ has to be determined during the system design and varies with the scenario.

A new linear combining technique has been recently proposed, named partial equalization (PE), whose coefficient G_m is given by (Conti et al., 2007)

$$G_m = \frac{H_m^*}{\left|H_m\right|^{1+\beta}} \tag{7}$$

where β is the PE parameter having values in the range of $[-1,1]$. It may be observed that, being parametric with β, (7) reduces to EGC, MRC and ORC for $\beta = 0$, -1, and 1, respectively. Hence, (7) includes in itself all the most commonly adopted linear combining techniques.

Note also that, while MRC, and ORC are optimum in the extreme cases of noise-limited and interference-limited systems, respectively, for each intermediate situation an optimum value of the PE parameter β can be found to optimize the performance. Moreover, the PE scheme has the same complexity of EGC, MRC, and ORC, but it is more robust to channel impairments and to MAI-variations (Conti et al., 2007).

2.2 Non-linear equalization

Linear equalization techniques compensate the distortion due to flat fading, by simply performing one complex-valued multiplication per sub-carrier. If the spreading code structure of the interfering signals is known, the MAI could not be considered in advance as noise-like, yielding to suboptimal performance.

Non-linear multiuser equalizers, such as interference cancellation (IC) and maximum likelihood (ML) detection, exploit the knowledge of the interfering users' spreading codes in the detection process, thus improving the performance at the expense of higher receiver complexity (Hanzo et al., 2003).

IC is based on the detection of the interfering users' information and its subtraction from the received signal before the determination of the desired user's information. Two kinds of IC techniques exists: parallel and successive cancellation. Combinations of parallel and successive IC are also possible. IC works in several iterations: each detection stage exploits the decisions of the previous stage to reconstruct the interfering contribution in the received signal. It can be typically applied in cellular radio systems to reduce intra-cell and inter-cell interference. Note that IC requires a feed back component in the receiver and the knowledge of which users are active.

The ML detection attains better performance since it is based on optimum maximum likelihood detection algorithms which optimally estimate the transmitted data. Many optimum ML algorithms have been presented in literature and we remind the reader to (Hanzo et al., 2003; K. Fazel, 2003) for further investigation which are out of the scope of the present chapter. However, since the complexity of ML detection grows exponentially with the number of users and the number of bits per modulation symbol, its use can be limited in practice to applications with few users and low order modulation. Furthermore, also in this case as for IC, the knowledge about which users are active is necessary to compute the possible transmitted sequences and apply ML criterions.

2.3 Objectives of the chapter

We propose a general and parametric analytical framework for the performance evaluation of the downlink of MC-CDMA systems with PE.[2] In particular,

- we evaluate the performance in terms of bit error probability (BEP);
- we derive the optimum PE parameter β for all possible number of sub-carriers, active users, and for all possible values of the SNR;
- we show that PE technique with optimal β improves the system performance still maintaining the same complexity of MRC, EGC and ORC and is close to MMSE;
- we consider a combined equalization (CE) scheme jointly adopting PE at both the transmitter and the receiver and we investigate when CE introduces some benefits with respect to classical single side equalization.

3. System model

We focus on PE technique, that being parametric includes previously cited linear techniques and allows the derivation of a general framework to assess the performance evaluation and sensitivity to system parameters.

3.1 Transmitter

Referring to binary phase shift keying (BPSK) modulation and to the transmitter block scheme depicted in Fig. 1(a), the transmitted signal referred to the $k^{\underline{th}}$ user, can be written as

$$s^{(k)}(t) = \sqrt{\frac{2E_b}{M}} \sum_{i=-\infty}^{+\infty} \sum_{m=0}^{M-1} c_m^{(k)} a^{(k)}[i] g(t - iT_b) \cos(\varphi_m) \tag{8}$$

---

[2] Portions reprinted with permission from A. Conti, B. M. Masini, F. Zabini, and O. Andrisano, "*On the down-link Performance of Multi-Carrier CDMA Systems with Partial Equalization*", IEEE Transactions on Wireless Communications, Volume 6, Issue 1, Jan. 2007, Page(s):230 - 239. ©2007 IEEE, and from B. M. Masini, A. Conti, "*Combined Partial Equalization for MC-CDMA Wireless Systems*", IEEE Communications Letters, Volume 13, Issue 12, December 2009 Page(s):884 – 886. ©2009 IEEE.

where E_b is the energy per bit, i denotes the data index, m is the sub-carrier index, c_m is the mth chip (taking value ±1)[3], $a_i^{(k)}$ is the data-symbol transmitted during the ith time-symbol, $g(t)$ is a rectangular pulse waveform, with duration $[0,T]$ and unitary energy, T_b is the bit-time, $\varphi_m = 2\pi f_m t + \phi_m$ where $f_m = f_0 + m \cdot \Delta f$ is the sub-carrier-frequency (with $\Delta f \cdot T$ and $f_0 T$ integers to have orthogonal frequencies) and ϕ_m is the random phase uniformly distributed within $[-\pi,\pi]$. In particular, $T_b = T + T_g$ is the total OFDM symbol duration, increased with respect to T of a time-guard T_g (inserted between consecutive multi-carrier symbols to eliminate the residual inter symbol interference, ISI, due to the channel delay spread). Note that we assume rectangular pulses for analytical purposes. However, this does not lead the generality of the work. In fact, a MC-CDMA system is realized, in practice, through inverse fast Fourier transform (IFFT) and FFT at the transmitter and receiver, respectively. After the sampling process, the signal results completely equivalent to a MC-CDMA signal with rectangular pulses in the continuous time-domain.

Considering that, exploiting the orthogonality of the code, all the different users use the same carriers, the total transmitted signal results in

$$s(t) = \sum_{k=0}^{N_u-1} s^{(k)}(t) = \sqrt{\frac{2E_b}{M}} \sum_{k=0}^{N_u-1} \sum_{i=-\infty}^{+\infty} \sum_{m=0}^{M-1} c_m^{(k)} a^{(k)}[i] g(t - iT_b) \cos(\varphi_m) \tag{9}$$

where N_u is the number of active users and, because of the use of orthogonal codes, $N_u \leq M$.

3.2 Channel model

Since we are considering the downlink, focusing on the nth receiver, the information associated to different users experiments the same fading. Due to the CDMA structure of the system, each user receives the information of all the users and select only its own data through the spreading sequence. We assume the impulse response of the channel $h(t)$ as time-invariant during many symbol intervals.

We employ a frequency-domain channel model in which the transfer function, $H(f)$, is given by

$$H(f) \simeq H(f_m) = \alpha_m e^{j\psi_m} \text{ for } |f - f_m| < \frac{W_s}{2}, \forall m \tag{10}$$

where α_m and ψ_m are the mth amplitude and phase coefficients, respectively, and W_s is the the transmission bandwidth of each sub-carrier. The assumption in (10) means that the pulse shaping still remains rectangular even if the non-distortion conditions are not perfectly verified. Hence, the response $g'(t)$ to $g(t)$ is a rectangular pulse with unitary energy and duration $T' \triangleq T + T_d$, being $T_d \leq T_g$ the time delay. Note that this assumption is helpful in the analytical process and does not impact in the generality of the work.

We assume that each $H(f_m)$ is independent identically distributed (i.i.d.) complex zero-mean Gaussian random variable (r.v.) with variance, σ_H^2, related to the path-loss L_p as $1/L_p = \mathbb{E}\{\alpha^2\} = \sigma_H^2$.

---

[3] We assume orthogonal sequences $\overline{c^{(k)}}$ for different users, such that:

$$<\overline{c^{(k)}}, \overline{c^{(k')}}> = \sum_{m=0}^{M-1} c_m^{(k)} c_m^{(k')} = \begin{cases} M & k = k' \\ 0 & k \neq k'. \end{cases}$$

3.3 Receiver

The received signal can be written as

$$r(t) = \sqrt{\frac{2E_b}{M}} \sum_{k=0}^{N_u-1} \sum_{i=-\infty}^{+\infty} \sum_{m=0}^{M-1} \alpha_m c_m^{(k)} a^{(k)}[i] g'(t - iT_b) \cos(\tilde{\varphi}_m) + n(t) \tag{11}$$

where $n(t)$ is the additive white Gaussian noise with two-side power spectral density (PSD) $N_0/2$, $\tilde{\varphi}_m = 2\pi f_m t + \vartheta_m$, and $\vartheta_m \triangleq \phi_m + \psi_m$. Note that, since ϑ_m can be considered uniformly distributed in $[-\pi, \pi]$, we can consider $\angle H(f_m) \sim \vartheta_m$ in the following.

The receiver structure is depicted in Fig. 1(b). Focusing, without loss of generality, to the lth sub-carrier of user n, the receiver performs the correlation at the jth instant (perfect synchronization and phase tracking are assumed) of the received signal with the signal $c_l^{(n)} \sqrt{2} \cos(\tilde{\varphi}_l)$, as

$$z_l^{(n)}[j] = \frac{1}{\sqrt{T}} \int_{jT_b}^{jT_b+T} r(t)\, c_l^{(n)} \sqrt{2} \cos(\tilde{\varphi}_l) dt. \tag{12}$$

Substituting (11) in (12), the term $z_l^{(n)}[j]$ results in (13)

$$z_l^{(n)}[j] = 2\sqrt{\frac{E_b}{MT}} \sum_{i=-\infty}^{+\infty} \int_{jT_b}^{jT_b+T} \sum_{k=0}^{N_u-1} \sum_{m=0}^{M-1} \alpha_m c_m^{(k)} c_l^{(n)} a^{(k)}[i]\, g'(t - iT_b)$$

$$\times\, \cos(\tilde{\varphi}_m)\cos(\tilde{\varphi}_l)dt + \overbrace{\int_{jT_b}^{jT_b+T} \sqrt{2}\, \frac{c_l^{(n)}}{\sqrt{T}} n(t)\cos(\tilde{\varphi}_l)dt}^{n_l[j]} \tag{13}$$

$$= \sqrt{\frac{E_b \delta_d}{M}} \alpha_l a^{(n)}[j] + \sqrt{\frac{E_b \delta_d}{M}} c_l^{(n)} \alpha_l \sum_{k=0, k \neq n}^{N_u-1} c_l^{(k)} a^{(k)}[j] + n_l[j]$$

where $\delta_d \triangleq 1/(1 + T_d/T)$ represents the loss of energy caused by the time-spreading of the impulse.

4. Decision variable

The decision variable, $v^{(n)}[j]$, is obtained by linearly combining the weighted signals from each sub-carrier as follows[4]

$$v^{(n)} = \sum_{l=0}^{M-1} |G_l|\, z_l^{(n)} \tag{14}$$

where $|G_l|$ is a suitable amplitude of the lth equalization coefficient. By considering PE, the weight for the lth sub-carrier is given by

---

[4] For the sake of conciseness in our notation, since ISI is avoided, we will neglect the time-index j in the following.

$$G_l = \frac{H^*(f_l)}{\left|H^*(f_l)\right|^{1+\beta}}, \quad -1 \le \beta \le 1. \tag{15}$$

Therefore, from (13) and (14) we can write

$$v^{(n)} = \overbrace{\sqrt{\frac{E_b\delta_d}{M}} \sum_{l=0}^{M-1} \alpha_l^{1-\beta} a^{(n)}}^{U} + \overbrace{\sum_{l=0}^{M-1} \alpha_l^{-\beta} n_l}^{N} + \overbrace{\sqrt{\frac{E_b\delta_d}{M}} \sum_{l=0}^{M-1} \sum_{k=0,k\neq n}^{N_u-1} \alpha_l^{1-\beta} c_l^{(n)} c_l^{(k)} a^{(k)}}^{I}. \tag{16}$$

At this point, the distribution of the test statistic can be obtained by studying the statistics of U, I and N in (16).

4.1 Interference term

Exploiting the properties of orthogonal codes, the interference term can be rewritten as

$$I = \sqrt{\frac{E_b\delta_d}{M}} \sum_{k=0,k\neq n}^{N_u-1} a^{(k)} \left(\overbrace{\sum_{h=1}^{\frac{M}{2}} \alpha_{x_h}^{1-\beta}}^{A_1} - \overbrace{\sum_{h=1}^{\frac{M}{2}} \alpha_{y_h}^{1-\beta}}^{A_2} \right), \tag{17}$$

where indexes x_h and y_h define the following partition

$$c^{(n)}[x_h]c^{(k)}[x_h] = 1 \tag{18}$$

$$c^{(n)}[y_h]c^{(k)}[y_h] = -1 \tag{19}$$

$$\{x_h\} \cup \{y_h\} = 0,1,2,....,M-1. \tag{20}$$

For large M, we can apply the central limit theorem (CLT) to each one of the internal sums in (17) obtaining

$$A_1, A_2 \sim \mathcal{N}\left(\sqrt{\frac{M}{2}} \mathbb{E}\{\alpha^{1-\beta}\}, \frac{M}{2} \zeta_\beta(\alpha) \right) \tag{21}$$

where $\zeta_\beta(\alpha)$ indicates the variance of $\alpha^{1-\beta}$ given by

$$\zeta_\beta(\alpha) \triangleq \mathbb{E}\{(\alpha^{1-\beta})^2\} - (\mathbb{E}\{\alpha^{1-\beta}\})^2. \tag{22}$$

Therefore, $A \triangleq A_1 - A_2$ is distributed as

$$A \sim \mathcal{N}\left(0, M \zeta_\beta(\alpha) \right). \tag{23}$$

By exploiting the symmetry of the Gaussian probability density function (p.d.f.) and the property of the sum of uncorrelated (and thus independent) Gaussian r.v.'s ($A_k = a^{(k)}A \sim (0,M\,\zeta_\beta(\alpha))$), the interference term results distributed as

$$I \sim \mathcal{N}\left(0, \sigma_I^2 \triangleq E_b\delta_d(N_u-1)\zeta_\beta(\alpha) \right). \tag{24}$$

4.2 Noise term

The thermal noise at the combiner output is given by

$$N = \sum_{l=0}^{M-1} \alpha_l^{-\beta} n_l \tag{25}$$

where terms α_l and n_l are independent and n_l is zero mean. Thus, N consists on a sum of i.i.d zero mean r.v.'s with variance $N_0/2\ \mathbb{E}\{\alpha^{-2\beta}\}$. By applying the CLT, we approximate the unconditioned noise term N as

$$N \sim \mathcal{N}\left(0, \sigma_N^2 \triangleq M\frac{N_0}{2}\mathbb{E}\{\alpha^{-2\beta}\}\right). \tag{26}$$

4.3 Useful term

By applying the CLT, the gain U on the useful term in (16) results distributed as

$$U \sim \mathcal{N}\left(\sqrt{E_b\delta_d M}\mathbb{E}\{\alpha_l^{1-\beta}\}, E_b\delta_d\zeta_\beta(\alpha)\right). \tag{27}$$

4.3.1 Independence between each term

By noting that $a^{(k)}$ is zero mean and statistically independent on α_l, A, and n_l, it follows that $\mathbb{E}\{I\ N\} = \mathbb{E}\{I\ U\} = 0$. Since n_l and α_l are statistically independent, the $\mathbb{E}\{N\ U\} = 0$. The fact that I, N and U are uncorrelated Gaussian r.v.'s implies they are also independent.

5. Bit error probability evaluation

From (24) and (26) we obtain

$$I + N \sim \mathcal{N}\left(0, E_b\delta_d(N_u - 1)\zeta_\beta(\alpha) + M\mathbb{E}\{\alpha^{-2\beta}\}\frac{N_0}{2}\right) \tag{28}$$

that can be applied to the test statistic in (16) to derive the BEP conditioned to the r.v. U as

$$P_b|_U = \frac{1}{2}\mathrm{erfc}\left\{\frac{U}{\sqrt{2(\sigma_I^2 + \sigma_N^2)}}\right\}. \tag{29}$$

By applying the law of large number (LLN), that is approximating $\sum_{l=0}^{M-1}\alpha_l^{1-\beta}$ with $M\mathbb{E}\{\alpha^{1-\beta}\}$, we can derive the unconditioned BEP as

$$P_b \approx \frac{1}{2}\mathrm{erfc}\left\{\sqrt{\frac{E_b\delta_d(\mathbb{E}\{\alpha^{1-\beta}\})^2}{2E_b\delta_d\dfrac{N_u - 1}{M}\zeta_\beta(\alpha) + \mathbb{E}\{\alpha^{-2\beta}\}N_0}}\right\} \tag{30}$$

where it can be evaluated that

$$\mathbb{E}\{\alpha^{1-\beta}\} = (2\sigma_H^2)^{\frac{1-\beta}{2}} \Gamma\left(\frac{3-\beta}{2}\right) \tag{31}$$

$$\mathbb{E}\{\alpha^{-2\beta}\} = \left(2\sigma_H^2\right)^{-\beta} \Gamma(1-\beta) \tag{32}$$

$$\zeta_\beta(\alpha) = (2\sigma_H^2)^{1-\beta}\left[\Gamma(2-\beta) - \Gamma^2\left(\frac{3-\beta}{2}\right)\right] \tag{33}$$

being $\Gamma(z)$ the Euler Gamma function. Hence, we can write

$$P_b \simeq \frac{1}{2}\mathrm{erfc}\sqrt{\frac{\Gamma^2\left(\frac{3-\beta}{2}\right)\bar{\gamma}}{2\frac{N_u-1}{M}\left[\Gamma(2-\beta) - \Gamma^2\left(\frac{3-\beta}{2}\right)\right]\bar{\gamma} + \Gamma(1-\beta)}}. \tag{34}$$

where

$$\bar{\gamma} \triangleq \frac{2\sigma_H^2 E_b \delta_d}{N_0} \tag{35}$$

represents the mean SNR averaged over small-scale fading.
Note that the BEP expression is general in β and it is immediate to verify that results in the expressions for EGC ($\beta = 0$) and MRC ($\beta = -1$) as in (Yee et al., 1993).
As a benchmark, note also that for MRC with one active user (i.e., $N_u = 1$), (34) becomes

$$P_b \simeq \frac{1}{2}\mathrm{erfc}\sqrt{\bar{\gamma}} \tag{36}$$

that is independent on the number of sub-carrier M and represents the well known limit of the antipodal waveforms in AWGN channel. This means that the approximation due to LLN is equivalent to assume that we have a number of sub-carriers (M) sufficiently high to saturate the frequency-diversity, then the transmission performs as in the absence of fading.

5.1 Optimum choice of the combining parameter

Now we will analyze the proposed PE technique with the aim of finding the optimum value of β, defined as the value within the range $[-1,1]$ that minimizes the BEP

$$\beta^{(\mathrm{opt})} = \arg\min_\beta\{P_b(\beta,\bar{\gamma})\}$$

$$\simeq \arg\max_\beta\left\{\frac{\Gamma^2\left(\frac{3-\beta}{2}\right)\bar{\gamma}}{2\frac{N_u-1}{M}\left[\Gamma(2-\beta) - \Gamma^2\left(\frac{3-\beta}{2}\right)\right]\bar{\gamma} + \Gamma(1-\beta)}\right\}. \tag{37}$$

It will be shown in the numerical results that the approximation on the BEP does not significantly affect $\beta^{(\mathrm{opt})}$. By forcing to zero the derivative of the argument in (37), after some mathematical manipulations we obtain the following expression

Wireless Multimedia Communications and Networking Based on JPEG 2000

Max AGUEH
ECE Paris
France

1. Introduction

Nowadays, more and more multimedia applications integrate wireless transmission functionalities. Wireless networks are suitable for those types of applications, due to their ease of deployment and because they yield tremendous advantages in terms of mobility of User Equipment (UE). However, wireless networks are subject to a high level of transmission errors because they rely on radio waves whose characteristics are highly dependent of the transmission environment.

In wireless video transmission applications like the one considered in this chapter and presented in Figure 1, effective data protection is a crucial issue.

JPEG 2000, the newest image representation standard, addresses this issue firstly by including predefined error resilient tools in his core encoding system (part 1) and going straightforward by defining in its 11th part called wireless JPEG 2000 (JPWL) a set of error resilient techniques to improve the transmission of JPEG 2000 codestreams over error-prone wireless channel.

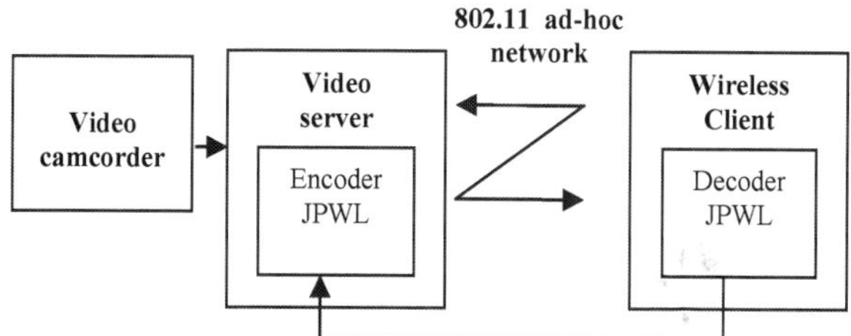

Fig. 1. Wireless video streaming system

JPEG 2000

JPEG 2000 is the newest image compression standard completing the existing JPEG standard (Taubman & Marcellin, 2001).

The interest for JPEG 2000 is growing since the Digital Cinema Initiatives (DCI) has selected JPEG 2000 for future distribution of motion pictures.

Its main characteristics are: lossy or lossless compression modes; resolution, quality and spatial scalability; transmission and progressive image reconstruction; error resilience for low bit rate mobile applications; Region Of Interest (ROI) functionality, etc.

Part 1 of the standard defines different tools allowing the decoder to detect errors in the transmitted codestream, to select the erroneous part of the code and to synchronise the decoder in order to avoid decoder crash. Even if those tools give a certain level of protection from transmission errors, they become ineffective when the transmission channel experiment high bit error rate. Wireless JPEG 2000 (JPEG 2000 11th part) addressed this issue by defining techniques to make JPEG 2000 codestream more resilient to transmissions errors in wireless systems.

Wireless JPEG 2000 (JPWL)

Wireless JPEG (JPWL) specifies error resilience tools such as Forward Error correction (FEC), interleaving, unequal error protection.

In this chapter we present a wireless JPEG 2000 video streaming system based on the recommendations of JPWL final draft (JPWL, 2005).

In (Dufaux & Nicholson, 2004), the description of the JPWL system is presented and the performance of its Error Protection Block (EPB) is evaluated. A fully JPEG 2000 Part 1 compliant backward compatible error protection scheme is proposed in (Nicholson et al, 2003). A memoryless Binary Symmetric Channel (BSC) is used for simulations both in (Nicholson et al, 2003) and (Dufaux & Nicholson, 2004). However, as packets errors mainly occur in bursts, the channel model considered in those works is not realistic. Moreover JPEG 2000 codestreams interleaving is not considered in (Nicholson et al, 2003).

In this chapter we address the problem of robust and efficient JPEG 2000 images and video transmission over wireless networks. The chapter is organized as follows: In section 2, we present a state of art of wireless JPEG 2000 multimedia communication systems along with the challenges to overcome in terms of codestreams protection against transmission errors. In section 3, we provide an overview of channel coding techniques for efficient JPEG 2000 based multimedia networking. Finally section 4, provides discussions and prospective issues for future distribution of motion JPEG 2000 images and video over wireless networks.

2. Wireless JPEG 2000 multimedia communication system and its challenges

In high error rate environments such as wireless channels, data protection is mandatory for efficient transmission of images and video. In this context, Wireless JPEG 2000 (JPWL) the 11th part of JPEG 2000 (JPWL, 2005) different techniques such as data interleaving, Forward Error Correction (FEC) with Reed-Solomon (RS) codes etc. in order to enhance the protection of JPEG 2000 codestreams against transmission errors.

In wireless multimedia system such as the one considered in this chapter (see Figure 1), a straightforward FEC methodology is applying FEC uniformly over the entire stream (Equal Error Correction - EEP). However, for hierarchical codes such as JPEG 2000, Unequal Error Protection (UEP) which assigns different FEC to different portion of codestream has been considered as a suitable protection scheme.

Since wireless channels' characteristics depend on the transmission environment, the packet loss rate in the system also changes dynamically. Thus a priori FEC rate allocation schemes such as the one proposed in (Agueh et al, 2007, a) are less efficient. Two families of data protection schemes address this issue by taking the wireless channel characteristics into where $P^{(0)} = \mathrm{diag}\{P_1^{(0)}, P_2^{(0)}, \cdots, P_N^{(0)}\}$ is the transmit power matrix of the DAs in the 0th cell. Unfortunately, it is quite difficult to get a more compact expression of the ergodic downlink capacity. Therefore, we propose the operation of "system scale-up" to study a simplified method to calculate the capacity as accurately as possible.

3.2 System scale-up

The basic idea of system scale-up is illustrated in Fig. 2. Assuming the proportion between the initial system and the scaled-up system to be t (a positive integer), we can summarize the characteristics of system scale-up as follows:

- Each DA with a single AE is scaled to a DA cluster with t AEs.
- The number of AEs equipped on the MT is increased from M to Mt.
- The system topology is not changed.
- The variance of $\mathcal{N}$ is not changed.
- The large-scale channel fading is changed from $\mathbf{L}^{(i)}$ to $\mathbf{L}^{(i)t}$, we have

$$\mathbf{L}^{(i)t} = \mathbf{L}^{(i)} \otimes \mathbf{I}_t. \tag{11}$$

The small-scale fading is changed from $H_w^{(i)} \in \mathbb{C}^{M \times N}$ to $H_w^{(i)t} \in \mathbb{C}^{Mt \times Nt}$, $i = 0,1,\cdots,6$, let $\mathbf{H}_{mn}^{(i)t} \in \mathbb{C}^{t \times t}, 1 \le m \le M, 1 \le n \le N, i = 0,1,\cdots,6$, we have

$$H_w^{(i)t} = \begin{bmatrix} \mathbf{H}_{11}^{(i)} & \cdots & \mathbf{H}_{1N}^{(i)} \\ \vdots & \ddots & \vdots \\ \mathbf{H}_{11}^{(i)} & \cdots & \mathbf{H}_{MN}^{(i)} \end{bmatrix}, i = 0,1,\cdots,6. \tag{12}$$

$H_w^{(i)t}$ is also a matrix with i.i.d. zero-mean unit-variance circularly symmetric complex Gaussian entries, which is the same as $H_w^{(i)}$.

- The total power consumption is not changed. In detail, the transmit power of each DA in the initial system will be equally shared by the t AEs within a DA cluster in the scaled-up system. We can express the new transmit power matrix as

$$P_t^{(0)} = \frac{1}{t} \mathrm{diag}\{P_1^{(0)}, P_2^{(0)}, ..., P_N^{(0)}\} \otimes \mathbf{I}_t. \tag{13}$$

It is well known that the channel capacity of a MIMO system can be well approximated by a linear function of the minimum number of transmit and receive antennas (Telatar, 1999) as follows:

$$\mathbb{C} \approx min(a,b) \times A, \tag{14}$$

where $\mathbb{C}$ is the capacity of a MIMO channel with a transmit antennas and b receive antennas, A is a corresponding fixed parameter determined by the total transmit power constraint. If the number of transmit antennas and receive antennas increase from a to ta, from b to tb, respectively, the channel capacity is derived as

$$\hat{\mathbb{C}} \approx min(ta, tb) \times A \approx t\mathbb{C}. \tag{15}$$

Communications and Networking

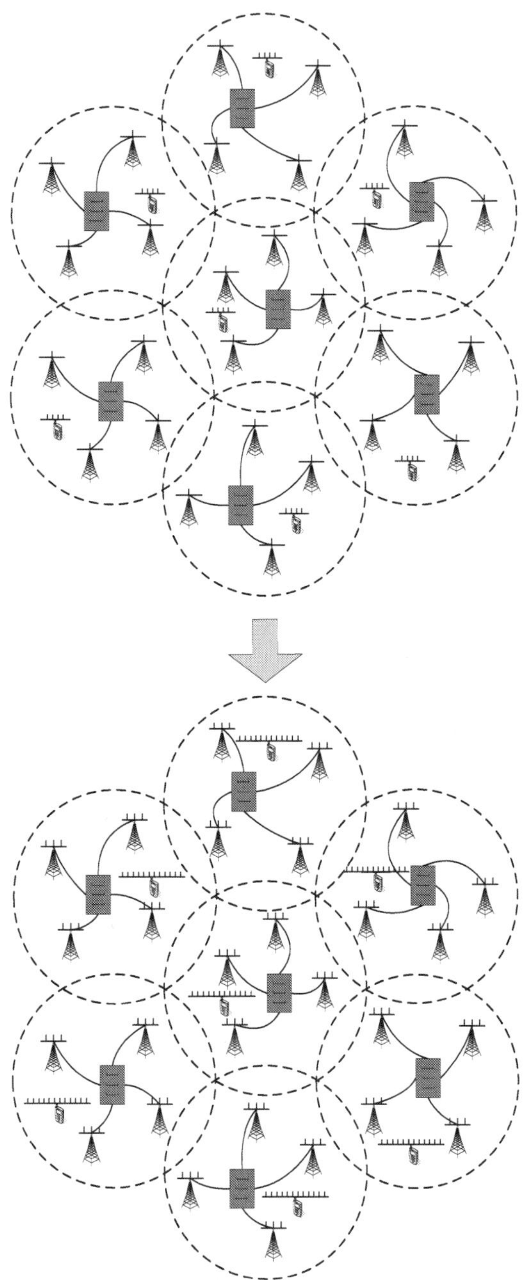

Fig. 2. Illustration of system scale-up.

Since the considered DAS is a special MIMO system, we directly hold that the system capacity scales linearly in the process of system scale-up, which can be partial testified by the following Theorem.

Theorem 1:

If the proportion between the initial system and the scaled-up system is t, an upper bound for the downlink capacity of the scaled-up system can be expressed as

$$C_t^{upper} = t \times M \log_2 \left(1 + \sum_{n=1}^{N} \frac{(l_n^{(0)})^2 P_n^{(0)}}{\sigma^2} \right). \tag{16}$$

Proof:

Based on (10), the capacity of the scaled-up system can be derived as

$$C_t = \mathbf{E}_{\mathbf{H}_w^{(0)t}} \left[\log_2 \det(\mathbf{I}_{Mt} + \frac{1}{\sigma^2} (\mathbf{H}_w^{(0)t} \mathbf{L}^{(0)t}) \mathbf{P}_t^{(0)} (\mathbf{H}_w^{(0)t} \mathbf{L}^{(0)t})^H) \right], \tag{17}$$

According to Hadamard Inequation, we have

$$C_t \leq \mathbf{E}_{\mathbf{H}_w^{(0)t}} \sum_{j=1}^{Mt} \log_2 (1 + \frac{1}{\sigma^2} \left[(\mathbf{H}_w^{(0)t} \mathbf{L}^{(0)t}) \mathbf{P}_t^{(0)} (\mathbf{H}_w^{(0)t} \mathbf{L}^{(0)t})^H \right]_{[jj]}), \tag{18}$$

Directly put E inside $\log_2$, according to Jenson Inequation, we have

$$C_t \leq \mathbf{E}_{\mathbf{H}_w^{(0)t}} \sum_{j=1}^{Mt} \log_2 (1 + \frac{1}{\sigma^2} \mathbf{E}_{\mathbf{H}_w^{(0)t}} \left[(\mathbf{H}_w^{(0)t} \mathbf{L}^{(0)t}) \mathbf{P}_t^{(0)} (\mathbf{H}_w^{(0)t} \mathbf{L}^{(0)t})^H \right]_{[jj]}), \tag{19}$$

Then, from (11), (12) and (13), we can further derive

$$C_t \leq t \times M \log_2 \left(1 + \sum_{n=1}^{N} \frac{(l_n^{(0)})^2 P_n^{(0)}}{\sigma^2} \right). \tag{20}$$

Thus,

$$C_t^{upper} = t \times M \log_2 \left(1 + \sum_{n=1}^{N} \frac{(l_n^{(0)})^2 P_n^{(0)}}{\sigma^2} \right). \tag{21}$$

∎

Let

$$C_0 = M \log_2 \left(1 + \sum_{n=1}^{N} \frac{(l_n^{(0)})^2 P_n^{(0)}}{\sigma^2} \right). \tag{22}$$

From Theorem 1, we have

$$C_t^{upper} = t \times C_0. \tag{23}$$

It is observed that the upper bound of the system capacity scales linearly in the process of system scale-up.

3.3 Calculation of the downlink capacity

Based on the foregoing argument, we derive an approximation of the downlink ergodic capacity as

$$C \approx \frac{1}{t} \mathbf{E}_{\mathbf{H}_w^{(0)t}} \left\{ \log_2 \det \left[\mathbf{I}_{Mt} + \frac{1}{\sigma^2} \mathbf{H}_t^{(0)} \mathbf{P}_t^{(0)} \mathbf{H}_t^{(0)H} \right] \right\}, \tag{24}$$

where $\mathbf{H}_t^{(0)}$ is the channel matrix of the scaled-up system

$$\mathbf{H}_t^{(0)} = \begin{bmatrix} l_1^{(0)} \mathbf{H}_{11}^{(0)} & \cdots & l_N^{(0)} \mathbf{H}_{1N}^{(0)} \\ \vdots & \ddots & \vdots \\ l_1^{(0)} \mathbf{H}_{M1}^{(0)} & \cdots & l_N^{(0)} \mathbf{H}_{MN}^{(0)} \end{bmatrix}. \tag{25}$$

We rewrite (24) as

$$C \approx \frac{1}{t} \mathbf{E}_{\mathbf{H}_w^{(0)t}} \left\{ \log_2 \det \left[\mathbf{I}_{Mt} + \frac{1}{\sigma^2} \mathcal{H} \mathcal{H}^H \right] \right\}, \tag{26}$$

where $\mathcal{H} \in \mathbb{C}^{Mt \times Nt}$ and

$$H = \begin{bmatrix} l_1^{(0)} \sqrt{\dfrac{P_1^{(0)}}{t}} \mathbf{H}_{11}^{(0)} & \cdots & l_N \sqrt{\dfrac{P_N^{(0)}}{t}} \mathbf{H}_{1N}^{(0)} \\ \vdots & \ddots & \vdots \\ l_1^{(0)} \sqrt{\dfrac{P_1^{(0)}}{t}} \mathbf{H}_{M1}^{(0)} & \cdots & l_N^{(0)} \sqrt{\dfrac{P_N^{(0)}}{t}} \mathbf{H}_{MN}^{(0)} \end{bmatrix}. \tag{27}$$

Theorem 2:

The ergodic downlink capacity described in (10) can be accurately approximated as

$$C \approx \bar{C} = \sum_{n=1}^{N} \log_2 \left(1 + \frac{1}{\sigma^2} [l_n^{(0)}]^2 P_n^{(0)} W^{-1} M \right) + M \log_2(W) - M \log_2 e \left[1 - W^{-1} \right], \tag{28}$$

where W is the solution of the following equation

$$W = 1 + \sum_{n=1}^{N} \frac{[l_n^{(0)}]^2 P_n^{(0)}}{\sigma^2 + [l_n^{(0)}]^2 P_n^{(0)} W^{-1} M}. \tag{29}$$

Proof:

Let $v^t : [0, M) \times [0, N) \to \mathbb{R}$ be the variance profile function of matrix $\mathcal{H}$, which is given by

$$v^t(x, y) = t \cdot Var(\mathcal{H}(i, j)), \quad x \in [\frac{i-1}{t}, \frac{i}{t}); y \in [\frac{j-1}{t}, \frac{j}{t}),$$

where $\mathcal{H}(i, j)$ is the entry of matrix $\mathcal{H}$ with index (i, j). We can further find that as $t \to \infty$, $v_t(x,y)$ converges uniformly to a limiting bounded function $v(x,y)$, which is given by

$$v(x,y) = [l_n^{(0)}]^2 P_n^{(0)}\}, \quad x \in [0,M); \ y \in [n-1,n). \tag{30}$$

Therefore, the constraints of Theorem 2.53 in (Tulino & Verdu, 2004) are satisfied, we can derive the Shannon transform (Tulino & Verdu, 2004) of the asymptotic spectrum of $\mathcal{H}\mathcal{H}^H$ as

$$\mathcal{V}_{\mathcal{H}\mathcal{H}^H}(v) = \lim_{t \to \infty} \frac{1}{t} E_{\mathbf{H}_w^{(0)t}}[\log_2 \det(\mathbf{I} + v\mathcal{H}\mathcal{H}^H)] \tag{31}$$

$$= E_{\mathbf{Y}}[\log_2(1 + v E_{\mathbf{X}}[v(\mathbf{X},\mathbf{Y})\Gamma_{\mathcal{H}\mathcal{H}^H}(\mathbf{X},v) \,|\mathbf{Y})])]$$
$$+ E_{\mathbf{X}}[\log_2(1 + v E_{\mathbf{Y}}[v(\mathbf{X},\mathbf{Y})Y_{\mathcal{H}\mathcal{H}^H}(\mathbf{Y},v) \,|\mathbf{X})])]$$
$$- v E_{\mathbf{X},\mathbf{Y}}[v(\mathbf{X},\mathbf{Y})\Gamma_{\mathcal{H}\mathcal{H}^H}(\mathbf{X},v)Y_{\mathcal{H}\mathcal{H}^H}(\mathbf{Y},v)]\log_2 e,$$

with $\Gamma_{\mathcal{H}\mathcal{H}^H}(.,.)$ and $Y_{\mathcal{H}\mathcal{H}^H}(.,.)$ satisfying the following equations

$$\Gamma_{\mathcal{H}\mathcal{H}^H}(x,v) = \frac{1}{1 + v E_{\mathbf{Y}}[v(x,\mathbf{Y})Y_{\mathcal{H}\mathcal{H}^H}(\mathbf{Y},v)]}, \tag{32}$$

$$Y_{\mathcal{H}\mathcal{H}^H}(y,v) = \frac{1}{1 + v E_{\mathbf{X}}[v(\mathbf{X},y)\Gamma_{\mathcal{H}\mathcal{H}^H}(\mathbf{X},v)]}, \tag{33}$$

where $\mathbf{X}$ and $\mathbf{Y}$ represent independent random variables, which are uniform on $[0,M)$ and $[0,N)$, respectively, v is a parameter in Shannon transform. Given v, based on (30), we can observe that $\Gamma_{\mathcal{H}\mathcal{H}^H}(x,v)$ is constant on $x \in [0,M)$ and $Y_{\mathcal{H}\mathcal{H}^H}(y,v)$ is constant on $y \in [n-1,n)$. Thus, we define

$$\Gamma_{\mathcal{H}\mathcal{H}^H}(x,v)|_{x\in[0,M)} = W^{-1}, \tag{34}$$

$$\mathbf{Y}_{\mathcal{H}\mathcal{H}^H}(y,v)|_{y\in[n-1,n)} = U_n^{-1}. \tag{35}$$

From (32) and (33), we have

$$W = 1 + v \sum_{n=1}^{N} [l_n^{(0)}]^2 P_n^{(0)} U_n^{-1}, \tag{36}$$

$$U_n = 1 + v [l_n^{(0)}]^2 P_n^{(0)} W^{-1} M, \quad 1 \le n \le N. \tag{37}$$

Assuming $v = \frac{1}{\sigma^2}$, we can further derive

$$C \approx \mathcal{V}_{\mathcal{H}\mathcal{H}^H}(\frac{1}{\sigma^2}) = \sum_{n=1}^{N} \log_2(1 + \frac{1}{\sigma^2}[l_n^{(0)}]^2 P_n^{(0)} W^{-1} M) + M\log_2(W) - M\log_2 e\left[1 - W^{-1}\right]. \tag{38}$$

Moreover, from (36) and (37), W can be calculated by solving the following equation

$$W = 1 + \sum_{n=1}^{N} \frac{[l_n^{(0)}]^2 P_n^{(0)}}{\sigma^2 + [l_n^{(0)}]^2 P_n^{(0)} W^{-1} M}. \tag{39}$$

∎

The unknown parameter W in Theorem 2 can be easily derived via an iterative method as presented in Table 1. The efficiency of the iterative algorithm will be demonstrated in Section 4.

$$
\begin{aligned}
&Initialization: \\
&\quad W^0 = 1; \; \epsilon = 1.0 \times 10^{-6}. \\
&Loopstep: \\
&\quad W^l = 1 + \sum_{n=1}^{N} \frac{[l_n^{(0)}]^2 P_n^{(0)}}{\sigma^2 + [l_n^{(0)}]^2 P_n^{(0)} (W^{l-1})^{-1} M} \\
&\quad until \, \Delta = \left[W^l - W^{l-1} \right]^2 < \epsilon. \\
&end.
\end{aligned}
$$

Table 1. The iterative method to calculate W.

4. Simulation results

In this section, Monte Carlo simulations are used to verify the validity of our analysis. The radius of a cell is assumed to be $1000m$. The path loss exponent is set to be 4, the shadowing standard deviation is set to be 4 according to field measurement for microcell environment (Goldsmith & Greenstein, 1993), and the noise power σ_2^n is set to be -107dBm. The per distributed antenna power constraint takes value from -30dBm to 30dBm.

Without loss of generality, four different simulation setups are considered as follows:

- Case 1: $N = M = 4$, with randomly-selected system topology as shown in Fig. 3-A;
- Case 2: $N = M = 4$, with randomly-selected system topology as shown in Fig. 3-B;
- Case 3: $N = M = 8$, with randomly-selected system topology as shown in Fig. 3-C;
- Case 4: $N = M = 8$, with randomly-selected system topology as shown in Fig. 3-D;

Both analysis and simulation results of the ergodic downlink capacity for the four cases are presented in Fig. 4. It is observed that the two kinds of results are quite accordant with each other, which implies the high accuracy of the approximation in Theorem 2.

The total error covariance (Δ in Table 1) of the iterative method to calculate W is illustrated in Fig. 5. We can observe that 40 iteration steps are enough to make Δ be less than 1.0×10^{-6}. In summary, we can conclude that the approximation is accurate and the iterative method is efficient.

5. Conclusions

In this chapter, the problem of characterizing the downlink capacity of a DAS with random antenna layout is addressed with the generalized assumptions: (a1) per distributed antenna power constraint, (a2) generalized mobile terminals equipped with multiple antennas, (a3) a multi-cell environment. Based on system scale-up, we derive a good approximation of the ergodic downlink capacity by adopting random matrix theory. We also propose an iterative method to calculate the unknown parameter in the approximation. The approximation is illustrated to be quite accurate and the iterative method is verified to be quite efficient by Monte Carlo simulations.

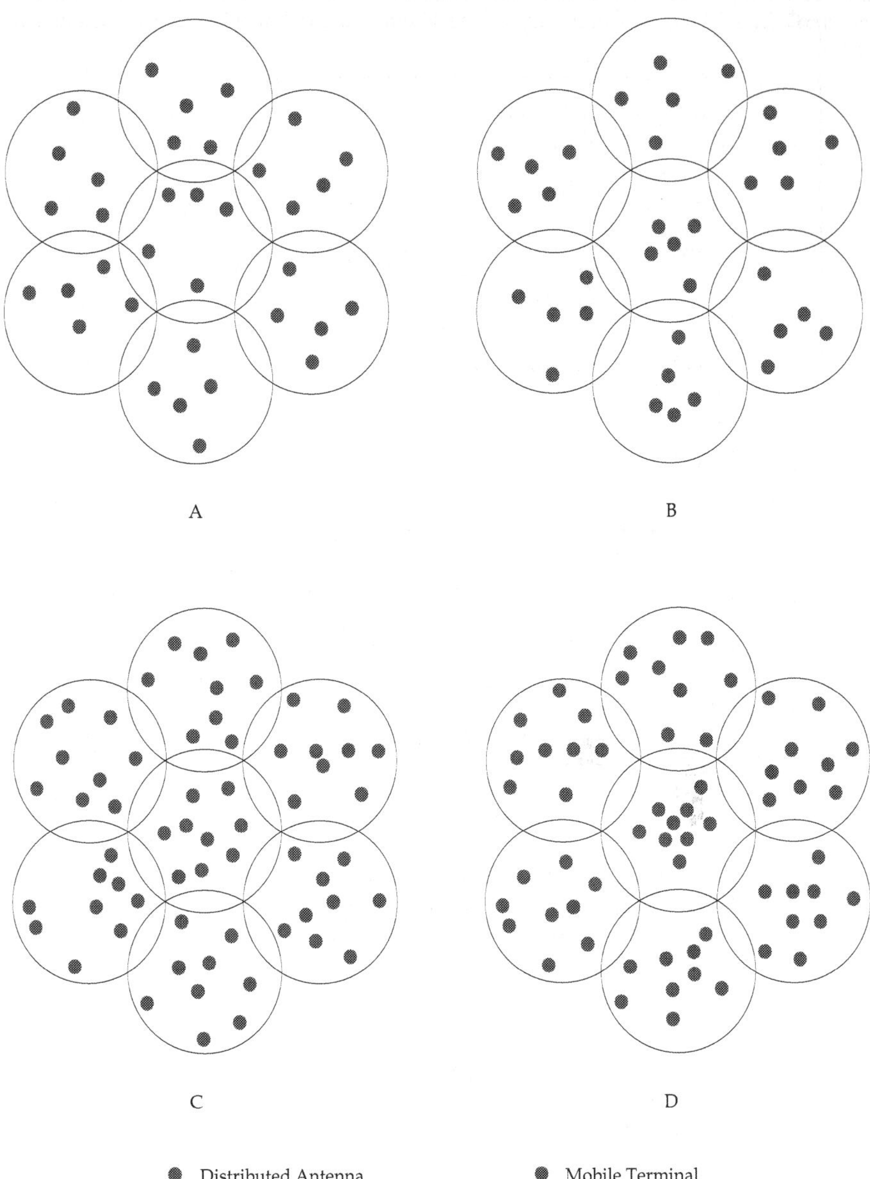

Fig. 3. Randomly-selected system topologies for simulations.

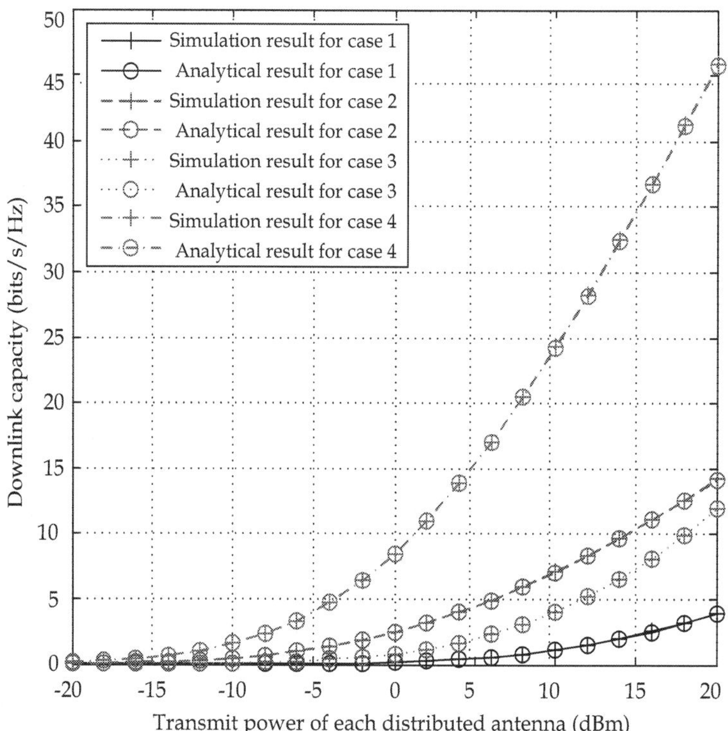

Fig. 4. Ergodic downlink capacity.

Finally, we consider the optimized Golden code (Belfiore et al, 2005) which is a full rate and fully diverse code. The Golden code is designed to maximize the rate such that the diversity gain is preserved for an increased signal constellation size. It is defined by:

$$\mathbf{X} = \frac{1}{\sqrt{5}} \begin{bmatrix} \beta(s_1 + \theta s_2) & \beta(s_3 + \theta s_4) \\ \mu \overline{\beta}(s_3 + \overline{\theta} s_4) & \overline{\beta}(s_1 + \overline{\theta} s_2) \end{bmatrix} \tag{8}$$

where $\theta = \frac{1+\sqrt{5}}{2}$, $\overline{\theta} = 1 - \theta$, $\alpha = 1 + j(1 - \theta)$, $\overline{\alpha} = 1 + j(1 - \overline{\theta})$.

To identify the most efficient ST code, the OFDM parameters are derived from those of the DVB-T standard (see Table 1). The spectral efficiencies 4 and 6 [b/s/Hz] are obtained for different ST schemes as shown in Table 2. In all simulations, we assume that two Rx antennas are used by the MT.

In the simulations results given hereafter, we separate the single layer case and the double layer case. For completeness point overview, we give first simulations results using a Rayleigh channel model in frequency domain i.e. we assume that the transmission from a transmitting antenna i to a receiving antenna j is achieved for each subcarrier n through a frequency non-selective Rayleigh fading channel. The use of the i.i.d. channel model is a first approach to justify our proposed 3D STS code. For this first step, the parameters β_i are chosen arbitrarily[1]. In a second step, we will present the results with more realistic channel model like the COST 207 TU-6 channel model (COST, 1989). In this case, the results will be given for both, open and gap area environments.

FFT size	8K
Sampling frequency (f_s=1/T_s)	9.14 MHz
Guard interval (GI) duration	1024×T_s=112 µs
Rate R_c of convolutional code	1/2, 2/3, 3/4
Polynomial code generator	$(133,171)_o$
Channel estimation	perfect
Constellation	16-QAM, 64-QAM, 256-QAM
Spectral Efficiencies	η= 4 and 6 [b/s/Hz]

Table 1. Simulations Parameters

Spectral Efficiency	ST scheme	ST rate R	Constellation	R_c
η=4 [bit/Sec/Hz]	Alamouti	1	64-QAM	2/3
	SM	2	16-QAM	1/2
	Golden	2	16-QAM	1/2
	3D code	2	16-QAM	1/2
η=6 [bit/Sec/Hz]	Alamouti	1	256-QAM	3/4
	SM	2	64-QAM	1/2
	Golden	2	64-QAM	1/2
	3D code	2	64-QAM	1/2

Table 2. Different MIMO schemes and efficiencies

---

[1] Since we model the channel in frequency domain, there is no CIR and hence no CIR delays in this case.

a.   Single Layer case: inter-cell ST coding

The received signal at the input of the MT could be written as:

$$\mathbf{y} = \mathbf{GBFs} + \mathbf{w} = \mathbf{G_{eq}s} + \mathbf{w} \qquad (9)$$

where the matrix $\mathbf{G}$ is composed of blocks $\mathbf{G_{j,i}}$ (j=1,...,M_R; i=1,..., $2M_T$) each having ($2T$, $2T$) elements, reflecting the channel coefficients (Khalighi et al., 2006) & (Nasser et al., 2008). $\mathbf{B}$ is the matrix reflecting the powers received from each antenna. $\mathbf{F}$ is composed of $2M_T$ blocks of $2T$ rows each i.e. the data transmitted on each antenna are gathered in one block having $2T$ rows and $2Q$ columns according to the ST coding scheme. $\mathbf{G_{eq}}$ is the equivalent channel matrix between $\mathbf{s}$ and $\mathbf{y}$. It is assumed to be known perfectly at the receiving side.

The optimal receiver is a ML (Rupp et al., 2004) receiver whose complexity increases exponentially with the number of antennas and the constellation size. In the case of orthogonal STBC (OSTBC), the optimal receiver is simply made of a concatenation of ST decoder and channel decoder modules. However, in the case of non-orthogonal STBC (NO-STBC) schemes, there is an IEI at the receiving side. The optimal receiver becomes more complex since it requires joint ST and channel decoding operations. Moreover, it requires large memory to store the different points of the trellis. In our work, we use a sub-optimal solution based on an iterative receiver where the ST detector and channel decoder exchange extrinsic information in order to enhance soft information metrics. The iterative detector shown in Fig. 4 is composed of a parallel interference canceller (PIC), a demapper which consists in computing the soft information of the transmitted bits, i.e. a log likelihood ratio (LLR) computation (Tosato & Bisaglia, 2002), a soft-input soft-output (SISO) decoder (Hagenauer & Hoeher,1989), and a soft mapper.

At the first iteration, the demapper takes the estimated symbols $\hat{\mathbf{s}}$, the knowledge of the channel $\mathbf{G_{eq}}$ and of the noise variance, and computes the LLR values of each of the coded bits transmitted per channel use. The estimated symbols $\hat{\mathbf{s}}$ are obtained via minimum mean square error (MMSE) filtering according to:

$$\hat{s}_p^{(1)} = \mathbf{g_p^{tr}} \left(\mathbf{G_{eq}} \cdot \mathbf{G_{eq}^{tr}} + \sigma_w^2 \mathbf{I} \right)^{-1} \mathbf{y} \qquad (10)$$

where $\mathbf{g_p^{tr}}$ of dimension ($2M_R T$, 1) is the pth column of $\mathbf{G_{eq}}$ ($1 \leq p \leq 2Q$). $\hat{s}_p^{(1)}$ is the estimation of the real part (p odd) or imaginary part (p even) of s_q ($1 \leq q \leq Q$). Once the estimation of the different symbols s_q is achieved by the soft mapper at the first iteration, we use this estimation for the next iterations process.

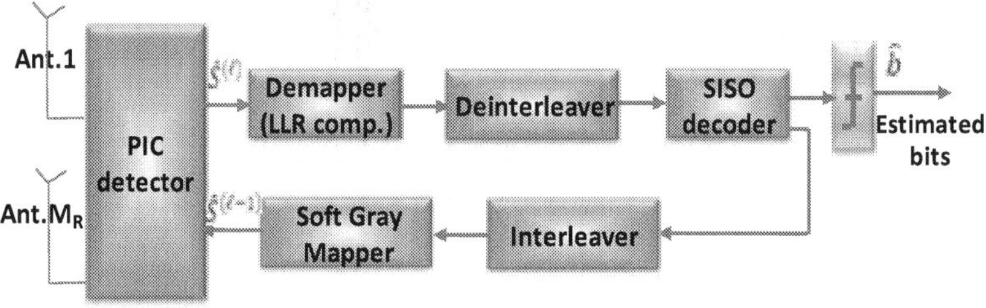

Fig. 4. Iterative receiver structure

From the second iteration, we perform PIC operation followed by a simple inverse filtering (instead of MMSE filtering at the first iteration). This block offers enhanced LLR values to be fed to the SISO decoder by suppressing the spatial interference. This interference cancellation is described by:

$$\hat{\mathbf{y}}_p = \mathbf{y} - \mathbf{G}_{eq,p}\tilde{\mathbf{s}}_p^{(1)}$$
$$\hat{s}_p^{(2)} = \frac{1}{\mathbf{g}_p^{tr}\mathbf{g}_p}\mathbf{g}_p^{tr}\hat{\mathbf{y}}_p \tag{9}$$

where $\mathbf{G}_{eq,p}$ of dimension $(2M_RT, 2Q\text{-}1)$ is the matrix $\mathbf{G}_{eq,p}$ with its pth column removed, $\tilde{\mathbf{s}}_p^{(1)}$ of dimension $(2Q\text{-}1, 1)$ is the vector $\tilde{\mathbf{s}}$ estimated by the soft mapper with its pth entry removed. In our proposition, we consider a sub-optimal iterative detector for non-orthogonal schemes in order to cancel the IEI. The iterative process used here converges after 3 iterations (Nasser et al., May 2008). Therefore, all the results given thereafter are obtained after 3 iterations.

In the case of single layer reception, we have one antenna by site. Then, the second layer matrix $\mathbf{X}^{(2)}$ in (5) resumes to one element. The multiple input component of the MIMO scheme is then only obtained by the single antenna in each site (M_T= 1). Due to the mobility, the MT is assumed to occupy different locations and the first layer ST scheme must be efficient face to unequal received powers. For equal received powers, we assume that the powers of the matrix $\mathbf{B}$ in (9) are equal to 0 dB.

Fig. 5 gives the required E_b/N_0 to obtain a BER=10^{-4} for a spectral efficiency η=4 [b/s/Hz]. Moreover, since we have one Tx antenna by site, we set β_1=0 dB and we change $\beta=\beta_2$. As expected, this figure shows that the Golden code presents the best performance when the Rx receives the same power from both sites (i.e. $\beta_1=\beta_2$=0 dB). When β_2 decreases, the Alamouti scheme is very efficient and presents a maximum loss of only 3 dB in terms of required E_b/N_0 with respect to equal received powers case. Indeed, for very small values of β, the

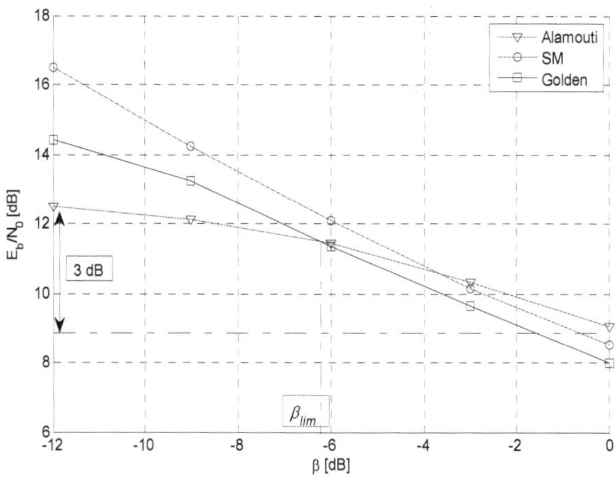

Fig. 5. Required Eb/N0 to obtain a BER=10^{-4}, single layer case, η=4 [b/s/Hz]

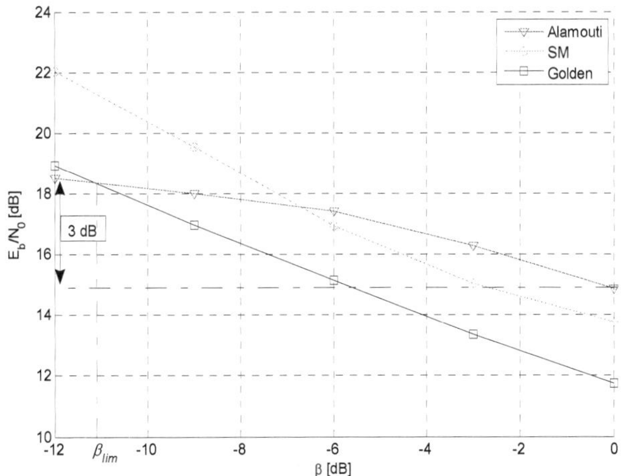

Fig. 6. Required Eb/N0 to obtain a BER=10⁻⁴, single layer case, η=4 [b/s/Hz]

transmission scenario becomes equivalent to a transmission scenario with one transmitting antenna. In this figure, the value β_{lim}= -6.2 dB presents the power imbalance limit where the Alamouti and the Golden code schemes have the same performance at a BER=10⁻⁴.

The same kind of results, shown in Fig. 6, are observed for a spectral efficiency η=6 [b/s/Hz]. The Alamouti scheme is more efficient than the Golden code when the power imbalance parameter β becomes less than a given limit value β_{lim} = -11.2 dB.

b.   Double Layer case: intra-cell ST coding

Considering the whole double layer space domain construction, one ST coding scheme has to be assigned to each layer of the proposed system. The resulting 3D STS code should be efficient for both environments in SFN architecture. We propose to construct the first layer, i.e. the inter-cell coding, with Alamouti scheme since it is the most resistant for the unequal received powers case. In a complementary way, we propose to construct the second layer, i.e. the intra-cell coding, with the Golden code since it offers the best results in the case of equal received powers. After combination of the two space layers with time dimension, (5) yields:

$$X = \frac{1}{\sqrt{5}} \begin{pmatrix} \alpha(s_1 + \theta s_2) & \alpha(s_3 + \theta s_4) & \alpha(s_5 + \theta s_6) & \alpha(s_7 + \theta s_8) \\ j\bar{\alpha}(s_3 + \bar{\theta} s_4) & \bar{\alpha}(s_1 + \bar{\theta} s_2) & j\bar{\alpha}(s_7 + \bar{\theta} s_8) & \bar{\alpha}(s_5 + \bar{\theta} s_6) \\ -\alpha^*(s_5^* + \theta^* s_6^*) & -\alpha^*(s_7^* + \theta^* s_8^*) & \alpha^*(s_1^* + \theta^* s_2^*) & \alpha^*(s_3^* + \theta^* s_4^*) \\ j\bar{\alpha}^*(s_7^* + \bar{\theta}^* s_8^*) & -\bar{\alpha}^*(s_5^* + \bar{\theta}^* s_6^*) & -j\bar{\alpha}^*(s_3^* + \bar{\theta}^* s_4^*) & \bar{\alpha}^*(s_1^* + \bar{\theta}^* s_2^*) \end{pmatrix} \tag{12}$$

where $\theta = \frac{1+\sqrt{5}}{2}$, $\bar{\theta} = 1-\theta$, $\alpha = 1+j(1-\theta)$, $\bar{\alpha} = 1+j(1-\bar{\theta})$.

3.1.4 Simulation results in open area environment

In an open area environment, the MT is in an unobstructed region with respect to each site antennas. Since the distance d between the transmitting antennas in one site is negligible with respect to the distance D (Fig. 1), the power attenuation factors in the case of our 3D code are such that $\beta_1=\beta_2=0$ dB and $\beta=\beta_3=\beta_4$.

Fig. 7 shows the results in terms of required E_b/N_0 to obtain a BER equal to 10^{-4} for different values of β and 3 STBC schemes i.e. our proposed 3D code scheme, the single layer Alamouti and the Golden code schemes assuming Rayleigh i.i.d frequency channel coefficients. In this figure, the value β corresponds to β_2 for the single layer case and to $\beta=\beta_3=\beta_4$ for our 3D code. Fig. 7 shows that the proposed scheme presents the best performance whatever the spectral efficiency and the factor β are. Indeed, it is optimized for SFN systems and unbalanced received powers. For $\beta=-12$ dB, the proposed 3D code offers a gain equal to 1.8 dB (respectively 3 dB) with respect to the Alamouti scheme for a spectral efficiency $\eta=4$ [b/s/Hz] (resp. $\eta=6$ [b/s/Hz]). This gain is greater when it is compared to the Golden code. Moreover, the maximum loss of our code due to unbalanced received powers is equal to 3 dB in terms of E_b/N_0. This means that it leads to a powerful code for SFN systems.

In a MIMO COST 207 TU-6 channel model, we assume that the MT is moving with a velocity of 10 km/h and the distance d_1 between the receiver and the reference antenna is equal to 5 km. The CIRs between different transmitters and the MT are delayed according to (3).

Fig. 8 gives the same kind of results of those given in Fig. 7. Once again, these results highlight the superiority of the proposed 3D code in real channel models whatever the spectral efficiency and the factor β i.e. the 3D code outperforms the others schemes in all cases. The gain could reach 1.5 dB for a spectral efficiency $\eta=4$ [b/s/Hz] and 3.1 dB for a spectral efficiency $\eta=6$ [b/s/Hz].

Fig. 9 evaluates the robustness of the different schemes to the MT velocity. We assume that the MT is moving within one cell with a velocity of 10 km/h and 60 km/h respectively. We show in this figure that the Alamouti scheme is very robust to the MT velocity. The degradation of the Golden code might reach 1 dB in terms of required Eb/N0 to reach a BER=10^{-4}. The degradation of the proposed 3D code due to the MT velocity and hence to the Doppler effect is of about 0.2 dB only.

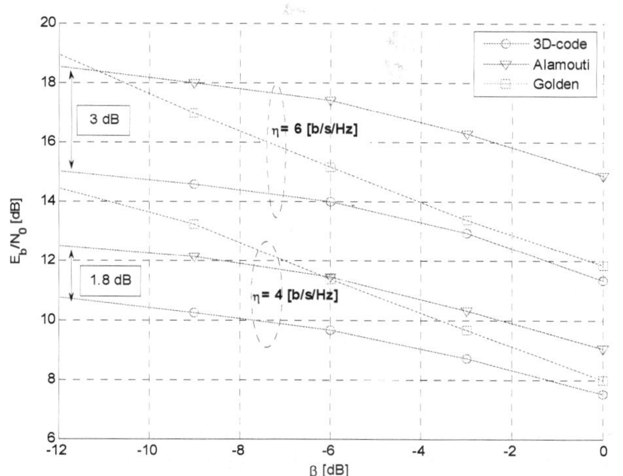

Fig. 7. Required Eb/N0 to obtain a BER=10^{-4}, double layer case, $\eta=4$ [b/s/Hz], $\eta=6$ [b/s/Hz], Rayleigh channel

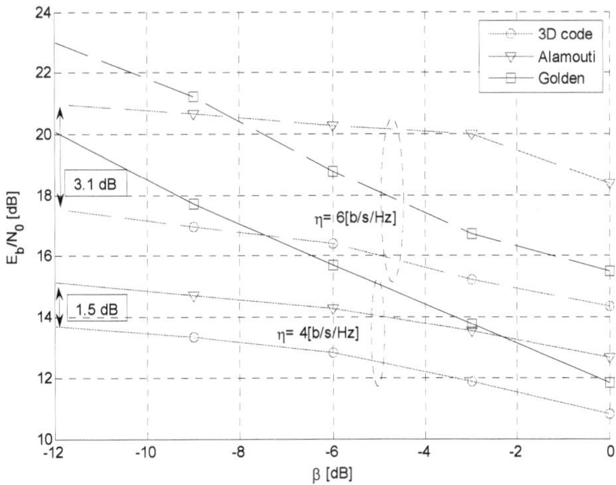

Fig. 8. Required E_b/N_0 to obtain a BER=10⁻⁴, double layer case, η=4 [b/s/Hz], η=6 [b/s/Hz], TU-6 channel

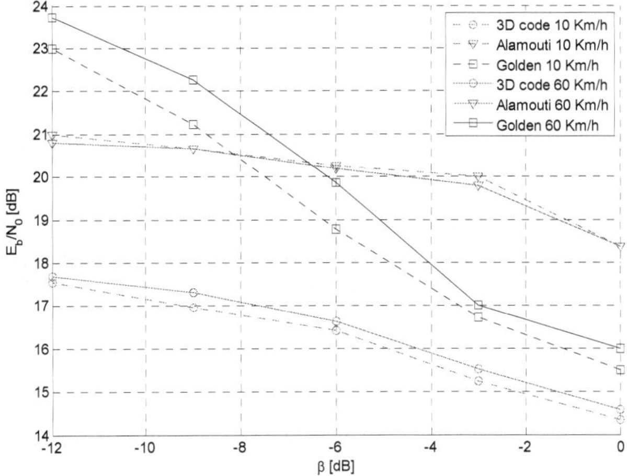

Fig. 9. Required E_b/N_0 to obtain a BER=10⁻⁴, η=6 [b/s/Hz], TU-6 channel, different values of MT velocity

3.1.5 Simulation results in gap area environment

In a gap area environment, the MT is in obstruction with respect to each site antennas. In this case, the gap filler receiving antennas become at the same situation of those of the MT in the open area environment i.e. a power imbalance is observed at the receiving side and it is related to the CIR delays by equation (4). However, due to the gap filler amplification, the power received by the MT in a gap area could be independent of these delays.

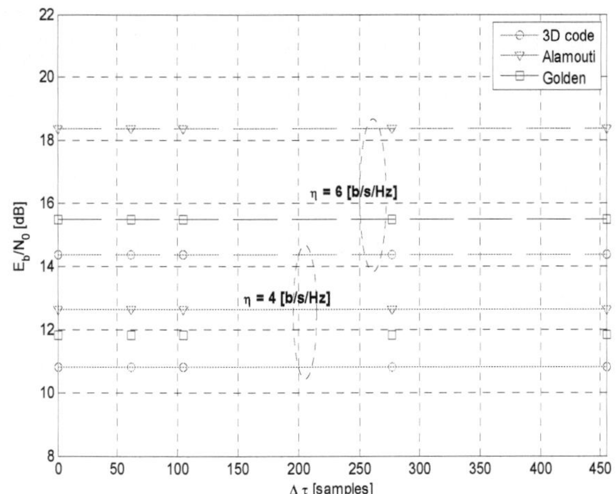

Fig. 10. Required E_b/N_0 to obtain a BER=10⁻⁴, η=4 [b/s/Hz], η=6 [b/s/Hz], TU-6 channel, gap area environment.

In Fig. 10, we give the required E_b/N_0 that a MT needs in a gap area to obtain a BER = 10⁻⁴ with respect to the CIR delays Δτ observed at the gap filler receivers. As expected, we show in this figure that the results are independent of these delays since they are smaller than the guard interval durations (GI= 1024 samples). In other words, as these delays are less than the guard interval duration, they produce only a phase rotation which is corrected by the equalizer in the frequency domain. The power imbalance is already corrected by the gap filler amplification.

3.2 System model in hybrid satellite terrestrial transmission

For hybrid SATT transmission, we propose to apply the MIMO scheme between the terrestrial and satellite sites as described in Fig. 11. Due to the links model difference, i.e. satellite link and terrestrial link, the proposed code has to cope with different transmission scenarios. More precisely, the MIMO scheme has to be efficient in the LOS region but also in shadowing regions (moderate and deep) with respect to the satellite antennas. In order to achieve that, we propose again to use the 3D MIMO scheme for such situations. The first layer corresponds to the inter-cell ST coding, i.e. between satellite and terrestrial antennas, while the second corresponds to the intra-cell ST coding, i.e. between the antennas of the same site. For the satellite links, we have considered the land mobile satellite (LMS) (Murr et al., 1995) adopted in DVB-SH (ETSI, 2008) and described by Fontan (Fontan et al., 2001), (Loo, 1985) & (Fontan et al., 1998). The LMS channel is modeled by Markov chain with three states. The state S1 corresponds to the LOS situation, while S2 and S3 correspond respectively to the moderate and deep shadowing situations. Generally speaking, the LMS channel in each state follows a Loo distribution (Loo, 1985). The latter is a Rice distribution where its mean follows a log-normal distribution having a mean μ and a standard deviation Σ. Table 3 shows that the different states of the Markov chain depend on the elevation angles and that each state has its specified mean and standard deviation. The parameter MP in this table reflects the multipath component power in the Rice distribution.

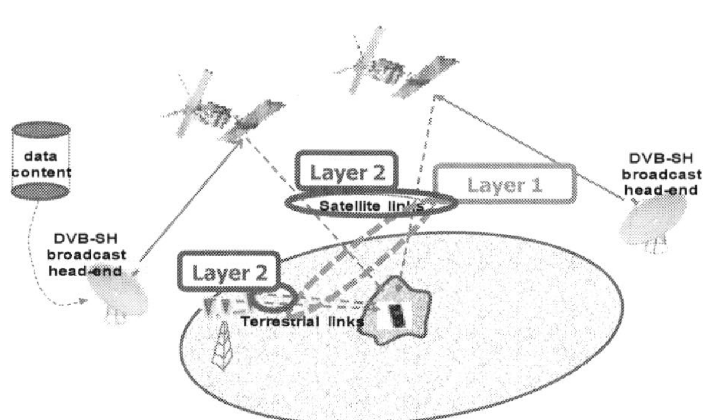

Fig. 11. Layered STS 3D code using SATT transmission scheme

3.2.1 First layer construction: SATT coding

In order to construct the first layer, we consider the same method as done for terrestrial transmission. First, we will construct the first layer using the well-known MIMO schemes, i.e. Alamouti and Golden codes. Second, due to the mobility, the MT is assumed to occupy different locations over a sufficient long route. Then, the first layer ST scheme must be efficient face to shadowing during its trajectory. Recall that the moderate and deep shadowing are dependent of the elevation angle. For example, in Table 3, the moderate shadowing for an elevation angle of 30° corresponds to a mean value μ= -4.7 dB and the deep shadowing corresponds to a mean value equal to -7 dB. It is clear from Table 3 that for an elevation angle equal to 30°, the system presents the highest signal power level since the moderate and deep shadowing are relatively acceptable comparing to other elevation angles θ. In the sequel, we will present first the results obtained with an elevation angle θ = 30° and θ = 50° and for the various spectral efficiencies using an Alamouti and Golden code scheme at the first layer. Fig. 12 shows the required E_b/N_0 to obtain a BER equal to 10^{-4} for a spectral efficiency η= 2, 4 and 6 b/s/Hz. As expected, we conclude from these results that for low spectral efficiency, i.e. η= 2, the Alamouti scheme outperforms the Golden scheme. However, for a spectral efficiency η= 4 and η= 6, the conclusion on the best performance is not immediate. It depends on the elevation angle and hence on the shadowing level. For high shadowing level (see Table 3, θ = 50°), the Alamouti code presents almost better

Elevation	S1: LOS			S2: Interm. Shadowing			S3: Deep Shadowing		
	μ	Σ	MP	μ	Σ	MP	μ	Σ	MP
10°	-0.1	0.5	-19	-8.7	3	-12	-12.1	6	-25
30°	-0.5	1	-15	-4.7	1.5	-19	-7	3	-20
50°	-0.5	1	-17	-6.5	2.5	-17	-14	2.5	-20
70°	-0.2	0.5	-15	-6.0	2.1	-17	-11.5	2	-20

Table 3. Average Loo model parameters in dB for various angles and suburban area (measurement results given in (Fontan et al., 1985))

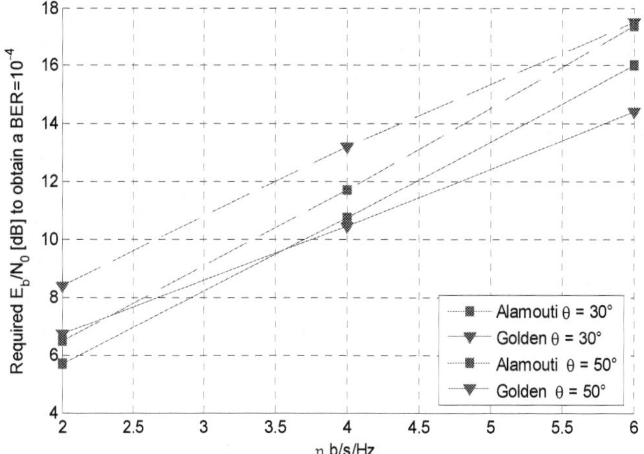

Fig. 12. Required E_b/N_0 to obtain a BER=10^{-4}, single layer case

performance. In summary, the Golden code scheme outperforms the Alamouti scheme only for high spectral efficiency and relatively low shadowing levels ($\theta = 30°$). This confirms our results in terrestrial transmission where the performance of the MIMO scheme depends on the power imbalance between the two signals received from each site.

3.2.2 Second layer construction: intra-site coding

Considering the whole layers' construction (i.e. $M_T > 1$), one ST coding scheme has to be assigned to the SATT coding and another ST coding scheme has to be assigned to the intra-site coding. The resulting layered ST coding should be efficient for low, moderate and deep shadowing levels. Considering the results and conclusions obtained in previous sub-section, we propose to construct the SATT layer with Alamouti scheme, since it is the most resistant for the deep shadowing levels. In a complementary way, we propose to construct the second layer with the Golden code since it offers the best results in the case of relatively low shadowing levels.

Fig. 13 shows the results in terms of required E_b/N_0 to obtain a BER equal to 10^{-4} for the various elevation angles, two spectral efficiencies $\eta = 2$ b/s/Hz and $\eta = 6$ b/s/Hz and the three considered codes i.e. our proposed 3D scheme, the single layer Alamouti scheme and the single layer Golden scheme. The results obtained in this figure show that the proposed 3D scheme outperforms the other schemes whatever the elevation angle and the spectral efficiency are. Moreover, as expected, the best performance is obtained for an elevation angle $\theta = 30°$. The gain of the 3D code compared to the Alamouti scheme is about 1 dB for $\eta = 2$ b/s/Hz and can reach 4 dB for $\eta = 6$ b/s/Hz. The conclusions of Fig. 13 are confirmed in Fig. 14 for $\eta = 4$ b/s/Hz. This means that the 3D code leads to a powerful code for next DVB-NGH systems.

3.3 Conclusions

In this work, we have presented a full rate full diversity 3D code, a promising candidate for next generation broadcast technologies. It is constructed using two layers: the first layer using Alamouti code and the second layer using Golden code. We showed that our proposed scheme is very efficient to cope with low, moderate and deep shadowing levels as well as various elevation angles. The proposed scheme is fully compatible with SFN and hybrid SATT scheme. It is then a very promising candidate for the broadcasting of the future terrestrial digital TV through NGH structures.

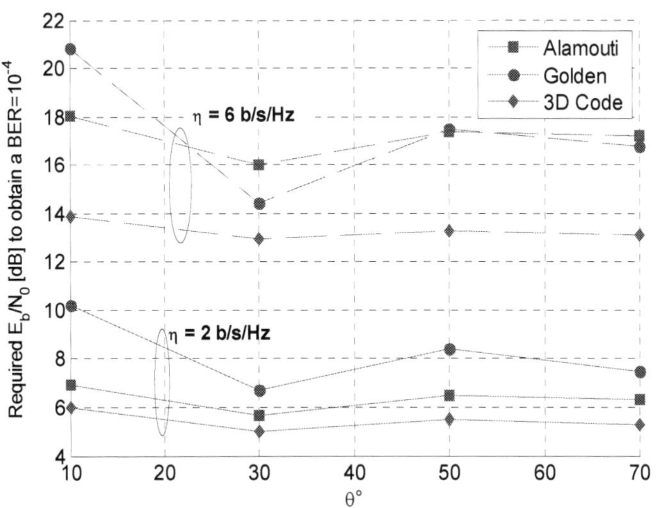

Fig. 13. Required E_b/N_0 to obtain a BER=10^{-4}, double layer construction, η variable

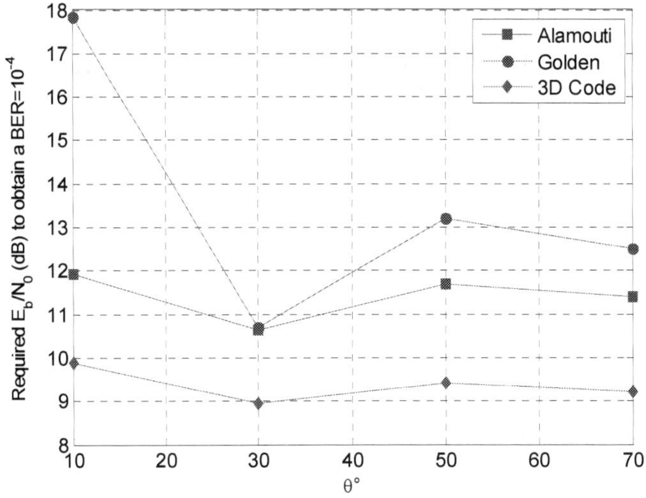

Fig. 14. Required E_b/N_0 to obtain a BER=10^{-4}, double layer construction, η=4 b/s/Hz

4. References

Mattson A. (2005), Single frequency networks in DTV, *IEEE Trans. on Broadcasting*, Vol. 51, Issue 4, Dec. 2005, pp. 413-422, ISSN : 0018-9316.

Zhang L., Gui L., Qiao Y., and Zhang W. (2004), Obtaining diversity gain for DTV by using MIMO structure in SFN, *IEEE Trans. on broadcasting*, Vol. 50, No. 1, March 2004, 83-90, ISSN: 0018-9316.

Kanbe Y., Itami M., Itoh K., and Aghvami A. (2002), Reception of an OFDM signal with an array antenna in a SFN environment, *Proc. of IEEE Personal Indoor and Mobile Radio Communications*, Vol. 3, 1310-1315, ISBN: 0-7803-7589-0, Sept. 2002.

Alamouti, S.M. (1998), A simple transmit diversity technique for wireless communications, *IEEE Journal on Selected Areas in Communications*, Vol. 16, No. 8, Oct. 1998, 1451-1458, ISSN: 0733-8716.

Rupp M., Gritsh G., Weinrichter H. (2004), Approximate ML detection for MIMO systems with very low complexity, *Proc. of the International conference on Acoustics, Speech, and Signal Processing*, Vol. 4, pp. 809-812, ISBN: 0-7803-8484-9, May 2004.

Foschini G. J. (1996), Layered space-time architecture for wireless communication in a fading environment when using multi-element antenna, *Bell Labs Tech. Journal*, Vol. 1, no. 2, 41–59.

Belfiore, J.-C., Rekaya G., & Viterbo E. (2005). The golden code: a 2 × 2 full-rate space-time code with non vanishing determinants, *IEEE Transactions in Information Theory*, Vol. 51, No. 4, April 2005, 1432–1436, ISSN : 0018-9448.

COST (1989), *COST 207 Report*, Digital Land Mobile Radio Communications, Commission of European Communities, Directorate General, Telecommunications Information Industries and Innovation, Luxemburg.

Khalighi M. A., Hélard J.-F., and Bourennane S. (2006), Contrasting Orthogonal and non orthogonal space-time schemes for perfectly-known and estimated MIMO channels, *Proc. of IEEE Int. Conf. on Communications systems*, 1-5, ISBN: 1-4244-0411-8, Oct. 2006, Singapore.

Nasser, Y.; Helard, J.-F. & Crussiere, M. (2008). System Level Evaluation of Innovative Coded MIMO-OFDM Systems for Broadcasting Digital TV. *International Journal of Digital Multimedia Broadcasting*, Vol. 2008, pages 12, doi:10.1155/2008/359206.

Nasser Y., Hélard J.-F., Crussiere M., and Pasquero O. (2008), Efficient MIMO-OFDM schemes for future terrestrial digital TV with unequal received powers, *Proc. of IEEE International Communications Conference*, 2021 - 2027, ISBN: 978-1-4244-2075-9, June 2008, Bejing, China.

Tosato F., and Bisaglia P. (2002), Simplified Soft-Output Demapper for Binary Interleaved COFDM with Application to HIPERLAN/2, *Proc IEEE Int. Conf. on Communications*, pp. 664-668, ISBN: 0-7803-7400-2, June 2002.

Hagenauer J., and Hoeher P. (1989), A Viterbi algorithm with soft-decision outputs and its applications, *Proc. of IEEE Global Telecommunications Conf.*, pp. 1680-1686, Nov. 1989, Dallas, USA.

Murr F., Kastner-Puschl S., Bolzano B., Kubista E. (1995), Land mobile Satellite narrowband propagation measurement campaign at Ka-Band, ESTEC contract 9949/92NL, Final report.

ETSI (2008). *DVB-SH Implementation Guidelines*. TM-SSP252r9f.

Fontan F., Vazquez-Castro M., Cabado C., Garcia J., Kubista E. (2001), Statistical modeling of the LMS channel, *IEEE Trans. on Vehicular Technology*, Vol. 50, No.6, Nov. 2001, 1549-1567, ISSN: 0018-9545.

Loo C. (1985), A Statistical Model for a Land Mobile Satellite Link, *IEEE Trans. Vehicular. Technology*, Vol. VT-34, No.3, August 1985, 122-127, ISSN: 0018-9545.

Fontan F., Vazquez-Castro M., Buonomo S., Baptista P., and Arbesser-Rastburg B. (1998), S-Band LMS propagation channel behavior for different environments, degrees of shadowing and elevation angles, *IEEE Trans. on Broadcasting*, Vol. 44, March 1998, 40-76, ISSN: 0018-9316.

Loo C. (1991), Further results on the statistics of propagation data at L-band (1542 MHz) for mobile satellite communications, *Proc. of IEEE Vehicular Technology Conference*, pp. 51-56, ISSN: 1090-3038, May 1991, Saint Louis, USA.

10

Throughput Optimization for UWB-Based Ad-Hoc Networks

Chuanyun Zou

School of Information Engineering, Southwest University of Science and Technology
China

1. Introduction

The increasing demand for portable, high data-rate communications has stimulated search for new wireless technologies. Ultra-wideband impulse radio (UWB-IR) is an emerging radio technology that can support data rates of megabit-per-second, while maintaining low average-power consumption. UWB uses very short, carrier-less pulses of bandwidth on the order of a few Gigahertz. Over the past decade, many individuals and corporations began asking the United States Federal Communications Commission (FCC) for permission to operate unlicensed UWB systems concurrent with existing narrowband signals. In 2002, the FCC decided to change the rules to allow UWB system operation in a broad range of frequencies between 3.1 and 10.6 GHz. The FCC defines UWB as a signal with either a *fractional bandwidth* of 20% of the center frequency or 500 MHz (when the center frequency is above 6 GHz). The formula proposed by the FCC commission for calculating the fractional bandwidth is $2(f_H-f_L)/(f_H+f_L)$ where f_H represents the upper frequency of the -10 dB emission limit and f_L represents the lower frequency limit of the -10 dB emission limit. What makes UWB systems unique is their large instantaneous bandwidth and the potential for very simple implementations. Additionally, the wide bandwidth and potential for low-cost digital design enable a single system to operate in different modes as a communications device, radar, or locator. Taken together, these properties give UWB systems a clear technical advantage over other more conventional approaches in high multipath environments at low to medium data rates. Communication over UWB is particularly attractive due to its wide range of bit-rates, resilience to multi-path fading, accurate ranging ability, low transmission power requirements, and low probability of interception. After substantial progress in research on the UWB physical layer, in recent years, researchers began to consider the design of UWB networks [1]-[9]. The maximum allowable UWB transmission power is limited to a very small value, since UWB shares the same frequency band with other existing wireless communication systems. Consequently, short-distance communications are the main uses considered and UWB networks will likely often be ad hoc in nature. In an ad-hoc network each node has to have a routing function and it is essential to use multihop transmission to reach nodes further away. Since each node has a network control function, even if one of the nodes is not working properly, its influence on the whole network is quite limited. Therefore, ad-hoc networks are excellent with respect to robustness. Ad-hoc network do not require any infrastructure, a feature which allows for instant deployment and rerouting of traffic around failed or congested nodes. Since in ad-hoc networks it is unnecessary to deploy base stations, the cost of a ad-hoc networks system is expected to be considerably lower than the corresponding cost of a cellular infrastructure. Furthermore, fault-tolerance (for example, due to richness of alternative routes [15]) of this type of networks is also significantly improved. Ad-hoc networks can be reconfigured to adapt its operation in diverse network environments. As the results of these characteristics, ad-hoc networks became of interest to the commercial and to the military markets. It is expected that UWB ad-hoc networks will be used for digital household electric appliances and peripheral equipment of PCs, for example, such as a wireless link between a PC and DVD player or a physical layer for a 'wireless USB' replacing traditional USB cables between devices. Examples of other applications that were considered are for networking among students in classrooms or among delegates at a convention centre. The mechanisms to best meet the requirements of the network layer for wireless ad hoc networks are a focus of current research and are certainly not well understood for UWB, which is a nascent networking technology. There are opportunities to leverage both radio link characteristics, using cross-layer design, and application requirements to optimize network layer protocols. For example, UWB devices in an ad hoc network may self-organize themselves into hierarchical clusters in ways that consider mutual interference, power conservation, and application connectivity requirements.

Throughput, which is defined as the bit rate of successfully received data, is a key performance measure for a data communication networks. In a wireless ad hoc network, throughput is a function of various factors, including the transmission power, the symbol rate (i.e., data rate), the modulation and the coding schemes, the network size, the antenna directionality, the noise and the interference characteristics, the routing and the multiple access control (MAC) schemes, and numerous other parameters. How to allocate resource and determine the optimal transmission power, transmission rate and schedule is a very challenging issue. There are several related papers [2]-[8] in the technical literature that study the throughput capacity and the optimization of UWB networks. They have suggested that: (1) an exclusion region around a destination should be established, where nodes inside the exclusion region do not transmit and the nodes outside the exclusion region can transmit in parallel [4], (2) the optimal size of the exclusion region depends only on the path-loss exponent, the background noise level, and the cross-correlations factor [6], (3) each node should either transmit with full power or not transmit at all [7], (4) the design of MAC is independent of the choice of a routing scheme [5].

In this chapter, we analyze and investigate the maximal total network throughput of UWB based ad hoc wireless networks. Understanding how this characteristic affects system performance and design is critical to making informed engineering design decisions regarding UWB implementation. The objectives of our work are: (1) to obtain theoretical results which demonstrate the dependencies among the maximum achievable throughput of a network, the number of active links in the network, the bit rate and the transmission power of active links, and other parameters, and (2) to determine the implications of these dependencies on the allocation and scheduling of the network resources. Our analysis show that the optimal allocation should: (1) allow the transmitters to either transmit at maximum power or be turned off, (2) allow more than one transmission when the maximum powers of the links are less than some value, which we term the critical power, (3) allow only one transmission when the maximum powers of the links are larger than the critical power, and (4) adjust the transmission rates to maintain the optimal transmission rates. We also derive an expression of the optimum transmission rate. As an example, we analytically calculate the critical transmission power for the case of two-links and for the case of a scenario of N-links. Our results imply that the design of the optimal MAC scheme is not independent of the choice of the routing scheme. Furthermore, we expect our results obtain in this chapter to be helpful to network protocol design as well.

This chapter is organized as follows. The next section describes the UWB transmission system and formalizes the throughput optimization problem. In Section 3, we demonstrate the solution for the case of two simultaneous transmitters, while in Section 4 we analyze a network with arbitrary number of transmitters. Section 5 discusses the implications of the results, and the summary is given in Section 6.

2. Analytical model

We consider an ad hoc wireless network (Fig. 1.) that consists of identical nodes, each equipped with a half-duplex UWB radio. A transmitting node (a source node) is associated with a single receiver node (a destination node) and a pair of source-destination nodes forms a communication link. Each link can be selected for transmission by the MAC protocol based on some traffic requirements.

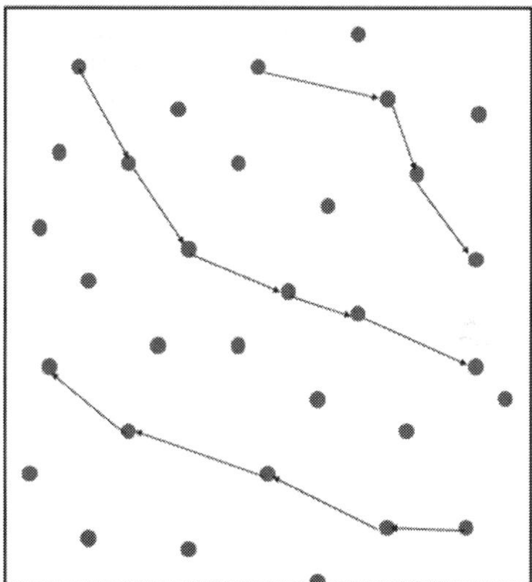

Fig. 1. A Multiple Hop Ad Hoc Network

We assume that the physical link layer is based on the *Time Hopping* with *Pulse Position Modulation* (TH-PPM) scheme, described in refs. [10--12]. In PPM, each monocycle pulse occupies a *frame*. Signal information is contained in pulse time position relative to the frame boundaries. Each bit is represented as L PPM-modulated pulses. An analytic TH-PPM representation of the transmitted signal of the k-th node is given by

$$s^k(t) = \sum_j w(t - jT_f - c_j^k T_c - \delta D_{\lfloor j/L \rfloor}^k) \tag{1}$$

where $w(t)$ denotes the monocycle pulse waveform, T_f is the nominal frame or pulse repetition interval, c^k_j is a user-unique pseudorandom TH code sequence (used for multiple access), T_c is the TH code chip period, $D^k_{\lfloor j/L \rfloor}$ is the k-th user's $\lfloor j/L \rfloor$-th data symbol, where $\lfloor j/L \rfloor$ is the integer part of j/L and a symbol is transmitted as L monocycles PPM-modulated pulses, and δ is the amount of time shift of the PPM pulse for a data bit of "1".

The UWB communication system considered in this chapter is a spread-spectrum communication system, which uses a multiple-access scheme. Time hopping is used for multiple accesses. The source and the destination of each link have a common pseudorandom time hopping sequence, which is independent of other links' sequences. In the multiple-access scheme, transmissions on other links contribute added interference to the received signal and, due to randomness in time-hopping codes, we model such an interference as having statistical properties of Gaussian noise. The total noise at a receiver is comprised of background noise and a sum of interferences from all other active transmitters. The communication channel is assumed to be an AWGN channel. Thus, supposing that N links are active at a given time, the signal-to-interference plus noise (SINR) at the i-th link's receiver is represented as γ_i and is defined as [10]

$$\gamma_i = \frac{p_i g_{ii}}{R_i T_f \left(\eta_i + \rho \sum_{k=1, k \neq i}^{N} p_k g_{ki} \right)} \qquad (2)$$

where R_i is the data transmission rate of i-th link and $R_i = 1/(LT_f)$, p_i is the average transmission power of the i-th link's transmitter, g_{ij} denotes path gain from the i-th link's transmitter to j-th link's receiver (g_{ii} is referred to as the i-th link's path gain and g_{ij} ($i \neq j$) is the interference path gain), η_i denotes the power of the background noise at i-th link's receiver, and ρ represents a parameter which depends on the shape of impulse((79) in ref. [10]).

In this work, a link is comprised of a pair of transmitter and receiver and the link is active if it is transmitting. When N links in a network are active at a given time, we define the throughput of the i-th link as the number of packets per second received without error at the i-th link's receiver:

$$T_i^N = R_i f(\gamma_i) \qquad (3)$$

where $f(\gamma_i)$ is the packet success rate; i.e., it is the probability that the i-th link's receiver decodes a data packet correctly as a function of γ_i. The actual form of $f(\gamma_i)$ depends on the UWB receiver's configuration, the packet size, the channel coding, and the radio propagation model. We do not impose any restrictions on the form of $f(\gamma_i)$, except that $f(\gamma_i)$ is a smooth monotonically increasing function of γ_i, and $0 \leq f(\gamma_i) \leq 1$.

The total network throughput of N active links in the network, which we term T^N, is the sum of the N individual throughputs T^N_i.

$$T^N = \sum_{i=1}^{N} T_i^N \qquad (4)$$

The aim of our optimization study is to determine the rate and the power assignments among the N links when the link gains and the background noise are given such that the total network throughput is maximized.

First we examine the properties of the throughput of link i, T^N_i, as a function of SINR. Using the following definition:

$$\mu_i = \frac{p_i g_{ii}}{T_f\left(\eta_i + \rho \sum_{k=1,k\neq i}^{N} p_k g_{ki}\right)} \tag{5}$$

eqs. (1) and (3) can now be represented respectively as

$$\gamma_i = \frac{\mu_i}{R_i} \tag{6}$$

$$T_i^N = \mu_i \frac{f(\gamma_i)}{\gamma_i} \tag{7}$$

Given the links' powers p_i ($i=1, ..., N$), the value of μ_i is fixed and SINR γ_i varies only with rate R_i. As the rate R_i increases, the SINR γ_i and the packet success rate $f(\gamma_i)$ decrease. From eq. (7), we can see that too large or too small SINR leads to reduced throughput; at small SINR, the throughput is limited by small packet transmission success probability; however, at large SINR, the throughput is limited by small data transmission rate. Thus, we expect that there is an optimal value of SINR or an optimal symbol rate which corresponds to the maximum throughput.

3. Optimization for the two-links case

Before analyzing the performance of an arbitrary number of active links, we examine the case of two active links ($N=2$). This will allow us to gain some insight into the optimum allocation of transmission rates and transmission powers based on maximization of the throughput.

In the case of two active links, the total throughput is

$$T^2 = \mu_1 \frac{f(\gamma_1)}{\gamma_1} + \mu_2 \frac{f(\gamma_2)}{\gamma_2} \tag{8}$$

To obtain the optimal values of SINRs, γ_1^* and γ_2^*, that maximize the total network throughput, when p_1 and p_2 are fixed, we differentiate eq. (8) with respect to γ_1 and γ_2, setting the first derivatives at zero and verifying that the second derivatives are negative. A simple calculation reveals that the conditions for both γ^*_1 and γ^*_2 are the same and, therefore, we can write $\gamma^*_1 = \gamma^*_2 = \gamma_c$ and state the conditions on γ_c as follows:

$$f(\gamma_c) = \gamma_c f'(\gamma_c) \tag{9}$$

$$f''(\gamma_c) < 0 \tag{10}$$

Then, from eq. (6), we calculate the optimal data rates:

$$R_1^* = \frac{\mu_1}{\gamma_c} = \frac{1}{\gamma_c T_f} \cdot \frac{g_{11} p_1}{\eta_1 + \rho g_{21} p_2}$$

$$R_2^* = \frac{\mu_2}{\gamma_c} = \frac{1}{\gamma_c T_f} \cdot \frac{g_{22} p_2}{\eta_2 + \rho g_{12} p_1}$$

(11)

And with the above conditions, the optimal total network throughput is

$$T^{2*} = f'(\gamma_c)(\mu_1 + \mu_2)$$

$$= \frac{f'(\gamma_c)}{T_f} \left(\frac{g_{11} p_1}{\eta_1 + \rho g_{21} p_2} + \frac{g_{22} p_2}{\eta_2 + \rho g_{12} p_1} \right)$$

(12)

When there is only a single active link in the network, either $p_2=0$ or $p_1=0$, the optimum total throughput is, respectively

$$T_1^{1*} = T^{2*}(p_2 = 0) = \frac{f'(\gamma_c)}{T_f} \cdot \frac{g_{11} p_1}{\eta_1}$$

$$T_2^{1*} = T^{2*}(p_1 = 0) = \frac{f'(\gamma_c)}{T_f} \cdot \frac{g_{22} p_2}{\eta_2}$$

(13)

If we can adapt the transmission rates to the transmission powers according to eq. (11), the optimal total network throughput is then a function of the two links' powers and its value is determined by eqs. (12) and (13). Next, we show how to allocate the transmission powers between the two links so as to maximize the total network throughput. To do so, we focus our attention on eq. (12). From eq. (12), the optimal total network throughput is a function of p_2 only for fixed value of p_1. In Figure 2, we depict a set of curves of the optimal total network throughput for different values of p_1. Note that the graph includes the value of T_2^{1*} (i.e., $T^{2*}(p_1=0)$) and that the values for $p_2=0$ correspond to the situation in which only the first link is active. We state two observations: Firstly, we note that the throughput increases for large enough values of p_2 and that for small values of p_1, the value of T^{2*} increases faster than for larger values of p_1, so that T_2^{1*} will eventually exceed T^{2*} for non-zero p_1. Secondly, we observe from the Figure that, there is a critical value, p_{c1}, such that if p_1 is larger than p_{c1}, T^{2*} will first decrease, take on a minimum, and then increase as p_2 grows. However, if p_1 is smaller than p_{c1}, T^{2*} will always be an increasing function of p_2, with a minimum at $p_2=0$ (i.e., when the second link is inactive). These two observations imply that, when the two powers are high enough, the optimal total network throughput of two active links will always be smaller than the throughput of a single active link, but if the power of the first link is smaller than p_{c1}, then the adding of the second link increases the optimal total network throughput. To obtain the value of p_{c1}, we set $\partial T^{2*}/\partial p_2$ at $p_2=0$ at zero, which results in

$$p_{c1} = \frac{\eta_2}{2\rho g_{12}} \left(\sqrt{1 + 4\frac{\eta_1^2 g_{12} g_{22}}{\eta_2^2 g_{21} g_{11}}} - 1 \right)$$

(14)

Also, if eq. (12) is seen as a function of single variable p_1 with p_2 being a parameter, we can obtain the critical value of p_2 as

$$p_{c2} = \frac{\eta_1}{2\rho g_{21}}(\sqrt{1 + 4\frac{\eta_2^2 g_{21} g_{11}}{\eta_1^2 g_{12} g_{22}}} - 1)$$ (15)

When p_2 is smaller than p_{c2}, T^{2*} will always be an increasing function of p_1. If the power p_1 and p_2 simultaneously satisfy the following two inequalities: $p_1 < p_{c1}$ and $p_2 < p_{c2}$, then the total network throughput, T^{2*}, is larger than the throughputs of the single active link case with the same power, T_1^{1*} and T_2^{1*}. In the example of Figure 2, we find that p_{c1}=90. 95 mW and p_{c2}=155.69 mW.

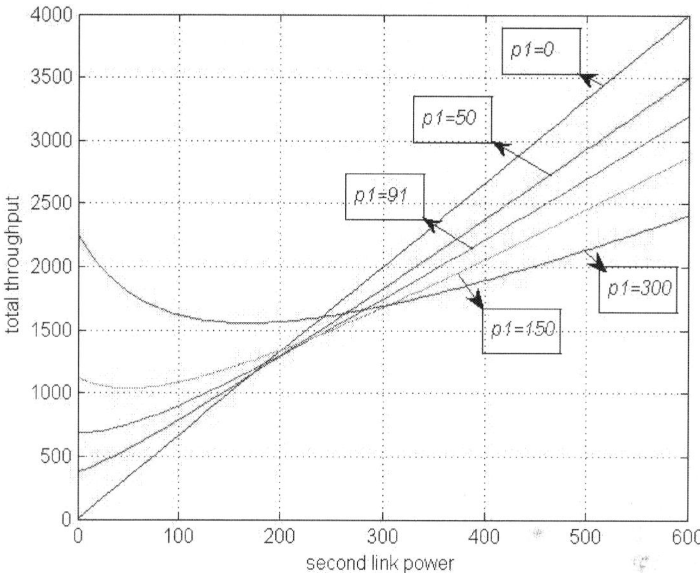

Fig. 2. The maximal total throughput vs. the power of the second link, the power of the first link as the parameter, and with the following values of parameters in (12): $f'(\gamma_c)/T_f$=1 bit/s, g_{11}=0.03, g_{22}=0.04, g_{21}=0.003, g_{12}=0.002, ρ=0.01, η_1=0.004 mW, η_2=0.006 mW, p_{c1}=90.95 mW, p_{c2}=155.69 mW

In any practical situation, transmission powers are not unlimited. But, using eq. (11), we can calculate the corresponding optimal transmission rates according to the attainable transmission power values and, so as to achieve the optimal throughput. We describe how to allocate the transmission powers, so as to maximize the throughput, when $0<p_1<P_1$ and $0<p_1<P_2$. Since the sign of the second derivatives of eq. (12) with respect to p_1 and p_2 is positive for any value of p_1 and p_2, the maximum throughput lies on the boundary of the attainable region, i.e., [$0<p_1<P_1$, $0<p_1<P_2$]. Based on our analytic results obtained so far, if $P_1 < p_{c1}$ and $P_2 < p_{c2}$, the optimum transmission power allocation is $p_1=P_1$ and $p_2=P_2$, i.e., the two links' transmitters transmit at their maximum powers and at the same time (Figure 3 is an example of such a case). However, if $P_1 > p_{c1}$ and $P_2 > p_{c2}$, the optimum allocation is $p_1=P_1$, $p_2=0$ or $p_1=0$, $p_2=P_2$, i.e., the transmitter of one link transmits at its maximum power, while the other is turned off (Figure 4 is an example of such a case).

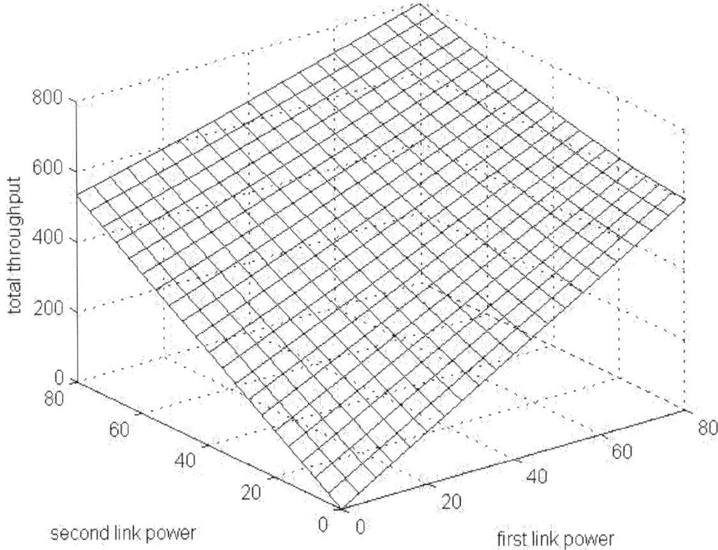

Fig. 3. The maximal total throughput vs. the transmission powers of the two link, when maximum attainable powers are smaller than the critical values, for the same parameters' values as in Figure 2 (the total throughput is maximum at p_1=80 mW, p_2=80 mW)

A transmitted signal attenuates according to a power law as a function of distance from its transmitter; i.e., if d_{ij} is the distance from the i-th link's transmitter to j-th link's receiver, then

$$g_{ij} = c \cdot d_{ij}^{-\alpha} \tag{16}$$

where c and a are constants. This is a commonly used attenuation model for wireless transmissions, and it has been verified as applicable to an UWB indoor propagation model [13][14]. Hence, p_{c1} and p_{c2} are functions of d_{12}, d_{21}, d_{11}, and d_{22}. From eqs. (14) and (15), we calculate the two critical distances, d_{c12} and d_{c21} for given values of P_1, P_2, d_{11}, d_{22}, and either d_{12} or d_{21}.

$$d_{c21} = \frac{d_{22}}{d_{11}} \cdot \left[\frac{(\rho c d_{12}^{-\alpha} P_1^2 + \eta_2 P_1)\rho c}{\eta_1^2} \right]^{\frac{1}{\alpha}} \tag{17}$$

$$d_{c12} = \frac{d_{11}}{d_{22}} \cdot \left[\frac{(\rho c d_{21}^{-\alpha} P_2^2 + \eta_1 P_2)\rho c}{\eta_2^2} \right]^{\frac{1}{\alpha}} \tag{18}$$

So, if $d_{12}<d_{c12}$ or $d_{21}<d_{c21}$, only one link should be active. This conclusion is equivalent to the concept of "the exclusion regions" in refs. [4--6], but in our case the exclusion regions sizes, d_{c12} and d_{c21}, depend on the transmission powers of the sources, the powers of background noises, the path-loss exponent, and the length of the links; thus our solution is different from the proposition in refs. [4--6].

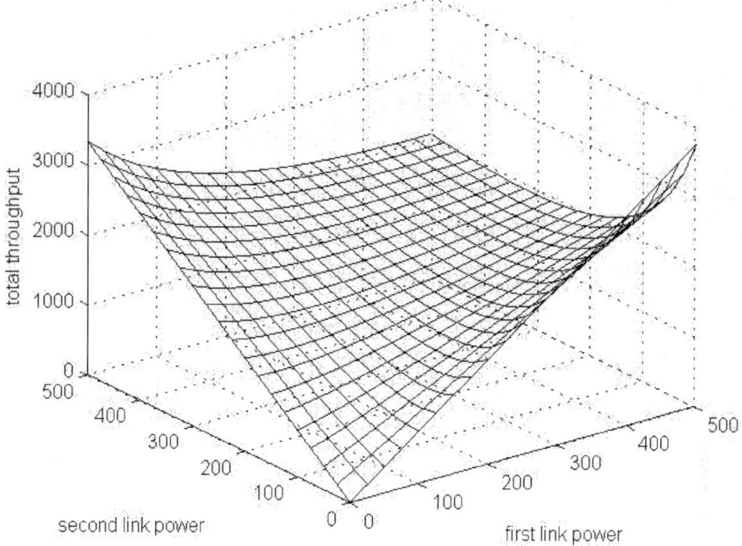

Fig. 4. The maximal total throughput vs. the transmission powers of the two link, when maximum attainable powers are larger than the critical values, for the same parameters' values as in Figure 2 (the total throughput is maximum at p_1=500 mW, p_2=0 mW)

4. Optimization for *N* links

We now expand our study to consider the optimization problem of eq. (4) for networks with N active links. Examining the first and second derivatives of (4) with respect to γ_i (i=1,…,N), we find that all the optimal values of SINRs, γ^*_i (i=1,…,N), correspond to one and the same value, γ_c, a value which satisfies eq. (9) and (10). So the N optimal rates are

$$R_i^* = \frac{\mu_i}{\gamma_c} = \frac{1}{\gamma_c T_f} \cdot \frac{g_{ii}p_i}{\eta_i + \rho \sum_{k=1,k\neq i}^{N} g_{ki}p_k} \qquad i = 1 \cdots N \tag{19}$$

Accordingly, the optimum total network throughput is

$$T^{N*} = \frac{f'(\gamma_c)}{T_f} \sum_{i=1}^{N} \frac{g_{ii}p_i}{\eta_i + \rho \sum_{k=1,k\neq i}^{N} g_{ki}p_k} \tag{20}$$

We fix all p_i (i=1,…, N) at some arbitrary values, except for p_j, and we consider eq. (20) as a function of a single free variable p_j. We can draw curves similar to those in Figure 2, but the values for p_j=0 are now the throughputs of the N-1 active links. The first and second partial derivatives of (20) with respect to p_j are

$$\frac{\partial T^{N*}}{\partial p_j} = \frac{f'(\gamma_c)}{T_f} \left[\frac{g_{jj}}{\eta_j + \rho \displaystyle\sum_{k=1,k\neq j}^{N} g_{kj}p_k} - \sum_{i=1,i\neq j}^{N} \frac{\rho g_{ji}g_{ii}p_i}{\left(\eta_i + \rho \displaystyle\sum_{k=1,k\neq i}^{N} g_{ki}p_k \right)^2} \right] \quad j=1...N \qquad (21)$$

$$\frac{\partial^2 T^{N*}}{\partial p_j^2} = \frac{f'(\gamma_c)}{T_f} \sum_{i=1,i\neq j}^{N} \frac{2\rho g_{ji}^2 g_{ii}p_i}{\left(\eta_i + \rho \displaystyle\sum_{k=1,k\neq i}^{N} g_{ki}p_k \right)^3} \quad j=1...N \qquad (22)$$

Because eq. (22) is always positive for any $p_j>0$ ($j=1...\,N$), T^{N*} is always a concave function, and hence its maximum is only attained either at $p_j=0$ or at the value of maximum transmission power, $p_j=P_j$. Of course, $p_j=0$ means that the link j is inactive, while $p_j=P_j$ means transmission at maximum attainable power. So to solve the maximal throughput problem, we need to determine how many links will be active (transmitting with maximal power). By setting eq. (21) at $p_j=0$ ($j=1...\,N$) at zero, we can compute a set of critical p_{cj} ($j=1...\,N$). When $P_j< p_{cj}$ ($j=1...\,N$), since eq. (21) is always positive, then the maximal total throughput of N active links, T^{N*}, is larger than the maximal throughput of single active link, T^{1*}, and larger than the maximal throughput of N-1 active links, $T^{(N-1)*}$. So the optimal scheduling is to allow all the N links to transmit, each at its maximal power. When $P_j>p_{cj}$ ($j=1...\,N$), the maximal total throughput of N active links might be less than the maximal throughput of a single active link. So, at any particular time, the optimal scheduling should allocate transmission of one active link with large enough power, while the other transmitters are turned off. We could also arrive at this conclusion by the following argument. If we allocate each link's transmitting power as $p_i=a_ip$ ($i=1...\,N$), a_i being a positive constant or zero, then eq. (20) becomes

$$T^{N*} = \frac{f'(\gamma_c)}{T_f} \sum_{i=1}^{N} \frac{g_{ii}a_i}{\dfrac{\eta_i}{p} + \rho \displaystyle\sum_{k=1,k\neq i}^{N} g_{ki}a_k} \qquad (23)$$

We can see that T^{N*} is an increasing function of p. When p is large enough (strictly, infinity), we can obtain

$$T^{N*} = \frac{f'(\gamma_c)}{T_f} \sum_{i=1}^{N} \frac{g_{ii}a_i}{\rho \displaystyle\sum_{k=1,k\neq i}^{N} g_{ki}a_k} \qquad (24)$$

When more than two links are active, the value of T^{N*} is limited. However, if just one link is active, for example, $a_i=0$ ($i=2...N$) but $a_1\neq0$, then T^{N*} tends to infinity.

We consider a special scenario when $g_{ii}=g$, $g_{ij}=g'(i\neq j)$, $\eta_i=\eta$, and $p_i=p$ ($i,j=1...N$). With these conditions, the single active link's maximal throughput is

$$T^{1*} = \frac{f'(\gamma_c)}{T_f} \frac{gp}{\eta}$$ (25)

However, the maximal total network throughput of N active links is in this case:

$$T^{N*} = \frac{f'(\gamma_c)}{T_f} \frac{Ng}{\frac{\eta}{p} + (N-1)\rho g'}$$ (26)

and each link's maximal throughput is

$$T_1^{N*} = \frac{f'(\gamma_c)}{T_f} \frac{g}{\frac{\eta}{p} + (N-1)\rho g'}$$ (27)

If we let p go to infinity, T^{1*} will approach infinity as well, but T^{N*} approaches the following finite value:

$$T^{N*} = \frac{N}{N-1} \cdot \frac{f'(\gamma_c)}{T_f} \cdot \frac{g}{\rho g'}$$ (28)

We can also see that T^{N*} is an increasing function of N. So with N increasing to infinity, eq. (27) decreases to zero, but eqs. (26) and (28) approach

$$T^{\infty*} = \frac{f'(\gamma_c)}{T_f} \cdot \frac{g}{\rho g'}$$ (29)

From comparison, eq. (26) will be smaller than eq. (25) when p is larger than the following value of p_c:

$$p_c = \frac{\eta}{\rho g'}$$ (30)

Using eq. (16), we calculate the critical value of the interference distance, d_c', for transmitted power p:

$$d_c' = (\frac{\rho c p}{\eta})^{\frac{1}{\alpha}}$$ (31)

In this special symmetric scenario, the critical power, p_c, is independent of N. and the critical interference distance, d_c', is independent of the link length. When $0 < p < p_c$, the maximal total network throughput is larger than the maximal single active throughput and the increment, $T^{N*} - T^{1*}$, is maximum when p is equal to the following value of p_m:

$$p_m = \frac{\eta}{(\sqrt{N}+1)\rho g'}$$ (32)

When $p=p_m$, eqs. (25) and (26) become, respectively

$$T_m^{1*} = \frac{f'(\gamma_c)}{T_f} \cdot \frac{g}{(\sqrt{N}+1)\rho g'} \tag{33}$$

$$T_m^{N*} = \frac{\sqrt{N}}{\sqrt{N}+1} \cdot \frac{f'(\gamma_c)}{T_f} \cdot \frac{g}{\rho g'}$$
$$= \frac{\sqrt{N}}{\sqrt{N}+1} T^{\infty*} \tag{34}$$
$$= \sqrt{N} T_m^{1*}$$

and the maximal throughput of each link is

$$T_1^{N*} = \frac{T_m^{N*}}{N} = \frac{T^{\infty*}}{N+\sqrt{N}}$$
$$= \frac{T_m^{1*}}{\sqrt{N}} \tag{35}$$

Actually, $T^{\infty*}$ is the maximal total network throughput capacity of a network with concurrently active links, and 90% of the maximal total network throughput can be attained when $N=81$. From eq. (29), the maximal total network throughput $T^{\infty*}$ is mainly determined by the physical layer, and it can be enhanced by increasing g (the signal gain) and $f'(\gamma_c)$ (packet transmission success probability increment rate at optimal SINR), and by decreasing T_f (pulse repetition interval), ρ (the shape factor of impulse), and g' (the interference gain). The values of $f'(\gamma_c)$, T_f, and ρ depend on design parameters, such as modulation, pulse shape, time-hopping sequences, and the size of data packets. The values of g and g' depend on the antenna design; e.g., multiple transmit and receive antennas (MIMO) [16] can increase g and decrease g'. However, g and g' are also affected by the routing and the MAC schemes.

5. Discussion and concluding remarks

While the fundamental principles of networking are the same regardless of the underlying physical layer, UWB has unique characteristics that influence how protocols and a UWB system are designed. A UWB network can be represented by a five-layer model, compatible with the TCP/IP suite, that includes a UWB physical layer, associated data link layer, network layer, transport layer, and application layer. Each layer provides services to the layer directly above it and uses services provided by the layer beneath it. The unique characteristics of the UWB physical layer have the greatest influence on the design of the data link layer. The characteristics of the physical layer and the design of the associated data link layer may also influence the design of the network layer, transport layer, and even application layer, especially if a design is to achieve optimal performance.

When designing a communication network, it is important to understand how much information such a network can transport, what parameters affect the maximal throughput of the network, and how to change the parameters so as to maximize the throughput. The two last sections provide us with some answers to these questions for UWB wireless ad hoc networks. We have established the dependencies among the maximum achievable throughput of the network, each active link's transmission rate and transmission power, the number of simultaneously active links in the network, the link and the interference paths gains, and the background noise.

In the MAC protocol of data link layer, time is divided into time slots, which are allocated for links according to the link-scheduling policy. There are two types of link-scheduling policies: single link policy which allows only one link to transmit in any slot, and concurrent links policy which allows multiple links to transmit simultaneously in a slot. These two policies require that the transmission rate of the active links be maintained at the optimal value according to eq. (19). Under this condition, the maximum total network throughput depends on each link's maximum power and on the interferences among the active links. Our results show that the single link policy suits transmissions with large power: the throughput increases linearly with the power (and, in theory, indefinitely), as shown in eq. (13) and (25). With this policy, the larger is the power, the larger is the throughput. With the concurrent links policy, the maximal total network throughput cannot increase indefinitely by continual increase in transmission powers. Actually, the maximal total network throughput is limited by the interference levels among the active links, and the throughput approaches a finite value when multiple powers are increased indefinitely. This is demonstrated by eqs. (24) and (28). So, on one hand, when the powers are large enough, the single active link maximal throughput exceeds the maximal total network throughput of concurrently active links. In this situation, it is better to choose the single link policy. On the other hand, the maximal total network throughput of the concurrently active links is larger than the maximal throughput of a single active link, if each link power is below the critical value or when the separation between any pair of active links is above their critical values. These critical values are computed in eqs. (14), (15), (30), (17), (18), and (31). Hence, the concurrent links policy is suitable for small powers or for sparse networks. In this situation, each link has an optimum power value which maximizes the throughput gain by increasing the number of the concurrently active links.

The maximal total network throughput with concurrent active links, or the network capacity, is calculated by eq. (29), and can be enhanced by decreasing the interference path gains or by increasing the link path gain, but not by increasing the power. As the number of concurrently active links, N, is increasing, each link throughput is decreased. Existing protocols (like 802.11) are based on the single link policy, but their rate might not be optimum. The regulatory bodies (like FCC) impose severe limitation on UWB power density to avoid interference on other existing wireless communication systems (such as GPS and 802.11 networks), since they share the same frequency band. The FCC regulation allows commercial UWB devices to emit no more than -41 dBm/MHz of average transmitted power, so the maximum transmitted power is limited to less than -2.2 dBm, or approximately half a Milliwatt. Consequently, the concurrent links policy may be a more suitable choice for UWB ad hoc networks.

Because the routing protocol of network layer determines the paths of data flow and interference gains between intended links, the design of an MAC protocol based on the concurrent links policy should be related to the choice of a routing protocol for maximization of the total network throughput. However, the design of an MAC protocol based on the single link policy should be independent of the choice of routing protocol. As the rate adaptation requires support of the physical layer, such adaptation is most efficiently performed if the design is based on cross-layer considerations. The application of our results to implementation of an MAC protocol based on the concurrent links policy with cross-layer design considerations is outside the scope of this chapter, but is left for future study.

When a mechanism for adaptation of transmission rates is incorporated into the design of the MAC protocol, by adjusting the transmission rates to their optimum values, the maximal total network throughput is limited by maximal transmission power and by the interference from other active links in the networks. The maximal total network throughput approaches a constant and each link's throughput approaches zero as the maximal transmission power and the simultaneously active links increase in number. For the case of a single active link, the maximal throughput increases linearly with the maximal transmission power and, barring a limit on transmission power, the maximal throughput can increase indefinitely. When the values of the maximal transmission power are large enough, the maximal throughput in the single active link case exceeds the maximal total network throughput of the multiple active links case. To maximize the total network throughput, the optimal transmission scheduling should allocate at any time transmission on one link only when the maximal transmission power is large and the interference is strong. However, when the maximal transmission power is small and the interference is weak, the optimal transmission scheduling should allocate at any time simultaneous transmission on multiple links.

6. Summary

In this chapter, we study the problem of radio resource allocation, both transmission rates and transmission powers, so as to maximize the throughput of UWB wireless ad-hoc networks. Our analysis is based on the packet-success function (PSF), which is defined as the probability of a data packet being successfully received as a function of the receiver's signal-to-interference-and-noise-ratio (SINR). We find an optimal link transmission rate, which maximizes the link's throughput and is dependent on the all active links transmission powers. If each link transmission rate is adapted to this optimal link transmission rate, then, with single-link operation (i.e., no other interference sources are present), the link's throughput is directly proportional to the transmitter's power and increases indefinitely with increasing transmission power. However, with multiple-links operation and interference each other, as each link transmitting power increases, so does the interference level, and the total network throughput approaches a constant other than infinite. Thus, for sufficiently small transmission power, the total network throughput of the multiple-links case exceeds the throughput of the single-link case, but the reverse happens for high power. In addition, this chapter reveals that, as the number of concurrently transmitting links increases, regardless of the power level, the maximal total network throughput approaches a constant, with each link's throughput approaching zero. To maximize the network throughput, for the case of small maximal transmission power with weak interference levels, the optimal transmission scheduling allocates simultaneous transmissions of multiple links, but for the case of large maximal transmission power with strong interference levels, the optimal policy assigns separate time for transmission on each link. The breakpoint of when to use one link or multiple links is termed the critical power. As an example of the analytical calculation of the critical link's power, we present here solutions for a two-link case and an N-link case. In contrast with previous studies, our results imply that the design of optimal MAC is dependent on the choice of a routing scheme.

7. Acknowledgement

This work is supported by the Scientific Foundation of Sichuan Education Department of China (Grant No. 2006A096), the Ph. D Foundation of Southwest University of Science and Technology (Grant No. 06zx7107), and the Scientific Research Foundation for the Returned Overseas Chinese Scholars, State Personnel Ministry (Grant No. 08ZD0106)

8. References

[1] Apsel A, Dokania R, Wang X. Ultra-low power radios for ad-hoc networks. In: IEEE International Symposium on Circuits and Systems, Taipei, 2009. 1433 – 1436

[2] Tang X, Hua Y. Capacity of ultra-wideband power-constrained Ad Hoc networks. IEEE Trans Inf Theory, 2008, 54(2): 916 – 920

[3] Zou C, Haas Z. Optimal Resource Allocation for UWB Wireless AD HOC Networks. In: IEEE 16th International Symposium on Personal, Indoor and Mobile Radio Communications, Berlin, 2005. 452-456

[4] Radunovic B, Boudec J-Y L. Optimal power control, scheduling, and routing in UWB networks. IEEE J Sel Area Commun, 2004, 22(7): 1252–1270

[5] Merz R, Boudec J-Y L, Widmer J, et al. A rate-adaptive MAC protocol for low-power ultra-wide band ad-hoc networks. In: Proceeding of 3rd International Conference on AD-HOC Networks and Wireless, Vancouver, 2004. 306–311

[6] Liu K H, Cai L, Shen X. Exclusive-region based scheduling algorithms for UWB WPAN. IEEE Trans Wireless Commun, 2008, 7(3): 933 – 942

[7] Cuomo F, Martello C, Baiocchi A, et al. Radio resource sharing for ad hoc networking with UWB. IEEE J Sel Area Commun, 2002, 20(12): 1722–1732

[8] Baldi P, Nardis L D, Benedetto M-G D. Modeling and optimization of UWB communication networks through a flexible cost function. IEEE J Sel Area Commun, 2002, 20(12): 1733–1744

[9] Zhu S, Leung KK, Constantinides A G. Distributed cooperative data relaying for diversity in impulse-based UWB Ad-Hoc networks. IEEE Trans Wireless Commun, 2009, 8(8): 4037 – 4047

[10] Win M, Scholtz R. Ultra-wide bandwidth time-hopping spread spectrum impulse radio for wireless multiple-access communications. IEEE Trans Commun, 2000, 48(4): 679–691

[11] Feng D, Ghauri S, Zhu Q. Application of the MUI model based on packets collision (PC) in UWB ad-hoc network. In: International Conference on Networking, Sensing and Control, 2009. 554 – 558

[12] Durisi G, Romano G. On the validity of Gaussian approximation to characterize the multiuser capacity of UWB TH PPM. In: Proceeding of IEEE Conference of Ultra-Wideband Systems Technologies, 2002. 151–161

[13] Molisch A F. Ultrawideband propagation channels-theory, measurement, and modeling. IEEE Trans Veh Technol, 2005, 54(5): 1528-1545

[14] Ghassemzadeh S S, Tarokh V. UWB path loss characterization in residential environments. In: Proceeding of IEEE Radio Frequency Integrated Circuits (RFIC) Symposium, 2003: 501–504

[15] Tsirigos A, Haas Z J. Analysis of multipath routing - Part I: The effect on the packet delivery ratio. IEEE Trans Wireless Commun, 2004, 3(1): 138-146, January

[16] Kaiser T, Zheng F, Dimitrov E. An overview of ultra-wide-band systems with MIMO. Proceedings of the IEEE, 2009, 97(2): 285-312

11

Outage Probability Analysis of Cooperative Communications over Asymmetric Fading Channel

Sudhan Majhi, Youssef Nasser and Jean François Hélard
National Institute of Applied Sciences of Rennes
France

1. Introduction

Cooperative relaying is a promising technology for future wireless communications. It is mostly applicable to the small dimensional and limited power devices, which cannot use the conventional multiple input multiple output (MIMO) technology to obtain the advantages of MIMO. It can benefit most of the leverages of MIMO such as array gain, diversity gain, spatial multiplexing gain and interference reduction without using the conventional MIMO technology Liu et al. (2009); Laneman et al. (2004); Paulraj et al. (2004). Since the original signal is forwarded by relay nodes, the performance of the relaying network depends on the relaying process of the relay nodes and fading characteristic of their links. Classically, relay network has three links source-destination (S-D), source-relay (S-R) and relay-destination (R-D) and the relaying processes are classified as amplify-and-forward (AF), decode-and-forward (DF) and compress-and-forward (CF) Krikidis & Thompson (2008); Nosratinia et al. (2004).

The diversity of the relaying network depends on the degree of freedom of the network. For repetition-based relaying, the degree of freedom increases with the number of relay nodes when the system is an half duplex and use a time division duplex Zhao et al. (2005, 2007). However, it suffers spectral efficiency with increase in the number of relay nodes in the network. On the other hand, opportunistic relaying uses only one relay node to forward source data to the destination and its degree of freedom is two. It has higher spectral efficiency and better outage performance than that of repetition-based relaying.

The performance of the relaying network depends on the fading characteristic of S-D, S-R and R-D links, i.e. diversity of the relaying networks depends on the location of the relay nodes and its surrounding environment. In practice, cooperative nodes are usually located in different geographical locations and at different distances with respect to S and D. The signal in one link may be in line of sight (LOS) situation and other links may be in NLOS situation. For example, fixed relay nodes are used for forwarding source's data to a specific region (e.g. tunnel, behind of the building) and they often use directional antennas, so the R-D link is likely to be a LOS situation. However, we cannot assume such scenario for other links specially when D is in a shadowing region with respect to S. In other words, one link may undergo Rician fading channel and others links may undergo Rayleigh fading channel. Such scenario is refereed to as asymmetric fading channel. This channel scenario can also be seen in cooperative cognitive radio where secondary terminal works as a relay. In addition, all the links, i.e., S to i^{th} relay (S-R_i) and i^{th} relay to D (R_i-D), may be independent but non-identically distributed (i.n.d) fading channels. Therefore, a complete outage performance study of cooperative relaying for such asymmetric and i.n.d fading channels is required.

The outage probability of relaying networks over symmetric fading channel, in which all the links undergo the same fading distribution, is provided in several works Hwang et al. (2007); Xu et al. (2009); Zhao et al. (2006); Savazzi & Spagnolini (2008); Michalopoulos & Karagiannidis (2008); Zou et al. (2009); Vicario et al. (2009). The outage probability for repetition-based AF relaying over Rayleigh channel is provided in Zhao et al. (2007). The outage probability of AF relaying over Rician fading is provided only in few articles Zhu et al. (2008). The asymmetric fading channel, mix of Rayleigh and additive white Gaussian noise, is introduced in Katz & Shamai (2009). The performance of AF relaying over asymmetric fading, mix of Rician & Rayleigh, is provided in independent work in Suraweera et al. (2009); Suraweera, Karagiannidis & Smith (2009). However, in the literature, none of the papers provided any closed form outage probability of AF relaying over asymmetric fading channels.

In this work, we provide a complete study of outage probability of repetition-based and opportunistic relaying over asymmetric fading channels. The closed form of outage probability is derived over i.n.d fading channel at high SNR regime. In this work, we adopted AF relaying networks over two different scenarios, called asymmetric channel I and asymmetric channel II given in Fig. 1. We provide analytical model of each of the asymmetric channel and verified through the Monte-Carlo simulation studies. The obtained results of asymmetric fading channel are compared with symmetric fading channel, i.e., with Rician fading channel and Rayleigh fading channel. When outage performance is compared between two asymmetric channels, asymmetric channel I provides better outage performance than asymmetric channel II and when it is compared between two diversity techniques, opportunistic AF relaying provides better outage performance than the repetition-based AF relaying.

The rest of the article is organized as follows. Section 2 discusses a two-hop AF relaying network and asymmetric channel models. Section 3 derives the outage probability of the repetition-based AF relaying over two different asymmetric fading channel scenarios at high SNR regime. Section 4 derives the outage probability of opportunistic AF relaying over asymmetric channel I and asymmetric channel II. Finally, conclusion is drawn in section 6.

2. System model

2.1 Signal model of AF relaying

In this framework, we consider a general 2-hop AF relaying network consisting of S, M relays, R_i, i=1, 2, ..., M, and D. We assume that D performs maximal ratio combining at the receiver. The network has $M+1$ time slots for M relay nodes Zhao et al. (2005). In the first time slot, S broadcasts data to D and all R_i. The received signals at D and R_i are given by

$$y_{sd} = h_{sd}x + \eta_d \tag{1}$$

$$y_{sr_i} = \alpha h_{sr_i}x + \eta_{r_i} \tag{2}$$

where x is the signal transmitted by S, η_d and η_{ri} are the zeromean complex Gaussian random variables at D and i^{th} relay, respectively. h_{sd} and h_{sri} are the fading coefficients of S-D and S-R_i links, respectively.

The received signal at D from R_i at the $(i+1)^{\text{th}}$ time slot is

$$y_{r_i d} = h_{r_i d} x' + \eta_d \tag{3}$$

where $\alpha = 1$, x' is the signal transmitted by the relay R_i for the case of repetition-based relaying and $h_{r_i d}$ is the fading coefficient of R_i-D link. For the opportunistic AF relaying, α is the amplifying factor and $x' = x$. In the 2nd time slot, the best opportunistic relay node forwards the source's signal to D.

2.2 Channel model of asymmetric fading channel

For simplicity, we use different notations of the random variables for different fading distributions. For the Rayleigh channel, in general, let $\gamma_{ab} = P_s |h_{ab}|^2$ be the instantaneous signal power of a-b link and for the Rician fading channel, the corresponding instantaneous signal power is denoted as ξ_{ab}. The transmitted power from source and relay is P_s. The probability density function (PDF) of γ_{ab} and ξ_{ab} are expressed respectively as

$$f_{\gamma_{ab}}(x) = \frac{1}{\overline{\gamma}_{ab}} e^{-x/\overline{\gamma}_{ab}} \tag{4}$$

$$f_{\xi_{ab}}(\xi) = \frac{K_{ab}+1}{\overline{\xi}_{ab}} e^{-\xi(K_{ab}+1)/\overline{\xi}_{ab} - K_{ab}} I_0\left(\sqrt{\frac{4K_{ab}(K_{ab}+1)\xi}{\overline{\xi}_{ab}}}\right) \tag{5}$$

where $I_0(.)$ is the 0th order modified Bessel function of first kind, $\overline{\gamma}_{ab} = E\{\gamma_{ab}\}$, $\overline{\xi}_{ab} = E\{\xi_{ab}\}$, and K_{ab} is the Rician factor.

Although there are several possibilities of asymmetric fading channel, in this work, we assume two asymmetric fading channels: namely asymmetric channel I and asymmetric channel II, shown in Fig. 1. For the asymmetric channel I, we assume that S-R link undergos Rayleigh distribution and S-D and R-D links undergo Rician fading distribution. For the asymmetric channel II, S-R link undergos Rician distribution and S-D and R-D links undergo Rayleigh distribution.

3. Repetition based AF relaying

The repetition-based AF relaying is introduced in Laneman et al. (2004). Due to the higher degree of freedom of repetition-based relaying and simple implementation for AF relaying, it gain its own importance in cooperative communications. The equivalent instantaneous end-to-end signal-to-noise ratio (SNR) for repetition-based AF relaying is given as Zhao et al. (2006)

$$\gamma = \frac{P_s |h_{sd}|^2}{N_{sd}} + \sum_{i=1}^{M} \frac{\dfrac{P_s |h_{sr_i}|^2}{N_{sr_i}} \dfrac{P_s |h_{r_i d}|^2}{N_{r_i d}}}{\dfrac{P_s |h_{sr_i}|^2}{N_{sr_i}} + \dfrac{P_s |h_{r_i d}|^2}{N_{r_i d}} + 1} \tag{6}$$

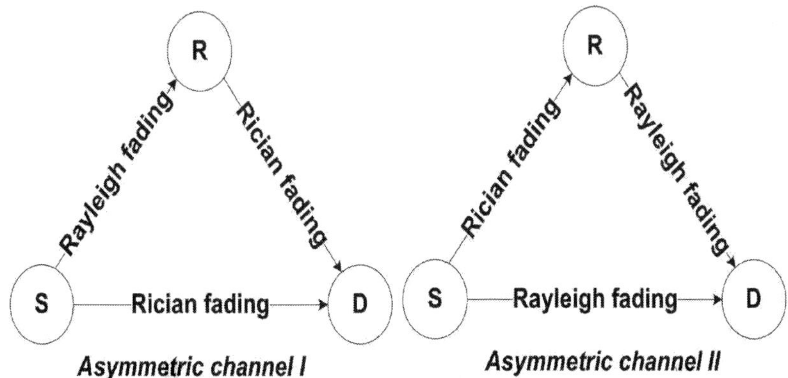

Fig. 1. Different asymmetric fading channels of a cooperative networks

The upper bound of instantaneous SNR for the above can be written as

$$\gamma_{max} = P_s \mid h_{sd} \mid^2 \gamma_0 + \sum_{i=1}^{M} \min\left(P_s \mid h_{sr_i} \mid^2 \gamma_0, P_s \mid h_{r_i d} \mid^2 \gamma_0\right) \tag{7}$$

In the following section, we provide the lower bound of outage probability of the opportunistic AF relaying for different asymmetric fading channels shown in Fig. 1.

3.1 Asymmetric channel I:

For the asymmetric channel I, S-R link experiences Rayleigh distribution and S-D and R-D links experience Rician fading distribution, so (7) can be written as

$$\gamma_{max} = \gamma_0 \gamma_{sd} + \gamma_0 \xi_{sum} \tag{8}$$

where $\gamma_{sd} = P_a \mid h_{sd} \mid^2$ is the exponential distribution, $\xi_{sum} = \sum_{i=1}^{M} \xi_{min,i}$, $\xi_{min,i} = \min(\xi_{sr_i}, \xi_{r_i d})$, ξ_{sr_i} and $\xi_{r_i d}$ are the random variables of noncentral Chi-square distribution. The corresponding outage probability can be defined as

$$p_{out} = Pr\left[\gamma_{ub} < \gamma\right] \tag{9}$$

where $\gamma_{ub} = \gamma_{max}/\gamma_0$, $\gamma = (2^{(M+1)R} - 1)/\gamma_0$. The outage probability provided in (9) is equivalent to the commutative distribution function (CDF) of γ_{ub}. The direct evaluation CDF of γ_{ub} is complicated, so we use the initial value theorem (IVT) of Laplace transformation (LT). Therefore, this derived analytical results are valid for high SNR regime. To evaluate this, first CDF of $\xi_{min,i}$ needs to be evaluated. The CDF of the random variable $\xi_{min,i}$ can be written as

$$F_{\xi_{min,i}}(\gamma) = 1 - \left(1 - Pr[\xi_{sr_i} < \gamma]\right)\left(1 - Pr[\xi_{r_i d} < \gamma]\right)$$

$$= 1 - Q_1\left(\sqrt{2K_{sr_i}}, \sqrt{\frac{2(K_{sr_i}+1)\gamma}{\bar{\xi}_{sr_i}}}\right) Q_1\left(\sqrt{2K_{r_i d}}, \sqrt{\frac{2(K_{r_i d}+1)\gamma}{\bar{\xi}_{r_i d}}}\right) \tag{10}$$

where $Q_1(.)$ is the Marcum Q-function of first order. The PDF of $\xi_{min,i}$ is obtained by differentiating the above, which can be expresses as

$$f_{\xi_{min,i}}(\gamma) = Q_1\left(\sqrt{2K_{sr_i}}, \sqrt{\frac{2(K_{sr_i}+1)\gamma}{\overline{\xi}_{sr_i}}}\right) f_{\xi_{r_id}}(\gamma) + Q_1\left(\sqrt{2K_{r_id}}, \sqrt{\frac{2(K_{r_id}+1)\gamma}{\overline{\xi}_{r_id}}}\right) f_{\xi_{sr_i}}(\gamma) \tag{11}$$

The LT of the random variable $\gamma_{ub} = \gamma_{sd} + \xi_{sum}$ is obtained by using IVT at high SNR regime. Since $\gamma \to 0$ as $\gamma_0 \to \infty$, we can write

$$\lim_{s\to\infty} s\mathcal{L}(f_{\gamma_{sd}}(\gamma)) = \lim_{\gamma\to\infty} f_{\gamma_{sd}}(\gamma) \tag{12}$$

This implies

$$\mathcal{L}(f_{\gamma_{sd}}(\gamma)) = \frac{1}{s} f_{\gamma_{sd}}(0) \tag{13}$$

Similarly the LT of the PDF of random variable ξ_{sum} can be expressed as

$$\mathcal{L}(f_{\xi_{sum}}(\gamma)) = \frac{1}{s^M} \prod_{i=1}^{M} f_{\xi_{min,i}}(0) \tag{14}$$

Now by using the multiplication properties of LT, the LT of the PDF of random variable γ_{ub} for i.n.d fading channel can be written as

$$\mathcal{L}\left(f_{\gamma_{sd}}(\gamma)\right) = \frac{1}{s^{M+1}} f_{\gamma_{sd}}(0) \prod_{i=1}^{M} f_{\xi_{min,i}}(0) \tag{15}$$

The PDF of random variable γ_{ub} is obtained by applying inverse LT (ILT) on the above

$$f_{\gamma_{ub}}(\gamma) = \frac{1}{M!} \gamma^M f_{\gamma_{sd}}(0) \prod_{i=1}^{M} f_{\xi_{min,i}}(0) \tag{16}$$

By integrating the above and substituting the value of $f_{\gamma_{sd}}(0)$ and $f_{\xi_{min,i}}(0)$, the outage probability can be expressed as

$$P_{out} = \frac{1}{(M+1)! \overline{\gamma}_{sd}} \prod_{i=1}^{M} \left(\frac{(K_{sr_i}+1)}{\overline{\xi}_{sr_i} e^{K_{sr_i}}} + \frac{(K_{r_id}+1)}{\overline{\xi}_{r_id} e^{K_{r_id}}}\right) \gamma^{M+1} \tag{17}$$

3.2 Asymmetric channel II:

For asymmetric channel II, signal in S-D and R-D links experience Rayleigh distribution and signal in S-R link experiences Rician distribution. For this scenario, we use $\xi_{sd} = P_s |h_{sd}|^2$, $\xi_{sr_i} = P_s |h_{sr_i}|^2$ and $\gamma_{r_id} = P_s |h_{r_id}|^2$. The end-to-end instantaneous SNR can be expressed as

$$\gamma_{ub} = \gamma_0 \xi_{sd} + \gamma_0 g_{sum} \tag{18}$$

where $g_{sum} = \sum_{i=1}^{M} g_{min,i}$ and $g_{min,i} = \min\left(\xi_{sr_i}, \gamma_{r_i d}\right)$. Similarly as the previous section, the PDF of $g_{min,i}$ is expressed as

$$f_{g_{min,i}}(\gamma) = Q_1\left(\sqrt{2K_{sr_i}}, \sqrt{\frac{2(K_{sr_i}+1)\gamma}{\overline{\xi}_{sr_i}}}\right) f_{\gamma_{r_i d}}(\gamma) + f_{\xi_{sr_i}}(\gamma)\left(1 - F_{\gamma_{r_i d}}(\gamma)\right) \tag{19}$$

where $F_{\gamma_{r_i d}}(\gamma)$ is the CDF of the random variable $\gamma_{r_i d}$..

Similarly as previous, the PDF of γ_{ub} for this asymmetric channel can be derived as

$$f_{\gamma_{ub}}(\gamma) = \frac{1}{M!}\gamma^M f_{\xi_{sd}}(0)\prod_{i=1}^{M} f_{g_{min,i}}(0) \tag{20}$$

By integrating (20), the outage probability for the asymmetric channel II can be expressed as

$$p_{out} = \frac{1}{(M+1)!}\frac{(K_{sd}+1)}{\overline{\xi}_{sd}e^{K_{sd}}}\prod_{i=1}^{M}\left(\frac{(K_{sr_i}+1)}{\overline{\xi}_{sr_i}e^{K_{sr_i}}} + \frac{1}{\overline{\gamma}_{r_i d}}\right)\gamma^{M+1} \tag{21}$$

4. Opportunistic AF relaying

In this section, we analyze the outage probability of opportunistic AF relaying over the same asymmetric fading scenario. For the relay selection, we use maximum SNR approach provided in Bletsas et al. (2007). The equivalent instantaneous end-to-end SNR for opportunistic AF relaying is given as Zhao et al. (2006)

$$\gamma = \frac{P_s\left|h_{sd}\right|^2}{N_{sd}} + \max_{i=\{1,2,\dots,M\}} \frac{\dfrac{P_s\,|h_{sr_i}|^2}{N_{sr_i}}\dfrac{P_s\,|h_{r_i d}|^2}{N_{r_i d}}}{\dfrac{P_s\,|h_{sr_i}|^2}{N_{sr_i}} + \dfrac{P_s\,|h_{r_i d}|^2}{N_{r_i d}} + 1} \tag{22}$$

The upper bound of instantaneous SNR for the above can be written as

$$\gamma_{max} = P_s\left|h_{sd}\right|^2\gamma_0 + \max_{i=\{1,2,\dots,M\}} \min\left(P_s\,|h_{sr_i}|^2\gamma_0, P_s\,|h_{r_i d}|^2\gamma_0\right) \tag{23}$$

4.1 Asymmetric channel I:

In asymmetric channel I, the outage performance can be expressed as

$$p_{out} = Pr\left[\gamma_{ub} < \gamma\right] \tag{24}$$

where $\gamma_{ub} = \gamma_{max}/\gamma_0$, $\gamma = (2^{2R}-1)/\gamma_0$, $\xi_{max} = \max(\xi_{min,1}, \xi_{min,2}, \dots, \xi_{min,M})$ and $\xi_{min,i} = \min\left(\xi_{sr_i}, \xi_{r_i d}\right)$. The CDF of the random variable ξ_{max} for i.n.d fading channel can be expressed as

$$F_{\xi_{max}}(\gamma) = \prod_{i=1}^{M} F_{\xi_{min,i}}(\gamma) \tag{25}$$

and the corresponding PDF of ξ_{max} is obtained as

$$f_{\xi_{max}}(\gamma) = \sum_{i=1}^{M} f_{\xi_{min,i}}(\gamma) \prod_{\substack{j=1 \\ j \neq i}}^{M} f_{\xi_{min,j}}(\gamma) \tag{26}$$

Since $F_{\xi_{min,i}}(0) = 0$, the $(M-1)^{\text{th}}$ order derivative of (26) at high SNR, i.e., at $\gamma = 0$ for $\gamma_0 \to \infty$, can be derived as

$$\frac{\partial^{M-1}}{\partial \gamma^{M-1}} f_{\xi_{max}}(\gamma)\Big|_{\gamma=0} = M! \prod_{i=1}^{M} f_{\xi_{min,i}}(0) \tag{27}$$

By using LT of Mth order differentiation, we can write

$$\mathcal{L}\left(\frac{\partial^{M-1}}{\partial \gamma^{M-1}} f_{\xi_{max}}(\gamma) \right) = s^{M-1} \mathcal{L}\left(f_{\gamma_{max}}(\gamma) \right) - s^{M-2} f_{\gamma_{max}}(0) - \dots - f_{\gamma_{max}}^{(M-2)}(0) \tag{28}$$

Since $f_{\gamma_{max}}(0) = f_{\gamma_{max}}^{(1)}(0) = \dots = f_{\gamma_{max}}^{(M-2)}(0) = 0$, by using the IVT of LT, we can write

$$\mathcal{L}(f_{\gamma_{max}}(\gamma)) = \frac{1}{s^M} \frac{\partial^{M-1}}{\partial \gamma^{M-1}} f_{\xi_{max}}(\gamma)\Big|_{\gamma=0} \tag{29}$$
$$\lim s \to \infty$$

The LT of the PDF of random variable $\gamma_{ub} = \gamma_{sd} + \xi_{max}$ over i.n.d can be written as

$$\mathcal{L}(f_{\gamma_{ub}}(\gamma)) = \mathcal{L}(f_{\gamma_{sum}}(\gamma)) \mathcal{L}(f_{\gamma_{max}}(\gamma))$$
$$= \frac{1}{s^{M+1}} f_{\gamma_{sd}}(0) \frac{\partial^{M-1}}{\partial \gamma^{M-1}} f_{\xi_{max}}(\gamma)\Big|_{\gamma=0} \tag{30}$$
$$= \frac{M!}{s^{M+1}} f_{\gamma_{sd}}(0) \prod_{i=1}^{M} f_{\xi_{min,i}}(0)$$

with respect to s, the PDF of γ_{ub} is obtained by applying the ILT on the above as

$$f_{\gamma_{ub}}(\gamma) = \gamma^M f_{\gamma_{sd}}(0) \prod_{i=1}^{M} f_{\xi_{min,i}}(0) \tag{31}$$

The corresponding outage probability or CDF of γ_{ub} is obtained by integrating the above as.

$$p_{out} = \frac{1}{(M+1)\bar{\gamma}_{sd}} \prod_{i=1}^{M} \left(\frac{K_{sr_i}+1}{\bar{\xi}_{sr_i} e^{K_{sr_i}}} + \frac{K_{r_id}+1}{\bar{\xi}_{r_id} e^{K_{r_id}}} \right) \gamma^{M+1} \tag{32}$$

4.2 Asymmetric channel II:

Similarly, in asymmetric channel II, the outage performance can be expressed as

$$p_{out} = Pr\left[\gamma_{ub} < \gamma \right] \tag{33}$$

where $\gamma_{ub} = \xi_{sd} + g_{max}$, $g_{max}=\max(g_{min,1}, g_{min,2}, ..., g_{min,M})$ and $g_{min,i}=\min(\gamma_0\xi_{sr_i}, \gamma_0\gamma_{r_id})$.

As the previously, the LT of the random variable of γ_{ub} over i.n.d fading channel can be written as

$$\mathcal{L}\left(f_{\gamma_{ub}}(\gamma)\right) = \frac{M!}{s^{M+1}} f_{\gamma_{sd}}(0)\prod_{i=1}^{M} f_{g_{min,i}}(0) \tag{34}$$

The PDF of γ_{ub} is obtained by applying the ILT on the above as

$$f_{\gamma_{ub}}(\gamma) = \gamma^{M} f_{\gamma_{sd}}(0)\prod_{i=1}^{M} f_{g_{min,i}}(0) \tag{35}$$

The corresponding outage probability or CDF of γ_{ub} is obtained by integrating the above as

$$p_{out}=\frac{1}{(M+1)\bar{\gamma}_{sd}}\prod_{i=1}^{M}\left(\frac{K_{sr_i}+1}{\bar{\xi}_{sr_i}e^{K_{sr_i}}}+\frac{1}{\bar{\gamma}_{r_id}}\right)\gamma^{M+1} \tag{36}$$

5. Numericale

In this section, analytical and Monte-Carlo simulation results are presented. Since the channel are i.n.d, we set different means for different S-R_i/R_i-D links. In the Rician fading channel, the Rician factor K_{ab} is uniformly distributed in [2,3] and the mean $\bar{\gamma}_{ab}$ of NLOS components are uniformly distributed in [0,1]. The LOS components are derived for a given value of K_{ab} and $\bar{\gamma}_{ab}$. The number of relay nodes is set to 2, 4, 5 and 6.

Fig. 2, Fig. 3 and Fig. 4 show the lower bound of outage probability of repetition-based AF relaying over asymmetric channel I, asymmetric channel II and a comparison among the different fading channels. Since the analytical outage probability are derived based on high SNR assumption, analytical results converge with Monte-Carlo simulation results at high SNR value. From Fig. 2 and Fig. 3, it is clear that the diversity of repetition-based AF relaying increases with the number of relay nodes.

From Fig. 4, it is clear that the outage performance over Rician fading channel outperforms all other fading scenarios due to the presence of LOS signal. On the other hand, due to the absence of LOS signals, Rayleigh fading channel has poorer outage performance than all other fading scenarios. When the outage performance is compared between two different asymmetric channels, asymmetric channel I provides better outage performance than the asymmetric channel II. It is because of S-R link experience LOS signal in asymmetric channel I, so, there is less chance to amplify the noise by relay nodes. However, for the asymmetric channel II, S-R is a NLOS situation, there is more chance to amplify the noise by relay nodes and send it to the destination.

Fig. 5, Fig. 6 and Fig. 7 show the lower bound of outage probability of opportunistic AF relaying over asymmetric channel I, asymmetric channel II and a comparison among the different fading channels. As similar as repetition-based relaying, analytical outage performance converges with Monte-Carlo simulation results at high SNR values. In opportunistic relaying, the performance as well as the diversity increase with the number of relay nodes. When the outage performance is compared among the fading channel, opportunistic relaying shows the same characteristic as repetition based relaying. Without providing any extra simulation, it is easily concluded that opportunistic AF relaying provides better outage performance than the repetition-based AF relaying.

6. Conclusions

This work investigates the outage performance of repetition-based and opportunistic AF relaying over two different asymmetric fading channel. The lower bound of outage probability is derived for high SNR regime and validated through the Monte-Carlo simulation studies. It is observed that asymmetric channel I has better outage performance than that of asymmetric channel II for both the repetition-based and opportunistic AF relaying, and opportunistic AF relaying provides better outage performance than the repetition-based AF relaying.

7. Acknowledgments

The authors would like to thank the European IST-FP7 WHERE project for support of this work.

8. References

Bletsas, A., Shin, H. and Win, M. Z. (2007). Cooperative communication with outage optimal opportunistic relaying, *IEEE Transactions on Wireless Communications* 6: 3450–3459.

Hwang, K.-S., Ko, Y.-C. and Alouini, M.-S. (2007). Outage probability of cooperative diversity systems with opportunistic relaying based on decode-and-forwards, *IEEE Transactions on Wireless Communications* 7: 5100–5106.

Katz, M. and Shamai, S. (2009). Relaying protocols for two colocated users, *IEEE Transactions on Information Theory* 52: 2329 – 2344.

Krikidis, I. and Thompson, J. (2008). Amplify-and-Forword with partial realy selection, *IEEE Communications Letters* 12: 235–237.

Laneman, J. N., Tse, D. N. C. and Wornell, G. W. (2004). Cooperative diversity in wireless networks: Efficient protocols and outage behavior, *IEEE Transactions of Information Theory* 50: 3062–3080.

Liu, K. J. R., Sadek, A. K., Su, W. and Kwasinski, A. (2009). *Cooperative Communications and Networking*, Canbridge.

Michalopoulos, D. and Karagiannidis, G. (2008). Performance analysis of single relay selection in Rayleigh fading, *IEEE Transactions on Wireless Communications* 7(10): 3718–3724.

Nosratinia, A., Hunter, T. E. and Hedayat, A. (2004). Cooperative communication in wireless networks, *IEEE Communications Magazine* 42: 74–80.

Paulraj, A., Gore, D., Nabar, R. and Bolcskei, H. (2004). An overview of mimo communications - a key to gigabit wireless, *Proceedings of the IEEE* 92(2): 198–218.

Savazzi, S. and Spagnolini, U. (2008). Cooperative fading regions for decode and forward relaying, *IEEE Transactions on Information Theory* 54(11): 4908–4924.

Suraweera, H., Karagiannidis, G. and Smith, P. (2009). Performance analysis of the dualhop asymmetric fading channel, *IEEE Transactions on Wireless Communications Letters* 8: 2783–2788.

Suraweera, H., Louie, R., Li, Y., Karagiannidis, G. and Vucetic, B. (2009). Two hop amplify-and-forward transmission in mixed Rayleigh and Rician fading channels, *IEEE Communications Letters* 13(4): 227–229.

Vicario, J., Bel, A., Lopez-Salcedo, J. and Seco, G. (2009). Opportunistic relay selection with outdated csi: outage probability and diversity analysis, *IEEE Transactions on Wireless Communications* 8(6): 2872–2876.

Xu, F., Lau, F. C. M., Zhou, Q. F. and You, D. W. (2009). Outage peformance of cooperative communication systems using opportunistic relaying and selection combining receiver, *IEEE Singal Processing Letters* 16: 113–116.

Zhao, Y., Adve, R. and Lim, T. (2007). Improving amplify-and-forward relay networks: optimal power allocation versus selection, *IEEE Transactions on Wireless Communications* 6(8): 3114–3123.

Zhao, Y., Adve, R. and Lim, T. J. (2005). Outage probability at arbitrary SNR with cooperative diversity, *IEEE Communications Letters* 9: 700–703.

Zhao, Y., Adve, R. and Lim, T. J. (2006). Symbol error rate of selection Amplify-and-Forward relay systems, *IEEE Communications Letters* 10: 757–759.

Zhu, Y., Xin, Y. and Kam, P.-Y. (2008). Outage probability of Rician fading relay channels, *IEEE Transactions on Vehicular Technology* 57(4): 2648–2652.

Zou, Y., Zheng, B. and Zhu, J. (2009). Outage analysis of opportunistic cooperation over Rayleigh fading channels, *IEEE Transactions on Wireless Communications* 8(6): 3077–3085.

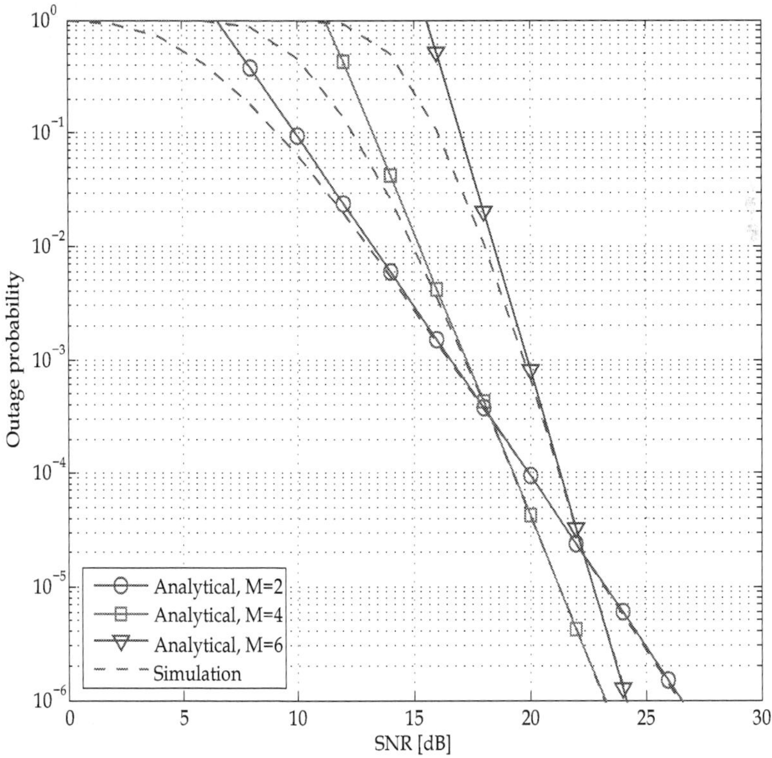

Fig. 2. The outage probability of repetition-based AF relaying over asymmetric channel I. The number of relay node is selected $M = 2$, $M = 4$ and $M = 6$.

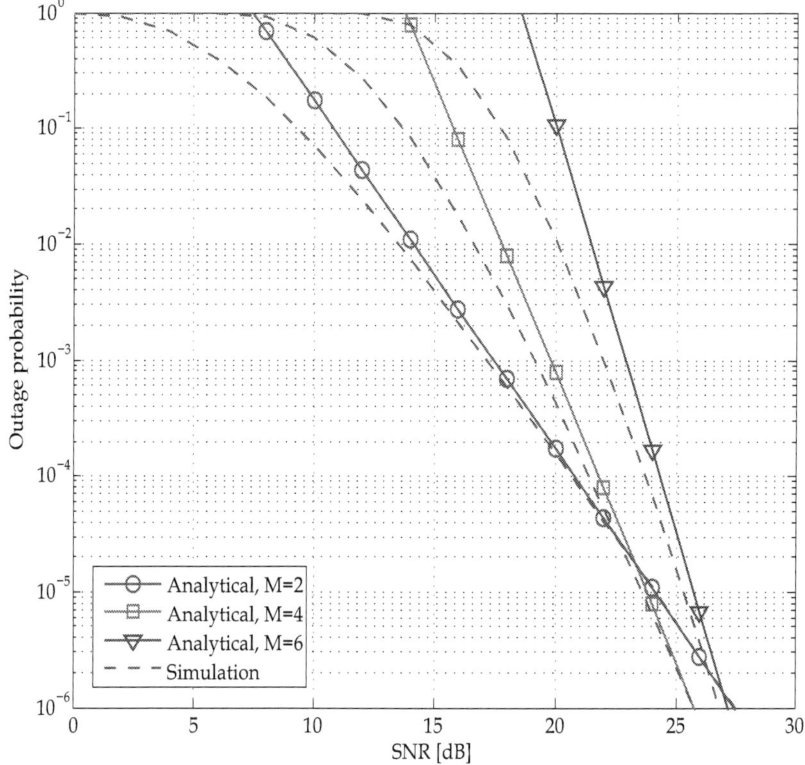

Fig. 3. The outage probability of repetition-based AF relaying over asymmetric channel II. The number of relay node is selected $M = 2$, $M = 4$ and $M = 6$.

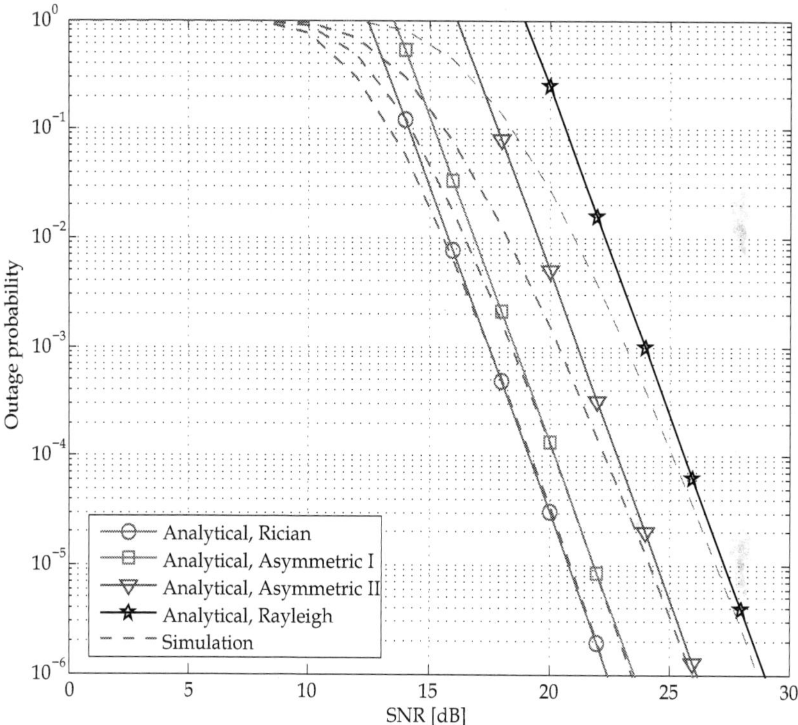

Fig. 4. The comparison of outage probability of repetition-based relaying over different fading channel such as Rician fading, Rayleigh fading, asymmetric channel I and asymmetric channel II. The number of relay nodes is of $M = 5$.

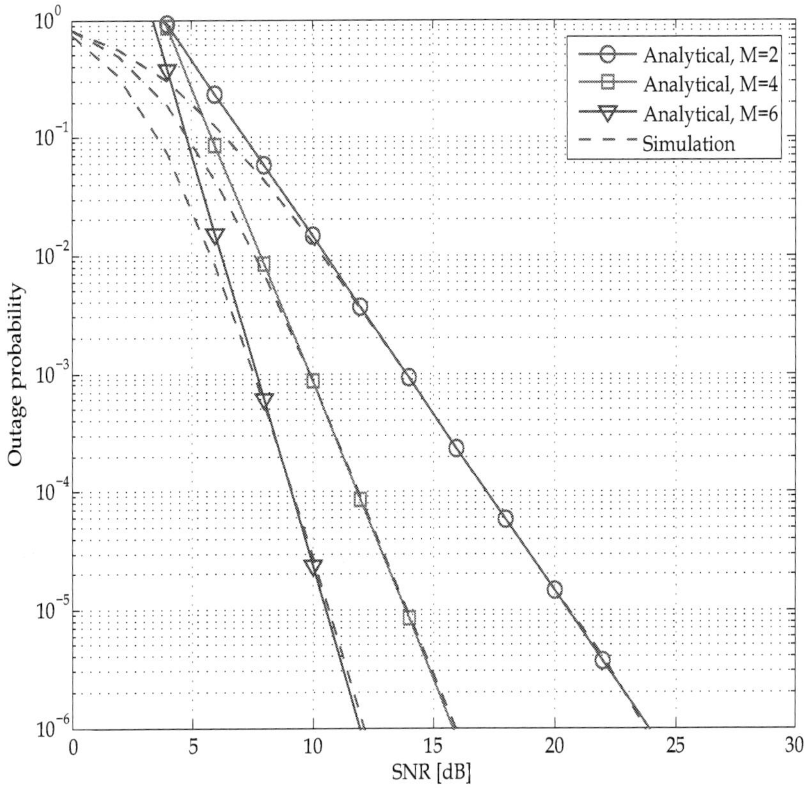

Fig. 5. The outage probability of opportunistic AF relaying over asymmetric channel I. The number of relay node is selected $M = 2$, $M = 4$ and $M = 6$.

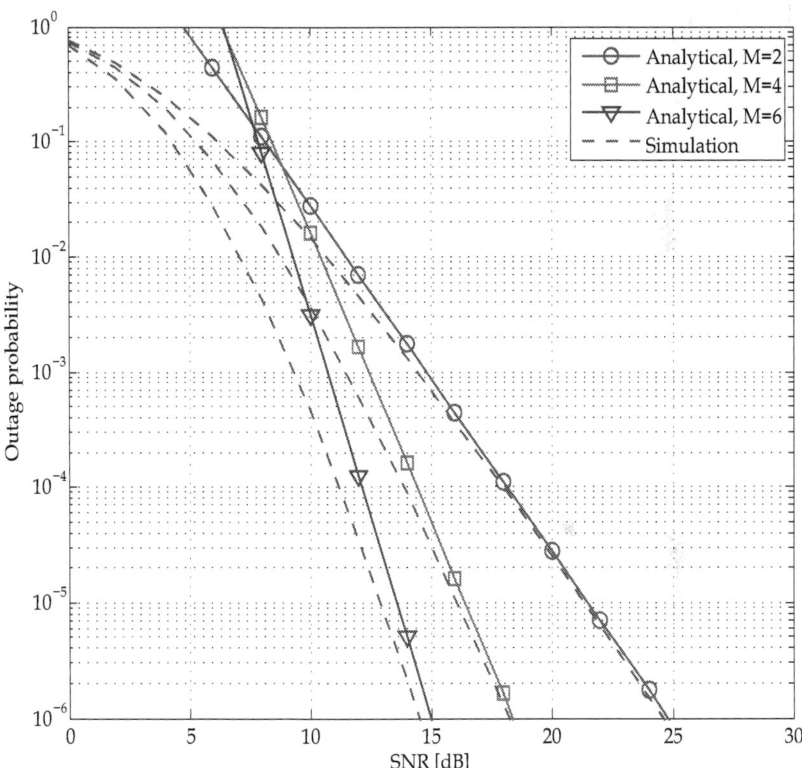

Fig. 6. The outage probability of opportunistic AF relaying over asymmetric channel II. The number of relay node is selected $M = 2$, $M = 4$ and $M = 6$.

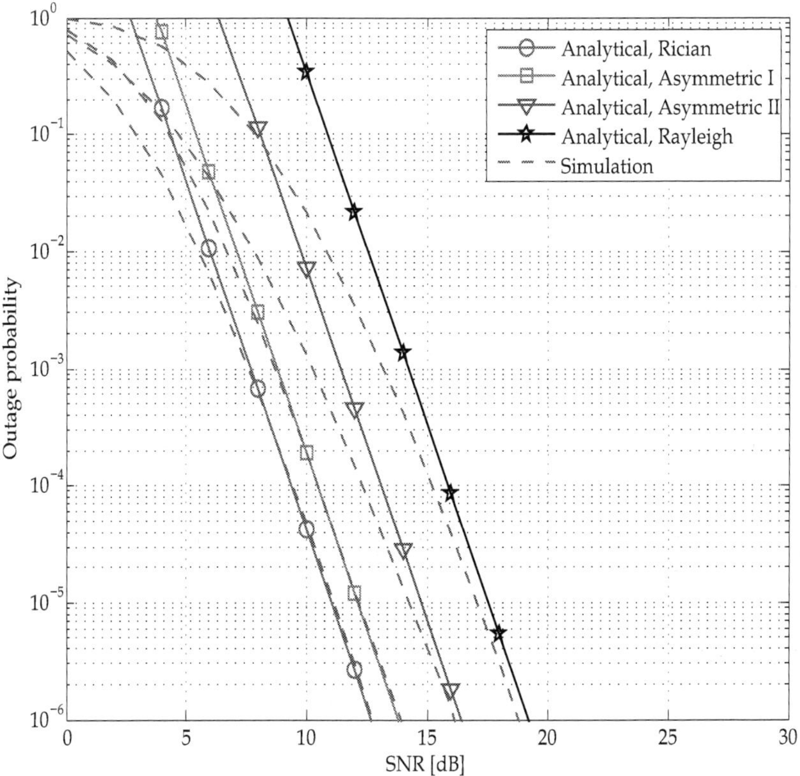

Fig. 7. The comparison of outage probability of opportunistic relaying over different fading channel such as Rician fading, Rayleigh fading, asymmetric channel I and asymmetric channel II. The number of relay nodes is of $M = 5$.

12

Indoor Radio Network Optimization

Lajos Nagy
Department of Broadband Communications and Electromagnetic Theory
Budapest University of Technology and Economics
Hungary

1. Introduction

The new focus of wireless communication is is shifting from voice to multimedia services. User requirements are moving from underlying technology to the simply need reliable and cost effective communication systems that can support anytime, anywhere, any device. The most important trends in global mobile data traffic forecast are:

Globally, mobile data traffic will double every year through 2014, increasing 39 times between 2009 and 2014.,
Almost 66 percent of the world's mobile data traffic will be video by 2014. (Cisco, 2010)

While a significant amount of traffic will migrate from mobile to fixed networks, a much greater amount of traffic will migrate from fixed to mobile networks. In many countries mobile operators are offering mobile broadband services at prices and speeds comparable to fixed broadband. Though there are often data caps on mobile broadband services that are lower than those of fixed broadband, some consumers are opting to forgo their fixed lines in favor of mobile.

There is a growing interest in providing and improving radio coverage for mobile phones, short range radios and WLANs inside buildings. The need of such coverage appears mainly in office buildings, shopping malls, train stations where the subscriber density is very high. The cost of cellular systems and also the one of indoor wireless systems depend highly on the number of base stations required to achieve the desired coverage for a given level of field strength. (Murch 1996)

The other promising technique is the Hybrid Fiber Radio (HFR)-WLAN which is combines the distribution and radio network. The advantages of using analogue optical networks for delivering radio signals from a central location to many remote antenna sites have long been researched and by using the high bandwidth, low loss characteristics of optical fiber, all high frequency and signal processing can be performed centrally and transported over the optical network directly at the carrier frequency. The remote site simplicity makes possible the network cheap and simple, requiring only optoelectronic conversion (laser diodes and photo-detectors), filtering and amplification. Such Remote Units (RU) would also be cheap, small, lightweight, and easy to install with low power consumption.

The design objectives can list in the priority order as RF performance, cost, specific customer requests, ease of installation and ease of maintenance. The first two of them are close related to the optimization procedure introduced and can take into account at the design phase of the radio network.

There are already numerous optimization methods published which can be applied to the optimal design of such indoor networks(Wu 2007, Adickes 2002, Portilla-Figueras 2009, Pujji 2009). The recently published methods use any heuristic technique for finding the optimal Access Point (AP) or RU positions. Common drawback of the methods are the slow convergence in a complex environment like the indoor one because all of the methods are using the global search space i.e. the places for AP-s are searched globally.

This chapter presents approaches in optimizing the indoor radio coverage using multiple access points for indoor environments. First the conventional Simple Genetic Algorithm (SGA) is introduced and used to determine the optimal access point positions to achieve optimum coverage. Next to overcome the disadvantage of SGA two optimization methods are applied Divided Rectangles (DIRECT) global optimization technique and a new hierarchic optimization method is introduced and comparisons are made for the methods deployed.

The main advantage of the proposed method is the reduction of the search space by using two step procedure starting with simple radio propagation method based AP position estimation and thereafter heuristic search using Motley Keenan radio propagation method with heuristic search.

2. Hybrid fiber radio architecture

Microwave radio-frequency transport over fibre, is an already widelly used approach which allows the radio functionality of several Base Stations (BS) to be integrated in a centralised headend unit (Schuh, 1999).

Moreover, it offers fixed and mobile wireless broadband access with a radio-independent fibre access network. Different radio feeder concepts such as Intermediate Frequency (IF) over fibre with electrical frequency conversion at the RAU or direct Radio Frequency (RF) transport are possible.

Few existing Hybrid Fiber Radio interfaces are

DECT - narrowband access for indoor multi-cell cordless telephony, with indoor range from 20 up to 50 metres, and for outdoor Wireless Local Loop (WLL) with a radio range up to a few kilometres.

GSM cellular mobile system provides narrowband access for speech and data services. Typical indoor DCS-1800 cell radius is from about 10 to 50 m and outdoor cell radius for GSM-900/DCS-1800 vary often between 50 to 1000 m.

W-LANs (IEEE 802.11) operate in 80 MHz of spectrum using the 2.4 GHz ISM band, giving indoor access originally designed to high data rates, up to 2 Mbit/s, with coverage areas up to 250 m.

UMTS will operate at ~2 GHz with up to 60 MHz of spectrum. It can provide features like 2nd generation mobile systems but will also offer multimedia services like video telephony, up to 2 Mbit/s for low mobility. Supported cell sizes for indoor applications are up to ~100 metres, and for outdoor applications cell size can be up to a few tens of kilometres (suburban areas), by supporting different mobility features. UMTS will be a public operated system.

One possible application of the HFR network is using analog optical links to transmit modulated RF signals. It serves to transmit the RF signals down- and uplink, i.e. to and from central units (CU) to base stations (BS) called also radio ports. Basic design is shown in Fig. 1, using wavelength duplex fiber star (T1) and fiber bus (T2) topology. This technique is the mostly used one in cellular HFR networks. [1,6]

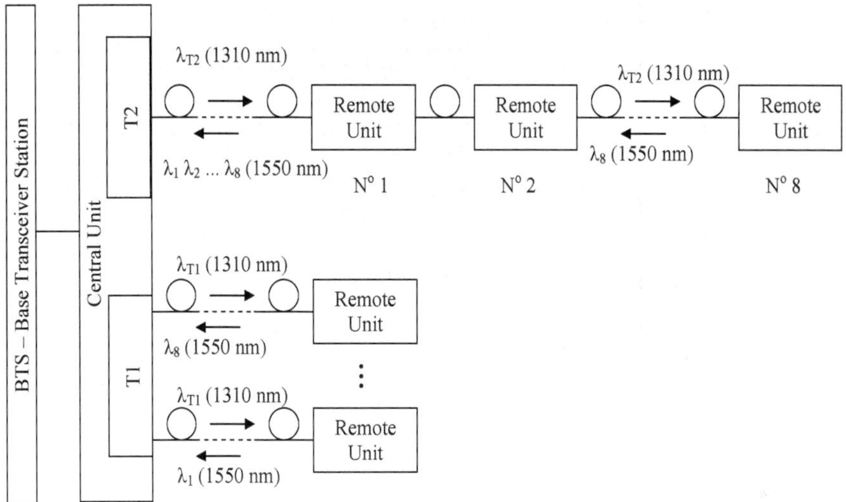

Fig. 1. HFR cellular architecture using one fiber star (T1) and one fiber bus (T2) topology

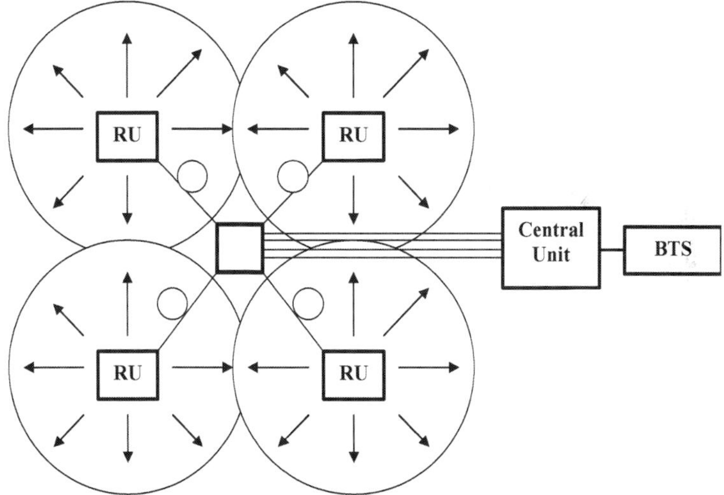

Fig. 2. HFR cellular architecture with Remote Units and Central Units

The other technique uses direct modulation of laser diode and more suitable for WLAN applications. The Fig. 3. shows the combination of IEEE 802.11a and 11.g WLAN services using HFR technology.

The main parts of the HFR network in Fig. 3. are the Local Transceiver Unit with circulator, electro-optical converters and the Remote Unit with electro-optical converters, antennas. The IEEE 802.11a and 11.g WLAN access points are used in unchanged form accessing to the wired internet network.

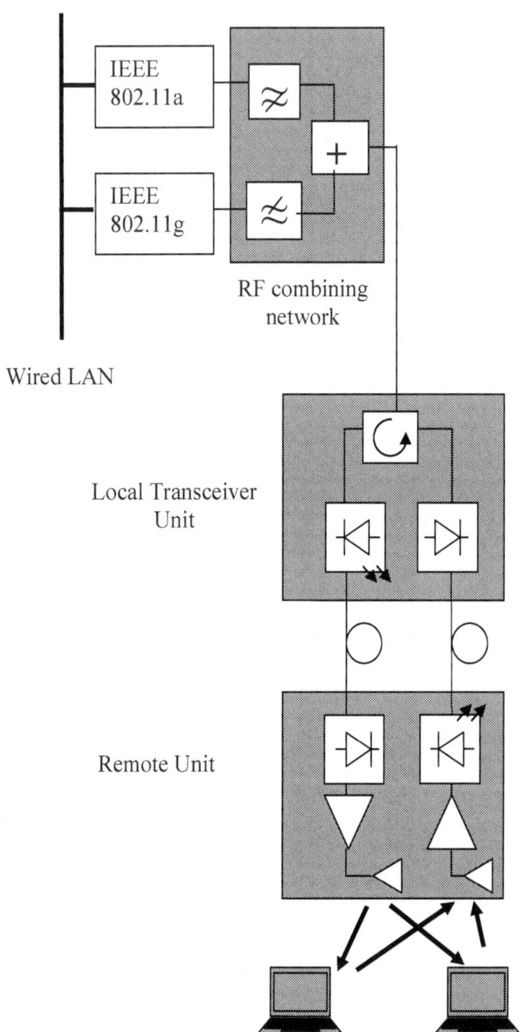

Fig. 3. HFR WLAN architecture

The indoor radio coverage of HFR network is basically determined by the RU positions. There are many factors on choosing these positions such as RF performance, cost, specific customer requests, ease of installation, ease of maintenance, but the optimal radio coverage achievable by a minimum number of the RUs is the most important one.

The next parts introduces the radio propagation modeling used in indoor environment and the optimization method for determining optimum RU positions for best radio coverage which is usually the main aim of the wireless design but the optimization method proposed can be easily amended of further objectives.

3. The indoor radiowave propagation model and the building database

In our article the Motley-Keenan (Keenan & Motley, 1990) model was used to analyze indoor wave propagation. This empirical type prediction model based on considering the influence of walls, ceilings and floors on the propagation through disparate terms in the expression of the path loss.

The overall path loss according to this model can be written as

$$L = L_F + L_a \tag{1}$$

where L_F is the free space path loss and L_a is an additional loss expressed as

$$L_a = L_c + \sum_{i=1}^{I} k_{wi} L_{wi} + \sum_{j=1}^{J} k_{fj} L_{fj} \tag{2}$$

where L_c is an empirical constant term, k_{wi} is the number of penetrated i type walls, k_{fj} is the number of penetrated floors and ceilings of type j, I is the number of wall types and J is the number of floor and ceiling types.

For the analyzed receiver position, the numbers k_i and k_j have to be determined through the number of floors and walls along the path between the transmitter and the receiver antennas. In the original paper (Keenan & Motley, 1990) only one type of walls and floors were considered, in order for the model to be more precise a classification of the walls and floors is important. A concrete wall for example could present very varying penetration losses depending on whether it has or not metallic reinforcement.

It is also important to state that the loss expressed in (Eq. 2) is not a physical one, but rather model coefficients, that were optimized from measurement data. Constant L_c is the result of the linear regression algorithm applied on measured wall and floor losses. This constant is a good indicator of the loss, because it includes other effects also, for example the effect of furniture.

For the considered office type building, the values for the regression parameters have been found. (Table 1.)

The Motley-Keenan model regression parameters have been determined using Ray Launching deterministic radiowave propagation model. These calculations were made for the office-type building floor of the Department of Broadband Infocommunication and Electromagnetic Theory at Budapest University of Technology and Economics (Fig. 4.). The frequency was chosen to 2450 MHz with a $\lambda/2$ transmitter dipole antenna mounted on the 3m height ceiling at the center of the floor.

The receiver antenna has been applied to evaluate the signal strength at (80x5)x(22x5)=44000 different locations in the plane of the receiver. At each location the received signal strength was obtained by RL method using ray emission in a resolution of 1^0. A ray is followed until a number of 8 reflections are reached and the receiver resolution in pixels has an area of 0.2*0.2 m². The receiver plane was chosen at the height of 1.2 m.

The wall construction is shown on Fig. 4. made of primarily brick and concrete with concrete ceiling and floor, the doors are made of wood. The coefficients of the model have been optimized on the data gathered by the RL simulation session described above.

The floor view and polygonal partitioning is shown on Fig. 5., which is based on the concept described next.

Wall type	Nr. of Layers	Layer widths	Regression parameter [dB]
Brick	1	Brick – 6 cm	4.0
Brick	1	Brick – 10 cm	5.58
Brick	1	Brick – 12 cm	6.69
Brick+ Concrete	3	Brick – 6 cm Concrete – 20 cm Brick – 6 cm	11.8
Brick+ Concrete	3	Brick – 10 cm Concrete – 12 cm Brick – 10 cm	14.8
Brick+ Concrete	3	Brick – 6 cm Concrete – 10 cm Brick – 6 cm	9.3
Brick	1	Brick – 15 cm	8.47
Concrete	1	Concrete – 15 cm	6.56
Concrete	1	Concrete – 20 cm	8
Concrete	3	Concrete – 15 cm Air – 2 cm Concrete – 15 cm	12.47
Glass	3	Glass – 3 mm Air – 10 cm Glass – 3 mm	0
Plasterboard	1	Plasterboard – 5 cm	4.5
Wood	1	Wood – 6 cm	0.92
Wood	1	Wood – 10 cm	0.17

Table 1. The regression parameters

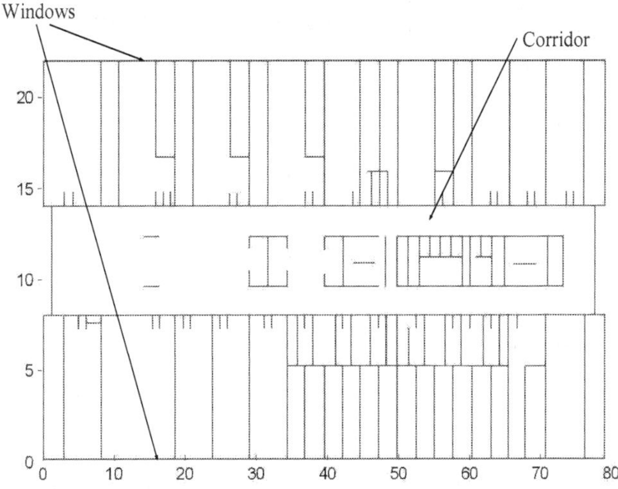

Fig. 4. The building database

Fig. 5. Floor view and polygon data base of V2 building at BUTE

The geometrical description of the indoor scenario is based on the same concept that the walls has to be partitioned to surrounding closed polygons and every such polygons are characterized by its electric material parameters.

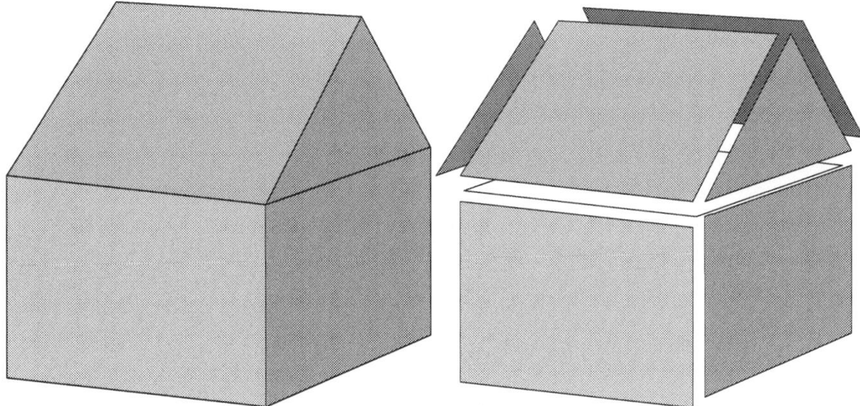

Fig. 6. Polygon representation of building structure

The data base for the ray tracing method in our applications can not contain cut-out surfaces directly, such as windows, doors. Therefore the cut-out surface description is based on surface partitioning of the geometry as can be seen in Fig. 7.

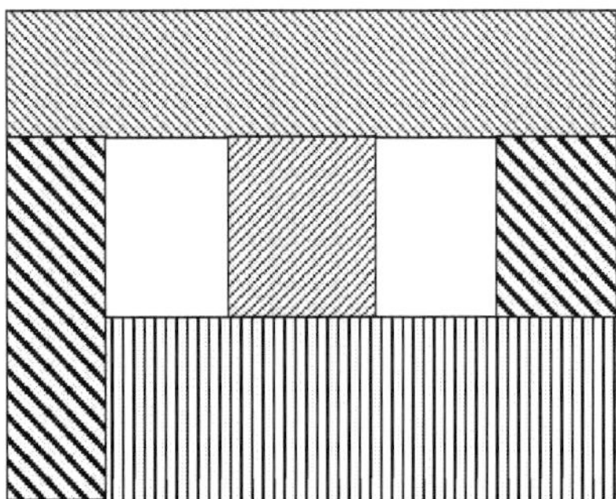

Fig. 7. A possible polygonal partitioning of windowed walls for ray tracing method

4. Optimization methods

There are already numerous optimization methods published which can be applied to the optimal design of such Hybrid Fiber Radio indoor networks (Wu 2007, Adickes 2002, Portilla-Figueras 2009, Pujji 2009). The recently published methods use any heuristic technique for finding the optimal Access Point (AP) or RU positions. Common drawback of the methods are the slow convergence in a complex environment like the indoor one because all of the methods are using the global search space i.e. the places for AP-s are searched globally.

Heuristic search and optimization is an approach for solving complex and large problems that overcomes many shortcomings of traditional (gradient type) optimization techniques. Heuristic optimization techniques are general purpose methods that are very flexible and can be applied to many types of objective functions and constraints. Another advantage of heuristic methods is their simplicity because of its gradient-free nature. Gradient free optimization methods are primarily based on the objective function values and are suitable for problems either with many parameters or with computationally expensive objective functions.

In the paper two global optimization methods the Simple Genetic Algorithm (SGA) and a method using Divided Rectangles (DIRECT) global search algorithm are used with wave propagation solver as can be seen in Fig. 8.

4.1 Optimization method through Simple Genetic Algorithms (SGA)

Genetic Algorithms (GA) are increasingly being applied to complex problems. Genetic Algorithm optimizers are robust, stochastic search methods modeled on the principles and concepts of natural selection. (Nagy 2000, Farkas 2001, Michielssen 1999, Michalewicz 1996) Genetic Algorithms (GA) are increasingly being applied to difficult optimization problems. GA optimizers are robust, stochastic search methods modeled on the principles and concepts of natural selection.

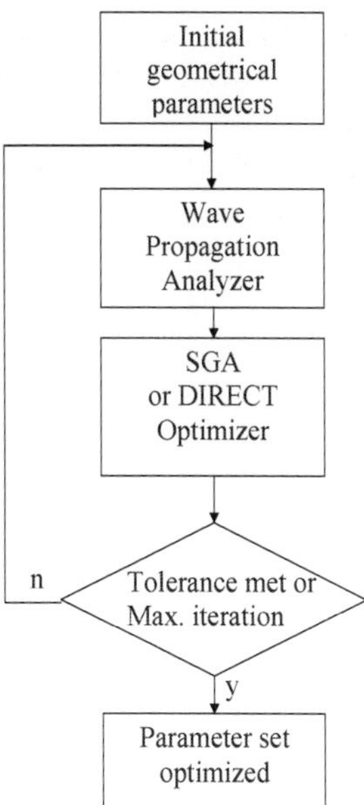

Fig. 8. Diagram of Wave Propagation analyzer and optimizer

If a receiver position that is fully described by N_{par} parameters arranged in a vector $x=\{x_i|\ i=1,...,N_{par}\}$ is considered, then the knowledge of x permits the evaluation of the objective function $f(x)$, which indicates the worth of a design (the area coverage percentage). It is assumed that x_i take on either real or discrete values, and that $f(x)$ needs to be maximized.

The GA does not operate on x but on a discrete representation or chromosome $p=\{g_i|\ i=1,...,N\}$ of x, each parameter x_i being described by a gene g_i. Each gene g_i in turn consists of a set of N_{all}^i all that are selected from a finite alphabet and that together decode a unique x_i.

The GA does not limit themselves to the iterative refinement of a single coded design candidate; instead the simple GA (SGA) simultaneously acts upon a set of candidates or population

$$\overline{p} = \left\{ p(i) \middle| i = 1,...,N_{pop} \right\} \tag{3}$$

where N_{pop} is the population size.

Starting from an initial population $\overline{p}^0$, the SGA iteratively constructs populations $\overline{p}^k, k = 1..N_{gen}$, with N_{gen} denoting the total number of SGA generations. Subsequent generations are constructed by iteratively acting upon $\overline{p}^0$ with a set of genetic operators. The operators that induce the transition $\overline{p}^k \rightarrow \overline{p}^{k+1}$ are guided solely by knowledge of the vector of objective function values

$$f^k = \left\{ f\left(x\left(p^k(i)\right)\right) \middle| i = 1..N_{pop} \right\} \tag{4}$$

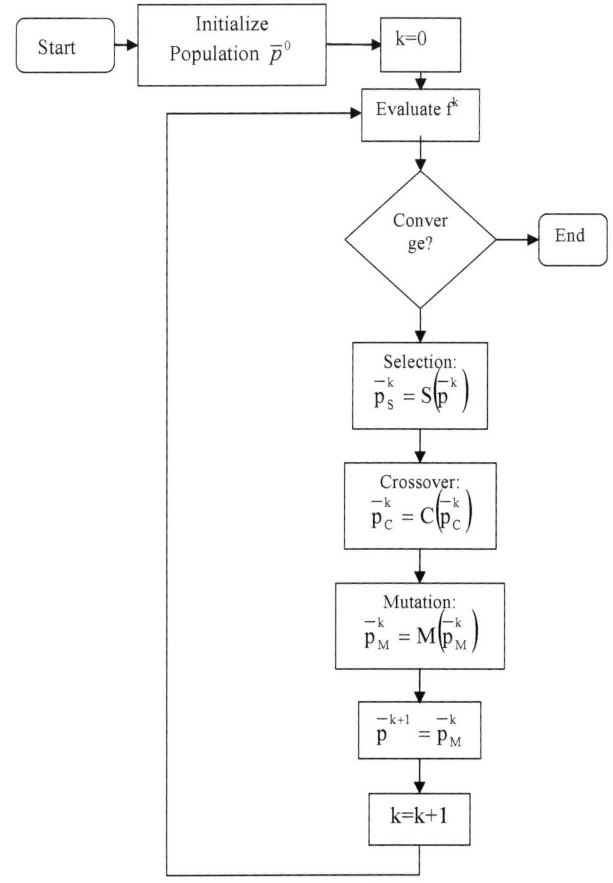

Fig. 9. The flowchart of a simple GA

and induce changes in the genetic makeup of the population leading to a $\bar{p}^{k+1}$ comprising individuals that are, on average better adapted to their environment than those in $\bar{p}^{k}$, i.e., they are characterized by higher objective function values.

This change is effected by three operators mentioned in the introduction: selection (S), crossover (C), and mutation (M).

The selection operator implements the principle of survival of the fittest. Acting on $\bar{p}^{k}$, S produces a new population $\bar{p}_S^k = S\left(\bar{p}^k\right)$ again of size N_{pop} that is, on average, populated by the better-fit individuals present in $\bar{p}^{k}$. Among the many existing schemes tournament selection has been chosen. The crossover operator mimics natural procreation. Specifically, C acts upon the population $\bar{p}_S^k$ by mating its members, thereby creating a new population

$$\bar{p}_C^k = \bigcup_{i=1}^{N_{pop}/2} C\left(ch\left(\bar{p}_S^k\right), ch\left(\bar{p}_S^k\right)\right) \tag{5}$$

where the chromosome crossover operator C selects a random crossover allele a_{Ncross} between the two chromosomes to be crossed upon which it acts with probability P_{cross}.

The mutation operator generates a new population of size by introducing small random changes into $\overline{p}_C^k$. The action of M can be represented in operator form as

$$\overline{p}_M^k = \bigcup_{i=1}^{N_{pop}} M\left(\overline{p}_C^k(i)\right) \tag{6}$$

The cost function of the optimization procedure has been the coverage percentage of the points for which the received power is greater than a given level.

$$c\left(P_{rec}\right) = \frac{\text{Number of points } (P_{thresh.} < P_{rec})}{\text{Total number of test points}} \tag{7}$$

The number of test points to evaluate the cost function above was 12000 on the floor level, and the P_{thresh} level was -70 dBm, respectively.

4.2 DIRECT algorithm

The DIRECT optimization algorithm is a derivative-free global algorithm that yields a deterministic and unique solution (Daniel E. Finkel, 2003). Its attribute of possessing both local and global properties make it ideal for fast convergence. An essential aspect of the DIRECT algorithm is the subdivision of the entire design space into hyper-rectangles or hyper-cubes for multidimensional problems.

The iteration starts by choosing the center of the design space as the starting point. Subsequently, at each iteration step, DIRECT selects and subdivides the set of hyper-cubes that are most likely to produce the lowest objective function. This estimation is based on Lipschitzian optimization method. Basically for one dimension a function is called Lipschitz continuous on domain R with Lipschitz constant α if

$$\left|f(x_1) - f(x_2)\right| \leq \alpha \left|x_1 - x_2\right| \quad x_1, x_2 \in R \tag{8}$$

where

$f(x)$ is the objective function for the optimization problem.

The complementary of the coverage percentage which has to be minimized was chosen as objective function for the DIRECT algorithm.

$$f(x) = 1 - c\left(P_{rec}\right) \tag{9}$$

The Lipschitzian function finds the global minimum point provided the constant α is specified to be greater than the largest rate of change of the objective function within the design space and that the objective function value is continuous. Within DIRECT, all possible values of the Lipschitzian constant α are used with the larger values of α chosen for global optimization (to find the basin of convergence of the optimum) followed by smaller values of α for local optimizations within this basin of convergence. As mentioned above, DIRECT divides the domain into multiple rectangles at each iteration. Thus, the convergence process is greatly sped up and the optimization algorithm achieves both local and global searching properties.

As illustration of subdividing the search region into hyper-rectangles and sampling, two dimensional problem optimization steps are shown in Fig. 10.

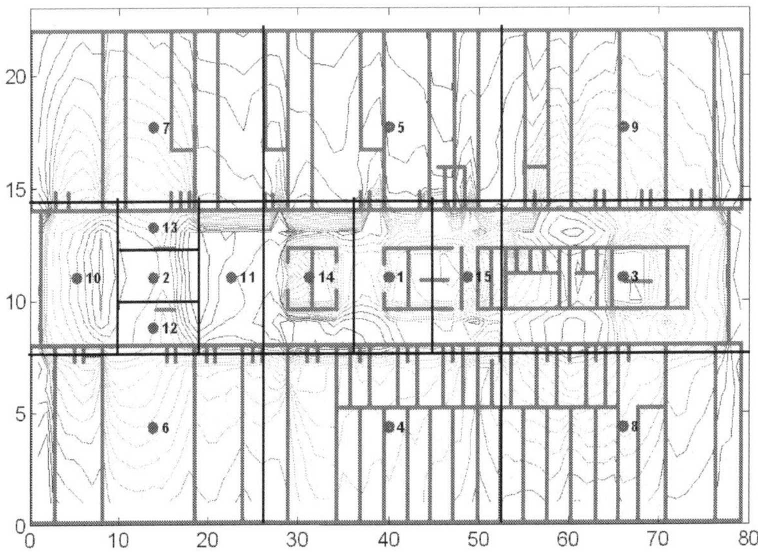

Fig. 10. DIRECT global optimizer search steps

The Algorithm DIRECT is stated as follows.

Algorithm DIRECT
Start point at the center of the user defined area ($0 \leq x \leq 80; 0 \leq y \leq 22$)
while $f_{objective} > f_{limit}$ **and iteration steps< iteration steps**$_{limit}$
        Divide the area of investigation space into three rectangles
        Set the centers of the three rectangles
        Use the Lipschitz constant α to select the rectangle has to be divided
end while

4.3 Hierarchic two level optimization method

The new proposed hierarchic optimization method uses a two level optimization procedure, in which the radio wave propagation models differ. The propagation models are:

indoor power law,

Motley-Keenan, (Motley & Keenan 1990)

The optimization procedure is based on simple GA and starts with simple power law model. At the point of non changing cost function the procedure switches to the more sophisticated model to Motley-Keenan model. In line with model change the mutation and crossover probabilities are decreased also.

A single approach of ITU-R model is used (ITU, 1238), except that the propagation exponent is accounted for explicitly by changing the path loss exponent. The model is assumed to produce the following total path loss model (in decibels)

$$L = 20\log\left(f_c^{[MHz]}\right) + 30\log\left(r^{[m]}\right) - 28 \tag{10}$$

where r is the distance between transmitter and receiver antennas.

The indoor power law model takes only account the distance to predict the received power therefore the first level of optimization procedure ends a coverage picture as can be seen on Fig. 11. for five AP-s. In this way the expensive propagation model take place only at refinement of the AP positions.

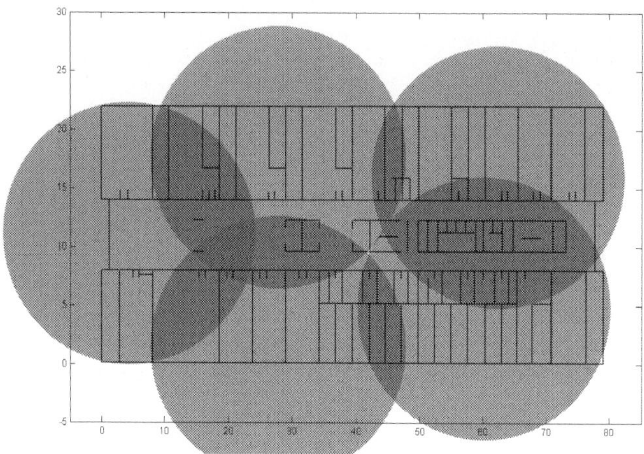

Fig. 11. Access Points positions after the first level optimization

The second optimization step assigns the AP regions based on the previous AP positions, as can be seen on Fig. 12.

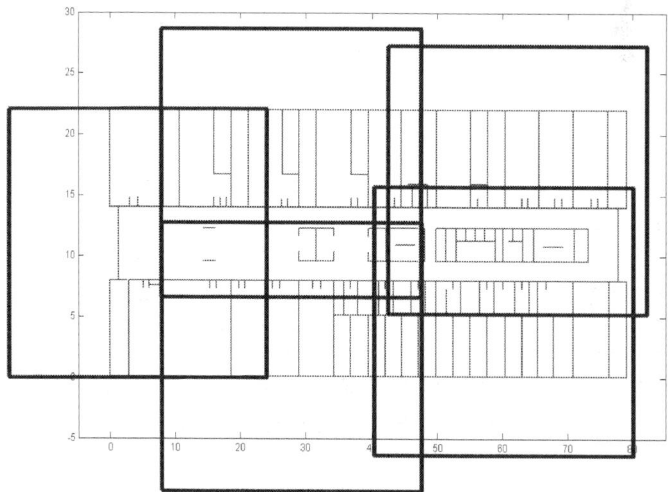

Fig. 12. AP regions for second level optimization

The second optimization step uses the Motley-Keenan model, which regression parameters have been determined using Ray Launching deterministic radiowave propagation model.

The most important innovation of the two steps method is the decrease the search area in the first search period using a homogeneous wave propagation model and to get quick results on candidate areas for access points for the second phase of search which is using genetic algorithm as well.

5. Results

The testing of the SGA optimization has been done with two testing cases at the office building in which first optimizing the coverage for part of the floor area and secondly for the whole level.

The results are shown for population size of 14, crossover probability – 0.12, mutation probability – 0.01, simple roulette wheel selection and simple elitist strategy.

The first scenario is an optimization on AP positions (circles in Fig. 13.) of the half part of the floor. The Fig. 13 shows the original 4 AP positions which were chosen to best coverage in laboratories and the corridor coverage was not an aim. The Fig. 14. shows the optimal AP positions using the cost function of (Eq. 7). The simulated distribution of received power for the two geometries is shown in Fig. 15-16. with the measured results.

To make the measurements we have chosen WLAN APs and the power levels were measured using laptops with external wireless adapter moved on the area of investigation. 90 sampling points in distances of 1 m were chosen on the level and the comparison of Fig. 15. and 16. show a good agreement for the received power distribution.

The most important change in the distributions of optimized and not optimized cases is increased number of points with proper coverage. (Table 2.)

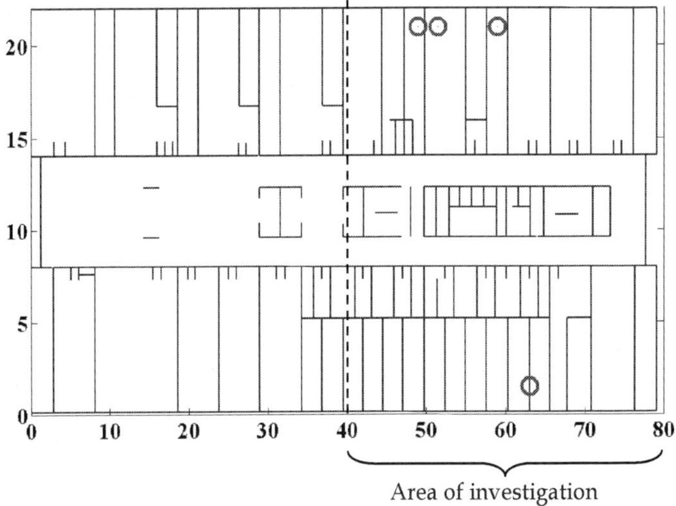

Fig. 13. Original (not optimized) AP positions

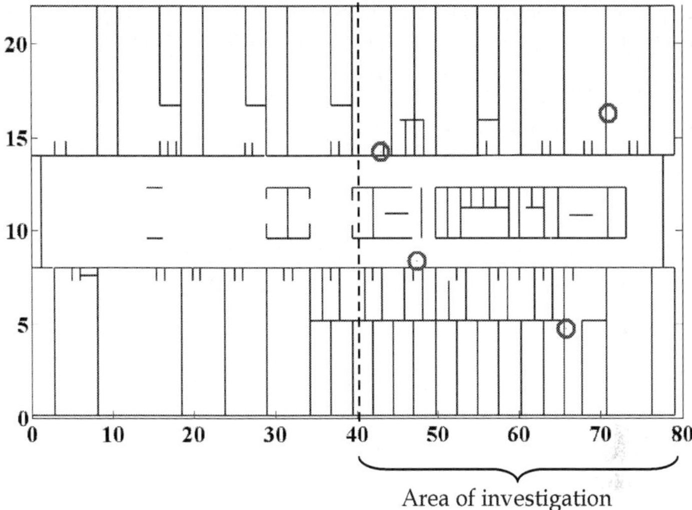

Fig. 14. Optimized AP positions

Configuration	Not optimized	Optimized
Coverage for P_{rec}>-60dBm (simulation)	40%	75%
Coverage for P_{rec}>-60dBm (measurement)	50%	80%

Table 2. Area Coverage for Optimized and not Optimized Case

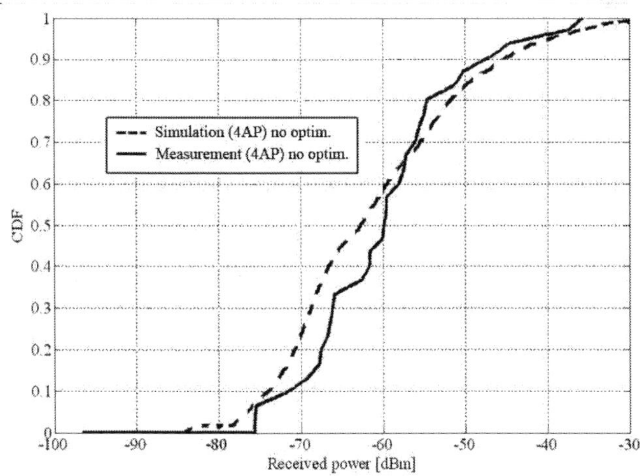

Fig. 15. Cumulative Density Function of received power level (not optimized)

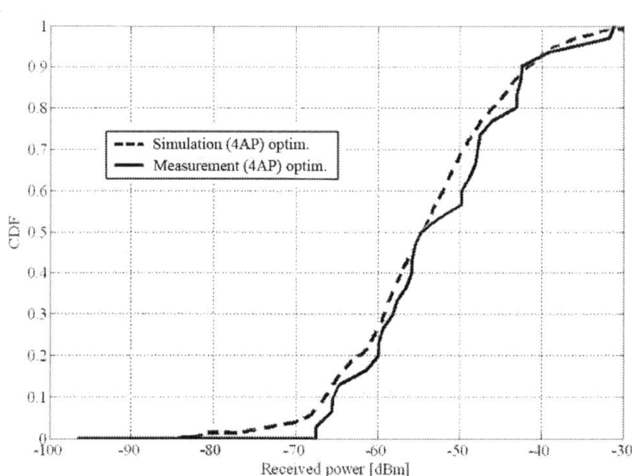

Fig. 16. Cumulative Density Function of received power level (optimized)

The convergence of the Genetic Algorithm can be improved by adjusting the crossover and mutation probability. The Fig. 17. shows the convergence dependence on these parameters for the same generation size.

The Fig. 17. shows a significant dependence of convergence on GA parameters and this results in a 1 to 10 running time ratio. The iteration step means that the number of necessary objective function evaluation can be calculated by multiplying with the population size.

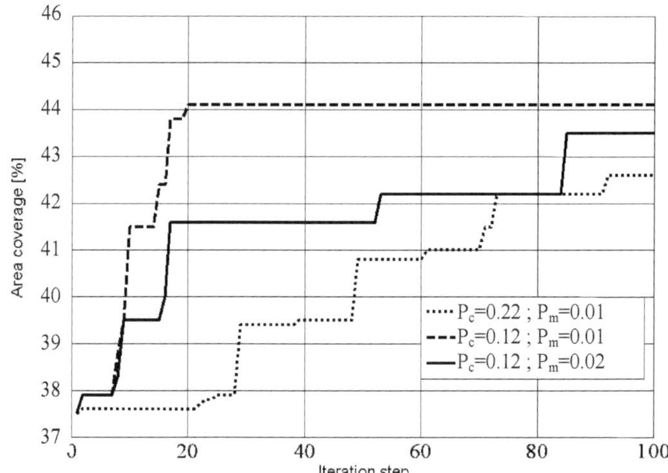

Fig. 17. Genetic Algorithm convergence

The second simulation is on the entire floor level and the aim of the simulation is to compare the necessary number of APs for the same area coverage.

The Fig. 18. shows plausible positions of APs and the Fig. 19. the optimized ones.

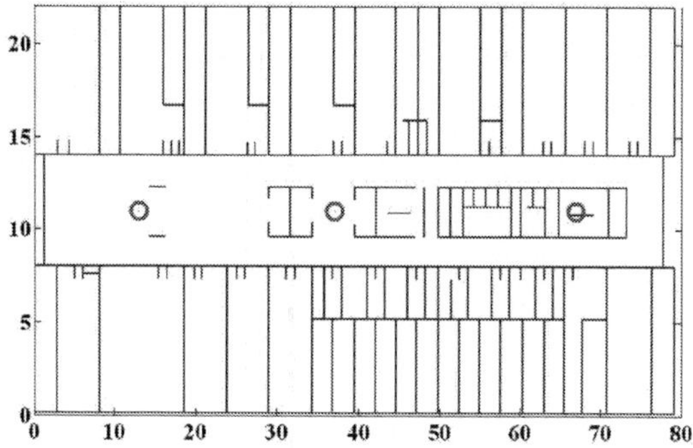

Fig. 18. Plausible AP positions

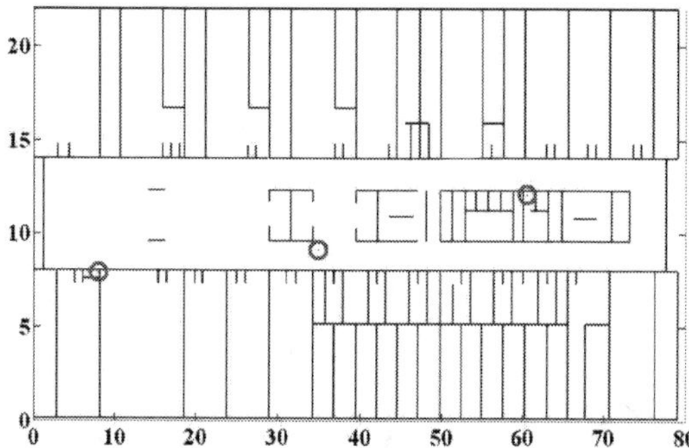

Fig. 19. Optimized AP positions

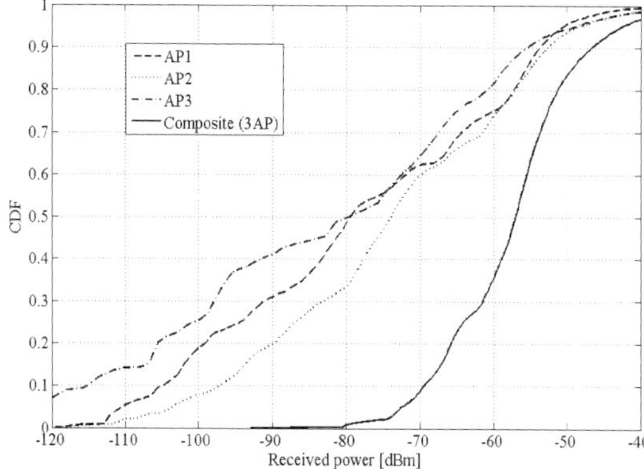

Fig. 20. Independent and composite CDF (optimized AP positions)

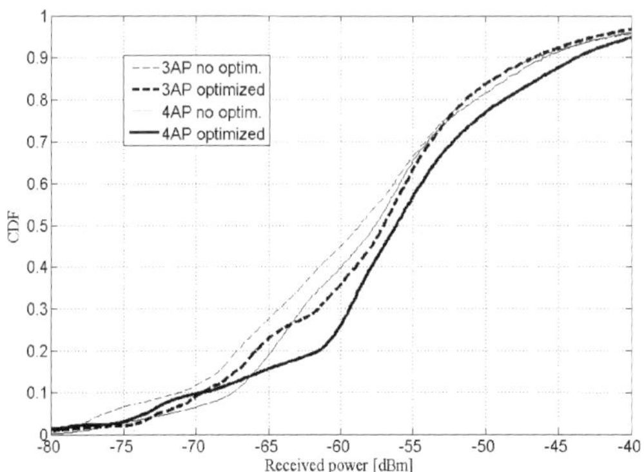

Fig. 21. Optimized and not optimized CDF using 3 and 4 APs

The Fig. 21. and Table 3 summarizes the importance of RU position of HFR. With the proper choice of the placement the optimized 3 AP network configuration results nearly the same coverage as the configuration 6 AP with APs installed in plausible positions.

Configuration	3AP	4AP	6AP
Coverage (not optimized)	55%	60%	66%
Coverage (optimized)	65%	75%	87%

Table 3. Area coverage for optimized and not optimized cases

These results (Table 3.) illustrate and justify well the importance of Remote Unit or Access Point installation positions in HFR networks in order to maximize the wireless coverage. Using the mentioned optimization procedure the network cost can be significantly reduced and the optical distribution network also can be simplified.

As we have shown the SGA is a powerful global optimization tool to improve the indoor coverage for HFR and other mobile radio systems. The main drawback of the method is the ambiguous convergence and therefore its application needs experience of the user. The DIRECT global optimization algorithm is a derivative-free global algorithm that yields a deterministic and unique solution. In the next simulation results will be shown using DIRECT for the same indoor AP position optimization problem. We are comparing DIRECT to SGA and the main point of comparison is the number of evaluation of objective function.

It is worth to investigate the candidate points for the AP position by the DIRECT algorithm. The simplest case is analyzed for one AP network and the investigated and best candidate points are shown in accordance with the objective function the area of coverage % in Fig. 24. The objective function was only evaluated 1 by 1 m resolution. It is well appreciable the testing of the attractive AP positions with high area coverage property.

Next the convergence of SGA and DIRECT will be compared in Fig. 25, 26 and 27. It can be point out that the DIRECT algorithm behaves well for 1 or 2 AP optimization problems (i.e. for 2 and 4 dimensional optimizations) but the convergence rate achieve is far below the SGA for 3 AP problem. Similar behavior can be experienced for higher dimensional optimization problems. Based on this investigations DIRECT algorithm can be proposed for low dimensional cases till 4 dimensions but the theoretically guaranteed fast and unique solution of global problem has to analyzed further.

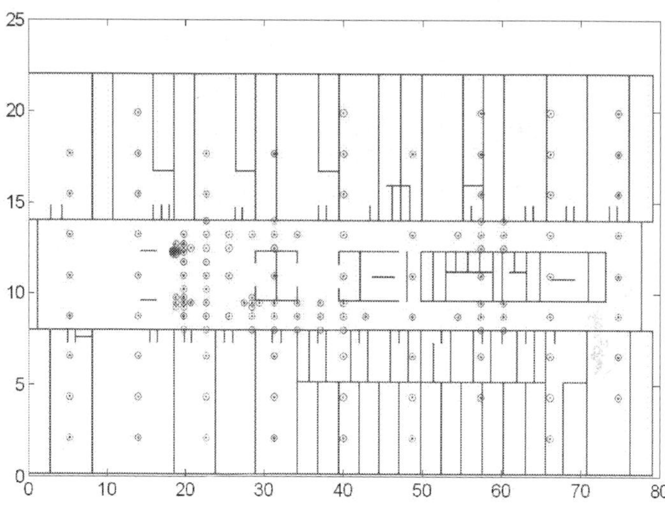

Fig. 22. Candidate points for AP position (after 12, 24, 36…iterations, DIRECT)

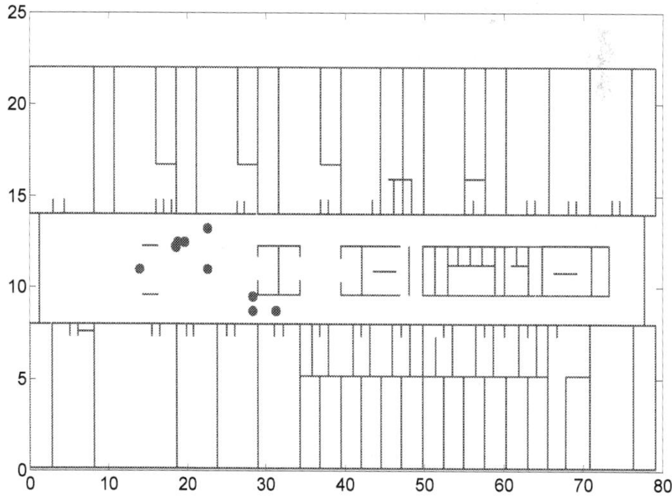

Fig. 23. Best candidate point for AP position (after 12, 24, 36…iterations, DIRECT)

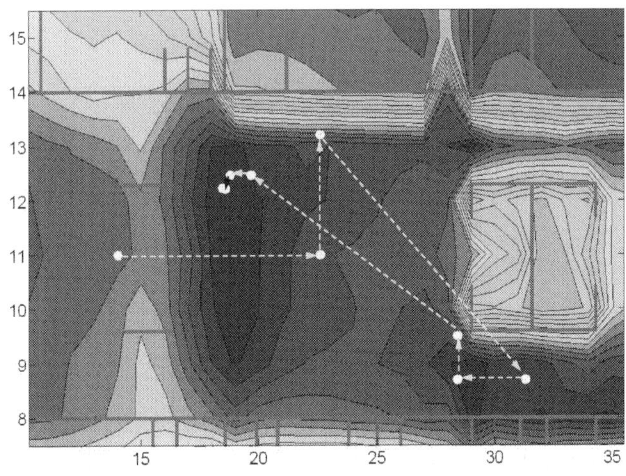

Fig. 24. Best candidate points for AP position (Area of coverage % is also shown)

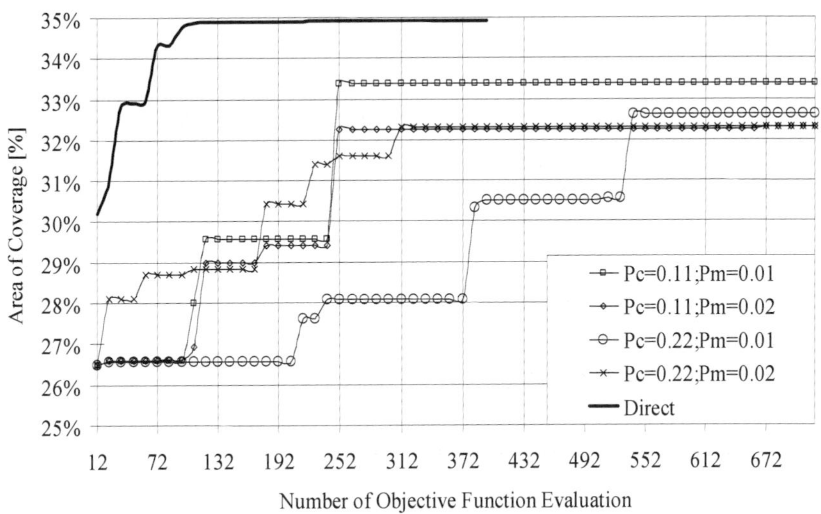

Fig. 25. Convergence of SGA and DIRECT for 1 Access Point

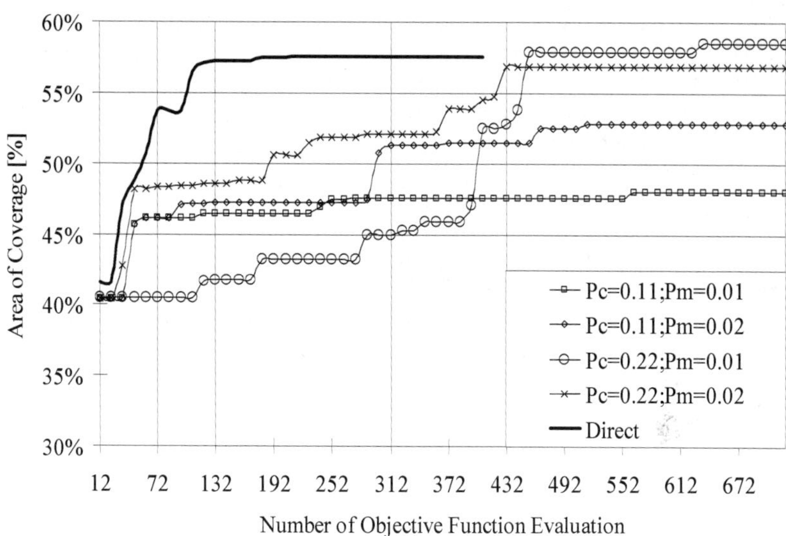

Fig. 26. Convergence of SGA and DIRECT for 2 Access Points

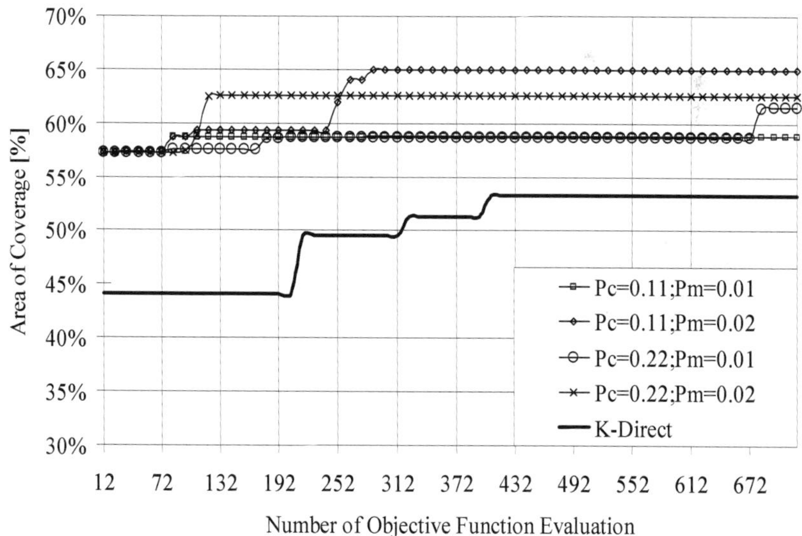

Fig. 27. Convergence of SGA and DIRECT for 3 Access Points

The next part shows the comparisons of SGA and the proposed hierarchic two steps optimization method, first the convergence of the simple Genetic Algorithm for different population sizes (Fig. 28.). Now we investigate 6 AP optimization cases in order to validate the two step method. As we have seen problems of dimensions above 4 can not be analyzed with DIRECT and therefore for comparison this 12 dimensional problem will be investigated. First the GA optimization is shown after performing the AP search by using power law path loss model i.e. the hierarchic approach. Finally the optimization results are analyzed.

Fig. 28 presents effect of values population size, crossover (C) and mutation (M) probability on convergence for 6 APs placement single GA optimization in our simulations.

The population size extension effect a better convergence (Figure 28) but the calculation time increase polynomial.

The most important observations are that the crossover and mutation probabilities have optimal values in this case for the geometry investigated these values are P_C=0.22 and P_M=0.01. (Fig. 28-29)

Next the proposed hierarchic optimization model is shown after performing the AP search by using power law path loss model. The limitation of the optimization areas for the AP positions results in much better convergence for each configuration (Fig. 30-31).

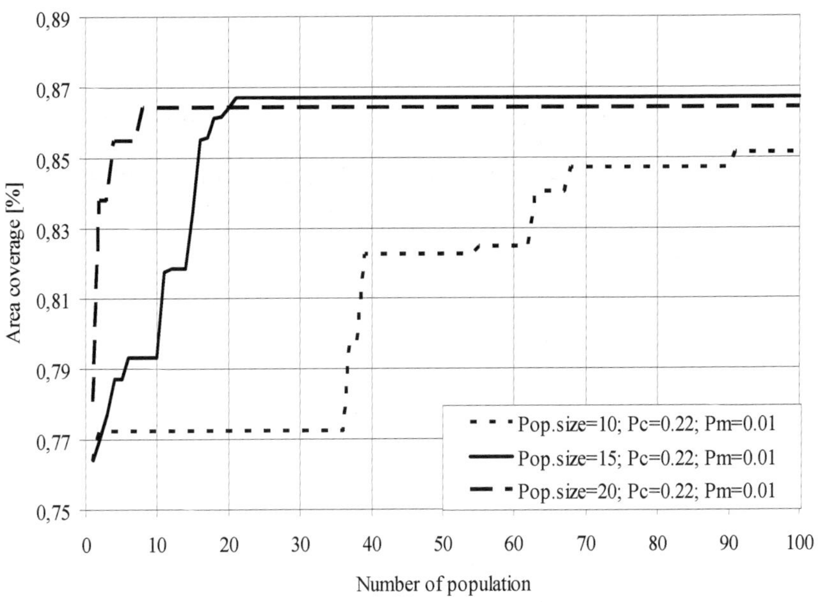

Fig. 28. Genetic Algorithm convergence (6AP whole floor)

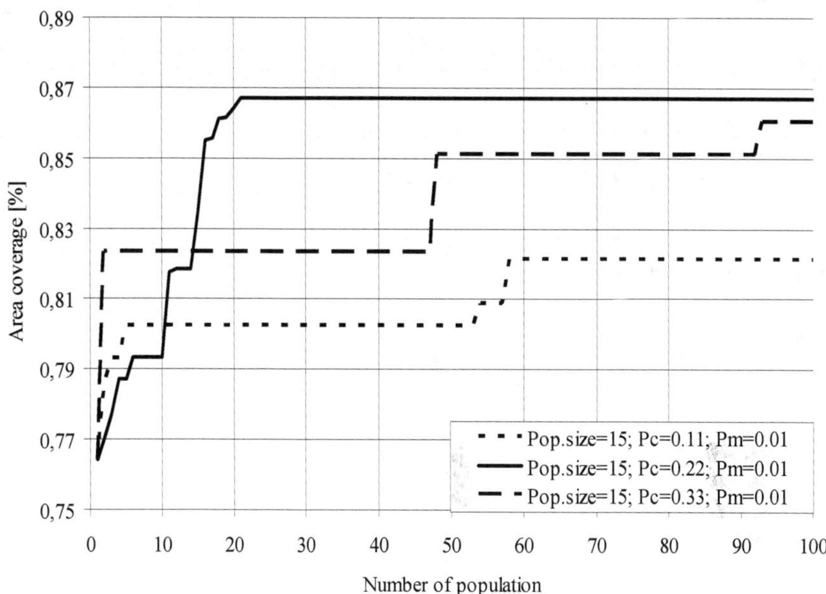

Fig. 29. Genetic Algorithm convergence (6AP whole floor)

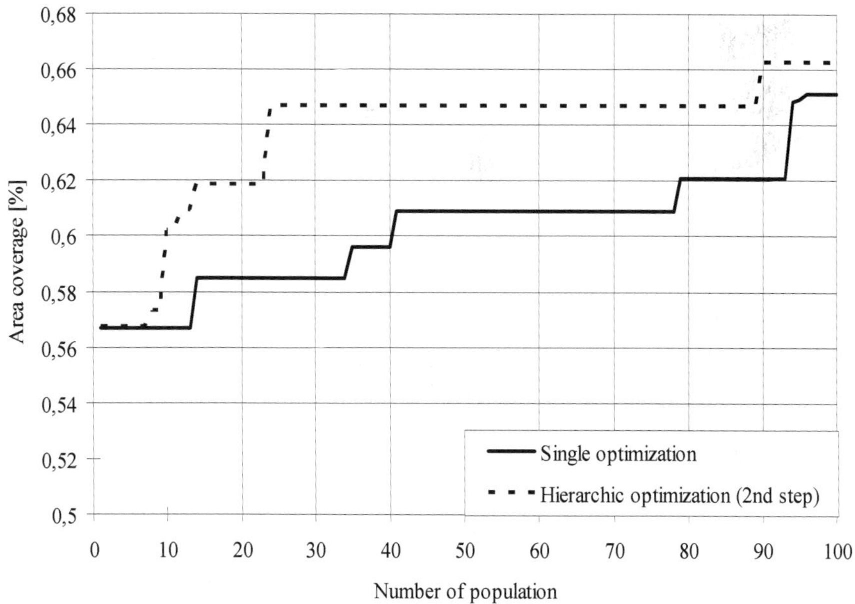

Fig. 30. Genetic Algorithm convergence (3AP whole floor)

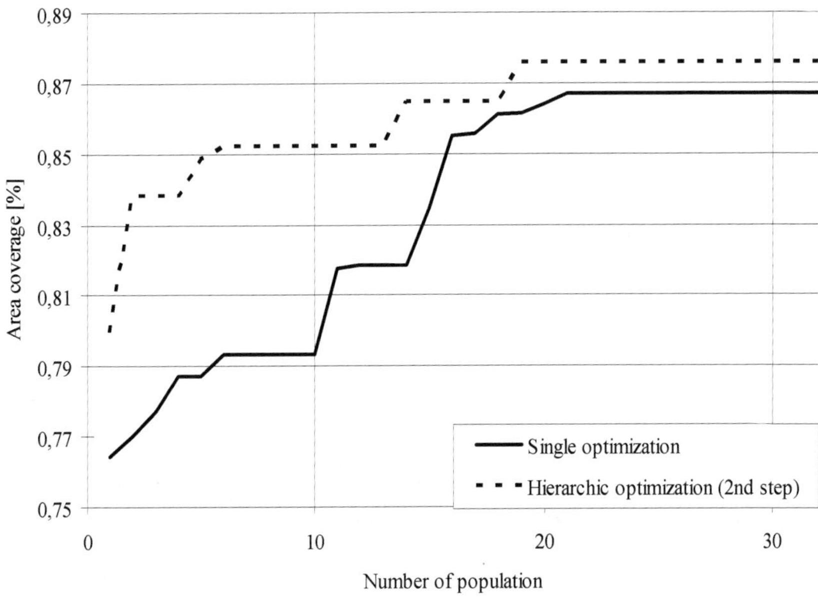

Fig. 31. Genetic Algorithm convergence (6AP whole floor)

6. Conclusion

The optimal Remote Unit position of Hybrid Fiber Radio is investigated for indoor environment. The article illustrates the possibility of optimization of HFR network using Genetic Algorithm in order to determine positions of APs. Two new approaches are introduced to solve the global optimization problem the DIRECT and a hierarchic two step optimization combined with genetic algorithm. The methods are introduced and investigated for 1,2, 3 and 6 AP cases. The influence of Genetic Algorithm parameters on the convergence has been tested and the optimal radio network is investigated. It has been shown that for finding proper placement the necessary number of APs can be reduced and therefore saving installation cost of WLAN or HFR.

It has been shown that for finding proper placement the necessary number of RU can be reduced and therefore saving installation cost of HFR. The results clearly justify the advantage of the method we used but further investigations are necessary to combine and to model other wireless network elements like leaky cables, fiber losses. Other promising direction is the extension of the optimization cost function with interference parameters of the wireless network part and with outer interference.

7. References

Martin D. Adickes, Richard E. Billo, Bryan A. Norman, Sujata Banerjee, Bartholomew O. Nnaji, Jayant Rajgopal (2002). Optimization of indoor wireless communication network layouts, IIE Transactions, Volume 34, Number 9 / September, 2002, Springer,

Cisco Visual Networking Index: Global Mobile Data Traffic Forecast Update, 2009-2014, (white paper), 2010
http://cisco.biz/en/US/solutions/collateral/ns341/ns525/ns537/ns705/ns827/white_paper_c11-520862.pdf

Lóránt Farkas, István Laki, Lajos Nagy (2001). Base Station Position Optimization in Microcells using Genetic Algorithms, ICT'2001, 2001, Bucharest, Romania

Daniel E. Finkel (2003). DIRECT Optimization Algorithm User Guide,
http://www.ncsu.edu/crsc/reports/ftp/pdf/crsc-tr03-11.pdf

J.M. Keenan, A.J. Motley (1990). Radio Coverage in buildings, BT Tech. J., 8(1), 1990, pp. 19-24.

Z. Michalewicz (1996). Genetic Algorithms + Data Structures = Evolution Programs, Springer-Verlag, Berlin, 1996.

E. Michielssen, Y. Rahmat-Samii, D.S. Weile (1999). Electromagnetic System Design using Genetic Algorithms, Modern Radio Science, 1999.

R.D. Murch, K.W. Cheung (1996). Optimizing Indoor Base-station Locations, XXVth General Assembly of URSI, 1996, Lille, France

Lajos Nagy, Lóránt Farkas (2000). Indoor Base Station Location Optimization using Genetic Algorithms, PIMRC'2000 Proceedings, Sept. 2000, London, UK

A. Portilla-Figueras, S. Salcedo-Sanz, Klaus D. Hackbarth, F. López-Ferreras, and G. Esteve-Asensio (2009). Novel Heuristics for Cell Radius Determination in WCDMA Systems and Their Application to Strategic Planning Studies, EURASIP Journal on Wireless Communications and Networking, Volume 2009 (2009)

Liza K. Pujji, Kevin W. Sowerby, Michael J. Neve (2009). A New Algorithm for Efficient Optimization of Base Station Placement in Indoor Wireless Communication Systems, 2009 Seventh Annual Communication Networks and Services Research Conference, Moncton, New Brunswick, Canada, ISBN: 978-0-7695-3649-1

R. E. Schuh, D. Wake, B. Verri and M. Mateescu, Hybrid Fibre Radio Access (1999) A Network Operators Approach and Requirements, 10th Microcoll Conference, Microcoll'99, Budapest, Hungary, pp. 211-214, 21-24 March, 1999

Yufei Wu, Samuel Pierre (2007).Optimization of 3G Radio Network Planning Using Tabu Search, Journal of Communication and Information Systems, Vol. 22, No. 1, 2007

13

Introduction to Packet Scheduling Algorithms for Communication Networks

Tsung-Yu Tsai[1], Yao-Liang Chung[2] and Zsehong Tsai[2]
[1]*Institute for Information Industry*
[2]*Graduate Institute of Communication Engineering, National Taiwan University*
[1,2]*Taipei, Taiwan, R.O.C.*

1. Introduction

As implied by the word "packet scheduling", the shared transmission resource should be intentionally assigned to some users at a given time. The process of assigning users' packets to appropriate shared resource to achieve some performance guarantee is so-called packet scheduling.

It is anticipated that packetized transmissions over links via proper packet scheduling algorithms will possibly make higher resource utilization through statistical multiplexing of packets compared to conventional circuit-based communications. A packet-switched and integrated service environment is therefore prevalent in most practical systems nowadays. However, it will possibly lead to crucial problems when multiple packets associated to different kinds of Quality of Service (QoS) (e.g. required throughput, tolerated delay, jitter, etc) or packet lengths competing for the finite common transmission resource. That is, when the traffic load is relatively heavy, the first-come-first-serve discipline may no longer be an efficient way to utilize the available transmission resource to satisfy the QoS requirements of each user. In such case, appropriate packet-level scheduling algorithms, which are designed to schedule the order of packet transmission under the consideration of different QoS requirements of individual users or other criteria, such as fairness, can alter the service performance and increase the system capacity . As a result, packet scheduling algorithms have been one of the most crucial functions in many practical wired and wireless communication network systems. In this chapter, we will focus on such topic direction for complete investigation.

Till now, many packet scheduling algorithms for wired and wireless communication network systems have been successfully presented. Generally speaking, in the most parts of researches, the main goal of packet scheduling algorithms is to maximize the system capacity while satisfying the QoS of users and achieving certain level of fairness. To be more specific, most of packet scheduling algorithm proposed are intended to achieve the following desired properties:

1. Efficiency:

The basic function of packet scheduling algorithms is scheduling the transmission order of packets queued in the system based on the available shared resource in a way that satisfies the set of QoS requirements of each user. A packet scheduling algorithm is generally said to be more efficient than others if it can provide larger capacity region. That is, it can meet the same QoS guarantee under a heavier traffic load or more served users.

2.   Protection:

Besides the guarantees of QoS, another desired property of a packet scheduling algorithm to treat the flows like providing individual virtual channels, such that the traffic characteristic of one flow will have as small effect to the service quality of other flows as possible. This property is sometimes refered as *flow isolation* in many scheduling contexts. Here, we simply define the term flow be a data connection of certain user. A more formal definition will be given in the next section.

Flow isolation can greatly facilitate the system to provide flow-by-flow QoS guarantees which are independent of the traffic demand of other flows. It is beneficial in several aspects, such as the per-flow QoS guarantee can be avoided to be degraded by some ill-behavior users which send packet with a higher rate than they declared. On the other hands, a more flexible performance guarantee service scheme can also be allowed by logically dividing the users which are associated to a wide range of QoS requirements and traffic characteristic while providing protection from affecting each other.

3.   Flexibility:

A packet scheduling algorithm shall be able to support users with widely different QoS requirements. Providing applications with vast diversity of traffic characteristic and performance requirements is a typical case in most practical integrated system nowadays.

4.   Low complexity:

A packet scheduling algorithm should have reasonable computational complexity to be implemented. Due to the fast growing of bandwidth and transmission rate in today's communication system, the processing speed of packets becomes more and more critical. Thus, the complexity of the packet scheduling algorithm is also of important concern.

Due to the evolution process of the communication technology, many packet scheduling algorithms for wireless systems in literatures are based on the rich results from the packet scheduling algorithms for wired systems, either in the design philosophy or the mathematical models. However, because of the fundamental differences of the physical characteristics and transmission technologies used between wired and wireless channels, it also leads to some difference between the considerations of the packet scheduling for wired and wireless communication systems. Hence, we suggest separate the existing packet scheduling algorithms into two parts, namely, wired ones and wireless ones, and illustrate the packet scheduling algorithms for wired systems first to build several basic backgrounds first and then go to that for the wireless systems.

The rest of the chapter is outlined as follows. In Section 2, we will start by introducing some preliminary definition for preparation. Section 3 will make a overview for packet scheduling algorithms in wired communication systems. Comprehensive surveys for packet scheduling in wireless communication systems will then included in Section 4. In Section 5, we will employ two case studies for designing packet scheduling mechanisms in OFDMA-based systems. In Section 6, summary and some open issues of interest for packet scheduling will be addressed. Finally, references will be provided in the end of this chapter.

2. Preliminary definitions

The review of the packet scheduling algorithms throughout this chapter considers a packet-switched single server. The server has an outgoing link with transmission rate C. The main task of the server is dealing with the packets input to it and forwarding them into the outgoing link. A packet scheduling algorithm is employed by the server to schedule the appropriate forwarding order to the outgoing link to meet a variety of QoS requirements associated to each packet. For wireline systems, the physical medium is in general regarded as stable and robust. Thus the packet error rate (PER) is usually ignored and C can be simply considered as a constant with unit bits/sec. This kind of model is usually referred as *error-free channel* in literatures. On the other hands, for wireless systems, the situation can become much more complicate. Whether in wireless networks with short transmission range (about tens of meters) such as WLAN and femtocell or that with long transmission range (about hundreds of meters or even several kilometers) such as the macrocell environments based on WCDMA, WiMAX and LTE, the packet transmission in wireless medium suffers location-dependent path loss, shadowing, and fading. These impairment make the PER be no longer ignorable and the link capacity C may also become varying (when adaptive modulation and coding is adopted). This kind of model is usually referred as *error-prone channel* in literatures.

Each input packet is associated to a *flow*. Flow is a *logical* unit which represents a sequence of input packets. In practice, packets associated to the same flows often share the same or similar quality of service (QoS) requirement. There should be a *classifier* in the server to map each input packets to appropriate flows.

The QoS requirement of a flow is usually characterized by a set of **QoS parameters**. In practice, the QoS parameters may include tolerant delay or tolerant jitter of each packet, or data rate requirement such as the minimum required throughput. The choice of QoS parameters might defer flow by flow, according to the specific requirement of different services. For example, in IEEE 802.16e [47], each data connection is associated to a service type. There are totally five service types to be defined. That is, unsolicited grant service (UGS), real-time polling service (rtPS), extended real-time polling service (ertPS), non-real-time polling service (nrtPS), and best effort (BE). Among these, rtPS is generally for streaming audio or video services, and the QoS parameters contains the minimum reserved rate, maximum sustained rate, and maximum latency tolerant. On the other hands, UGS is designed for IP telephony services without silence suppression (i.e. voice services with constant bit rate). The QoS parameters of UGS connections contains all the parameters of rtPS connections and additionally, it also contains a parameter, jitter tolerance, since the service experiment of IP telephony is more sensitive to the smoothness of traffic. Moreover, for nrtPS, which is mainly designed for non-real-time data transmission service such as FTP, the QoS parameters contains minimum reserved data rate and maximum sustained data rate. Unlike rtPS and UGS, which required the latency of each packet to be below certain level, nrtPS is somewhat less sensitive to the packet latency. It allows some packets to be postponed without degrading the service experiment immediately, however, an average data rate should still be guaranteed, since throughput is of the most concern for data transmission services.

The server can be further divided into two categories, according to the *eligible time* of the input packets. Eligible time of a packet is defined as the earliest time that the packet begins being transmitted. Additionally, a packet is called eligible when it is available to be transmitted by the server. If all packets immediately become eligible for transmission upon arrival, the system is called *work-conserving*, otherwise, it is called *nonwork-conserving*. A direct consequence of a system being work-conserving is that the server is never idle whenever there are packets queued in the server. It always forwards the packets when the queues are not empty.

3. Packet scheduling algorithms in wireline systems

In this section, we will introduce several representative packet scheduling algorithms of wireline systems. Their merits and expense will be examined respectively.

3.1 First Come First Serve (FCFS)

FCFS may be the simplest way for a scheduler to schedule the packets. In fact, FCFS does not consider the QoS parameters of each packets, it just sends the packets according to the order of their arrival time. Thus, the QoS guarantee provided by FCFS is in general weak and highly depends on the traffic characteristic of flows. For example, if there are some flows which have very bursty traffic, under the discipline of FCFS, a packet will very likely be blocked for a long time by packets burst which arrives before it. In the worst case, the unfairness between different flows cannot be bounded, and the QoS cannot be no longer guaranteed. However, since FCFS has the advantage of simple to implement, it is still adopted in many communication networks, especially the networks providing *best effort* services. If some level of QoS is required, then more sophisticated scheduling algorithm is needed.

3.2 Round Robin

Round Robin (RR) scheme is a choice to compensate the drawbacks of FCFS which also has low implementation complexity. Specifically speaking, newly arrival packets queue up by flow such that each flow has its respective queue. The scheduler polls each flow queue in a cyclic order and serves a packet from any-empty buffer encountered; therefore, the RR scheme is also called flow-based RR scheme. RR scheduling is one of the oldest, simplest, fairest and most widely used scheduling algorithms, designed especially for time-sharing systems. They do offer greater fairness and better bandwidth utilization, and are of great interest when considering other scenarios than the high-speed point-to-point scenario. However, since RR is an attempt to treat all flows equally, it will lead to the lack of flexibility which is essential if certain flows are supported to be treated better than other ones.

3.3 Strict priority

Strict priority is another classical service discipline which assigns *classes* to each flow. Different classes may be associated to different QoS level and have different *priority*. The eligible packets associated to the flow with higher-priority classes are send ahead of the eligible packets associated to the flow with lower-priority classes. The sending order of packets under strict priority discipline only depends on the classes of the packets. This is why it called "strict" since the eligible packets with lower-priority classes will never be sent before the eligible packets with higher-priority classes. Strict priority suffers from the same problem as that of FCFS, since a packet may also wait arbitrarily long time to be sent. Especially for the packets with lower-priority classes, they may be even starved by the packets with higher-priority classes.

3.4 Earliest Deadline First (EDF)

For networks providing real-time services such as multimedia applications, earliest deadline first (EDF) [5][6] is one of the most well-known scheduling algorithms. Under EDF discipline, each flow is assigned a tolerant delay bound d_i; a packet j of flow i arriving at time a_{ij} is naturally assigned a deadline $a_{ij} + d_i$. Each eligible packet is sent according to the

Non-real-time group: Non-real-time flows are not sensitive to delay and jitter. The QoS matrix of non-real-time services is the average throughput. A parameter λ_j is used to describe the traffic characteristic of non-real-time session j. Where λ_j is the minimum reserved data rate (normalized to slots/frame).

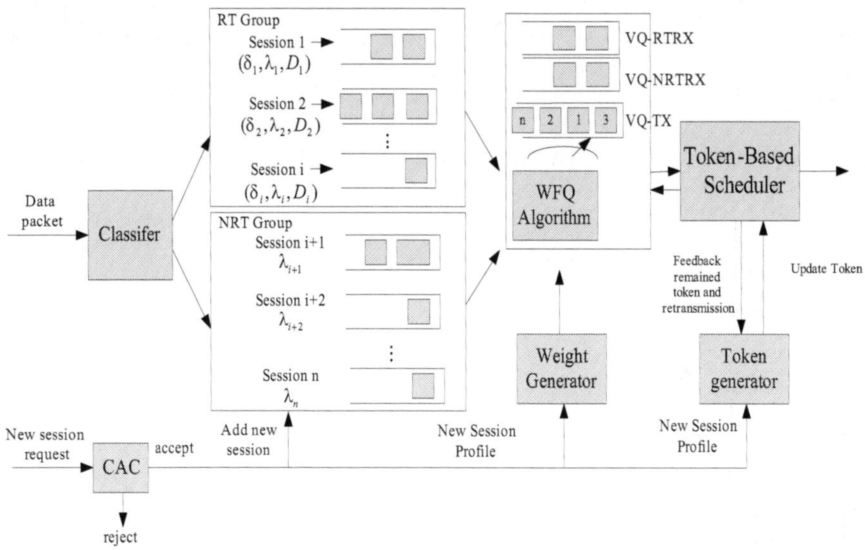

Fig. 5.2 The system architecture of our packet scheduler

Packet Scheduler and Weight Generator

In the following sections, we introduce the main part of our packet scheduling scheme. Some useful notations are as follows:

S_{RT}: The set of all real-time flows

S_{NRT}:The set of all non-real-time flows

b_i: The minimum required capacity to achieve the QoS requirement of flow i (normalized to slots/frame). For real-time services, the QoS marix is the tolerant delay of a packet, and for non-real-time services, the QoS matrix is the average throughput

w_i: The *weighting factor* of flow i in the WFQ scheduler

t_i: The current token value of flow i. If a packet of flow i is scheduled to transmit in the next frame. It must take the token value equal to the size of the packet (normalize to slot) away

T_i: The maximum token value flow i can keep

α_i : The protecting factor of flow i. A number which is larger than or equal to 1. The more α_i is, the more *protected capacity* for flow i.

r_i: The token incremental rate of flow i. At the beginning of a frame, the token value of flow i is updated to $max(t_i+r_i, T_i)$. r_i can be regard as the *protected capacity* for flow i. $r_i = b_i * \alpha_i$.

R: The sum of the *protected capacity* of real-time flows, $R = \sum_{i \in S_{RT}} r_i$

N: The sum of the *protected capacity* of non-real-time flows, $N = \displaystyle\sum_{i \in S_{NRT}} r_i$

N_{max}:The maximum value of the sum of *protected capacity* of non-real-time flows

C: The available slots for downlink traffic per frame. Intuitively, $C \geq R + N$

Our packet scheduling scheme has two stages. The first stage is a work conserving packet scheduler. When a packet arrives from upper layer, it first enters the first stage. The actual conditions in the lower layer such as the channel status or the allocation of slot are transparent to the first stage. It always assumes there is an error-free channel with fixed capacity C' in the lower layer. The main purpose of the first stage packet scheduler is to emulate the transmission order of a work conserving system in an ideal condition and be a reference system to our scheme. The packet order in the reference system is not certainly the actual transmission order in our packet scheduling scheme. The task of determining which packet should be scheduled to transmit in the next frame is executed by the token-based slot scheduler which is in the second stage of our scheme. The detail of the operation of the token-based slot scheduler will be illustrated in the next section.

There is no constraint to the scheduling discipline adopted in the first stage packet scheduler. But to achieve a better resource allocation and isolation among each flow, weight-based scheduling disciplines such as WFQ, VC, are suggested. In our packet scheduling scheme, we take WFQ as the reference system. When a packet arrives from the upper layer, it enters the packet scheduler in the first stage, the packet scheduler then schedules the transmission order of this packet with WFQ algorithm. The packet order scheduled by the packet scheduler is recorded in a *virtual queue*. *Virtual queue* is not really buffered the packets but store the pointers of packet which is the input of the token-based slot scheduler in the second stage.

There are three virtual queues with strict priorities. They are virtual queue for real-time retransmission (VQ-RTRX), virtual queue (VQ-NRTRX) for non-real-time retransmission, and virtual queue for first time transmission (VQ-TX) according to their priorities. The packets which have not been transmitted are recorded their pointer in the VQ. The real-time packets which have transmitted but not received successfully by the receiver, their pointers are moved from VQ to VQ-RTRX. The non-real-time packets which have transmitted but not received successfully by the receiver, their pointers are moved from VQ to NRTRVQ . The token-based packet scheduler checks the packet pointers from the virtual queue with highest priority (RTRVQ) to that with lowest priority (VQ) and determines which packets will be scheduled to transmit in the next frame. The algorithm determining which packets will be scheduled will be discussed in the next section in detail. Figure 5.3 is the queueing model of our packet schedulingscheme.

To indicate the resource sharing of the flows, each flow i associates a *weighting factor* w_i. The *weighting factor* is an important parameter as the weight in packet scheduler in the first stage and in the *debt allocation procedure* in token-based slot scheduler. We will return to discuss the procedure of weight allocation after we introduce the token-based slot scheduler and its algorithm in the next section.

Token-Based Scheduler

We use a token-based scheduler to determine which packet should be scheduled to transmit in the next frame. The fundamental operation of the token-based slot scheduler is as follows. For convenience of illustration, we define some notation as follows:

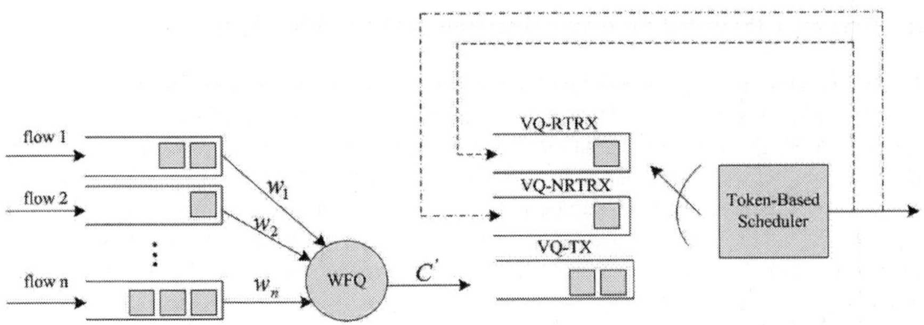

Fig. 5.3 The queueing model of our proposed packet scheduling scheme

l : The size of the packet that is checked by the token-based scheduler

l_i^j : The j$_{th}$ packets of flow i which is scheduled in the next frame

L_i : The total length of the scheduled packets of flow i. That is, $L_i = \sum_j l_i^j$

remained_slots :The remained slots available for scheduling. *remained_slot* $= C - \sum_i \lceil L_i \rceil$

Assume that there are C slots available for downlink traffic each frame. Each flow i maintains a *token value* t_i. The *token value* of every session i has a fixed *token incremental rate* r_i , the unit of r_i is slots/frame. At every beginning of a frame, the *token value* of session i is increased by r_i slots. The task of updating the token value of each flow at the beginning of a frame is operated by the *token generator*. When a packet of flow i with size l (normalized to slots) is scheduled to transmit, it must take the token value equal to the amount of the size of the packet (normalized to slots) away. And the number of slots available for scheduling is also decreased by That is,

When a packet of flow i with size l is scheduled

$$t_i \leftarrow t_i - 1 \tag{5.1}$$

$$L_i + = l \tag{5.2}$$

$$remained\_slot = C - \sum_i \lceil L_i \rceil \tag{5.3}$$

There should be an upper bound of the token value t_i, where we denote it by T_i. The setting of T_i can affect the system performance. We will discuss the issue of the effect of T_i later. Thus, when a new frame start

$$t_i \leftarrow max(t_i + r_i, T_i), \text{ for each flow } I \tag{5.4}$$

We can regarded r_i as the *protected capacity* of flow i. The configuration of r_i can affect the system performance significantly. We introduce the detailed algorithm of token-based slot scheduler in this section. Then we will return to discuss the guideline of the setting of token incremental rate in the next section.

The basic principle of scheduling is as follows:

1. The packet which has sufficient token value to transmit it has the higher priority, or it has the lower priority
2. For the packets with the same priority, the scheduling order is according to the order in WFQ scheduler (i.e. the order of the virtual finish time in the WFQ)

The process of our token-based packet scheduler algorithm can be divided into two phases. At the beginning of scheduling, the token-based packet scheduler enters the first phase. It checks the packet pointers sequentially in each virtual queue from high priority to low priority. We call the first step *packet selection procedure*. If the checked packet has sufficient token value (that is, $t_i \geq l$) and there are suffienct slots to transmit it in the next frame (that is, $remained\_slots \geq \lceil L_i + l \rceil - \lceil L_i \rceil$). It is scheduled in the next frame. And the token value of this flow is decreased by the size of the packet.

Otherwise, the token-based slot scheduler will skip it, and to keep the packets of the same flow to be transmitted in order, other packets from the same flow which have not been checked are also skipped in the first phase. For convenience of discussion, we say that this flow is *blocked* in this phase. After all the packets are checked, the slot scheduler enters the second phase.

During the second phase, the slot scheduler continues to find other packets can be transmitted with the remained slots in the next frame. The token-based scheduler does it by checking the packets which have not been scheduled in the first phase. Again, the order of checking is the same as the first phase. If there are still sufficient slots to transmit the checked packet (that is, $remained\_slots \geq \lceil L_i + l \rceil - \lceil L_i \rceil$), the packet is scheduled in the next frame, or the packet is skipped and the flow of this packet is *blocked* which is the same as the first phase. When the checked packet is scheduled, the token value of the scheduled packet must runs out and become a negative number, it implies that the session of this packet uses more capacity than its protected capacity. The additional consumed token value exceeding the *protected capacity* is regarded as the *debt* draw from other flows. For example, if t_i=30, now flow i has a packet with size 50 slots and is scheduled to transmit in the next frame by the scheduler. The *debt* is 20. If t_i= -10, a packet with the same size is scheduled, the *debt* is 50.

We can represent *debt* as follows:

$$debt = -1 * \max(-l, t_i - l), \ l \geq t_i \tag{5.5}$$

In our algorithm, we prefer to give real-time sessions more opportunity to increase its token value, since if we clean the packets of real-time sessions as soon as possible, it is more likely to have more remained resource to improve the throughput of non-real-time traffic in the operation of our token-based algorithm, thus meet the QoS requirement of both. So the *debt* is allocated to the token value of all real-time flows in proportion to their weight. That is,

$$t_i = \max(T_i, t_i + \frac{w_i}{\sum_{j \in S_{RT}} w_j} * debt), \text{ for all } i \in S_{RT} \tag{5.6}$$

We call the second step *debt allocation procedure*. For example, there are three flows. Flow 1 and 2 is real-time flows with *weighting factor* 0.3 and 0.2 respectively, flow 3 is non-real-time flows with *weighting factor* 0.5. And their *token value* is -10, 40, 20. Now flow 2 has a packet of size 50 slots be scheduled by the token-based slot scheduler. Since the packet size is larger than the token value of flow 2. We can calculate the *debt* is 10 and allocate it to the token value of real-time flows, that is, flow 1 and flow 2. Finally, the token value of flow 1 is $-10 + \dfrac{10*0.3}{0.2+0.3} = -4$, the token value of flow 2 is $40 - 50 + \dfrac{10*0.2}{0.2+0..3} = -6$. The token value of flow 3 is not changed. The debt allocation procedure is finished when all the packets are checked. Then in the slot the scheduler transmits the scheduled packet and receives ARQ from the receivers.

The chosen of T_i can affect system performance significantly. If the T_i is set too large, suppose flow i is in good channel status for a long time and it accumulates a large amount of token value from the token generator and the *debt* of other flows, now it incurs burst error and the channel is in bad channel for an long interval of time. Then flow i will waste a large amount of system resource to transmit error packet because it accumulates too much token value when it is in good channel. Thus is unfavorable. On the other hand, if the maximum token value is set too small. Then it is hard to differentiate the flows behave well and give it more opportunity to be scheduled. Thus is difficult to show the advantage of our algorithm. Furthermore, the traffic characteristic also should be taken into consider. Generally, we suggest that the maximum token value of non-real-time flows has better larger than that of real-time flows, because most non-real-time flow are TCP traffic, which is composed of several burst.

The flow chart of all procedures of the token-based slot scheduler is shown in Fig. 5.4. The checking procedure and the debt allocation procedure is the core of our slot scheduler. The pseudo codes of these two procedures are shown in Fig. 5.5 and Fig. 5.6, respectively.

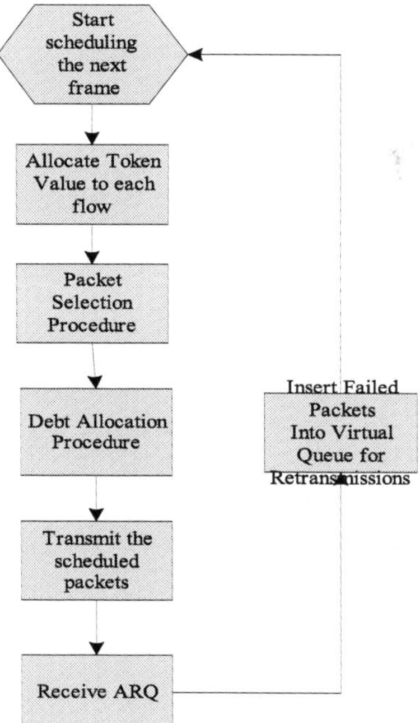

Fig. 5.4 The flow chart of the procedure of the token-based scheduler

```
packet-selection-procedure(system_capacity){
remained_slot←system_capacity;
for(each flow j){
   blockⱼ=0;
}
for(each virtual queue, from highest priority to lowest priority)
while(packets not checked in the virtual queue){
     i← the flow the packet belong to;
     l←the size of the checked packet;
     if( remained_slot ≥ ⌈Lᵢ+l⌉-⌈Lᵢ⌉ and l ≤ tᵢ and blockᵢ==0){

       schedule this packet in the next frame;
       remained_slot- = ⌈Lᵢ+l⌉-⌈Lᵢ⌉;

       tᵢ- = l;

     }
     else
       blockᵢ=1;  /* the other packet of flow i is also skipped in this procedure */
}
}
debt-allocation-procedure(remained_slot);
}
```

Fig. 5.5 The pseudo code of packet selection procedure

Weight Allocation and Token Generator

In this section, we discuss the functions of *token generator,* and the relationship between . The main tasks of token generator are calculating the *token incremental **rate*** of each flow, and allocating token value to all the flows per frame. In this section, we address the issues of the chosen of *weighting factor* and *token incremental rate.*

The different configuration of the *token incremental rate* alters the system performance. We suggest that the *token incremental rate* of flow i is set to its *minimum required capacity* b_i multiplies a *protecting factor* α_i. The *minimum required capacity* of flow i is the minimum capacity need to reserved for flow i to satisfy its QoS requirement. That is, the capacity to make flow i's QoS acceptable in the assumption that no channel error occurs. For real-time services, the QoS matrix is the tolerable delay of a packet. A real-time flow i with traffic profile *{δi, λi, Di}*, the ***minimum required capacity*** is $\max(\frac{\delta_i}{D_i}, \lambda_i)$. For non-real-time services, the QoS matrix is the average throughput. A non-real-time flow j with traffic profile λj, the *minimum required capacity* is λj. Thus, b_i is calculated as follows:

$$b_i = \begin{cases} \max(\frac{\delta_i}{D_i}, \lambda_i), i \in S_{RT} \\ \\ \lambda_i, i \in S_{NRT} \end{cases}$$

(5.7)

The purpose of *protecting factor* α_i is to expand the *protected capacity* of flow i by multiplying the *minimum required capacity* by a number larger than or equal to 1. The larger the *protecting*

```
debt_allocation_procedure(remained_slot){
  for(each flow j)
    block_i ← 0;

  for(each virtual queue, from the highest priority to the lowest priority){

    while(packets not checked and not scheduled in the virtual queue){
      i ← the flow the packet belong to;
      l ← the size of the packet;
```

$$\text{if}(\ remained\_slot \geq \lceil L_i + l \rceil - \lceil L_i \rceil\ \text{and}\ block_i\,!=1)\{$$

```
        schedule the packet in the next frame;
```

$$debt \leftarrow -1 * \max(t_i - l, -l)\,;$$

$$t_i\,-\,=l;$$

$$remained\_slot\,-\,= \lceil L_i + l \rceil - \lceil L_i \rceil\,;$$

```
        for(all real-time flows k){
```

$$t_k = \max(t_k + \frac{w_k * debt}{\sum\limits_{j \in RT} w_j}, T_k)\,;$$

```
        }
      }
      else
```

$$block_i \leftarrow 1;\quad \text{/* the other packet of flow i is also skipped in this procedure */}$$

```
    }
  }
}
```

Fig. 5.6 The pseudo code of debt allocation procedure

factor, the larger the *protected capacity*. It implies that providing a flow more protection by giving it more resource than it required to compensate the loss due to wireless channel error. The tuning of *protecting factors* is also important and closely relative to system performance. If the *protecting factor* of a flow is too large, it may be unfair to other flows and also cause waste of resource, which will be harmful to overall system performance. In our scheme, we set the *protecting factors* of real-time flows to 1, and set the *protecting factors* of non-real-time flows to a number slightly larger than 1, for example, Since in our token-based scheduler, we give real-time flows more opportunity to increase their token value than that of non-real-time flows by allocating all the *debt* to real-time flows. So we compensate non-real-time flows by regulating their *protecting factors* to be larger than that of real-time flows'. Additionally, setting the *protecting factor* of real-time flows to 1 means the *protected capacity* of a real-time flow is the same as its *minimum required capacity*. It brings benefits to differentiate the flows with good channel status and the flows with bad channel status. Because when a flow suffers burst error, it will use more capacity than its minimum required, so it soon runs out of its token value, and other real-time flows in good channel status get additional token value. It makes the real-time flows in good channel status has higher priority to be transmitted, and improve the efficiency of the use of system resource.

In many real situations, we may degrade some resource sharing of non-real-time flows to make the system to accommodate more real-time flows. That is, satisfy more real-time users at the cost of some average throughput of non-real-time services. We can achieve this by bounding the sum of the *token generating rate* of non-real-time flows. When the sum of the *token generating rate* of all non-real-time flows exceeds a defined value N_{max}, the *token generating ratse* of all non-real-time flows degrade proportionally to make their sum not larger than N_{max}.

Thus, the sum of the token rate of all non-real-time flows N can be represented as

$$N = \min\left(N_{max}, \sum_{i \in S_{NRT}} (\alpha_i * b_i)\right) \tag{5.8}$$

and the token rate of a non-real-time flow can be calculated as

$$r_i = N * \frac{b_i}{\sum_{i \in S_{NRT}} b_i} \tag{5.9}$$

The *weighting factor* is for indicating the resource allocation of the WFQ in the first stage of our scheme. The WFQ emulates a work-conserving system with error-free channel. The *weighting factor* of flow i is proportional to its *protected capacity* divided by its protecting factor. That is,

$$w_i = \frac{r_i / \alpha_i}{\sum_j r_j / \alpha_j} \quad \text{for all flow } i \tag{5.10}$$

5.3 PF schemes for OFDMA systems

Recently, for the higher rate data transmission, interest in wireless communications has shifted in the direction of broadband systems such as multicarrier transmission systems such like the OFDMA system. There has been a growing interest in defining radio resource allocation for a physical layer based on the OFDMA technology for 4G cellular system. While throughput–optimal scheduling can be achieved by using the multi–user diversity effect, it can generate unfairness as users with bad channel conditions have a lower probability to get a resource.

Based on the definition of the standard PF scheduling scheme [45], the theorem of the modified PF scheduling for multi-carrier transmission systems was proposed in [40]. Notice that the proof of this theorem is omitted and can be referred to [40].

Theorem: *A scheduling P is 'proportional fair' for a multicarrier transmission system, if and only if, for any feasible scheduling S, it satisfies:*

$$P = \arg\max_S \prod_{i \in U} \left(1 + \frac{\sum_{k \in C_i} r_{i,k}}{(T-1)\bar{R}_i}\right),$$

where U is the set of selected users by S, C_i is the set of carriers allocated to user i, $r_{i,k}$ is the instantaneous transmittable data rate of carrier $k \in C_i$ at the current slot, $\bar{R}_i$ is the average rate of user i at the previous slot, and T is the average window size.

With OFDMA, there are multiple transmission channels that can be used, where scheduling schemes considering the PF algorithms have widely been studied in many papers. See, for example, [39 41-42]. Papers [39] and [42] had proposed heuristic approaches by simply applying PF of the single carrier case in each subcarrier to adapt for the multi–carrier case in a suboptimal manner. Additional the QoS requirement for each user was considered in [41]. Furthermore, readers are suggested to refer to [43-44] for more complete investigation of related modified PF schemes in multi-carrier systems.

6. Summary and the discussion of open issues

Packet scheduling is one of most important radio resource management functions. It is responsible for determining which packet is to be transmitted such that the resources are fully utilized. The design of an efficient algorithm to be used for the scheduling of packet transmissions in wireless communication networks is a still a open issue for research. This Chapter has widely covered the conceptual description of many representative packet scheduling algorithms deployed in high-speed point-to-point wireline and wireless scenarios. Well designing algorithms with low complexity offering fairness among and potentially differentiation between different data-flows is important in the evolution of communication networks. The rapidly growing demand of network nodes capable of taking into account the different QoS requirements of different flows to better utilize the available resources at the same time as some degree of fairness is maintained, makes more intelligent packet scheduling a central topic in future development of communication technologies.

7. Acknowledgement

The authors wish to express their sincere appreciation for financial support from the National Science Council of the Republic of China under Contract NSC 98-2221-E-002-002.

8. References

[1] A. Parekh, R. G. Gallager, "A generalized processor sharing approach to flow control in integrated services networks: The single-node case," *IEEE/ACM Trans. on Networking*, Vol. 1, June 1993

[2] A. Parekh, R. G. Gallager, "A generalized processor sharing approach to flow control in integrated services networks: The multiple-node case," *IEEE/ACM Trans. On Networking*, Vol. 2, April 1994

[3] R. Cruz, "Quality of Service Guarantees in Virtual Circuit Switched Networks," *IEEE J. Select. Areas Commun.*, Special issue on "Advances in the Fundamentals of Networking," August, 1995.

[4] A. Demers, S. Keshav, and S. Shenkar, "Analysis and simulation of a fair queueing algorithm," *Internet. Res. Amd Exper., vol. 1, 1990*

[5] D. Ferarri, "Real-time communication in an internetwork," *J. High Speed Networks*, vol. 1, no. 1, pp. 79-103, 1992

[6] D. Ferrari and D. Verma. "A scheme for real-time channel establishment in wide-area networks," *IEEE Journal on Selected Areas in Communications*, 8(3):368–379, April 1990.

[7] J. R. Piney, S. Sallent, "Performance Evaluation of a Normalized EDF Service Discipline," *in Proc. IEEE MELECON 2004, Dubrovnik, Croatia, May 2004*

[8] S. Chaudhry, and A. Choudhary, "Tune dependent priority scheduling for guaranteed QoS Systems," *in Proc. Sixth International Conference on Computer Communications and Networks, pp. 236-241, Sept. 1997*

[9] L. Georgiadis, R. Guerin, A. Parekh, "Optimal multiplexing on a single link: delay and buffer requirements," *IEEE Trans. On Information Theory, 43(5), pp. 1518-1535, Sep. 1997*

[10] K. Zai, Y. Zhang, Y. Viniotis, "Achieving end-to-end delay bounds by EDF scheduling without traffic shaping," *in Proc. Infocom'01, 2001*

[11] V. Sivaraman, F. M. Chiussi, Mario Gerla, "End-to-End Statistical Delay Service under GPS and EDF Scheduling: A Comparison Study," *in Proc. Infocom'01, 2001*

[12] H. Zhang, "Service disciplines for guaranteed performance service in packet-switching networks," *Proceedings of the IEEE, vol. 83, No. 10, Oct. 1995*

[13] J. Liebeherr, D. Wrege and D. Ferrari, "Exact admission control in networks with bounded delay services," IEEE/ACM Trans. Networking, vol. 4, pp. 885-901, 1996.

[14] S. Lu and V. Bharghavan, "Fair Scheduling in Wireless Packet Networks," *IEEE/ACM Trans. Neetworking, vol. 7, no. 4, pp. 473-489, 1999.*

[15] Y. Cao, and VICOR O. K. Li, "Scheduling Algorithms in Broad-Band Wireless Networks," *Proceedings of the IEEE, Vol. 89, No. 1, Jan. 2001.*

[16] F. Tsou, H. Chiou, and Z. Tsai, "WDFQ: An Efficient Traffic Scheduler with Fair Bandwidth Sharing for Wireless Multimedia Services," *IEICE TRANS. COMMUNICATIONS*, Vol. E00-A, No. 1, Jan. 2000

[17] T. S. Eugene Ng, I. Stoica, and H. Zhang, "Packet Fair Queueing Algorithms for Wireless Networks with Location-Dependent Errors," *in Proc. INFOCOM'98*, Mar. 1998, pp. 1103-1111.

[18] J. Gomez, A. T. Campbell, and H. Morikawa, "The Havana Framework for Supporting Application and Channel Dependent QOS in Wireless Networks," *in Proc. Seventh International Conference on Network Protocols*, 1999.

[19] T. E. Kolding, K. I. Pedersen, J. Wigard, F. Frederiksen, and P. E. Mogensen, "High Speed Downlink Packet Access: WCDMA Evolution," *IEEE Vehicular Technology Society News*, February 2003, pp. 4-10.

[20] P. Viswanath, D. Tse, and R. Laroia , "Opportunistic beam forming using dumb antennas," *IEEE Transactions on Information Theory*, vol. 48, no. 6, June 2002.

[21] D. Tse, "Multiuser diversity in wireless networks," *Wireless Communication Seminar*, Stanford University, April 2001.

[22] J. M. Holtzman, "Asymptotic analysis of Proportional Fair algorithm," *IEEE Proc. Personal Indoor Mobile Radio Communications (PIMRC)*, September 2001, pp. 33-37.

[23] T. E. Kolding, "Link and system performance aspects of Proportional Fair scheduling in WCDMA/HSDPA," *Proceedings of 58th IEEE Vehicular Technology Conference (VTC)*, Florida USA, October 2003, pp. 1454-1458.

[24] "Guidelines for the evaluation of radio transmission technologies for IMT-2000," Recommendation ITU-R M.1225, 1997.

[25] A. Jalali, R. Padovani, and R. Pankaj, "Data throughput of CDMA-HDR a high efficiency-high data rate personal communication wireless system," *in Proc. IEEE. Veh. Technol. Conf. Spring*, Tokyo, Japan, May 2000, pp. 1854-1858.

[26] S. Borst, "User-level performance of channel-aware scheduling schemes in wireless data networks," *IEEE INFOCOM*, Mar. 2003, vol. 1, pp. 321–331.

[27] A. Jalali, R. Padovani, and R. Pankaj, "Data throughput of CDMA-HDR a high efficiency-high date rate personal communication wireless system," *in Proc. IEEE VTC*, May 2000, pp. 1854-1858.

[28] M. Kazmi and N. Wiberg, "Scheduling schemes for HSDSCH in a WCDMA mixed traffic scenario," *in Proc. IEEE Int. Symp. PIMRC*, Beijing, China, Sep. 2003, pp. 1485-1489.

[29] J. M. Holtzman, "Asymptotic Analysis of Proportional Fair Algorithm", *IEEE International Symposium on Personal, Indoor and Mobile Radio Communications*, Vol. 2, October 2001

[30] L. Erwu, and K. K. Leung, "MAC 20-5 - Proportional Fair Scheduling: Analytical Insight under Rayleigh Fading Environment", *IEEE Wireless Communications and Networking Conference*, April 2008

[31] P. Viswanath, D. N. C. Tse, and R. Laroia, "Opportunistic Beamforming using Dumb Antennas", *IEEE Transactions on Information Theory*, Vol. 48, Issue 6, June 2002

[32] P. Mueng, W. Yichuan, and W. Wenbo, "Joint an Advanced Proportionally Fair Scheduling and Rate Adaptation for Multi-services in TDD-CDMA Systems", *IEEE 59th Vehicular Technology Conference*, Vol. 3, May 2004

[33] K. Kuenyoung, K. Hoon, and H. Youngnam, "A Proportionally Fair Scheduling Algorithm with QoS and Priority in 1xEV-DO", *IEEE Symposium on Personal, Indoor and Mobile Radio Communications*, Vol. 5, September 2002

[34] O. S. Shin, and K. B. Lee, "Packet Scheduling over a Shared Wireless Link for Heterogeneous Classes of Traffic", *IEEE International Conference on Communications*, Vol. 1, June 2004

[35] J. A.C. Bingham, "Multi carrier modulation for data transmission: an idea whose time has come," *IEEE Communications Magazine*, pp. 5-14, May 1990.

[36] J. Jang and K. Lee, "Transmit power adaptation for multiuser OFDM systems," *IEEE Journal on Selected Areas in Communications*, 21(2): 171-178, Feb. 2003.

[37] Y. J. Zhang and K. B. Letaief, "Multiuser adaptive subcarrier-and bit allocation with adaptive cell selection for OFDM systems," *IEEE Transactions on Wireless Communications*, 3(4): 1566-1575, Sept. 2004.

[38] Z. Shen, J. G. Andrews, and B. L. Evans, "Adaptive resource allocation for multiuser OFDM with constrained fairness," *IEEE Transactions on Wireless Communications*, 4(6): 2726-2737, Nov. 2005.

[39] W. Anchun, X. Liang, Z. Shidong, X. Xibin, and Y. Yan, "Dynamic resource management in the fourth generation wireless systems," *in Proc. ICCT*, vol. 2, April 2003, pp. 1095-1098.

[40] H. Kim and Y. Han, "A proportional fair scheduling for multicarrier transmission systems," *IEEE Communications Letters*, vol. 9, no. 3, pp. 210–212, March 2005.

[41] Y. Lu, C. Wang, C. Yin ,and G. Yue, "Downlink scheduling and radio resource allocation in adaptive OFDMA wireless communication system for user-individual QoS," *International Journal of Electrical, Computer, and Systems Engineering* 2009

[42] N. Ruangchaijatupon and Y. Ji, "Simple proportional fairness scheduling for OFDMA frame-based wireless system," *IEEE WCNC* 2008

[43] M. Kaneko, P. Popovski, and J. Dahl, "Proportional fairness in multi-carrier system with multi-slot frames: upper bound and user multiplexing algorithms," *IEEE Transactions Wireless Communications*, vol. 7, no. 1, January 2008

[44] N. Ruangchaijatupon and Y. Ji, "Proportional fairness with minimum rate guarantee scheduling in a multiuser OFDMA wireless network," *ACM IWCMC*, Leipzig, Germany, 2009

[45] F. P. Kelly, A. K. Maulloo, and D.K.H. Tan., "Rate control in communication networks: shadow prices, proportional fairness and stability," *J. of the Operational Research Society*, vol.49, pp. 237-252, April 1998.

[46] T.-Y. Tsai and Z. Tsai, "Design of a packet scheduling scheme for downlink channel in IEEE 802.16 BWA systems," *IEEE WCNC* 2008.

[47] IEEE 802.16e-2005, "IEEE Standard for Local and Metropolitan Area Networks – Part 16: Air Interface for Fixed and Mobile Broadband Wireless Access Systems – Amendent for Phisical and Medium Access Control Layers for Combined Fixed and Mobile Operation in Licensed Bands," Dec. 7, 2005.

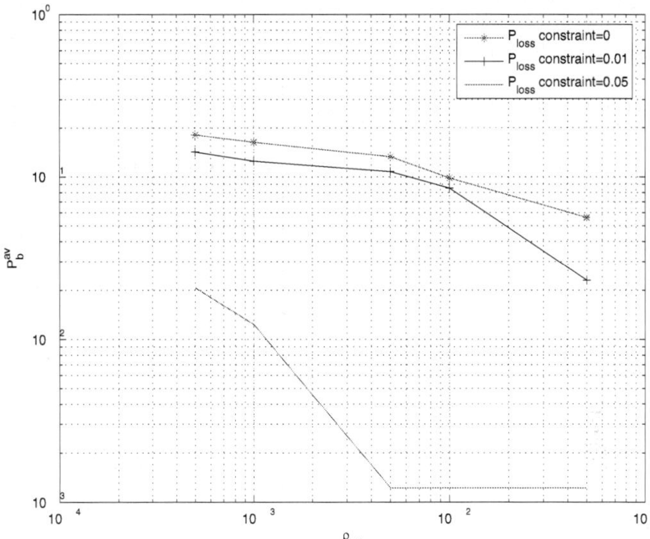

Fig. 3. Blocking probability as a function of ρ_{av}.

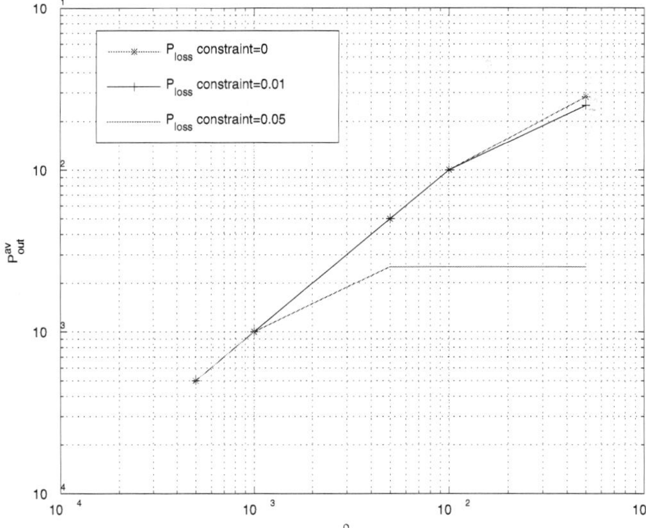

Fig. 4. Outage probability as a function of ρ_{av}.

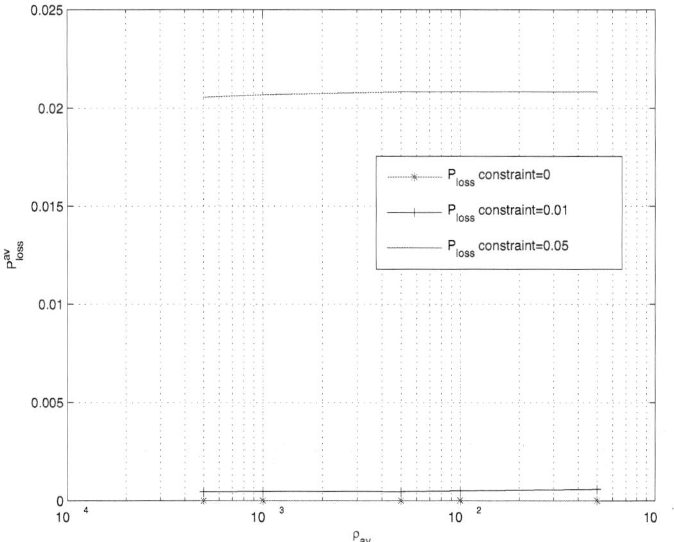

Fig. 5. Average packet loss probability as a function of ρ_{av}.

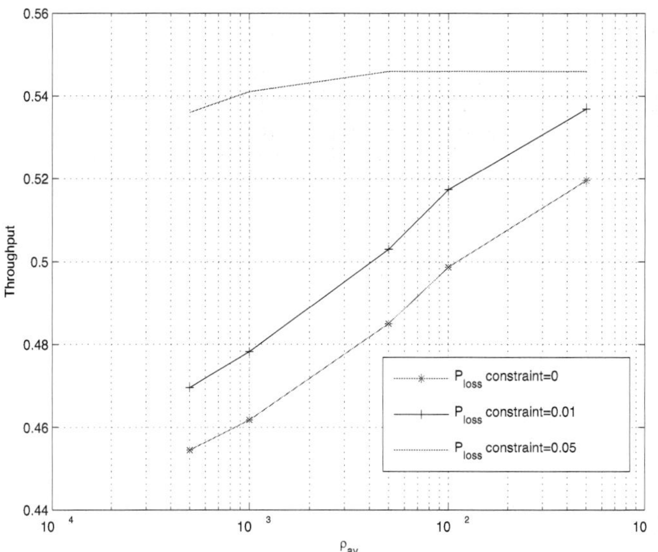

Fig. 6. Throughput as a function of ρ_{av}.

network layer, while simultaneously improving the overall system throughput. This can be explained by the fact that with a given physical layer performance, a large packet loss probability constraint allows more users to access the network. In the system we investigate, with $\rho_{av} = 10^{-2}$, relaxing the packet loss probability constraint from 0 to 0.05 can reduce the blocking probability from 10^{-1} to 10^{-3}, i.e., by 99%, while improving the throughput from 0.5 to 0.545, i.e., by 9%.

We note that the achieved packet loss probability in Figure 5 is obtained by averaging the measurements over a long-term period, while P_{loss} *constraint* denotes the maximum allowed packet loss probability for each system state.

With a CAC policy in a circuit-switched network, e.g., the work discussed in [6], a zero packet-loss-probability can be ensured. As observed in Figures 3-6, in a packetized system which allows a non-zero packet loss probability, this zero packet loss probability leads to an inefficient utilization of the system resource and as a result degrades the connection level performance as well as the overall system throughput.

B. Performance by employing packet retransmissions

Figures 7-9 compare the performance between a system without ARQ, e.g., [8] [16], and a system with ARQ. In these figures, ARQ = i is equivalent to $L_1 = L_2 = i$. The blocking probability is set to 0.1 for both classes and the target overall PERs are set to $\rho_1 = 10^{-4}$ and $\rho_2 = 10^{-6}$, respectively. The packet loss probability constraints are set to 0.05 for both classes.

From Figure 7, it is observed that with ARQ, the blocking probability and outage probability can be reduced. This represents a tradeoff between transmission delay and system performance. For example, with $\rho_{av} = 10^{-3}$, employing an ARQ scheme with $L_j = 1$ can decrease the blocking probability from 10^{-3} to 10^{-4}, i.e., by 90%, while simultaneously reducing the outage probability from 10^{-3} to almost 10^{-6}, i.e., by 99%.

In the above, we have studied the physical and network layer performance by employing ARQ. We now investigate how ARQ schemes affect the packet level performance. As shown in (4), with an increased L_j, the departure rate is decreased due to retransmissions, which increases the packet loss probability. However, at the same time, an increased L_j also reduces the transmission error, allowing more virtual channels simultaneously presented in the system, which in turn decreases the packet loss probability. Therefore, the packet loss probability is determined by the above positive and negative impacts of ARQ. If the positive impact dominates, the packet loss probability is reduced by employing ARQ, as shown in the upper figure in Figure 8. Otherwise, if the negative impact dominates, the packet loss probability is degraded by employing ARQ, as shown in the lower figure in Figure 8. We note that the above degradation is not very significant. As shown in Figure 9, by employing ARQ, the overall system throughput can be improved.

Although increasing L_j may further improve system performance, it dramatically increases the computational complexity of the SMDP-based connection admission control policy. In [15], it has been shown that when L_j exceeds a certain level, further increasing L_j cannot improve the performance significantly. Therefore, there is no need to choose a large L_j. A detailed discussion on the impact of ARQ and how to choose L_j can be found in [15], in which a packet-level AC is discussed which employs an ARQ-based algorithm to reduce probability of outage. In this chapter, we have only addressed the connection admission control policy for a given L_j. The optimization of L_j is beyond the scope of this discussion.

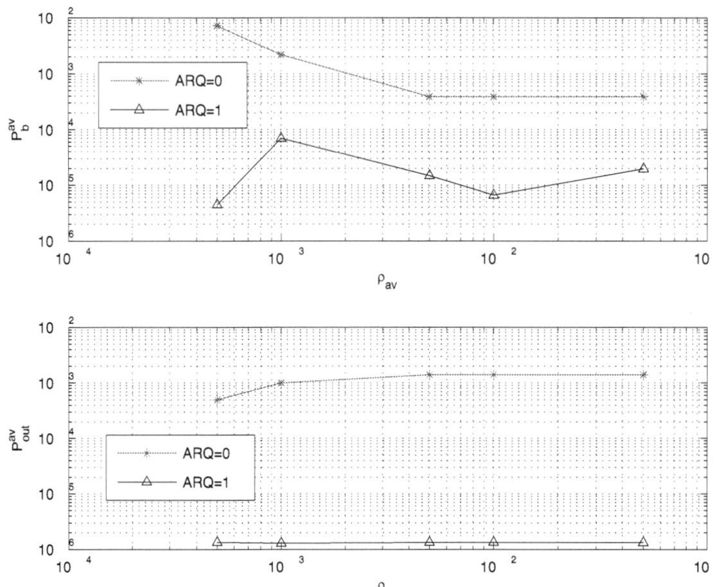

Fig. 7. Blocking and outage probabilities as a function of ρ_{av}.

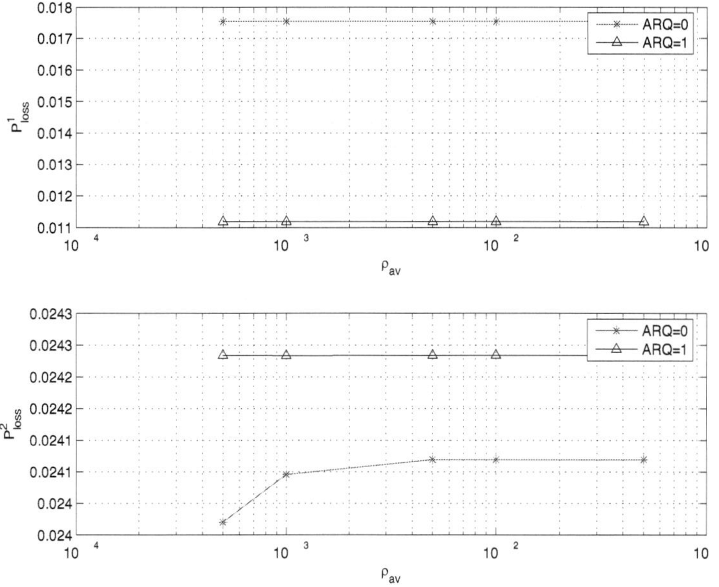

Fig. 8. Packet loss probability as a function of ρ_{av}.

allocated. This provides the flexible resource allocation framework required for opportunistic scheduling.

The frame structure supposed a perfect time and frequency synchronization between the mobiles and the access point as described in (Van de Beek et al., 1999). Additionally, perfect knowledge of the channel state is supposed to be available at the receiver (Li et al., 1999). The current channel attenuation on each subcarrier and for each mobile is estimated by the access node based on the SNR of the signal sent by each mobile during the uplink contention subframe. Assuming that the channel state is stable on a scale of 50 ms (Truman & Brodersen, 1997), and using a frame duration of 2 ms, the mobiles shall transmit their control information alternatively on each subcarrier so that the access node may refresh the channel state information once every 25 frames

3. Scheduling techniques in OFDM wireless networks

This chapter focuses on the two major scheduling techniques which have emerged in the litterature: Maximum Signal-to-Noise Ratio (MaxSNR), Proportional Fair (PF). Furthermore, it will present an improvement of PF scheduling which avoid fairness deficiencies: the Compensated Proportional Fair (CPF).

3.1 Classical scheduling: Round Robin

Before studying opportunistic schedulers, we bring to mind the characteristics of classical schedulers. Round Robin (RR) (Nagle, 1987; Kuurne & Miettinen, 2004) is a well-attested bandwidth allocation strategy in wireless networks. RR allocates an equal share of the bandwidth to each mobile in a ring fashion. However, it does not take in consideration that far mobiles have a much lower spectral efficiency than closer ones which does not provide full fairness. Moreover, the RR does not take benefit of multiuser diversity which results in a bad utilization of the bandwidth and in turn, poor system throughput.

3.2 Maximum Signal-to-Noise Ratio

Many schemes are derived from the Maximum Signal-to-Noise Ratio (MaxSNR) technique (also known as Maximum Carrier to Interference ratio (MaxC/I)) (Knopp & Humblet, 1995; Wong et al., 1999; Wang & Xiang, 2006). MaxSNR exploits the concept of opportunistic scheduling. Priority is given to the mobile which currently has the greatest signal-to-noise ratio (SNR). Profiting of the multiuser diversity and continuously allocating the radio resource to the mobile with the best spectral efficiency, MaxSNR strongly improves the system throughput. It dynamically adapts the modulation and coding to allow always making the most efficient use of the radio resource and coming closer to the Shannon limit. However, a negative side effect of this strategy is that the closest mobiles to the access point have disproportionate priorities over mobiles more distant since their path loss attenuation is much smaller. This results in a severe lack of fairness as illustrated in Fig. 1.

3.3 Proportional Fair

Proportional Fair (PF) algorithms have recently been proposed to incorporate a certain level of fairness while keeping the benefits of multiuser diversity (Viswanath et al., 2002; Kim et al., 2002; Anchun et al., 2003; Svedman et al., 2004; Kim et al., 2004). In PF based schemes, the basic principle is to allocate the bandwidth resources to a mobile when its channel conditions are the most favourable with respect to its time average. At a short time scale, path loss variations are negligible and channel state variations are mainly due to multipath fading, statistically similar for all mobiles. Thus, PF provides an equal sharing of the total available bandwidth among the mobiles as RR. Applying the opportunistic scheduling technique, system throughput maximization is also obtained as with MaxSNR. PF actually combines the advantages of the classical schemes and currently appears as the best bandwidth management scheme.

In PF-based schemes, fairness consists in guaranteeing an equal share of the total available bandwidth to each mobile, whatever its position or channel conditions. However, since the farther mobiles have a lower spectral efficiency than the closer ones due to pathloss, all mobiles do not all benefit of an equal average throughput despite they all obtain an equal share of bandwidth. This induces heterogeneous delays and unequal QoS. (Choi & Bahk, 2007; Gueguen & Baey, 2009; Holtzman, 2001) demonstrate that fairness issues persist in PF-based protocols when mobiles have unequal spatial positioning.

3.4 Compensated Proportional Fair

This QoS and fairness issues can be solved by an improvement of the PF called Compensated Proportional Fair (CPF). CPF introduces correction factors in the PF in order to compensate the path loss negative effect on fairness while keeping the PF system throughput maximization properties. With this compensation, CPF is aware of the path loss disastrous effect on fairness and adequate priorities between the mobiles are always adjusted in order to ensure them an equal throughput. This scheduling finely and simultaneously manages all mobiles. Keeping a maximum number of flows active across time but with relatively low traffic backlogs, CPF is designed for best profiting of the multi-user diversity taking advantage of the dynamics of the multiplexed traffics. Thus, preserving the multiuser diversity, CPF takes a maximal benefit of the opportunistic scheduling technique and maximizes the system capacity better than MaxSNR and PF access schemes. Well-combining the system capacity maximization and fairness objectives required for 4G OFDM wireless networks, an efficient support of multimedia services is provided.

At each scheduling epoch, the scheduler computes the maximum number of bits $B_{k,n}$ that can be transmitted in a time slot of subcarrier n if assigned to mobile k, for all k and all n. This number of bits is limited by two main factors: the data integrity requirement and the supported modulation orders.

The bit error probability is upper bounded by the symbol error probability (Wong & Cheng, 1999) and the time slot duration is assumed equal to the duration T_s of an OFDM symbol. The required received power $P_r(q)$ for transmitting q bits in a resource unit while keeping below the data integrity requirement BER_{target} is a function of the modulation type, its order and the single-sided power spectral density of noise N_0. For QAM and a modulation order M on a flat fading channel (Proakis, 1995):

$$P_r(q) = \frac{2N_0}{3Ts}\left[erfc^{-1}\left(\frac{BER_{target}}{2} \right)\right]^2 (M-1),\tag{1}$$

where $M = 2^q$ and $erfc$ is the complementary error function. $P_r(q)$ may also be determined in practice based on BER history and updated according to information collected on experienced BER. Additionally, the transmit power $P_{k,n}$ of mobile k on subcarrier n is upper bounded to a value P_{max} which complies with the transmit Power Spectral Density regulation:

$$P_{k,n} \leq P_{\max} \, . \tag{2}$$

Given the channel gain $a_{k,n}$ experienced by mobile k on subcarrier n (including path loss and multipath fading):

$$P_r(q) \leq a_{k,n} P_{\max} \, . \tag{3}$$

The channel gain model on each subcarrier considers free space path loss a_k and multipath Rayleigh fading $\alpha_{k,n}^2$ (Parsons, 1992):

$$a_{k,n} = a_k \, \alpha_{k,n}^2 \, . \tag{4}$$

a_k is dependent on the distance between the access point and mobile k. $\alpha_{k,n}^2$ represents the flat fading experienced by mobile k on subcarrier n. $\alpha_{k,n}$ is Rayleigh distributed with an expectancy equal to unity. Consequently, the maximum number of bits $q_{k,n}$ of mobile k which can be transmitted on a time slot of subcarrier n while keeping below its BER target is:

$$q_{k,n} \leq \left\lfloor \log_2 \left(1 + \frac{3 P_{\max} \, T_s \, a_k \, \alpha_{k,n}^2}{2 N_0 \left[erfc^{-1} \left(\frac{BER_{target}}{2} \right) \right]^2} \right) \right\rfloor . \tag{5}$$

We further assume that the supported QAM modulation orders are limited such as q belongs to the set $S = \{0, 2, 4, \ldots, q_{max}\}$. Hence, the maximum number of bits $B_{k,n}$ that will be transmitted on a time slot of subcarrier n if this resource unit is allocated to the mobile k is:

$$B_{k,n} = \max\{q \in S, q \leq q_{k,n}\} \, . \tag{6}$$

At each scheduling epoch and for each time slot, MaxSNR based schemes allocate the subcarrier n to the active mobile k which has the greatest $B_{k,n}$ value while the PF scheme consists in allocating the subcarrier n to the mobile k which has the greatest factor $F_{k,n}$ defined as:

$$F_{k,n} = \frac{B_{k,n}}{R_{k,n}} \, , \tag{7}$$

where $R_{k,n}$ is the time average of the $B_{k,n}$ values. However, considering rounded $B_{k,n}$ values in the allocation process have a negative discretization side effect on the PF performances. Several mobiles may actually have a same $F_{k,n}$ value with significantly different channel state with respect to their time average. More accuracy is needed in the subcarrier allocation process for prioritizing the mobiles. It is more profitable to allocate the subcarrier n to the mobile k which has the greatest $f_{k,n}$ value defined by:

$$f_{k,n} = \frac{b_{k,n}}{r_{k,n}} \, , \tag{8}$$

where:

$$b_{k,n} \leq \log_2 \left(1 + \frac{3 P_{\max} \, T_s \, a_k \, \alpha_{k,n}^2}{2 N_0 \left[\mathit{erfc}^{-1} \left(\dfrac{BER_{t\arg et}}{2} \right) \right]^2} \right),$$
(9)

and $r_{k,n}$ is the $b_{k,n}$ average over a sliding time window.

PF outperforms MaxSNR providing an equal system capacity and partially improving the fairness (Gueguen & Baey, 2009). Based on the PF scheme, this chapter presents a new scheduler that achieves high fairness while preserving the system throughput maximization. It introduces a parameter called "Compensation Factor" (CF_k), that takes into account the current path loss impact on the average achievable bit rate of the mobile k. It is defined by:

$$CF_k = \frac{b_{ref}}{b_k}.$$
(10)

b_{ref} is a reference number of bits that may be transmitted on a subcarrier considering a reference free space path loss a_{ref} for a reference distance d_{ref} to the access point and a multipath fading equal to unity:

$$b_{ref} \leq \log_2 \left(1 + \frac{3 P_{\max} \, T_s \, a_{ref}}{2 N_0 \left[\mathit{erfc}^{-1} \left(\dfrac{BER_{t\arg et}}{2} \right) \right]^2} \right).$$
(11)

b_k represents the same quantity but considering a distance d_k to the access point:

$$b_k \leq \log_2 \left(1 + \frac{3 P_{\max} \, T_s \, a_{ref} \left(\dfrac{d_{ref}}{d_k} \right)^{\beta}}{2 N_0 \left[\mathit{erfc}^{-1} \left(\dfrac{BER_{t\arg et}}{2} \right) \right]^2} \right),$$
(12)

with β the experienced path loss exponent.

The distance d_k of the mobile k to the access point is evaluated thanks to the channel state estimation time average (Jones & Raleigh, 1998). The CPF scheduling consists then in allocating a time slot of subcarrier n to the mobile k which has the greatest $CPF_{k,n}$ value:

$$CPF_{k,n} = f_{k,n} \, CF_k = \left(\frac{b_{k,n}}{r_{k,n}} \right) CF_k.$$
(13)

The CPF scheduling algorithm is detailed in Fig. 2. The distance correction factor CF_k adequately compensates the lower spectral efficiencies of far mobiles and the resulting

$CPF_{k,n}$ parameters bring high fairness in the allocation process. Far mobiles get access to the resource more often than close mobiles and inverse proportionally to their spectral efficiency. Thereby, an equal throughput is provided to each mobile. Moreover, CPF also keeps the PF opportunistic scheduling advantages thanks to the $f_{k,n}$ parameters which take into account the channel state. In contrast with MaxSNR and PF which satisfy much faster the mobiles which are close to the access point, the CPF keeps more mobiles active but with a relatively low traffic backlog. Satisfaction of delay constraints is more uniform and, preserving the multiuser diversity, a better usage of the bandwidth is made. This jointly ensures fairness and system throughput maximization.

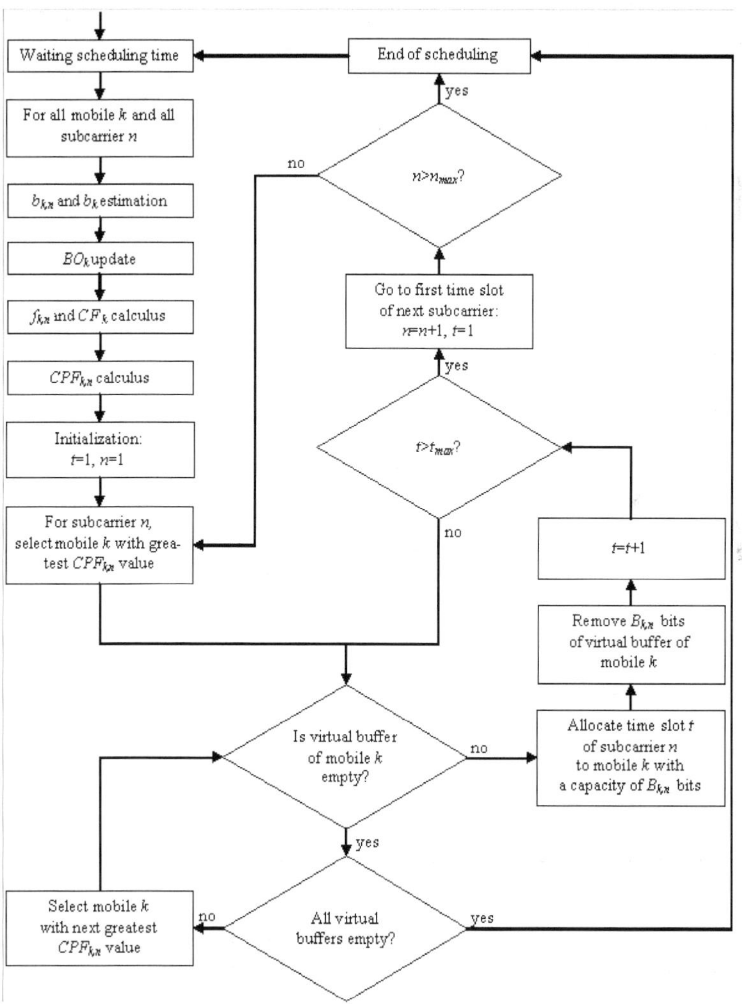

Fig. 2. CPF scheduling algorithm flow chart.

4. Performance evaluation

In this section an extend performance evaluation using OPNET discrete event simulations is proposed. We focus on two essential performance criteria: fairness and offered system capacity.

In the simulations, a frame is composed of 5 time slots and 128 subcarriers. β is assumed equal to 2 and the maximum transmit power satisfies:

$$10\log_{10}\left(\frac{P_{max}T_s}{N_0} \times a_{ref}\right) = 24 \ dB \ . \tag{14}$$

All mobiles run a videoconference application. The traffic is composed of an MPEG-4 video stream (Baey, 2004) multiplexed with an AMR voice stream (Brady, 1969). This demanding type of application generates a high volume of data with high sporadicity and requires tight delay constraints which substantially complicates the task of the scheduler. The average bit rate of each source is 80 Kbps. The traffic load is set by varying the number of mobiles. This allows to study the ability of each scheduler to take advantage of the multiuser diversity.

A crucial objective for modern multiple access schemes is the full support of multimedia transmission services. Evaluating the QoS offered by a scheduling scheme should not only focus on the classical delay and jitter analysis. Indeed, a meaningful constraint regarding delay is the limitation of the occurrences of large values. In this aim, we define the concept of *delay outage* by analogy with the concept of outage used in system coverage planning. A mobile transmission is in delay outage when its packets experience a delay greater than a given threshold. The delay experienced by each mobile is tracked all along the lifetime of its connection. At each transmission of a packet of mobile k, the ratio of the total number of packets whose delay exceeded the threshold divided by the total number of packets transmitted since the beginning of the connection is computed. The result is called Packet Delay Outage Ratio (PDOR) of mobile k and is denoted $PDOR_k$. Fig. 3 illustrates an example cumulative distribution of the packet delay of a mobile at a given time instant.

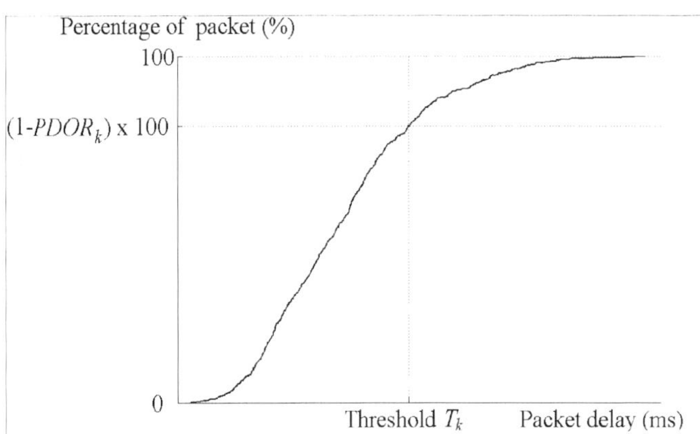

Fig. 3. Example packet delay CDF and experienced PDOR.

The PDOR target is defined as the maximum ratio of packets of mobile k that may be delivered after its delay threshold T_k. This characterizes the delay requirements of any mobile in a generic approach. In the following, the PDOR target is set to 5 % and the threshold time T_k is fixed to the value of 80 ms considering real time constraints. The BER_{target} value is taken equal to 10^{-3}.

Note that the problem we are studying in this chapter is quite different with the sum-rate maximization with water-filling for instance. The purpose of the schedulers presented in this chapter is to maximize the traffic load that can be admitted in the wireless access network while fulfilling delay constraints. This is achieved by both taking into account the radio conditions but also the variations in the incoming traffic. In this context, it cannot be assumed for instance that each mobile has some traffic to send at each scheduling epoch. Traffic overload is not realistic in a wireless access network because it corresponds to situations where the excess traffic experiences an unbounded delay. This is why, in the showed simulations, the traffic load (offered traffic) does not exceed the system capacity. In these conditions the offered traffic is strictly equal to the traffic carried over the wireless interface and all mobiles get served sooner or later. The bit rate sent by each mobile is equal to its incoming traffic. Fairness in terms of bit rate sent by each mobile is rigorously achieved. The purpose of the scheduler is to dynamically assign the resource units to the mobiles at the best time in order to meet the traffic delay constraints. This is why the PDOR is adopted as a measure of the fairness in terms of QoS level obtained by each mobile.

4.1 Static scenario

In order to study the influence of the distance on the scheduling performances, a first half of mobiles are positioned close to the access point at a distance of 1.5 d_{ref}. The second half of mobiles are twice over farther. With these settings, the values of $B_{k,n}$ for the two groups of mobiles are respectively 4 and 2 bits when $\alpha_{k,n}^2$ equals unity.

Fairness is the most difficult objective to reach. It consists in ensuring the same ratio of packets in delay outage to all mobiles, below the PDOR target. Fig. 4 displays the overall PDOR for various traffic loads. The influence of distance on the scheduling is also studied.

Classical RR yields bad results (Fig. 4a). Indeed, since multiuser diversity is not exploited, the overall spectral efficiency is small and system throughput is low. Consequently, the delay targets are exceeded as soon as the traffic load increases. Based on opportunistic scheduling, MaxSNR (Fig. 4b), PF (Fig. 4c) and CPF (Fig. 4d) provide better system performances. However, with MaxSNR and PF, close mobiles easily respect their delay requirement but the farther experience much higher delays and go beyond their PDOR target when the traffic load increases. This shows their difficulty to ensure fairness when the mobiles have heterogeneous positions. Indeed, with MaxSNR, unnecessary priorities are given to close mobiles who easily respect their QoS constraints while more attention should be given to the farther. These inadequate priority management dramatically increases the global mobile PDOR and mobile dissatisfaction. PF brings slightly more fairness and allocates more priority to far mobiles. The result on global overall PDOR indicates that some flows can be slightly delayed to the benefit of others without significantly affecting their QoS.

The CPF was built on this idea. The easy satisfaction of close mobiles (with better spectral efficiency) offers a degree of freedom which ideally should be exploited in order to help the farther ones. CPF dynamically adapts the priorities function of the mobile location. This results in allocating to each mobile the accurate share of bandwidth required for the

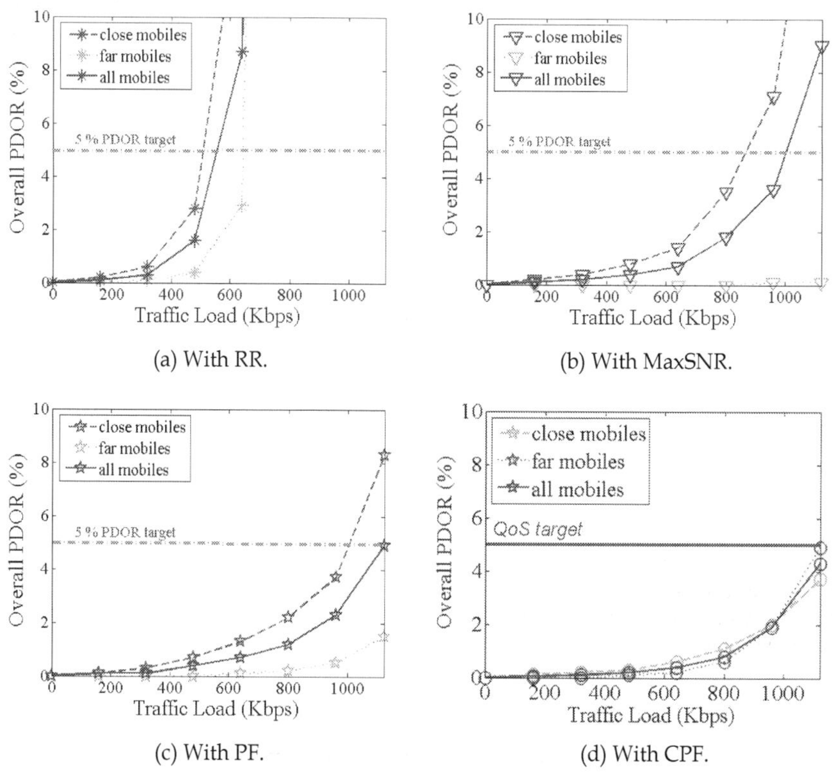

(a) With RR.   (b) With MaxSNR.

(c) With PF.   (d) With CPF.

Fig. 4. Measured QoS with respect to distance.

satisfaction of its QoS constraints, whatever its position. Like this, the problem of fairness is solved with CPF which provides comparable QoS levels to all mobiles whatever their respective location and allows to reach higher traffic loads with an acceptable PDOR (below the PDOR target). Additionally, observing the global PDOR value (for all mobiles), we can notice that, besides ensuring high fairness, CPF provides a better overall QoS level as well.

Fig. 5 shows the average number of bits carried per allocated Resource Unit by each tested scheduler under various traffic loads. Looking at the cost of this high fairness and mobile satisfaction in terms of system capacity, it appears that no system throughput reduction has been done with CPF. As expected, the non opportunistic Round Robin scheduling provides a constant spectral efficiency, i.e. an equal bit rate per subcarrier whatever the traffic load since it does not take advantage of the multiuser diversity. The three other tested schedulers show better results. In contrast with RR, with the opportunistic schedulers (MaxSNR, PF, CPF), we observe a characteristic inflection of the spectral efficiency curves when the traffic load increases. Exploiting the supplementary multiuser diversity, the system capacity is highly extended. This result also shows that the CPF scheduling has slightly better performances than the two other opportunistic schedulers. This improved multiplexing efficiency is obtained by processing all service flows jointly and opportunistically. Keeping

Medium Access Control in Distributed Wireless Networks

Jun Peng
University of Texas - Pan American, Edinburg, Texas
United States of America

1. Introduction

Medium access control (MAC) is a fundamental and challenging problem in networking. This problem is at the data link layer which interfaces the physical layer and the upper layers. A solution to this problem in a particular network thus needs to factor in the characteristics of the physical layer and the upper layers, which makes the MAC problem both a challenging and evolving problem. Medium access control in distributed wireless networks is one of the most active research areas in networking because distributed wireless networks are diverse and evolving fast.

One of the most well-known problem in medium access control in distributed wireless networks is the hidden terminal problem. Hidden terminals are interesting but problematic phenomena in distributed wireless networks. Basically, even if two nodes in a wireless network cannot sense each other, they may still cause collisions at the receiver of each other (1). If the hidden terminal problem is not well addressed, a wireless network may have a significantly degraded performance in every aspect, since frequent packet collisions consume all types of network resources such as energy, bandwidth, and computing power but generate no useful output.

There are basically two existing approaches to the hidden terminal problem. One is the use of an out-of-band control channel for signaling a busy data channel when a packet is in the air (2; 3; 4; 5). This approach is effective in dealing with hidden terminals but requires an additional control channel. The more popular approach to the hidden terminal problem is the use of in-band control frames for reserving the medium before a packet is transmitted (6; 7; 8; 9; 10). The popular IEEE 802.11 standard (11) uses this approach in its distributed coordination function (DCF).

Basically, before an IEEE 802.11 node in the DCF mode transmits a packet to another node, it first sends out a Request to Send (RTS) frame after proper backoffs and deferrals. If the receiver successfully receives the RTS frame and the channel is clear, the receiver responds with a Clear to Send (CTS) frame, which includes a Duration field informing its neighbors to back off during the specified period. In an ideal case, the hidden terminals of the initiating sender will successfully receive the CTS frame and thus not initiate new transmissions when the packet is being transmitted.

However, control frames have limited effectiveness in dealing with hidden terminals because they may not be able to reach all the intended receivers due to signal attenuation, fading, or interference (12). In addition, control frames have considerably long airtimes because they are recommended to be transmitted at the basic link rate in both narrow-band and broadband IEEE 802.11 systems. Moreover, they have relatively long physical layer preambles and headers. In-band control frames therefore introduce significant network overhead, even though they do not use an out-of-band control channel.

This article introduces a new approach of *bit-free* control frames to addressing the disadvantages of the traditional control frames. Basically, with the new approach, control information is carried by the *airtimes* instead of the *bits* of control frames. The airtime of a frame is robust against interference and channel effects. In addition, a bit-free control frame carries no meaningful bits so that no preamble or header is needed for it (Section 6 presents a fundamental view on bit-free control frames).

In investigating the performance of the new approach, we have first analyzed the potential performance gains of the IEEE 802.11 DCF if its traditional control frames are replaced by bit-free control frames. We have then modified the original protocol with the new approach of bit-free control frames and done extensive simulations. Our investigation has shown that the modified protocol improves the average throughput of a wireless network from fifteen percent to more than one hundred percent.

The rest of this article is organized as follows. Section 2 introduces our observations and analysis. Section 3 presents our modifications to the IEEE 802.11 DCF. We then show in Section 4 the comprehensive simulation results comparing the modified protocol to the original one. We introduce the related work in Section 5 and a fundamental view on the presented approach in Section 6. Finally, we give our conclusions in Section 7.

2. Observations and analysis

Our first observation is that the CTS frame of an IEEE 802.11 node may not be able to reach all the hidden terminals of the initiating sender, which was also studied in some related work such as (12). One source of the problem is that recovering the bits in a frame is a delicate process so that to corrupt a frame being received by a node is usually much easier than to correctly receive a frame from the same node. In general, if a node is receiving a frame at the power level L, then another node may corrupt the frame by generating a power of level l at the receiver in the channel that is several times lower than L. In particular, when $\frac{L}{l}$ is lower than the "capture" power ratio threshold, then the frame will be corrupted.

An example is shown in Fig. 1. We assume in the example that the network is a homogeneous network, which means that all the nodes are the same in terms of parameters such as transmission power and receive/carrier sense power thresholds. We also assume that the signal power deteriorates at a rate of $(\frac{1}{d})^4$ where d is the propagation distance (i.e., the receiver is beyond the crossover distance from the sender), the carrier sense range of a node is twice of its transmission range r, and the capture power ratio threshold is 10, as used as the default settings in ns-2 and in some other studies (12). Under these assumptions, node C shown in Fig. 1 is a hidden terminal to node A. Meanwhile, node C cannot correctly receive a frame from node B, since it is out of node B's transmission range. However, node C can still corrupt a frame at node B that is from node A. Therefore, node C is a hidden terminal of node A that cannot be addressed by the CTS control frame sent by node B. Actually, all nodes falling into the closed region enclosing node C are hidden terminals of node A that cannot be addressed by the CTS frames of node B.

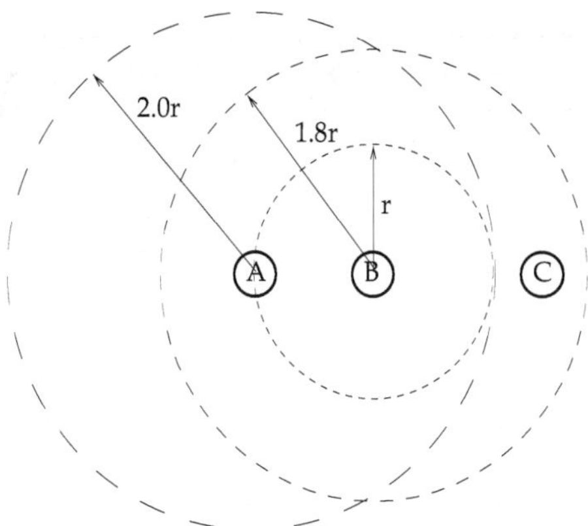

Fig. 1. A Case of a Failed CTS Frame for Reserving the Medium

Besides their limited effectiveness in dealing with hidden terminals, the control frames of IEEE 802.11 DCF also introduce significant overhead. There are two factors increasing the overhead. First, the control frames are recommended in both narrow-band and broadband IEEE 802.11 systems to be transmitted at the basic link rate for rate compatibility among competing nodes, which makes the bits in a control frame "flow" relatively slowly. Second, a bit-based frame, whatever the number of payload bits in it, needs a physical layer preamble and header for successful bit delivery.

As specified in IEEE 802.11, a DSSS (Direct Sequence Spread Spectrum) physical layer introduces 192-bit overhead (144-bit preamble plus 48-bit header) to each frame, while a FHSS (Frequency-Hopping Spread Spectrum) physical layer has an overhead of 128 bits (96-bit preamble plus 32-bit header). In the DSSS case, a RTS frame only uses 36% of its air time for delivering specific MAC information. It is even worse for a CTS frame, for which the percentage is 26%. The situation is relatively better in the FHSS case. The percentages are, however, still low at 44% and 33% for a RTS frame and a CTS frame, respectively.

We may use some analysis to demonstrate how a protocol that overcomes the two disadvantages of the IEEE 802.11 DCF may decrease the control overhead and thus improve the throughput of a network. After proper deferrals and backoffs, an IEEE 802.11 sender in the DCF mode starts to transmit the RTS frame. With a probability of p_c, however, the RTS frame may encounter a contention collision because another contending sender may have drawn a similar backoff delay. Even if there is no contention collision, the RTS frame may still face a collision later because of the possible existence of hidden terminals. We may assume the probability of such a collision as p_h. Therefore, a RTS frame with a transmission time of t_{rts} consumes a medium time of

$$T_{rts} = \frac{1}{(1 - p_c) \times (1 - p_h)} \times (T_{bo} + t_{rts}) \ (1)$$

before it is successfully received by the intended receiver, where T_{bo} is the average backoff time in a contention and the interframe space times are considered as negligible.

If the RTS frame is successfully received by the intended receiver, we may assume that the CTS frame will not have a collision at the initiating sender, considering that the RTS frame has already reserved the medium around the initiating sender. However, there is still a probability of $f \times p_h$ (f is the hidden terminal residual factor of DCF and $f \leq 1$) that the data packet may encounter a collision because some hidden terminals of the initiating sender may have failed to receive the CTS frame, as explained earlier. When the data packet has a collision, the RTS/CTS/Data process needs to be repeated. If we denote the transmission time of a CTS frame and of an ACK frame by t_{cts} and t_{ack}, respectively, then the medium time consumed for delivering a data packet and all its retransmissions is as follows

$$T = \frac{1}{1 - f \times p_h} \times (T_{rts} + t_{cts} + t_{data}) + t_{ack}. \tag{2}$$

We also assume here that the ACK may not have a collision, as in the CTS frame case.

The average time for successfully sending a packet will be decreased if the 802.11 DCF is modified with the new approach of bit-free control frames. We may use $\frac{1}{r}$ ($r < 1$) to denote the improvement factor of the effectiveness of the control frames in reducing the probability of collisions caused by hidden terminals. We may also denote the length reduction factor for the control frames by v ($v < 1$). Then, the medium time needed for successfully sending a RTS frame with the modified protocol is

$$T'_{rts} = \frac{1}{(1 - p_c) \times (1 - p_h)} \times (T_{bo} + v \times t_{rts}), \tag{3}$$

and the time for successfully sending a packet in such a case is

$$T' = \frac{1}{1 - r \times f \times p_h} \times (T'_{rts} + v \times t_{cts} + t_{data}) + v \times t_{ack}. \tag{4}$$

We now show by an example how the modified protocol with bit-free control frames may reduce the control overhead and thus increase the throughput of a network. For easy reference, we named the modified MAC protocol as CSMA/FP, which denotes Carrier Sense Multiple Access with Frame Pulses (bit-free frames may be regarded as a type of in-band pulses). In the example, the network has a DSSS physical layer, the control and data frames are transmitted at 1 Mb/s and 2 Mb/s, respectively, and each packet has a size of 512 bytes. In addition, p_h assumes a value of 0.2, which means that a frame without medium reservation has a probability of 0.2 to encounter a collision caused by hidden terminals. The hidden terminal residue factor f assumes a value of 0.2 for the IEEE 802.11 DCF in the example. T_{bo} takes the value of 2 ms for a high network load case, which is a typical value shown by our simulation results in Section 4. Finally, r and v assume values of 2 and 0.4, respectively, in the example.

Fig. 2 shows the average medium time consumed for successfully delivering a packet with the two protocols in our example as the probability of a contention collision on a frame increases (i.e., as the number of nodes and/or the traffic load increase in the network[1]). As shown in the figure, the performance gains of CSMA/FP over IEEE 802.11 DCF may be more than ten percent in our example.

---

[1] Although these factors may also affect p_h, we assign p_h a fixed value for the simplicity of demonstration.

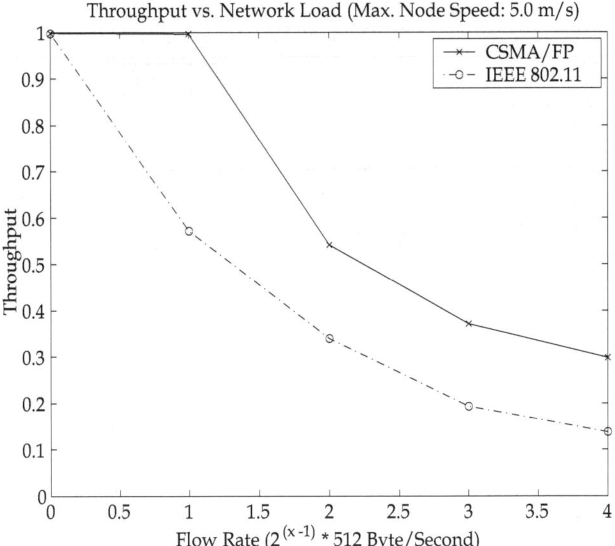

Fig. 6. Flow Throughput, Max Node Speed 5.0 m/s

Fig. 6 shows the throughput of the test flow versus the flow rate in the network, which determines the network load in our simulations. As shown in the figure, when the rate of the background flows is 0.5*512 B/s, almost all packets of the test flow are successfully delivered by the network with either MAC protocol. However, as the network load increases, more packets of the test flow are delivered by the network with the modified MAC protocol.

Particularly, when the rate of the background flows is 1*512 or 2*512 B/s, the throughput of the test flow increases by at least 50% as the modified MAC protocol replaces the original one. When the rate of the background flows is further increased above 4*512 B/s, the relative performance gains of CSMA/FP reach more than 100%. In summary, the modified protocol shows higher relative performance gains when the network load is higher.

In addition, as shown by the comparison of Fig. 6 to Fig. 4, the modified protocol shows higher performance gains in multihop ad hoc networks than in wireless LANs. These results are expected because there are hidden terminals in the multihop ad hoc network and the modified protocol is more effective in dealing with hidden terminals than the original protocol.

4.4 More hidden terminals

This section shows how the modified protocol performs when there is a higher probability of hidden terminals for a transmitter in the network. To increase the probability of hidden terminals, we increased the carrier sense (CS) power threshold of a node from less than one twentieth to half of its packet receive power threshold. The increase of the CS power threshold shrinks the carrier sense range of a node in the network.

Fig. 7 shows the throughput of the test flow when the CS power threshold has been increased in the network. As shown in Fig. 7, the relative performance gain of the modified protocol is, on average, more than 100% in the case of a higher probability of hidden

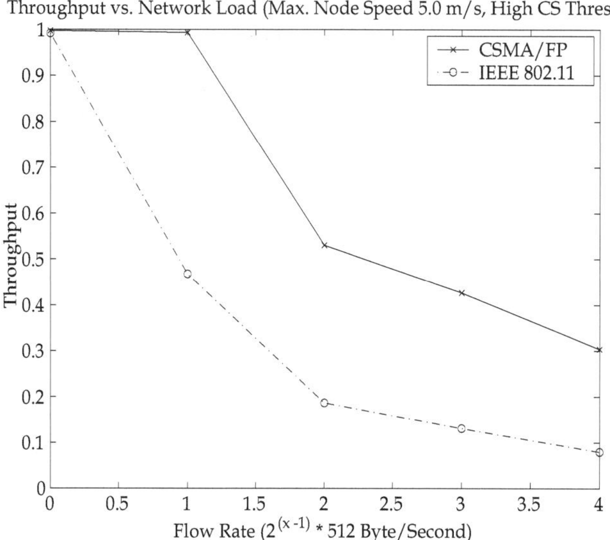

Fig. 7. Higher CS Power Threshold Case

terminals. By comparing Fig. 7 to Fig. 6, we find that the modified protocol has higher performance gains as the probability of hidden terminals is increased in the network. These results further show that the modified protocol is better in dealing with hidden terminals than the original protocol.

4.5 Rayleigh fading channel

By default, the two-ray ground channel model is used in ns-2. We have also investigated the impact of a Rayleigh fading channel on the performance of the modified protocol. The bit-free control frames of the modified protocol are robust against channel effects because of their low receive power threshold. However, a traditional, bit-based control frame may be easily lost in a fading channel.

Fig. 8 shows the results for the case of a Rayleigh fading channel. As shown by the comparison of Fig. 8 to Fig. 6, a fading channel increases the relative performance gains of the modified protocol over the original protocol. These results are expected because traditional control frames are sensitive to fading while any loss of a control frame makes all preceding related transmissions wasted.

4.6 Environmental noise

Besides the impact of channel effects, we have also investigated the impact of environmental noise on the modified protocol. On one hand, the bit-free control frames are robust against environmental noise in the sense that a noise signal may not change the length of a bit-free control frame but may corrupt a bit-based control frame. On the other hand, environmental noise may be falsely interpreted as control frames by a node with the modified MAC protocol. As explained in Section 3, a noise signal must have the right length, arrive at the right node, and possibly arrive at the right time for it to be harmful.

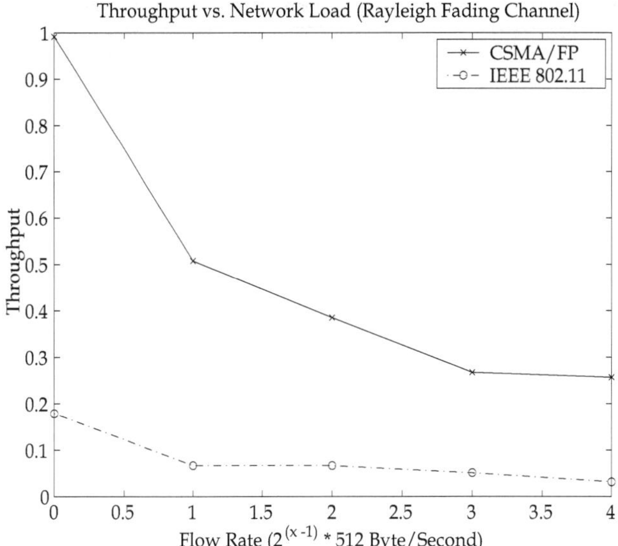

Fig. 8. Rayleigh Fading Channel Case

To test the impact of environmental noise,we placed a noise source at the center of the network and let it generate random-length noise signals at an average rate of 100 signals per second. Moreover, we restricted the noise signal lengths to the range from $1\mu s$ to $200\mu s$, which were the range designated for the bit-free control frames. The simulation results for this scenario are shown in Fig. 9. As shown by the comparison of Fig. 9 to Fig. 6, the modified protocol is not more sensitive to noise than the original one. In fact, after the noise source is introduced in the network, the modified protocol shows higher *relative* performance gains over the original one.

4.7 Protocol resilience

The above subsections are about how external factors may impact the performance of the modified protocol. This subsection shows how the parameters of the protocol affect its performance. We have investigated the three most important parameters of the protocol, which are the receive power thresholds for control frames, the length set for control frames, and the base n of the Mod-n calculations for obtaining RTS frame lengths.

Fig. 10 shows how the modified protocol performs when all its control frames use the same receive power threshold as data frames, which deprives the modified protocol of its advantage of better hidden terminal handling. As shown in the figure, the protocol still maintains significant gains over the original protocol.

Fig. 11 shows the performance of the modified protocol as the average length of its control frames becomes similar to the average length of the bit-based control frames of the original protocol. As shown in this figure, the performance of the modified protocol degrades gracefully in this case.

Fig. 12 shows how the modified protocol performs as the base n of the Mod-n calculation is halved. Halving the n is similar to doubling the node density of the network in terms of

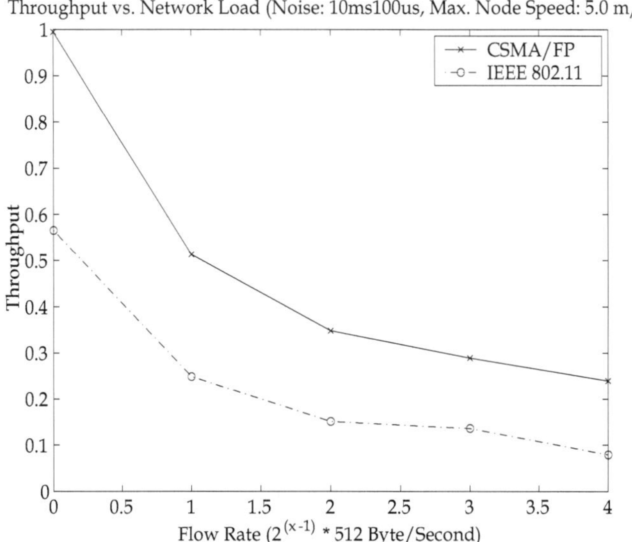

Fig. 9. Environmental Noise Case

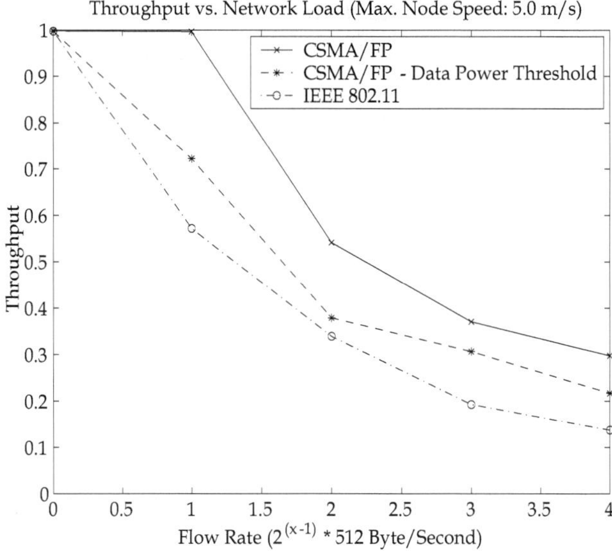

Fig. 10. Data Receive Power Threshold Case

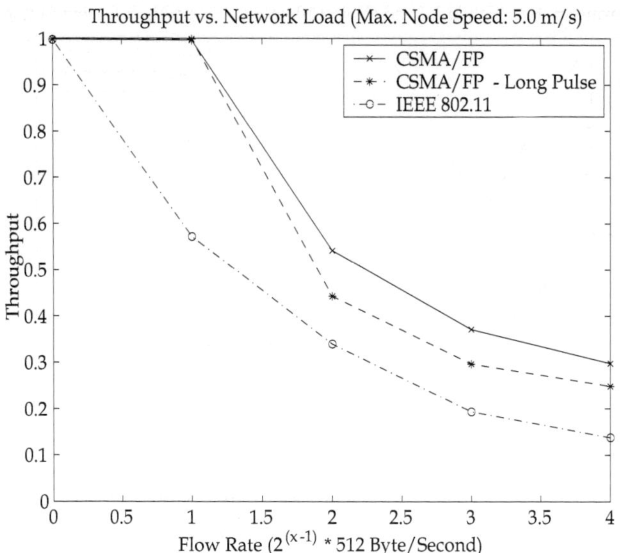

Fig. 11. Long Bit-Free Control Frames Case

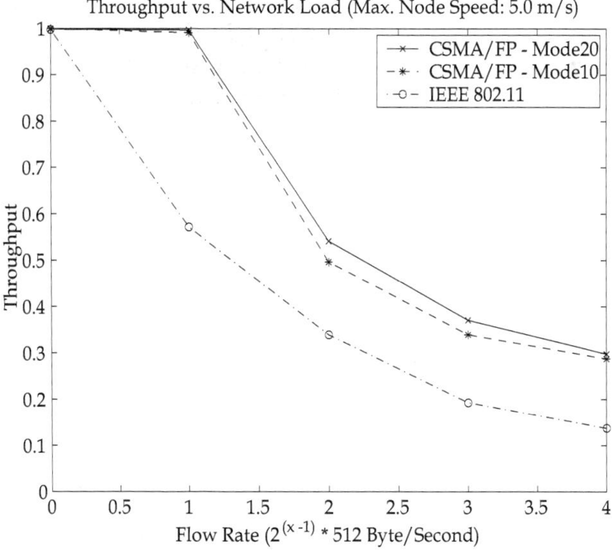

Fig. 12. Mod-n: n Changes from 20 to 10

investigating how the redundant CTS frames for a RTS frame may affect the performance of the protocol. As shown in Fig. 12, the performance of the modified protocol has a graceful degradation when the n is halved.

5. Related work

We introduce in this section some recent efforts on improving the IEEE 802.11 DCF in the community. Many efforts have been made to modify the backoff algorithm of the DCF. Cali et al. proposed an algorithm that enables each node to tune its backoff algorithm at run-time (15). Bianchi et al. proposed the use of a Kalman filter to estimate the number of active nodes in the network for dynamically adjusting the CW (16). Kwon et al. proposed a new CW adjustment algorithm that is to double the CW of any node that either experiences a collision or loses a contention (17). On the other hand, Ma et al. proposed a centralized way to dynamically adjust the backoff algorithm (18). From a theoretical perspective, Yang et al. investigated the design of backoff algorithms (19).

Another interesting scheme on backoff algorithms, named *Idle Sense*, was proposed by Heusse et al (20). With Idle Sense, a node monitors the number of idle timeslots between transmission attempts and then adjusts its contention window accordingly. This method uses interference-free feedback signals and the authors showed its fairness and flexibility among other features. Instead of modifying the backoff algorithm, some other works proposed diverse ways to improve the performance of the IEEE 802.11 DCF. Peng et al. proposed the use of out-of-band pulses for collision detection in distributed wireless networks (5). Sadeghi et al. proposed a multirate scheme that exploits the durations of high-quality channel conditions (21). Cesana et al. proposed the embedding of received power and interference level information in control frames for better spatial reuse of spectrum (22). Sarkar et al. proposed the combination of short packets in a flow to form large frames for reducing control and transmission overhead (23). Additionally, Zhu et al. proposed a multirate scheme that uses relay nodes in the MAC sub-layer (24).

Different from the work mentioned above, the work in this article is to improve the effectiveness and the efficiency of the collision avoidance (CA) part of the IEEE 802.11 DCF. The proposed method may work with other schemes that improve the backoff algorithm of the DCF protocol (i.e., the CSMA part of the protocol).

6. A fundamental view

Finally, we provide a fundamental view on bit-free control frames from the perspectives of information theory and digital communications. The basic goals of bit-free control frames are to increase the range, reliability, and efficiency of control information delivery for medium access control.

Information theory states that the capacity of a channel decreases as the signal to noise ratio decreases. For example, the capacity of a band-limited Gaussian channel is

$$C = W \log(1 + \frac{P}{N_0 W}) \tag{6}$$

where the noise spectral density is $N_0/2$. This equation basically states that when the received power P is lower, then the channel capacity is smaller. Therefore, if the control information for medium access control needs to be delivered in a larger range without sacrificing reliability, then the transmission power may need to be increased (the bandwidth W is usually fixed).

There are, however, two issues with the approach of higher power for control frames. One is that the transmission power for control frames has to be increased by at least multiple times because signals deteriorate fast in wireless channels. For example, if the transmission range of a control frame needs to be doubled, then the transmission power may have to be increased by more than ten times even in free space. The other issue is that when the transmission range of a control frame is increased, then its carrier sense range is also increased at the same ratio, which causes unnecessary backoff for some nodes.

Instead, the capacity of the channel may be traded, as shown by Equation 6. The first step in this direction is to trim the control information for medium access control, which is to only deliver indispensable control information. The second step is to find away to realize the tradeoff by using new physical layer mechanisms. With bit-free control frames, the medium access control information is not translated into *bits* and then goes through the *bit* delivery process. Instead, the control information is directly modulated by the airtimes of control frames. From this perspective, the bit-free control frame approach is a cross-layer approach with which control information is delivered with a simple modulation method that trades capacity for transmission range and information reliability.

7. Conclusions

We have presented in this article a new approach of *bit-free* control frames to collision avoidance in distributed wireless packet networks. With the new approach, medium access control information is not delivered through bit flows. Instead, the information is encoded into the airtimes of bit-free control frames. Bit-free control frames are robust against channel effects and interference. Furthermore, bit-free control frames can be short because they do not include headers or preambles. We have investigated the new approach by analysis and extensive simulations. We have shown how hidden terminals, a fading channel, and environmental noise may impact the performance of the new approach. Additionally, we have examined the impact of the average length, the receive power thresholds, and the length set size of control frames on the performance of the new approach. Our conclusion is that the new bit-free control frame approach improves the throughput of a wireless LAN or ad hoc network from fifteen percent to more than one hundred percent.

8. References

[1] F. A. Tobagi and L. Kleinrock, "Packet switching in radio channels: Part II - the hidden terminal problem in carrier sense multiple access and the busy tone solution," *IEEE Transactions on Communications*, vol. 23, pp. 1417–1433, 1975.

[2] L. Kleinrock and F. A. Tobagi, "Packet switching in radio channels: Part i - carrier sense multiple-access modes and their throughput- delay characteristics," *IEEE Transactions on Communications*, vol. 23, pp. 1400–1416, 1975.

[3] C. Wu and V. O. K. Li, "Receiver-initiated busy-tone multiple access in packet radio networks," in *Proc. of the ACM SIGCOMM*, Stowe, Vermont, August 1987.

[4] Z. J. Haas and J. Deng, "Dual Busy Tone Multiple Access (DBTMA) - a multiple access control scheme for ad hoc networks," *IEEE Transactions on Communications*, vol. 50, pp. 975–985, June 2002.

[5] J. Peng, L. Cheng, and B. Sikdar, "A new MAC protocol for wireless packet networks," in *IEEE GLOBECOM 2006*, San Francisco, CA, Nov.-Dec. 2006.

[6] A. Colvin, "CSMA with collision avoidance," *Computer Commun.*, vol. 6, pp. 227–235, 1983.

[7] P. Karn, "MACA - a newchannel accessmethod for packet radio," in *Proc. of the 9th ARRL Computer Networking Conference*, Ontario, Canada, 1990.

[8] C. L. Fullmer and J. J. Garcia-Luna-Aceves, "Floor acquisition multiple access (FAMA) for packet-radio networks," in *Proc. of the ACM SIGCOMM*, September 1995.

[9] V. Bharghavan, A. Demers, S. Shenker, and L. Zhang, "MACAW: a medium access protocol for wireless LANs," in *Proc. of the ACM SIGCOMM*, London, United Kingdom, August 1994.

[10] C. L. Fullmer and J. J. Garcia-Luna-Aceves, "Solutions to hidden terminal problems in wireless networks," in *Proc. of the ACM SIGCOMM*, French Riviera, France, September 1997.

[11] IEEE 802.11 wireless local area networks. [Online]. Available: http://grouper.ieee.org/groups/802/11/

[12] K. Xu,M. Gerla, and S. Bae, "How effective is the IEEE 802.11 RTS/CTS handshake in ad hoc networks?" in *Proc. of the IEEE GLOBECOM*, Taipei, Taiwan, November 2002.

[13] The network simulator - ns-2. [Online]. Available: http://www.isi.edu/nsnam/ns/

[14] D. B. Johnson, D. A. Maltz, and Y.-C. Hu, "The dynamic source routing protocol for mobile ad hoc networks (DSR)," *IETF Interet draft, draft-ietf-manet-dsr-10.txt*, July 2004.

[15] F. Cali, M. Conti, and E. Gregori, "Dynamic tuning of the IEEE 802.11 protocol," *IEEE/ACM Transactions on Networking*, vol. 8, pp. 785 – 799, Dec. 2000.

[16] G. Bianchi and I. Tinnirello, "Kalman filter estimation of the number of competing terminals in an IEEE 802.11 network," in *Proc. of the IEEE INFOCOM*, 2003.

[17] Y. Kwon, Y. Fang, andH. Latchman, "A novelMAC protocolwith fast collision resolution for wireless LANs," in *Proc. of the IEEE INFOCOM*, 2003.

[18] H.Ma, H. Li, P. Zhang, S. Luo, C. Yuan, and X. Li, "Dynamic optimization of IEEE 802.11 CSMA/CA based on the number of competing stations," in *Proc. of the IEEE ICC*, 2004.

[19] Y. Yang, J. Wang, and R. Kravets, "Distributed optimal contention window control for elastic traffic in wireless LANs," in *Proc. of the IEEE INFOCOM*, 2005.

[20] M. Heusse, F. Rousseau, R. Guillier, and A. Duda, "Idle Sense: An optimal accessmethod for high throughput and fairness in rate diverse wireless LANs," in *Proc. of the ACM SIGCOMM*, 2005.

[21] B. Sadeghi, V. Kanodia, A. Sabharwal, and E. Knightly, "Opportunistic media access for multirate ad hoc networks," in *Proc. of the ACM MOBICOM*, 2002.

[22] M. Cesana, D. Maniezzo, P. Bergamo, and M. Gerla, "Interference aware (IA) MAC: an enhancement to IEEE802.11b DCF," in *Proc. of the VTC*, 2003.

[23] N. Sarkar and K. Sowerby, "Buffer unit multiple access (BUMA) protocol: an enhancement to IEEE 802.11b DCF," in *Proc. of the IEEE GLOBECOM*, 2005.

[24] H. Zhu and G. Cao, "rDCF: A Relay-enabled Medium Access Control Protocol for Wireless Ad Hoc Networks," in *Proc. of the IEEE INFOCOM*, 2005.

Then define

$$\lambda = \lambda_1/\lambda_2 \quad (\ 0<\lambda_1 <\lambda_2<1) \tag{3}$$

θ in equation (1) stands for the function of T_n, shown in equation (2). It is used to adjust the weighting between historical STV and current evaluation. When historical STV is close to the original trust value, current evaluation should be emphatically considered. On the contrary, when historical trust value is far away from the original trust value, historical evaluation should be focused on.

In equation (3), λ_1 and λ_2 indicate respectively the increasing and decreasing extent of STV after each successful transaction, while λ shows the ratio of increasing extent to decreasing extent. Generally, decreasing extent is greater than increasing extent, controlled by λ. Furthermore, the algorithm can also be designed as: when the STV decreases to a given threshold even though the later transaction is honest, the increasing extent of STV will still be less than the decreasing one. In this way, the malicious behaviors can be published dramatically.

Since updating algorithms of RTV and STV are the same, there is no further discussion here.

4.2 Attacks and defenses

Strategy node attacks

Generally, strategy nodes achieve high trust value through some small transactions. Afterwards, they execute a big cheat. Repeatedly, they obtain the maximum benefits with minimum cost. Therefore, our reputation model needs to make the rising of trust value be slower. Specifically, we can adjust the value of λ in equation (3). Decreasing the value of λ, which means that the decreasing extent of trust value is much larger than the increasing extent, can prevent strategy nodes from gaining benefits.

Imputation attacks and boosts attacks

If some honest nodes are slandered by some malicious ones, their STV will decrease to quite a low level. Therefore, reputation model should be able to offer nodes the chance to regain their STV. Meanwhile, the request trust value of malicious nodes will decrease accordingly. In this way, when request trust value of malicious nodes decreases to some threshold, there are no nodes which would like to respond to them in networks. In this way, the requests of malicious nodes will be constrained, and malicious nodes would not dare to defame other nodes.

It's not comprehensive to accumulate the trust value based on only a few transactions with nodes, because boost attacks will be easy to come up among a few nodes. Therefore trust evaluation should be collected deep and extensively (Wang, Mokhta, et al., 2008). According to this idea, if transaction successful times reach out to a given value, the STV updating algorithm will change, that is, increasing extent will be slower. Specifically, we can change the λ_1 in equation (1) into $\lambda_1 \times 1/n$ (n stands for transaction successful times between two nodes) to control the deep collection of trust information.

Collusion attacks

Collusive nodes always cooperate with each other (for instance, virtual transactions) to increase their trust value, and organize together to slander other nodes with higher STV. This kind of "teamwork" attack is more harmful than single imputation or boost attack. However, since what we discuss in this chapter is logic network where information is transmitted in flooding; login server automatically creates logical neighbours for new-joining nodes and randomly distributes them to other nodes as neighbours, a collusion group is hard to form between nodes, which can restrict collusion attacks to some extent.

Sybil attacks (Douceur &Donath, 2002) **and Newcomer attacks** (Resnick & Zeckhauser, 2000)

A malicious node can make Sybil attacks to reputation model by pretending to be different nodes in networks with different IDs each time. In this way, different IDs can share the decreasing of trust value so that a single ID of malicious node suffers less punishment.

If a malicious node can easily join in a network as a fresh one, it will delete its bad trust records by frequently entering and leaving the network. This is so-called Newcomer attacks. Two schemes as below can resolve these two kinds of attacks.

Scheme 1: Login server needs some evidences to ensure that each node has one system ID. To keep login server from being open to attacks, such as DoS attack, the function of login server should be decentralized. However, fewer users would like to login if authentic and sensitive information is required. If we just bind the IP address with node ID instead of using login server, sybil attacks will be hard to fight against. SybilGuard (Yu, Kaminsky, et al., 2008) can be seen as a reference, for Yu et al. have proposed an effective protocol to wipe off "attack edge".

Scheme 2: This chapter mainly focuses on reputation model, not only encouraging new-joining nodes but also preventing newcomer attacks. Therefore, we can adopt a mechanism that nodes trust value can slowly reach a certain level which is not too high, if they succeed in previous transactions with a given number. When malicious nodes find it difficult to gain as much benefit as new-joining ones, newcomer attacks will be reduced. For example, a node trust value can finally reach the highest trust value 0.6 after previous 10 successful transactions, while the trust value is easy to drop once nodes process malicious behaviour.

Free riding attacks

There are some nodes referred as free riders in networks. They only receive the service provided by other nodes, but are not willing to provide any service or trust evaluation for other nodes. In our reputation model, the service and request trust value of these nodes all maintain at an initial level, so they can only get very limited resources. In addition, the incentive mechanism (for example, they can obtain the priority of network resources if STV reaches out to some extent) can be adopted in this model to motivate free riders to provide service and trust evaluation.

5. Performance evaluation

To verify the effectiveness of our reputation model, we presented a Java-based simulation program. We firstly checked whether the updating algorithm of trust value can control the STV of strategy nodes. Subsequently, we compared the dual trust values of nodes with expected values when malicious nodes existed in networks. At last, we analyzed how our model resisted the boost attacks.

In simulation environment, we adopted Gnutella routing architecture, with a central server storing trust value. There are totally 1000 nodes and 100 resources in simulation network and each node randomly chooses at most 5 nodes as neighbors and obtains 5 resources. The proportion of malicious nodes is not more than 50%. Averagely, each node sends 100 requests and the Time To Live (TTL) of resource request is 3. We assume that malicious nodes are always the most active ones to respond to any resource request messages. Besides, we also suppose that honest nodes provide honest service and evaluations while malicious nodes provide fake resources and evaluations. The other common parameters for all the simulation are listed in Table 1. The results are the mean value from several simulations, demonstrated from Fig. 7 to Fig. 12.

Parameters	Description	Default
λ	Ratio of increasing extent to decreasing extent	1/8
λ_1	Trust value increasing extent	0.1
λ_2	Trust value decreasing extent	0.8

Table 1. Simulation Settings

Experiment 1: When all the nodes in network are honest nodes except one strategy node, we observed the change of STV of that strategy node, as is shown in Fig. 7.

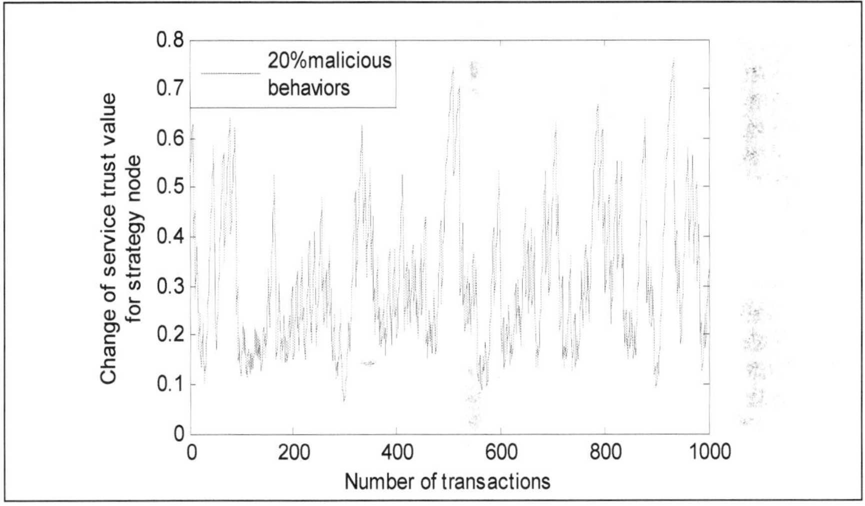

Fig. 7. Changes of STV for Strategy Nodes

In Fig. 7, when strategy node had 20% malicious service, the trust value of that node was controlled at 0.3, at most 0.75. In this case, the strategy node failed to be trusted by resource requester, which made less effect of malicious service on network.

Experiment 2: We set the network with about 30% malicious nodes and 70% honest nodes, and defined that no request could be provided when the RTV of nodes was less than 0.2. Afterwards, we run the updating algorithm of trust value to update dual trust value. After 100000 transactions, we checked whether the STV and RTV of both malicious and honest nodes were within the expected range. The results are presented from Fig. 8 to 10.

Fig. 8 indicates all the STVs of malicious nodes decreased to less than 0.5, which means honest nodes no longer chose these malicious nodes as cooperators. In Fig. 9, all the RTVs of malicious nodes reached 0.195, which was less than 0.2. In this way, these malicious nodes failed to request service. From Fig. 10 we can see that the STV of a minority of honest nodes dropped to 0.5 or less due to imputation attacks from malicious nodes. However, most of honest nodes became trustful nodes, whose STVs approached 1. For those honest nodes whose trust values decreased, our reputation model allowed them to regain the opportunities to be trusted by offering some new services. Fig. 11 shows that the RTV of honest nodes were all more than 0.5, which means that malicious nodes, as responding nodes, could be controlled after a few transactions, and could not be selected by honest nodes again. Thus the effect was less on the RTV of honest nodes.

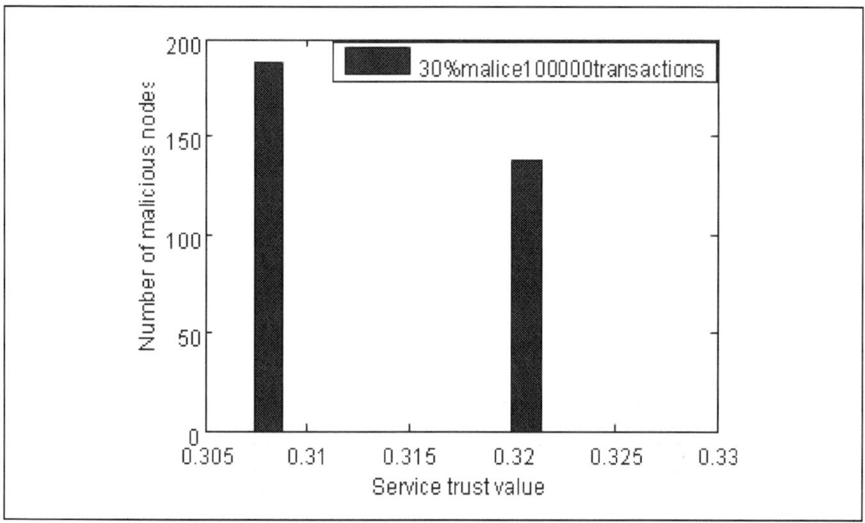

Fig. 8. STV Distribution of Malicious Nodes

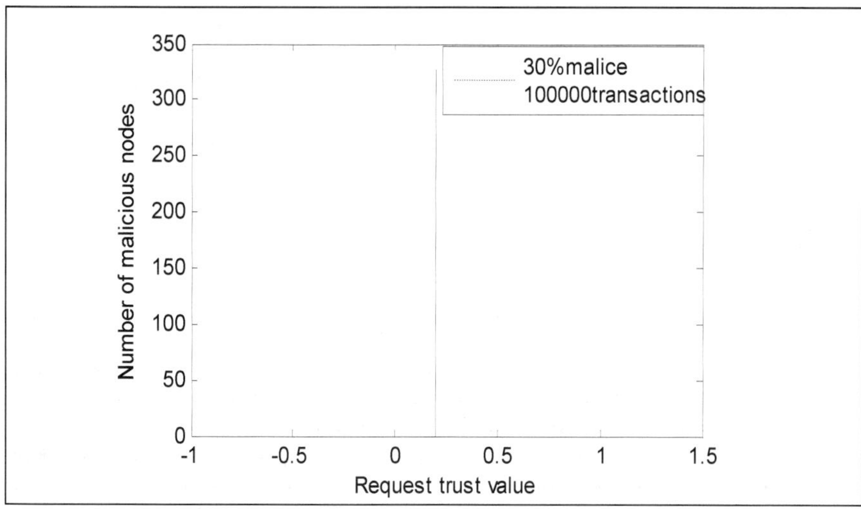

Fig. 9. RTV Distribution of Malicious Nodes

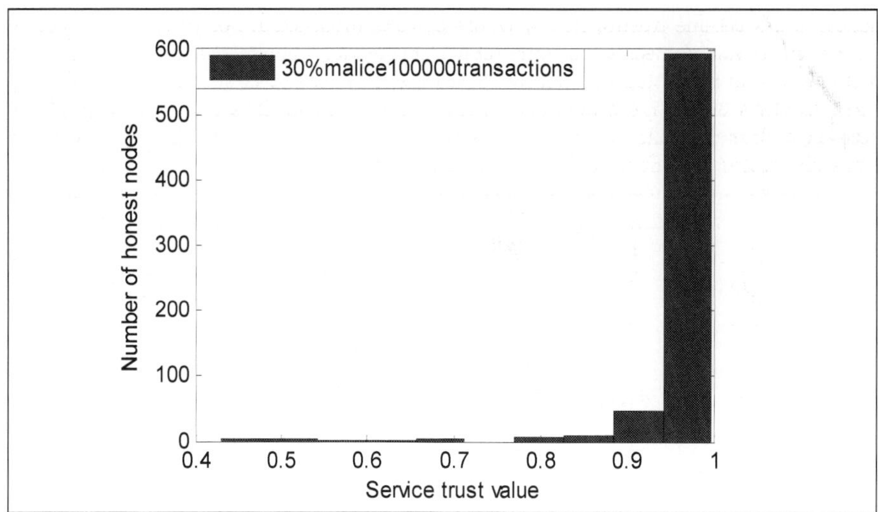

Fig. 10. STV Distribution of Honest Nodes

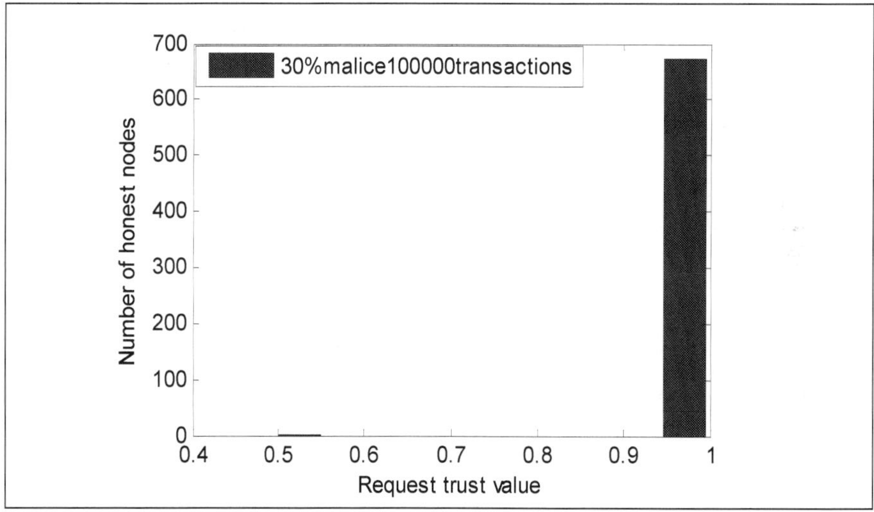

Fig. 11. RTV Distribution of Honest Nodes

Experiment 3: Boost attacks among the nodes in the network will degrade the network performance, causing more damages when happen among malicious nodes. Furthermore, boost attacks can make the STV of malicious nodes rise, hence deceiving honest nodes to transact with them. To avoid this attack, we adopted the updating algorithm with changing λ_1 into $\lambda_1 \times 1/n$. After experiments, we analyzed the changes of STV of some nodes in three conditions: non-boost, 80% boost and 100% boost, as shown in Fig. 12.

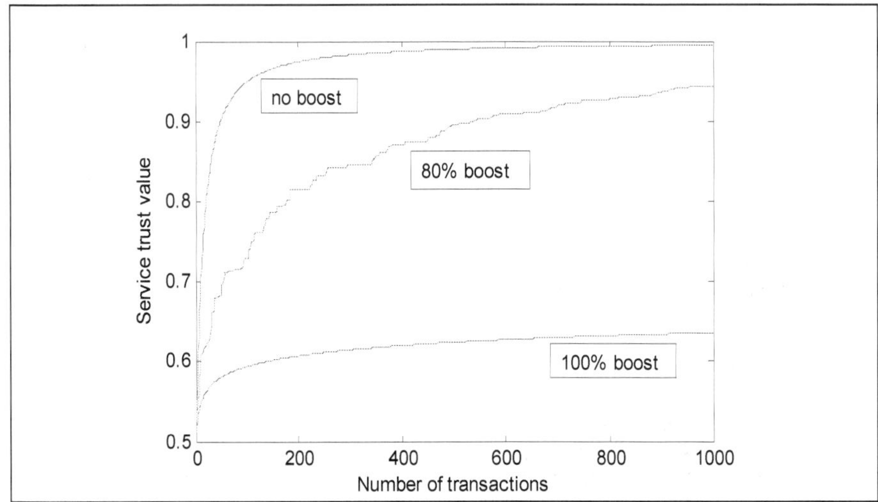

Fig. 12. Comparison of STV for Boost and Non-boost Cases

Fig. 12 illustrates the STV of that node rose slowly in condition of 80% boost, compared with the condition of non-boost. If requesting the same service, this node was selected as service provider. However, due to some honest transactions, the STV can also reach relatively high level after 1000 transactions. On the other hand, we can also see that the STV of malicious nodes in 100% boost achieved 0.6 or so. Once this node responded to honest nodes and is selected as service provider, its STV dropped to less than 0.5 right away. The comparison among these three conditions indicates that our model can effectively resist boost attacks to a certain extent.

6. Discussions and future work

Recommendation mechanism is an important component in any trust evaluation systems. The effectiveness of recommendation is closely related with communication overhead. For example, at the beginning of trust evaluation when few interactions have taken place in the network, higher mobility requires higher overhead. Then, after the trust evaluation system has been running for a long time, a mobile node has had opportunities to interact with many other nodes. Compared with a stationary node, a mobile node has a larger probability to interact with recommenders. In this case, the overhead of requesting recommendations for a node with high mobility can be reduced.

On the other hand, since trust evaluation can effectively improve network performance and detect malicious nodes, trust evaluation itself is an attractive target for attackers (Marmol & Penez, 2009).

A well-known attack is bad-mouthing attack (Dellarocas, 2000), that is, malicious parties providing dishonest recommendations to frame up good parties and/or boost trust values of malicious peers. The defense against the bad-mouthing attack has been considered in the design of the proposed trust evaluation system. First, the action trust and the recommendation trust records are maintained separately. Only the nodes who have provided good recommendations previously can earn high trust. Second, according to the necessary conditions of trust propagation, only the trust from the entities with positive trust can propagate. Third, the fundamental axioms limit the power of the entities with low trust. Trust evaluation may also be vulnerable to the Sybil attack and the newcomer attack. If a malicious node can create several faked IDs, the trust evaluation system suffers from the Sybil attack. Here, the faked IDs can share or even take the blame, which otherwise should be given to the malicious node. If a malicious node can easily register as a new user, the trust evaluation suffers from the newcomer attack. Here, malicious nodes can easily remove their bad history by registering as a new user. The defense against the Sybil attack and newcomer attack does not rely on the design of trust evaluation system, but the authentication and access control mechanisms, which make registering a new ID or a faked ID difficult.

In terms of security issues in trust model, some literatures related to our work have done a lot researches in trust mechanism. Here I will compare some typical models with our work in detail.

S. F. Peng, et. al. showed a weighted trust formula and presented an integrated trust update method. They used abnormal trust value sequence and statistical analysis to detect malicious recommenders and false recommendation trust values in the whole lifetime of trust. In addition, trust value update analysis aims at protecting against untrue recommendation, such as the collusion problem. However, authors adopted a common formula $T\ (n,\ m)= \alpha \times T_d+(1-\alpha)\ T_r$ to do the trust evaluation, which is different from our model. Meanwhile, the update of α was not considered in the paper, so we do not know the impact of α on trust formalization when it changes.

P. Victor, et. al. advocated the use of a centralized trust model in which trust scores are (trust, distrust)couples, drawn from a bilattice that preserves valuable trust provenance information including gradual trust, distrust, ignorance, and inconsistency. Authors presented a collection of four operators simultaneously in one model, especially the distrust information, which is their novel contribution. However, proposed trust techniques require a central authority to propagate and aggregate trust values; however, as the amount of nodes continues to grow, it will get more and more difficult to manage all trust information in one place, so a decentralized approach may be more appropriate. Furthermore, privacy of data is becoming increasingly important in applications, and nodes may refuse to disclose their personal trust. Authors didn't discuss the security issues in the paper.

J. H. Luo, et. al. promoted RFSTrust, a trust model based on fuzzy trust similarity to quantify and to evaluate the trustworthiness of nodes, which includes five types of fuzzy trust relationships based on the fuzzy relation theory and a mathematical description for MANETs. RFSTrust has some identification and containment capability in synergies cheating, promotes data packets forwarding between nodes, and improves the performance of the entire MANETs. But authors discuss only one type of situation when selfish nodes attack. No other types of nodes attacks are considered.

J. S. Liu and V. Issarny presented a reputation model, which incorporates two essential dimensions, time and context, along with mechanisms supporting reputation formation, evolution and propagation. Their model shows effectiveness in distinguishing truth-telling and lying agents, obtaining true reputation of an agent, and ensuring reliability against attacks of defame and collusion. The common ground of their work and ours is that we both take the time dimension of trust update into consideration, while the main difference is that Liu regards node's new behavior as a part of trust value, while we see the service and request from other nodes as a key proportion of trust establishment.

X. M. Li, et. al. gave us a global trust model, which is based on the distance-weighted recommendations under P2P circumstance (Li & Wang, 2009). Their model uses distributed methods to quantify and evaluate the credibility of peers to identify and restrain some common collective cheatings. The global credibility relies on distance between nodes in their model, and Distributed Hash Table (DHT) is used to designate peers to mange the credibility. That is to say, hash function needs using in their model, which is different from ours.

Besides these known attacks in the literatures, a malicious node may also reduce the effectiveness of trust evaluation through other methods. While the focus of this chapter is to lay the foundation of trust evaluation with meaningful trust metrics, we do not investigate all possible attacks in this chapter. Therefore, more security issues of cooperative communication in Ad Hoc networks are our following targets.

7. Conclusion

The creditability of multi-hop networks can achieve from the aspects of authentication, authorization, access control, as well as the reputation-based trust management model (Wang & Lin, 2008). In this chapter we propose a reputation model based on global STV and RTV. Afterwards, we discuss five attacks on the model in the progress of establishing reputation, and testify the model robustness of anti-attacks by simulations. Since the proposed model takes no consideration of the location issue of nodes for computing and storing trust information, our model can be applied in both structured multi-hop networks and unstructured ones.

8. Acknowledgements

We acknowledge a financial support from Six Talented Eminence Foundation of Jiangsu Province(06-E-043); Scientific Research Foundation of NJUPT (NY209016);

9. References

Aameek, S. & Liu, L. (2003). TrustMe: anonymous management of trust relationships in decentralized P2P systems, *Proceedings of IEEE 3rd International Conference on Peer-to-Peer Computing*, pp. 142-149, ISBN: 0-7695-2023-5, Sweden, September 2003, IEEE Press, Linkoping

Boukerche, A. & Ren, Y. L. (2008). A trust-based security system for ubiquitous and pervasive computing environments. *Computer Communications*, Vol. 31, No. 18, page numbers (4343-4351), ISSN: 0140-3664

Buchegger, S. & LeBoudec, J. Y. (2002). Performance Analysis of the CONFIDANT Protocol (Cooperation of Nodes-Fairness in Dynamic Ad-Hoc NeTworks, *Proceedings of the 3rd ACM International Symposium of Mobile MANET Networking and Computing*, pp. 80-91, ISBN: 1-58113-501-7, Switzerland, June 2002, ACM Press, Lausanne

Caronni, G. (2000). Walking the Web of trust, *Proceedings of the IEEE 9th International Workshops on Enabling Technologies: Infrastructure for Collaborative Enterprises*, pp. 153-159, ISBN: 0-7695-0798-0, USA, June 2000, IEEE Press, MD

Chang,B. J. & Kuo, S. L. (2009). Markov Chain Trust Model for Trust-Value Analysis and Key Management in Distributed Multicast MANETs. *IEEE Transactions on Vehicular Technology*, Vo l. 58, No. 4, page numbers (1846-1863), ISSN: 0018-9545

Dellarocas, C. (2000). Mechanisms for coping with unfair ratings and discriminatory behavior in online reputation reporting systems, *Proceedings of the Intenational Conference on Intelligent Systems*, pp. 520-525, ISBN: ICIS2000-X, Australia, December 2000, AIS Press, Brisbane, Queensland owned by the Karlskrona commune, is on behalf of the municipality commune to cooperate with *The Cloud* to let the city be wireless (Affärsverken, 2006).

3.1 Wireless city of Karlskrona in Sweden and its motivations

The motivations and benefits of building a wireless city in Karlskrona have closely linked to the history and development strategies of the city. These are:

Making the city more attractive to IT and Telecom companies - A wireless enabled city can be more attractive to new IT and Telecoms companies, as well as facilitate business of companies in Karlskrona. Karlskrona, which was previously known as a 300-year-old fortress as well as an old ship-building yard, has now successfully created a new type of city based on its strategy to support IT and telecom industries after 1990s. Wireless city gives these companies a new approach to provide services as service providers. In addition, becoming a service partner of *The Cloud* can deliver their local services internationally without investing on the network infrastructures.

Delivery of social municipal and tourist services - Wireless city gives local residents more freedom to acquire information through wireless broadband at anywhere in anytime. It is easy to access public internet resources, such as transportation, education, leisure services, and society activities. Additionally, wireless city can assist tourists to access the local websites in Karlskrona via different Wi-Fi enabled terminals.

A natural expansion of the city's broadband network and increasing traffic - Wireless city can be naturally regarded as an expansion of the city fixed fiber network, which is owned and managed by *Affärsverken*. Since all the wireless network operators have to be the partner of *Affärsverken* in the business model, traffic passing through the fiber network is accordingly increases, thererfore brings more revenue to this municipal company.

The main motivation for the wireless network operator *The Cloud* is the predicted increase usage of wireless network by local companies and residents. The sustainable strategy of city attracts growing attention and investment on IT and Telecom industries, and facilities internet connection for residents. For example, customers of *Telenor* can access *The Cloud*'s network for free, and therefore generate traffic passing through the network of *The Cloud*. It is also predicted that mobile broadband is going to replace the fixed broadband in the future, which creates a profitable market for wireless network operator.

3.2 The business model and SWOT analysis
3.2.1 Implementation and strength

The business model implemented in the wireless city of Karlskrona can be generally categorized as the Public-Wholesale model (Cloud, 2007), where the local fixed network operator has established partnership with wireless network operator. Based on the partnership with *The Cloud*, *Affärsverken* can accordingly extend its fixed fibre network to include wireless infrastructure at nearly zero cost, and subsequently achieve the goal of wireless city. It has to be noticed that the Karlskrona municipality has branded the network as *"Wireless City of Karlskrona"* and fully owned the brand. It indicates that the municipality absolutely controls the wireless city network, and implements a neutral and open business model. New service providers and network operators can freely cooperate with *Affärsverken* and access to the business model.

In Karlskrona, *The Cloud* establishes the wireless network infrastructure and works actively with service providers, device providers and application partners to bring a range of services into its sites (Cloud, 2010). Consequently, *Affärsverken* can share the revenue of *The*

Cloud based on the traffic passing through its fiber network, and fully control activities of *The Cloud* for the purpose of a fair competition environment for different service providers and network operators. Fig. 3 shows the areas with wireless city service available in Karlskrona in 2007.

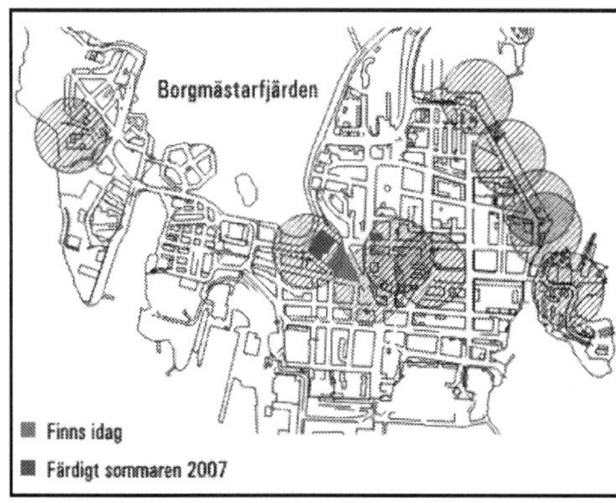

Fig. 3. Wireless city services available in the city centre of Karlskrona in 2007

Different roles of public and private actors involved in the business model are listed below:

Local authority - The Karlskrona municipality initializes the wireless city and provides funding to *Affärsverken* on behalf of the municipality to act as a public force to build wireless city. The local authority also gives access to buildings and light poles for mounting access equipment (Cisco, 2010).

Fixed network operator - *Affärsverken* provides backbone and shares revenue of the wireless network operator (Bar & Park, 2006). At the same time, it also acts as a regulator, which takes control over the network on behalf of the Municipality.

Wireless Network Operator - *The Cloud* mainly acts as a wireless network operator and brings services to end users. Being a network operator, it deploys and maintains the wireless network infrastructure in the wireless city. It is also responsible for managing and outsourcing the network capacity for service providers, and subsequently shares the revenue of service providers (Cisco, 2010). At the same time, *The Cloud* also provides an internet connection to end users paying through the Credit Card Company or mobile operator by sending messages through mobile phones.

Service Provider - It pays the network operator to let its customers to access the wireless network for free, or attracts new customers in the wireless city. In wireless city of Karlskrona, *The Cloud* has established partnership with various service partners, e.g. *Telenor, iPass, Spring PCS, Boingo, Trustive, Echovox SMS, AT&T*.

Technology Partner - It manufactures and sells devices to network operators as well as end users.

Credit Card Company or 3rd party - In wireless city of Karlskrona, it is responsible for charging and identifying end users, who don't have partner accounts of *The Cloud* in order to access the network. The payment module is widely used and gives a convenient way for users to subscribe services in the wireless city.

The business model of the wireless city in Karlskrona is shown in Fig. 4. By implementing the business model, Municipality can manage different actors in network rolling out, service

$$\tilde{d}_{ij,k} = d_{ij} + n_{ij,k},\qquad(2)$$

where $n_{ij,k}$ is assumed to be a Gaussian random variable with zero mean and variance σ_{ij}^2. Let $\mathcal{M}: \mathbb{R}^{N \times N \times K} \to \mathbb{R}^{N \times N}$ denote the functional model of the data-processing block and let $\overline{\mathbf{D}}$ be the smoothed EDM computed as

$$\overline{\mathbf{D}} \triangleq \mathcal{M}(\{\tilde{\mathbf{D}}_k\}),\qquad(3)$$

where K is the total number of EDM samples.

Then a non-parametric formulation of the LT problem is given by the following weighted least square (WLS) minimization

$$\hat{\mathbf{X}} = \arg\min_{\hat{\mathbf{X}} \in \mathbb{R}^{N \times \eta}} \ \frac{1}{2} \cdot \left\| \mathbf{W} \circ \left(\overline{\mathbf{D}}^{\circ q} - \mathcal{D}(\hat{\mathbf{X}})^{\circ q} \right) \right\|_F^2,\qquad(4)$$

$$\text{subject to}\quad \hat{\mathbf{x}}_i = \mathbf{x}_i \ \forall i = 1,\dots,N_{\mathrm{A}}$$

where $\hat{\mathbf{X}} \in \mathbb{R}^{N \times \eta}$ indicates an estimate of $\mathbf{X}$, $\mathbf{W}$ is a weighing matrix that relates to the reliability of $\overline{\mathbf{D}}$, q is an exponent typically chosen amongst the values $\{1,2\}$ and $\circ$ inidicates the point-wise (Hadamard) power or product, respectively.

The proposed WLS approach is widely used in the literature for several reasons. First, under the assumption of $N_{\mathrm{T}} = 1$ and $q = 2$, the exact solution of the minimization problem can be computed with a close-form algorithm Beck et al. (2008). Second, under the assumption of low noise, the WLS objective function can be linearized without compromising the accuracy of the location estimates Cheung et al. (2004); Guvenc et al. (2008). Third, under the assumption of a zero-mean Gaussian noise and $q = 1$, the WLS approach is equivalent to the maximum-likelihood (ML) formulation of the LT problem Patwari et al. (2003); Biswas, Liang, Toh & Wang (2006). Indeed, by computing the likelihood function of $\hat{\mathbf{X}}$

$$p(\hat{\mathbf{X}} \mid \overline{\mathbf{D}}) = \frac{1}{(2\pi)^{\eta}} \prod_{e_{ij} \in E} \exp\left(-\frac{(\overline{d}_{ij} - \|\hat{\mathbf{x}}_i - \hat{\mathbf{x}})_j\|_2)^2}{\sigma_{ij}^2 / K_{ij}} \right),\qquad(5)$$

where K_{ij} is the number of measurements of d_{ij}, e_{ij} indicates an connected link between the ith and the j-th nodes, and E as the set of all connected link, and taking the logarithm it follows that

$$\ln\left(p(\hat{\mathbf{X}} \mid \overline{\mathbf{D}}) \right) = \frac{1}{(2\pi)^{\eta}} \sum_{e_{ij} \in E} \frac{K_{ij}}{\sigma_{ij}^2} \cdot \left(\overline{d}_{ij} - \|\hat{\mathbf{x}}_i - \hat{\mathbf{x}}_j)\|_2 \right)^2,\qquad(6)$$

which is equivalent to equation 4 rewritten as

$$\sum_{e_{ij} \in E} w_{ij}^2 \cdot \left(\overline{d}_{ij}^q - \|\hat{\mathbf{x}}_i - \hat{\mathbf{x}}_j)\|_2^q \right)^2,\qquad(7)$$

with $w_{ij}^2 = \dfrac{K_{ij}}{\sigma_{ij}^2}$ and $q = 1$.

4. Ranging post-processing

As shown in figure 2, while block-1 deals with the detection, acquisition and association problem, block-2 pre-filters the data to improve the signal to noise ratio for the measurements. Although several algorithms can be used to smooth the observations, *e.g.* moving average, exponential, autoregressive moving average, Kalman filters and so forth, here after we will focus on a low-complex wavelet-based pre-filtering that has been proved to suit the localization and target tracking scenarios.

4.1 Wavelet-based smoothing

The Wavelet Transform (WT) makes use of a unique dilated window (the wavelet function) to analyze signals. This allows good time resolution (for short windows) at high frequency and good frequency resolution (corresponding to long-window) at low frequency S.Mallat (1998). The decomposition is based on a family of functions $\sqrt{s}\psi(s(x-u))_{(s,u)\in\mathbb{R}^2}$ corresponding to the translated and dilated version of the *wavelet* function $\psi(x)$, also called *mother* wavelet, and with s and u corresponding to the *scaling* and *translation* factors.

Given a continuous function $f(x)$, its continuous wavelet transform, here denoted as $Wf(s,u)$, corresponds to the inner product $\langle f(x),\psi_s(x-u)\rangle$, meaning the cross-correlation between the original function and the scaled wavelet shifted at u. In S.Mallat & S.Zhong (1992) it is shown that choosing $\psi(x) = d\phi(x)/dx$, with $\phi(x)$ as smoothing function, then it is possible to characterize the shape of irregular functions $f(x)$ through $Wf(s,u)$. In addition, using the properties of the convolution operator it follows that

$$Wf_s(x) = f * \left(s\frac{d\phi_s}{dx} \right)(x) = s\frac{d}{dx}\left(f * \phi_s \right)(x), \tag{8}$$

which allows to interpret $Wf(s,u)$ as the derivative of a local average of $f(x)$, with smoothing degree depending on the scale factor s.

Amongst the several algorithm to compute the wavelet transform of discrete signals, because of its low complexity and its redundant representation of the signal $f(x)$ across the scales, which has been proved to be particularly suitable in filtering applications, we use the *á trous* algorithm briefly summarized in the following.

Let $a_0[n]$ be the discrete signal to be analyzed, with n as the discrete time index and assume the value for $a_0[n]$ in n equivalent to the local average between the original continuos function $f(x)$ and a kernel function $\phi(x-n)$ (namely $\langle f(x),\phi(x-n)\rangle$), then at any scale $j > 0$, a smoothed version of $a_0[n]$ is computed as $\langle f(x),\phi_{2^j}(x-n)\rangle$, with

$$\phi_{2^j}(t) = \frac{1}{\sqrt{2^j}}\phi\left(\frac{x}{2^j} \right). \tag{9}$$

The function $\phi(x)$ is called *scaling function* and it corresponds to a low-pass filter, while the coefficient for the dyadic WT are obtains by $z_{2^j}[n] = Wf(s,n) = \langle f(x),\psi_{2^j}(x-n)\rangle$ with $\psi_{2^j}(x-n)$ defined similarly to equation 9. Once the low-pass filter $h[n]$ and high-pass filter $g[n]$ are designed then $a_0[n]$ is decomposed by repetitively computing

$$a_{j+1}[n] = a_j * \tilde{h}_j[n],$$
$$d_{j+1}[n] = a_j * \tilde{g}_j[n], \tag{10}$$

with $h_j[n]$ obtained from $h[n]$ inserting $2^j - 1$ zeros between each sample of the filter (similarly for $g_j[n]$) and $0 < j < J$.

We use the WT to study each time series corresponding to subsequent ranging measured at the devices. We restrict ourselves to LoS target tracking scenarios, and we suggest a scheme to adaptively pre-filtering the observations $f[n]$ in a completely non-parametric fashion. To do so we use the output of the DWT to estimate σ_d and δ, namely the noise level affecting the observations and the target dynamic perceived at each anchor via ranging.

As mentioned above, the wavelet coefficients $d_j[n]$ computed at the different scales j include the high frequency components for the original signal and it is therefore used to characterize σ_d. Similarly, the output of the scaling function is used to infer δ. Clearly the approach works at best if the signal can be decomposed in high frequency components of short duration and a low frequency part of relatively long duration. From equations 8 and 10 it is clear that the wavelet coefficients $d_j[n]$ at the scale $j = 1$ represents a simple differential operator, therefore under static ($\hat{v} = 0$) or anyway scenario characterized by a small dynamic $\hat{v}$, an estimate of $\hat{\sigma}_d$ can be inferred from $d_1[n]$.

However, when the target dynamic ($\hat{v}$) increases, $d_1[n]$ starts including part of the energy associated to $f[n]$ and eventual estimates of $\hat{\sigma}_d$ would be affected by error. To overcome this problem $\hat{\sigma}_d$ is estimated as the standard deviation of $d_1[n]$ computed from subsets of subsequent observations characterized by the same polarity value in the support function

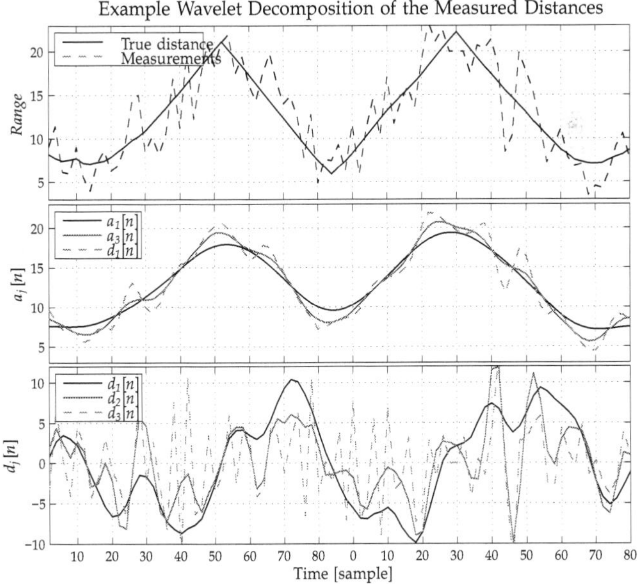

Fig. 3. Example wavelet decomposition of TOA ranging.

described in section 5.1.2. To distinguish the long term time process associated to the real TOA measurements (low-pass filtered version of $f[n]$), we use an averaged version of $a_1[n]$ in the same way proposed in Macagnano & de Abreu (2008), meaning that at each sampling time we compute the DWT on a window of size 2^J and centered at n.

From this averaged $a_1[n]$ we compute the parameter δ approximating the perceived dynamic at the specific anchor with respect to the considered target. The decomposition of $f[n]$ in its high/low frequency components is performed subject to the boolean operator Θ defined in section 5.1.2.

Using Θ, computed at each time n and for each anchor-to-target link, we decide whether the real ToA observation is better approximated by the measured ranging ($f[n]$) or it low-pass filtered version ($a_1[n]$). The only price paid using this wavelet smoothing based on Θ, is the introduction of a lag of $2^J - 1$ samples in the computation.

5. LT algorithm

The LT problem formulation considered in this chapter is the WLS-ML approach

$$\hat{\mathbf{X}} = \arg\min_{\hat{\mathbf{X}} \in \mathbb{R}^{N \times \eta}} \sum_{e_{ij} \in E} w_{ij}^2 \cdot \left(\overline{d}_{ij} - \| \hat{\mathbf{x}}_i - \hat{\mathbf{x}}_j \|_F \right)^2 \tag{11}$$

$$\text{subject to} \quad \hat{\mathbf{x}}_i = \mathbf{x}_i \ \forall i = 1,\ldots,N_A.$$

The challenges faced in this optimization problem are: the computation of the weights and the minimization of the objective function. In the sequel, we will tackle both issues and we will describe in details very effective solutions.

5.1 Weighing strategies

In the optimization problem posed in equation 11, the purpose of the weights is *"to reflect differing levels of concern about the sizes of the terms"* in the objective function. In other words, higher the weight tighter is the concern Boyd & Vandenberghe (2004).

The first proposed strategy, nevertheless optimal in the ML sense, can be derived directly from equation 6,

$$w_{ij}^* = \frac{K_{ij}}{\sigma_{ij}^2}, \ \ \forall \ \sigma_{ij}^2 \neq 0. \tag{12}$$

For the special case of $\sigma_{ij}^2 = 0$, *i.e.* no error, $w_{ij}^* = 0$ but in equation 11, we add the equality constraint

$$\hat{d}_{ij} = \tilde{d}_{ij}. \tag{13}$$

In most cases, however, $\sigma_{ij}^{2\prime}$s are not known *a priori*, therefore, alternative weighing strategies will be considered. The first alternative referred to as binary weight or unweighted is

$$w_{ij}^u = \begin{cases} K_{ij}, & \forall e_{ij} \in E, \\ 0, & otherwise \end{cases}. \tag{14}$$

$$[\mathbf{K}]_{1:\eta,1:\eta} = -\frac{1}{2}\left([\mathbf{D}]_{1:\eta,1:\eta} + \mathbf{C}_1 \otimes \mathbf{1}_\eta \mathbf{1}_\eta^\mathrm{T} - \mathbf{C}_2 \otimes \mathbf{1}_\eta^\mathrm{T} - \mathbf{C}_3 \otimes \mathbf{1}_\eta\right), \tag{30}$$

$$[\mathbf{K}]_{1:\eta,\eta+1:N} = -\frac{1}{2}\left([\mathbf{D}]_{1:\eta,\eta+1:N} + \mathbf{C}_1 \otimes \mathbf{1}_\eta \mathbf{1}_{N-\eta}^\mathrm{T} - \mathbf{C}_2 \otimes \mathbf{1}_{N-\eta}^\mathrm{T} - \mathbf{C}_4 \otimes \mathbf{1}_\eta\right), \tag{31}$$

where $\otimes$ denotes the Kronecker product and

$$\mathbf{C}_1 = \frac{1}{\eta^2} \cdot \left[\mathbf{1}_\eta^\mathrm{T} \cdot [\mathbf{D}]_{1:\eta,1:\eta} \cdot \mathbf{1}_\eta\right], \tag{32}$$

$$\mathbf{C}_2 = \frac{1}{\eta} \cdot \left[[\mathbf{D}]_{1:\eta,1:\eta} \cdot \mathbf{1}_\eta\right], \tag{33}$$

$$\mathbf{C}_3 = \frac{1}{\eta} \cdot \left[\mathbf{1}_\eta^\mathrm{T} \cdot [\mathbf{D}]_{1:\eta,1:\eta}\right], \tag{34}$$

$$\mathbf{C}_4 = \frac{1}{\eta} \cdot \left[\mathbf{1}_\eta^\mathrm{T} \cdot [\mathbf{D}]_{1:\eta,\eta+1:N}\right]. \tag{35}$$

Finally, invoke the relation (Dattorro, 2005, pp. 196)

$$\tilde{\mathbf{D}} = \left(\mathbf{1}_N \cdot \mathrm{diag}(\tilde{\mathbf{K}})^\mathrm{T} + \mathrm{diag}(\tilde{\mathbf{K}}) \cdot \mathbf{1}_N^\mathrm{T} - 2 \cdot \tilde{\mathbf{K}}\right). \tag{36}$$

Equation 36 yields a complete set of distances associated with $\tilde{\mathbf{K}}$, such that any missing entries of $[\mathbf{D}]_{\eta+1:N,\eta+1:N}$ can be replaced by corresponding entries from $\tilde{\mathbf{D}}$.

At this point, let us emphasize that $[\mathbf{D}]_{1:\eta,1:\eta}$ contains the distances amongst anchors and consequently $[\mathbf{K}]_{1:\eta,1:\eta}$, $\mathbf{C}_1$, $\mathbf{C}_2$ and $\mathbf{C}_3$ are all *constant*, such that $\tilde{\mathbf{K}}$ can be updated very efficiently.

Furthermore, the elements of $[\mathbf{D}]_{1:\eta,\eta+1:N}$ are the distances from anchors to targets, and therefore constitute the least (reasonable) amount of information required by tracking applications, such that this "completion" procedure can always[2] be applied.

In the extreme case of $[\mathbf{D}]_{\eta+1:N,\eta+1:N} = \mathbf{0}_{N-\eta}$, then to recover $[\mathbf{X}]_{\eta+1:N,1:\eta}$ only the eigendecomposition of $[\tilde{\mathbf{K}}]_{1:\eta,1:\eta}$ is required C. Fowlkes & Malik (2004).

Indeed, let $[\tilde{\mathbf{K}}]_{1:\eta,1:\eta} = \mathbf{Q} \cdot \Lambda \cdot \mathbf{Q}_\mathrm{T}$ as the eigendecomposition of $[\tilde{\mathbf{K}}]_{1:\eta,1:\eta}$. From equation 28 it follows that $[\mathbf{X}]_{1:\eta,1:\eta} = \mathbf{Q} \cdot \Lambda^{\frac{1}{2}}$, and because $[\tilde{\mathbf{K}}]_{1:\eta,\eta+1:N} = [\mathbf{X}]_{1:\eta,1:\eta} \cdot [\mathbf{X}]_{\eta+1:N,1:\eta}^\mathrm{T}$ then

$$[\mathbf{X}]_{\eta+1:N,:} = [\mathbf{X}]_{1:\eta,1:\eta}^\mathrm{T} \cdot [\tilde{\mathbf{K}}]_{1:\eta,\eta+1:N} = \mathbf{Q} \cdot \Lambda^{\frac{1}{2}} \cdot [\tilde{\mathbf{K}}]_{1:\eta,\eta+1:N}, \tag{37}$$

In conclusion, if an incomplete EDM is observed the aforementioned steps can be followed to complete $\mathbf{D}$ before constructing the MDS kernel $\mathbf{K}^*$ described in equations 27a.

---

[2] Even the case of sparse incomplete EDMs in which *none* of the rows of $\mathbf{D}$ is complete could, in principle, also be dealt with by combining the NyStöm solution with standard completion algorithms applied to a restricted subset of η rows of $\mathbf{D}$ Shang & Ruml (2004). This case, however, is of relatively little interest to tracking applications and outside the scope of the article.

5.2.3 SMACOF

The SMACOF technique is a well-known iterative algorithm that attempts to find the minimum of a non-convex function by tracking the global minima of the so-called majored convex functions $\mathcal{T}(\hat{\mathbf{X}}, \mathbf{Y})$ successively constructed from the original objective and basis on the previous solutions. In our context, the objective function to majorize is that one given in equation 7. Thus, we have

$$\mathcal{T}(\hat{\mathbf{X}}, \mathbf{Y}) = \sum w_{ij}^2 \cdot \bar{d}_{ij}^2 + \mathrm{tr}\left(\hat{\mathbf{X}}^{\mathrm{T}} \cdot \mathbf{H} \cdot \hat{\mathbf{X}}\right) - 2 \cdot \mathrm{tr}\left(\hat{\mathbf{X}}^{\mathrm{T}} \cdot \mathbf{A}(\mathbf{Y}) \cdot \mathbf{Y}\right), \tag{38}$$

where $\mathrm{tr}(\cdot)$ denotes the trace, $\mathbf{Y} \in \mathbb{R}^{N \times \eta}$ is an auxiliary variable and the entries of $\mathbf{H}$ and $\mathbf{A}(\mathbf{Y})$ are given by

$$h_{ij} = \begin{cases} \sum_{\substack{i=1 \\ i \neq j}}^{N} h_{ij} , i = j, \\ \\ -w_{ij}^2 , i \neq j, \end{cases} \tag{39a}$$

$$a_{ij} = \begin{cases} \sum_{\substack{i=1 \\ i \neq j}}^{N} a_{ij} , i = j, \\ \\ w_{ij}^2 \cdot \dfrac{\bar{d}_{ij}}{\| \mathbf{y}_i - \mathbf{y}_j \|_2} , i \neq j, \end{cases} \tag{39b}$$

where $w_{ij} > 0$ if $e_{ij} \in E$ and $w_{ij} = 0$ otherwise.

At the ℓ-th iteration the global minimum $\hat{\mathbf{X}}^{(\ell)}$ of the majored function $\mathcal{T}(\hat{\mathbf{X}}, \mathbf{Y})$ with $\mathbf{Y} = \hat{\mathbf{X}}^{(\ell-1)}$, is computed via the Guttman transform,

$$\hat{\mathbf{X}}^{(\ell)} = \mathbf{H}^{\dagger} \cdot \mathbf{A}\left(\hat{\mathbf{X}}^{(\ell-1)}\right) \cdot \hat{\mathbf{X}}^{(n-1)}, \tag{40}$$

where $\dagger$ denotes the pseudoinverse.

5.2.4 Linear global distance continuation

While the C-MDS and the Nyström approximation are algebraic approaches and SMACOF relies on the initialization point $\hat{\mathbf{X}}^{(0)}$, the algorithm proposed below, performs a low-complexity unconstrained global optimization. The approach is based on an iterative global smoothing technique, in which the global minimum is sought (with probability close to 1) after L number of iterations. The overall worse-case complexity of the method is equal to $L \times O$, where O is the worse-case complexity of the optimization technique used at the ℓ-th iteration. For convenience, we use a Quasi-Newton line search method whose complexity is $\mathcal{O}(N^2)$ Nocedal & Wright (2006). The proposed technique will be hereafter referred to as linear-global distance continuation (L-GDC) method, inspired by More & Wu (1997).

5.2.4.1 Fundamentals of the L-GDC

The objective of this subsection is to provide the fundamental Definitions, Theorems and Lemmas used in the L-GDC algorithm. Given the limited number of pages, we omit all proofs which can be found in Destino & Abreu (2010); More & Wu (1997).

Definition 1 (Gaussian kernel) *Let $g(u,\lambda)$ be the Gaussian kernel defined as*

$$g(u,\lambda) \triangleq e^{-u^2/\lambda^2}. \tag{41}$$

Definition 2 (Gaussian transform) *Let $\langle s \rangle_\lambda(\mathbf{x})$ denote the Gaussian transform (smoothed function) of a function $s(\mathbf{x})$, and given by*

$$\langle s \rangle_\lambda(\mathbf{x}) \triangleq \frac{1}{\pi^{n/2}\lambda^n} \int_{\mathbb{R}^n} s(\mathbf{u}) e^{-\frac{\|\mathbf{x}-\mathbf{u}\|_F^2}{\lambda^2}} d\mathbf{u}, \tag{42}$$

where $\mathbf{u},\mathbf{x} \in \mathbb{R}^n$ and $\lambda \in \mathbb{R}^+$ is a parameter that controls the degree of smoothing ($\lambda \gg 0$ strong smoothing).

Theorem 1 (Continuation method) *Let $\{\lambda^{(\ell)}\}$ with $\{1 \le \ell \le L\}$ be any sequence of λ's converging to zero, i.e. $\lambda^{(L)} = 0$. If $\mathbf{x}^{(\ell)}$ is a global minimizer of $\langle s \rangle_{\lambda^{(\ell)}}(\mathbf{x})$ and $\{\mathbf{x}^{(\ell)}\}$ converges to $\mathbf{x}^*$, then $\mathbf{x}^*$ is a global minimizer of $\langle s \rangle_{\lambda^{(\ell)}}(\mathbf{x})$.*

Theorem 2 (WLS-ML Smoothed Function) *Let $s(\hat{\mathbf{X}})$ equal to the objective function in equation 7, and for simplicity consider $\eta = 2$. Then, the smoothed function $\langle s \rangle_\lambda(\hat{\mathbf{X}})$ is given by*

$$
\begin{aligned}
\langle s \rangle_\lambda(\hat{\mathbf{X}}) &= \frac{1}{\pi} \int_{\mathbb{R}^n} \sum_{ij} w_{ij}^2 \left(\tilde{d}_{ij} - \hat{d}_{ij,u} \right)^2 \exp(\|\mathbf{u}\|_F^2)\, d\mathbf{u}, \\
&= \sum_{ij} w_{ij}^2 \left(\lambda^2 + \tilde{d}_{ij}^2 + \hat{d}_{ij}^2 - 2\lambda\tilde{d}_{ij}\Gamma\left(\frac{3}{2}\right) {}_1F_1\left(\frac{3}{2};1;\frac{\hat{d}_{ij}^2}{\lambda^2}\right)\exp\left(\frac{-\hat{d}_{ij}^2}{\lambda^2}\right) \right),
\end{aligned}
\tag{43}
$$

where $\hat{\mathbf{X}} \in \mathbb{R}^{N \times \eta}$ is a matrix whose i-th row-vector is $\hat{\mathbf{x}}_i$, $\hat{d}_{ij,u} \triangleq \|\hat{\mathbf{x}}_i - \hat{\mathbf{x}}_j + \lambda\mathbf{u}\|_F$ with $\mathbf{u} \in \mathbb{R}^n$, $\Gamma(a)$ is the gamma function and ${}_1F_1(a; b; c)$ is the confluent hypergeometric function Abramowitz & Stegun (1965).

Theorem 3 (Convexity condition) *Let $s(\hat{\mathbf{X}})$ equal to the objective function in equation 7 and $\langle s \rangle_\lambda$ given by 43, then $\langle s \rangle_\lambda$ is convex if*

$$\lambda^* \ge \frac{\sqrt{\pi}\,\max_{ij}\tilde{d}_{ij}}{2}. \tag{44}$$

Lemma 1 (Minimal $\{\lambda^{(\ell)}\}$ for source localization)
Let $N_T = 1$ and let $\hat{\mathbf{x}}$ denote the target location estimate. Consider an ordered set of ranging measurement $\{\bar{d}_\ell\}$, , such that $\tilde{d}_1 \ge \tilde{d}_2 \ge \dots \tilde{d}_\ell$, where $L = N_A$. Then the minimal set $\{\lambda^{(\ell)}\}$ is given by

$$\lambda^{(\ell)} = \frac{\sqrt{\pi}\tilde{d}_\ell}{2}, k = 1 \dots L. \tag{45}$$

5.2.4.2 Implementation of the L-GDC

Invoking Theorems 1,2 and 3 the L-GDC algorithm is given by

$$\mathbf{x}^{(\ell)} = \underset{\mathbf{x} \in \mathbb{R}^n}{\arg\min}\, \langle s \rangle_{\lambda^{(\ell)}}(\mathbf{x}),\ 1 \le \ell \le L, \tag{46}$$

with

$$\lambda_0 = \frac{\sqrt{\pi}\,\max_{ij}\overline{d}_{ij}}{2}. \tag{47}$$

Notice that the ML-transformed objective function involves the hypergeometric function then the numeric evaluation of equation 43 requires care, especially when λ is very small. Numerically stable computations can be achieved using the equivalences Abramowitz & Stegun (1965)

$$_1F_1\left(\frac{3}{2};1;z\right) = 1 + \sum_{m=1}^{+\infty}\left(z^m \cdot \prod_{k=1}^{m}\frac{(1/2+k)}{k^2}\right), z < 10. \tag{48}$$

$$_1F_1\left(\frac{3}{2};1;z\right) \approx \frac{z^{-3/2}}{\Gamma(-\frac{1}{2})}\left(\sum_{m=0}^{M-1}\frac{(-z)^{-m}}{m!}\prod_{k=0}^{m-1}\left(\frac{3}{2}+k\right)^2\right) + \frac{e^z z^{1/2}}{\Gamma(\frac{3}{2})}\left(\sum_{p=0}^{P-1}\frac{z^{-p}}{p!}\prod_{k=0}^{p-1}\left(k-\frac{1}{2}\right)^2\right), z \geq 10, \tag{49}$$

where $z \triangleq \frac{\tilde{d}^2}{\lambda^2}$ and M and P are sufficiently large numbers to ensure an accurate approximation (typically $(M,P) \geq 5$).

In order to use a Newton's based optimization method, gradient and Hessian of $\langle s\rangle_{\lambda^{(t)}}(\mathbf{x})$ are required. The gradient is given by

$$\nabla_{\hat{\mathbf{X}}}\langle s\rangle_{\lambda}(\hat{\mathbf{X}}) = \sum_{ij} w_{ij}^2 s'_{ij}(\hat{d}_{ij};\lambda)\nabla_{\hat{\mathbf{X}}}(\hat{d}_{ij}), \tag{50}$$

where the i-th and the j-th $1 \times \eta$ blocks of $\nabla_{\hat{\mathbf{X}}}(\hat{d}_{ij})$ are

$$\left[\nabla_{\hat{\mathbf{X}}}(\hat{d}_{ij})\right]_i = \frac{\hat{\mathbf{x}}_j - \hat{\mathbf{x}}_i}{\|\hat{\mathbf{x}}_i - \hat{\mathbf{x}}_j\|_2}, \tag{51}$$

$$\left[\nabla_{\hat{\mathbf{X}}}(\hat{d}_{ij})\right]_j = -\frac{\hat{\mathbf{x}}_j - \hat{\mathbf{x}}_i}{\|\hat{\mathbf{x}}_i - \hat{\mathbf{x}}_j\|_2}, \tag{52}$$

and the function $s'_{ij}(\hat{d}_{ij};\lambda)$ is the first derivative of

$$s_{ij}(\hat{d}_{ij};\lambda) \triangleq \overline{d}_{ij}^2 + \hat{d}_{ij}^2 + \lambda^2 - \lambda\tilde{d}_{ij}\sqrt{\pi}\,_1F_1\left(\frac{3}{2},1,\frac{\hat{d}_{ij}^2}{\lambda^2}\right)\exp\left(\frac{-\hat{d}_{ij}^2}{\lambda^2}\right), \tag{53}$$

and is equal to

$$s_{ij'}(\hat{d}_{ij};\lambda) = 2\hat{d}_{ij} + \frac{\hat{d}_{ij}\sqrt{\pi}\overline{d}_{ij}}{\lambda}S_1(\hat{d}_{ij};\lambda), \tag{54}$$

where

$$S_1(\hat{d}_{ij};\lambda) \triangleq \exp\left(\frac{-\hat{d}_{ij}^2}{\lambda^2}\right)\left(2\,_1F_1\left(\frac{3}{2},1,\frac{\hat{d}_{ij}^2}{\lambda^2}\right) - 3\,_1F_1\left(\frac{5}{2},2,\frac{\hat{d}_{ij}^2}{\lambda^2}\right)\right). \tag{55}$$

The Hessian matrix of $\langle s \rangle_\lambda(\hat{\mathbf{X}})$, denoted by $\nabla_{\hat{\mathbf{X}}}^2 \langle s \rangle_\lambda(\hat{\mathbf{X}})$, is computed as

$$\nabla_{\hat{\mathbf{X}}}^2 \langle s \rangle_\lambda(\hat{\mathbf{X}}) = \sum_{ij} w_{ij}^2 \left(s_{ij}''(\hat{d}_{ij};\lambda) \nabla_{\hat{\mathbf{X}}}^{\mathrm{T}}(\hat{d}_{ij}) \nabla_{\hat{\mathbf{X}}}(\hat{d}_{ij}) + s_{ij}' \nabla_{\hat{\mathbf{X}}}^2(\hat{d}_{ij}) \right), \tag{56}$$

where $\nabla_{\hat{\mathbf{X}}}^2(\hat{d}_{ij}) \in \mathbb{R}^{N\eta \times N\eta}$ is given by a symmetric block-matrix where the ii-th and ij-th blocks are

$$\left[\nabla_{\hat{\mathbf{X}}}^2(\hat{d}_{ij}) \right]_{ii} = \frac{1}{\hat{d}_{ij}} \left(\mathbf{I} - \left[\nabla_{\hat{\mathbf{X}}}(\hat{d}_{ij}) \right]_i^{\mathrm{T}} \left[\nabla_{\hat{\mathbf{X}}}^2(\hat{d}_{ij}) \right]_i \right), \tag{57}$$

$$\left[\nabla_{\hat{\mathbf{X}}}(\hat{d}_{ij}) \right]_{ij} = -\left[\nabla_{\hat{\mathbf{X}}}(\hat{d}_{ij}) \right]_{ii}, \tag{58}$$

and the second derivative of $s_{ij}(\hat{d}_{ij};\lambda)$, denoted by $s_{ij}''(\hat{d}_{ij};\lambda)$, is

$$s_{ij}''(\hat{d}_{ij};\lambda) = 2 + \frac{\sqrt{\pi}\,\bar{d}_{ij}}{\lambda} S_1(\hat{d}_{jj};\lambda) + \frac{\sqrt{\pi}\,\bar{d}_{ij}\hat{d}_{ij}}{\lambda^3}(S_2(\hat{d}_{ij};\lambda) - S_1(\hat{d}_{ij};\lambda)), \tag{59}$$

with

$$S_2(\hat{d}_i;\lambda) \triangleq e^{-\frac{\hat{d}_i^2}{\lambda^2}} \left(3\,_1F_1\left(\frac{5}{2};2;\frac{\hat{d}_i^2}{\lambda^2} \right) - \frac{15}{4}\,_1F_1\left(\frac{7}{2};3;\frac{\hat{d}_i^2}{\lambda^2} \right) \right). \tag{60}$$

In what follows, we provide an example of source localization problem in $\eta = 1$ dimension. Let $N_A = 2$ and $N_T = 1$. The anchors' and target coordinates are $\mathbf{a}_1 = 0.2$, $\mathbf{a}_2 = 0.5$ and $\mathbf{x} = 0.5$, respectively. We assume no noise, thus $\tilde{d}_i = d_i$. Invoking Theorem 3 we compute $\lambda^{(0)} = 0.3988$ such that $\langle s \rangle_\lambda(\hat{x})$ is convex. Next, we apply the L-GDC technique summarized in equation 46 where, invoking Theorem 2, we choose the set of λ's such that $\lambda^{(0)} = 0.3988$, $\lambda^{(L)} = 0$ and $\lambda^{(\ell)} = \lambda^{(\ell-1)} - 0.05$.

The light-gray lines shown shown in figure 8 indicate the smoothed function computed with the aforementioned set. At each iteration the level of smoothing is decreased and $\langle s \rangle_\lambda(\hat{x})$ approaches more and more $s(\hat{x})$.

The bold lines correspond, instead, to the smoothed function computed for the set of λ's {0.3988, 0.3420, 0.1706,0} using the Lemma 1. In this case, it is shown that $\langle s \rangle_\lambda(\hat{x})$ is recomputed only when a new concave region appears, thus we drastically reduce the computational efficiency of the L-GDC method while preserving optimal performance.

6. Simulation results

In this section, the performance of the non-parametric WLS-ML LT approach considered in this chapter will be evaluated using different optimization algorithms and adopting different weighing strategies. We will use the root-mean-square-error (RMSE) to measure the accuracy of the estimated positions $\hat{\mathbf{X}}$

$$\mathrm{RMSE} \triangleq \sqrt{\frac{1}{RP} \sum_{p=1}^{P} \sum_{r=1}^{R} \|\hat{\mathbf{X}}_{rp} - \mathbf{X}\|_2^2}, \tag{61}$$

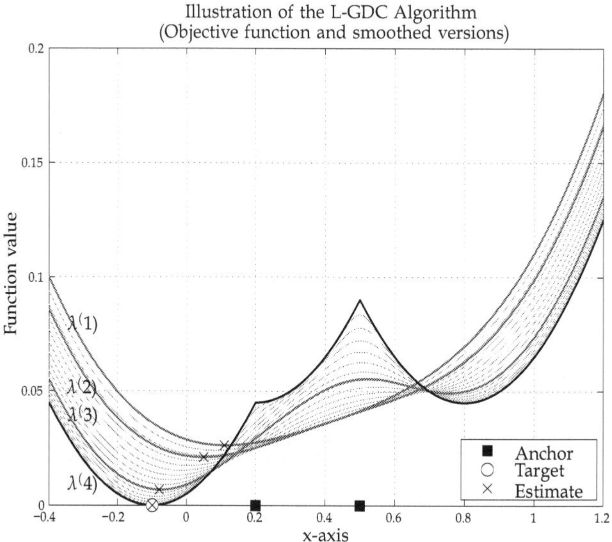

Fig. 8. Illustration of the L-GDC method and the smoothing process. Light-gray lines indicate smoothed versions of the objective functions obtained with a linear decreasing sequence of λ's. Bold lines indicate the smoothed objective with the optimized λ selection criteria.

where R and P are respectively, the number of realizations and networks considered.
For the purpose of comparison, we also benchmark the results to the Cramér-Rao lower bound (CRLB) derived in Jourdan et al. (2006) Patwari et al. (2003) and given by

$$\text{CRLB} \triangleq \text{tr}(\mathbf{F}^\dagger), \tag{62}$$

where $\mathbf{F}$ is the Fisher information matrix, that for $\eta = 2$ is equal to

$$\mathbf{F} \triangleq \begin{bmatrix} \mathbf{F}_{xx} & \mathbf{F}_{xy} \\ \mathbf{F}_{xy}^{T} & \mathbf{F}_{yy} \end{bmatrix}, \tag{63}$$

where

$$\left[\mathbf{F}_{xx}\right]_{jl} = \begin{cases} \displaystyle\sum_{e_j \in E} \frac{K_{il}}{\sigma_{il}^2} \frac{(x_l - x_i)^2}{d_{il}^2}, & j = l \\[4mm] -\dfrac{K_{il}}{\sigma_{il}^2} \dfrac{(x_l - x_j)^2}{d_{jl}^2}, & j \neq l \text{ and } e_{jl} \in E \end{cases} \tag{64}$$

$$\left[\mathbf{F}_{yy}\right]_{jl} = \begin{cases} \displaystyle\sum_{e_j \in E} \frac{K_{il}}{\sigma_{il}^2} \frac{(y_l - y_i)^2}{d_{il}^2}, & j = l \\[4mm] -\dfrac{K_{il}}{\sigma_{il}^2} \dfrac{(y_l - y_j)^2}{d_{jl}^2}, & j \neq l \text{ and } e_{jl} \in E \end{cases} \tag{65}$$

$$\left[\mathbf{F}_{xy}\right]_{jl} = \begin{cases} \displaystyle\sum_{e_j \in E} \frac{K_{il}}{\sigma_{il}^2} \frac{(x_l - x_i)(y_l - y_i)}{d_{il}^2}, & j = l \\[2ex] -\dfrac{K_{il}}{\sigma_{il}^2} \dfrac{(x_l - x_j)(y_l - y_j)}{d_{jl}^2}, & j \neq l \text{ and } e_{jl} \in E \end{cases} \tag{66}$$

where e_j indicates the set of links connected to the j-th node.

The first case-of-study is a network with $N_A = 4$ anchors and one target deployed in a square area of size $[-10,10] \times [-10,10]$. The target location is generated as a random variable with uniform distribution within the size of the square while anchors, are located at the locations $\mathbf{x}_1 = [-10,-10]$, $\mathbf{x}_2 = [10,-10]$, $\mathbf{x}_3 = [10,10]$ and $\mathbf{x}_4 = [-10,10]$. We assume that all nodes are connected and the distance of each link is measured K_{ij} times, with $K_{ij} \in [2,7]$. We use the ranging model given in equation 2 to generate distance measurements, and we consider $\sigma_{ij} \in (1e\text{-}4, \sigma_{max})$.

In figure 9, we show the RMSE obtained with different localization algorithms and unitary weight (unweighted strategy). In this particular study, all algorithms have very similar performance, and the reason is due to the convexity property of the WLS-ML objective function. Indeed, if the target is inside the convex-hull formed by the anchors and the noise is not sufficiently large, then the objective function in typically convex. However, all algorithms do not attain the CRLB because, under the assumption that σ_{ij}'s are all different, the unitary weight is not optimal.

In figure 10 we show the RMSE obtained with the L-GDC algorithm using different weighing strategy, namely, the optimal, the unweighted, the exponential and the dispersion weighing strategy given in equations 12, 14, 17, and 20, respectively. The results show that the L-GDC algorithm using w_{ij}^* is able to achieve the CRLB, whereas the others stay above.

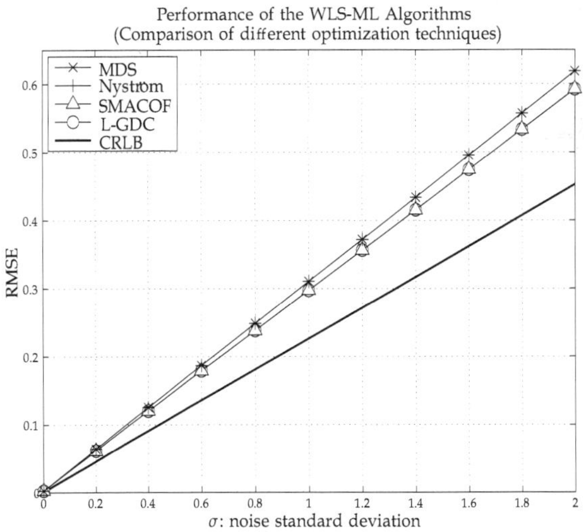

Fig. 9. Comparison of different optimization techniques and using binary weight (unweighted strategy) for a localization problem with $N_A = 4$, $N_T = 1$, $K_{min} = 2$, $K_{max} = 7$, $\sigma_{max} = 1$ and $\sigma_{min} = 1e\text{-}4$.

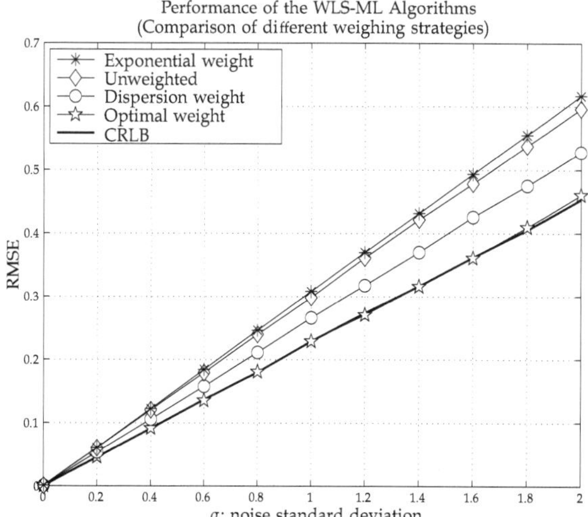

Fig. 10. Comparison of different weighing strategies and using L-GDC optimization method for a localization problem with $N_A = 4$, $N_T = 1$, $K_{min} = 2$, $K_{max} = 7$, $\sigma_{max} = 1$ and $\sigma_{min} = $ 1e-4.

However, to use the optimal weighing strategy we assumed that σ_{ij}'s are known a priori. Therefore, if we reconsider the LT problem under the assumption that the noise statistics are unknown, then the proposed dispersion weight provides the best performance. Indeed, using w_{ij}^L we are able to rip $\approx 50\%$ of gain from the unweighted and exponential strategies towards the CRLB.

In the second case-of-study, we consider instead a network with $N_A = 4$ anchors and $N_T = 10$ targets. As before, anchors are located at the corners of a square area while targets are randomly distributed. For this type of simulations, we evaluate the performance of the WLSML algorithms as functions of the *meshness ratio* defined as

$$m \triangleq \frac{(|E| - N + 1)}{(|E_F| - N + 1)}, \tag{67}$$

where E_F indicates the set of links of the fully connected network and $|\cdot|$ indicates the cardinal number of a set Adams & Franzosa (2008)Destino & De Abreu (2009).

This metric is commonly used in algebraic topology and Graph theory to capture, in one number, information on the planarity of a Graph. For example, under the constraint of a connected network, $m = 0$ results from $|E| = N - 1$, which implies that the network is reduced to a tree. In contrast, $m = 1$ results from $|E| = |E_F|$, which implies that the network is not planar, except for the trivial cases of $N \leq 4$. More importantly, the mesheness ratio is an indicator of the connectivity of the network, in a way that is more relevant to its localizability than the simpler connectivity ratio $|E| / |E_F|$.

In figures 11 and 12, the results confirm that the L-GDC is the best optimization technique and, the dispersion weight is the best performing weighing strategy. Similarly to the first case-of-study, also in this case the WLS-ML method based on L-GDC and using the dispersion weights rips about 50% of the error from the alternatives towards the CRLB. Furthermore, from the results shown in figure 11, the L-GDC algorithm is the only one to maintain an almost constant gap from the CRLB within the entire range of meshness ratio. This let us infer that the L-GDC algorithm finds the global optimum of the WLS-ML function with high probability, while SMACOF of the algebraic methods find sub-optimal solutions.

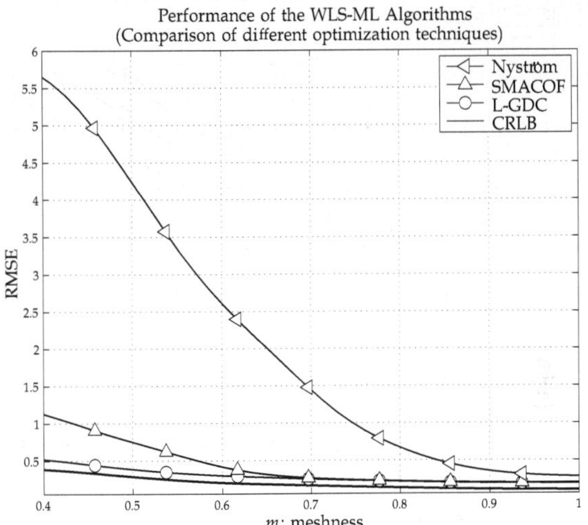

Fig. 11. Comparison of different optimization techniques and using binary weight (unweighted strategy) for a localization problem with $N_A = 4$, $N_T = 10$, $K_{min} = 2$, $K_{max} = 7$, $\sigma_{max} = 1$ and $\sigma_{min} = $ 1e-4.

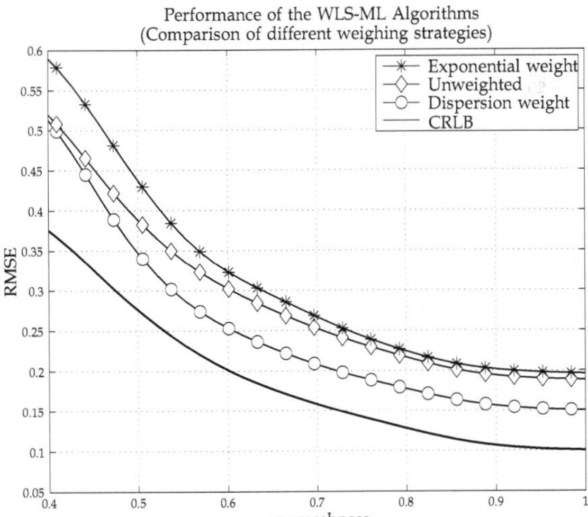

Fig. 12. Comparison of different weighing strategies and using L-GDC optimization method for a localization problem with $N_A = 4$, $N_T = 10$, $K_{min} = 2$, $K_{max} = 7$, $\sigma_{max} = 1$ and $\sigma_{min} = $ 1e-4.

The third and final case-of-study, is the tracking scenario. The network consists of 4 anchor nodes placed at the corner of a square in a $\eta = 2$ dimensional space with 1 targets that moves following an autoregressive model of order 1 within space defined by the anchors. It is assumed full anchor-to-anchor and anchor-to-target connectivity and measurements are perturbed by zero-mean Gaussian noise.

We use the L-GDC optimization method to perform successive re-localization of the target and we employ different weighing strategies. The result shown in figure 14 illustrates the performance of the WLS-ML algorithm as a function of σ considering a velocity $v = 1$.

Since the tracking is treated as a mere re-localization, the dynamics only affect the output of the filter block and it is seen from the localization algorithm as an additive noise.

For this reason, the trend of the RMSE is similar to that one obtained in a static scenario. From figure 14 the impact of the velocity on the performance of the WLS-ML algorithm with wavelet-based filter is revealed more clearly. The effect of velocity, indeed, is yet similar to a gaussian noise.

Finally, from both results we observe that the dispersion weight is the best weighing strategy.

7. Conclusions and future work

In this chapter we considered the LT problem in mesh network topologies under LOS conditions. After a general description of the system we focused on a wavelet based filter to smooth the observations and a centralized optimization technique to solve the WLS-ML localization problem. The proposed algorithm was compared with state-of-the-art solutions and it was shown that by combining the wavelet-based filter together with the dispersion weighing strategy and the L-GDC algorithm it is possible to get close to the CRLB.

The work described in this chapter did not address the problem of NLOS channel conditions which needs to be taken into consideration in most of the real life applications. To cope with the biases introduced by NLOS condition two main strategies can be distinguished. In the

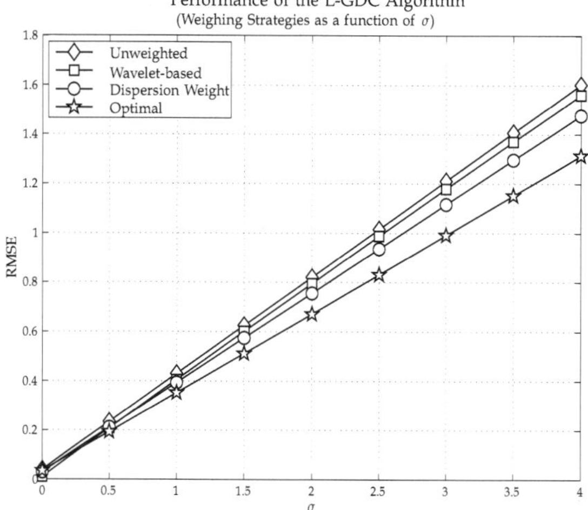

Fig. 13. Performance for the L-GDC algorithm for the different weighing strategies. Scenario measurements at the 4 anchor nodes subject to normal noise process with standard deviation between 0 and σ.

capabilities. It comprises of more than 150 cGPS stations across New Zealand. All seismic and GPS data are transmitted continuously to two data centers using radio, land-based or VSAT systems employing Internet Protocol data transfer techniques.

The Sumatran continuous-Global Positioning System Array (SuGAr) is located along Sumatra, Indonesia. As at the end of 2009, it consists of 32 operational GPS stations spanning 1400 km from north to south of Sumatra (Fig. 1). Stations are located either in remote islands or in rural areas near the tectonic place boundary which is one of the most active plates in the world. Due to the lack of local data communication network infrastructure, satellite telemetry is the only means of communicating with the GPS stations. All of the stations are equipped with a scientific-grade GPS receiver, a GPS antenna, a satellite modem, solar panels and batteries.

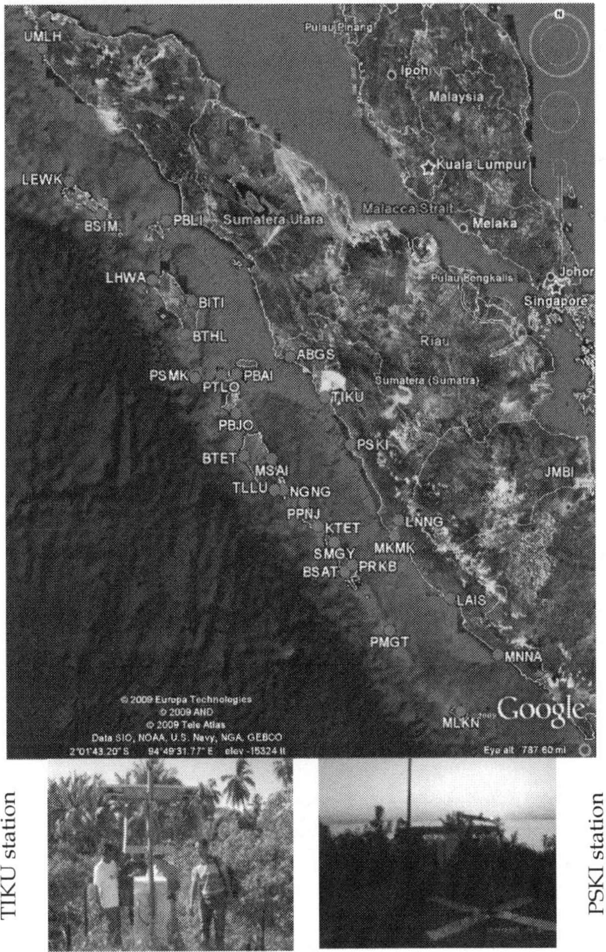

Fig. 1. Geographical distribution of the SuGAr stations

4. Utilisation of mesh networking

Mesh networking is proposed in this chapter to reduce the number of satellite links and bandwidth requirement for transmission of GPS data. To analyze the optimization achieved by the use of mesh networking on the SuGAr network, evaluation was performed using the archived SuGAr observation data from the last two months (61 days) of 2007. Only 24 stations were taken into account in this case study, as only 24 GPS stations were able to provide the complete GPS dataset for this entire period. This experiment data set can be accessed from the SOPAC website (http://sopac.ucsd.edu/).

Several assumptions were made for the evaluations presented in this study as follows:

- All GPS stations have enough energy to deal with the overheads cause by the additional communication equipments and data computation required. This assumption can be satisfied by adding more batteries and solar panels to the existing nodes.
- To simplify the analysis, the terrain information between the GPS stations was not taken into consideration in this analysis. In practice, construction of tall antenna towers as well as the use of multi-hop relays/repeaters can be used to overcome obstructions if required.
- The transmission overheads for the long range radios, such as packet formatting and control protocols, were not included in the evaluation as they will not have an impact on the analysis presented in this study.

The two main performance attributes of interest in this study are the reduction of the number of satellite links as well as the total amount of data transmitted via these links.

4.1 Removal of co-related data and reduction of uplink requirements

Mesh networking and clustering can be used to reduce the number of satellite links required for data telemetry between the GPS stations and the remote server. Wireless mesh networks can be established using long-range radios such as those developed by companies like FreeWave or Intuicom. These radios provide a point-to-point line-of-sight (LoS) wireless communication link with a maximum range of more than 96 kilometres (60 miles) and a maximum over-the-air throughput of 154 Kbps. For communication links over a longer distance, multi-hop communications can be utilized by deploying relay stations. The use of relay stations may also overcome LoS obstructions between GPS stations as well as provide for extended mesh networking capabilities such as redundancy. Depending on the cost, geographical, power or latency considerations, the number of hops and the radio range supported may be limited. In this case, clusters of GPS stations will be formed and a cluster-head would be selected for each cluster. Each cluster-head will have satellite communication capabilities and will be responsible for collecting all the observation data from the GPS stations within the cluster and transmitting them to the remote centralized data server. This greatly reduces the number of satellite links needed, as each cluster requires a minimum of only one satellite link. The various possible mesh network setups using the current geographical locations of the GPS station in the SuGAr array will also be presented.

In this study, each GPS station can be equipped with one or more long-range radios such as the FreeWave FGR-115RE. These radios specify a maximum range of over 90 km and can be used to form peer-to-peer wireless mesh networks between GPS stations. Assuming the maximum range of 90 km, the absence of relay stations or repeaters and the geographical locations of the 24 GPS stations, Fig.2 shows the network topology of GPS stations that will be formed using the FreeWave radios. It will contain one cluster with eight nodes, one cluster with three nodes, two clusters with two nodes, and nine clusters with one node. Assuming that only one satellite uplink is required for each cluster, 13 satellite links will have to be maintained.

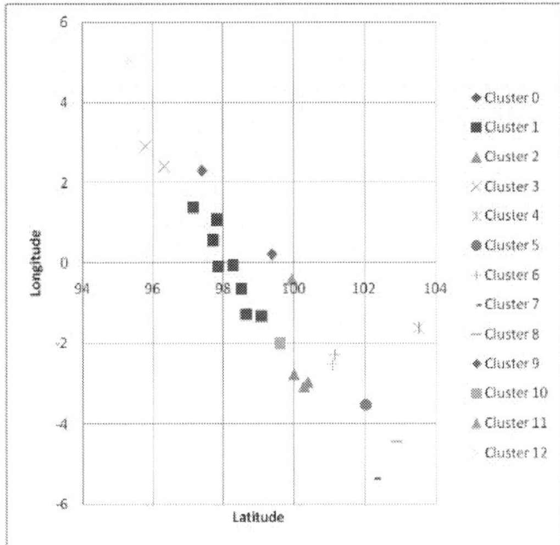

Fig. 2. Clusters of GPS station using 90 kilometer radio range

The range of the radio can be extended through the use of relay stations or repeaters. Thus, using the geographical locations of the 24 GPS stations, the minimum number of uplinks required and cluster size across various radio ranges can be determined. Fig. 3 shows the number of uplinks required for the various ranges. From the figure, it can be seen that given a maximum radio range of 20 km, only two GPS stations can be linked together and all other GPS stations were out of range from each other. Therefore, 23 satellite uplinks were required in this case. However, given a maximum radio range of 250 km, all GPS stations were grouped into one cluster using only one uplink.

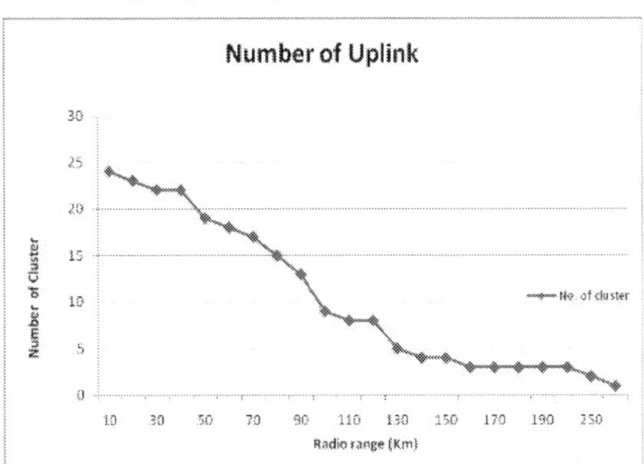

Fig. 3. Number of satellite uplinks required across various radio ranges

Fig. 4 provides the graph showing the average and the maximum number of GPS stations in a cluster across a radio range from 10 km to 250 km. As the number of GPS stations in a cluster increases, the data aggregated at the cluster-head will also increase in size. This will lead to better compression ratio at the cluster-heads and this phenomenal will be presented in more detail in the later part of this secion.

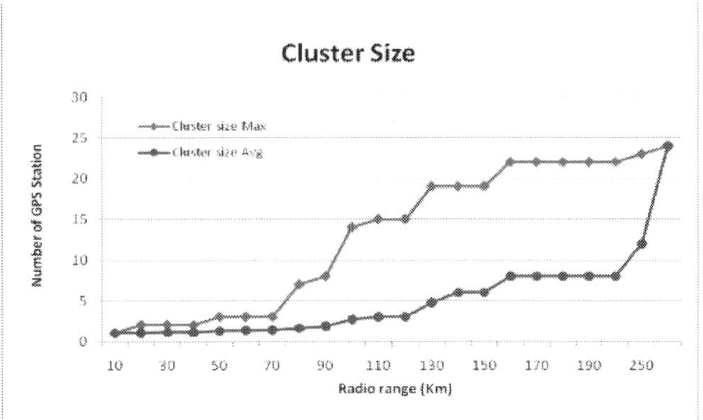

Fig. 4. Cluster sizes characteristics based on the various radio ranges

4.2 Collaborative compression of data

Cluster-based compression at the cluster-heads will be introduced where each cluster-head will compress the observation data from all GPS stations within the cluster using the LZMA (Ziv & Lempel, 1977) algorithm prior to transmission via the satellite link. Compared to the existing SuGAr deployment where each GPS station transmits the observation data independently, the use of mesh networking allows larger datasets to be formed through the aggregation of observation data from each GPS station within the cluster. Given that the compression ratio generally increases in proportion to the size of the dataset to be compressed, the number of bytes transmitted via the satellite will be significantly reduced.

Currently, the SuGAr sends collected data daily through dedicated satellite links from each GPS station. For this analysis, the GPS measurements will be converted locally to CRINEX format at each GPS station. Fig. 5 shows the total number of data bytes transmitted via all the satellite links using three different setups as follows:

- **Setup 1**: For the first setup, CRINEX data was uploaded via dedicated satellite links from each GPS stations without further compression.
- **Setup 2**: For the second setup, the CRINEX data was compressed using the LZMA algorithm prior to transmitting via dedicated satellite links at each GPS station.
- **Setup 3**: For the third and final setup, clusters of GPS stations were formed using long range radios with various maximum transmission ranges. In each cluster, one GPS station will be designated as the cluster-head and all other stations will forward their CRINEX data to the cluster-head. The cluster-head will perform further compression using LZMA algorithm on the aggregated data as a whole prior to transmitting the compressed data to the data server via a satellite link.

From Fig. 5, it can be seen that for Setup 2, the total number of bytes transmitted via all the satellite links over a 61 days period were reduced by about 67% when compared to Setup 1.

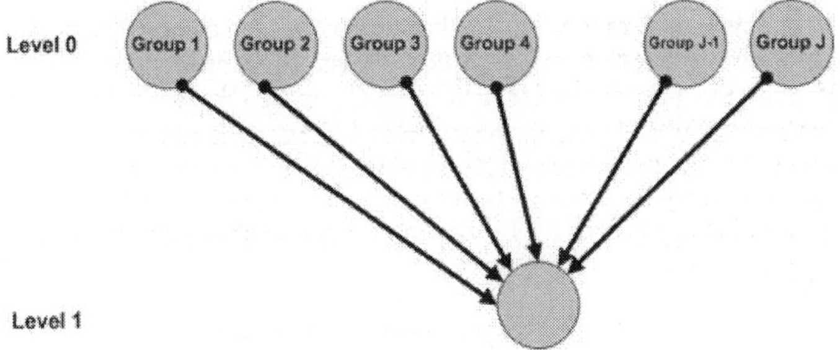

Fig. 8. One level parallel processing

groups is ζR. For simplicity, suppose the number of common measurement proportional to ζ is given by ζm and the remaining measurements are equally divided between groups, $(1-\zeta)m/J$, for each group. The number of parameters and measurements at level zero for each group is thus derived as

$$n_{0,i} = \kappa n + \frac{(1-\kappa)n}{J} \quad and \quad m_{0,i} = \zeta m + \frac{(1-\zeta)m}{J} \tag{6}$$

Arithmetic operations required are proportional to $n_{0,i}^2 m_{0,i}$, thus from equation (5)

$$B_{0,i} \propto \left(\frac{(1+(J-1)\kappa)n}{J}\right)^2 \frac{(1+(J-1)\zeta)m}{J} \tag{7}$$

in which $B_{0,i}$ is the number of arithmetic operations required at any group i $(1 \leq i \leq J)$ at level zero. There are J groups in this level with the same number of arithmetic operations so the total number of operations is equal to J multiplied by the number of operation of one representative group $B_{0,1}$. Hence, the total number of arithmetic operations at level zero is equal to

$$B_0 = \sum_{i=1}^{J} B_{0,i} = J * B_{0,1} \tag{8}$$

Finally, the parameter estimation processing at level 1 is the refinement of J group at level zero. It includes n parameters and the number of measurement equaling to the total number of estimated parameter of J groups at level zero. Using equation (5), the computation burden is derived as

$$B_1 \propto n^2 \sum_{i=1}^{J} n_{0,i} = n^2 \left(1+(J-1)\kappa\right)n \tag{9}$$

Thus, the total number of operations B is equal to the sum of all computation burdens at level zero and level one as follows,

$$B = B_0 + B_1 \propto n^2(1+(J-1)\kappa)(\frac{(1+(J-1)\kappa)(1+(J-1)\zeta)m}{J^2}+n) \tag{10}$$

The computation reduction percentage χ is equal to number of operations divide by the number of operation n^2m required for simultaneous parameter evaluation.

$$\chi = \frac{B}{n^2 m} \quad \propto \quad (1+(J-1)\kappa)(\frac{(1+(J-1)\kappa)(1+(J-1)\zeta)}{J^2} + \frac{n}{m}) \tag{11}$$

The value of χ approaches unity when ζ and κ approaches 1 assuming n/m is small. Therefore, if all the parameters and receivers are common between groups, parallel processing is ineffective.

This method is applied for the Sumatra continuous GPS (cGPS) array (Tran & Wong, 2009) and the results are evaluated for two different configurations using the parameters X = 24, $\Omega/4\pi$ = 0.25, Δ = 24h, σ = 2 min, d = 2, a = 29, b = 10, c = 5. For the first configuration, the number of receivers R equal to 40 which include 32 GPS stations of Sumatra cGPS array and 8 International GNSS Service (IGS) reference stations. In the second configuration, only 32 Sumatra cGPS stations were used without reference stations.

In the first configuration, we have ζ equal to the number of reference stations divide by the total number of stations, thus, $\zeta=8/40=0.2$. The number of common parameters equal to the sum of the parameters of the common reference stations, the transmitter parameters and the polar motion. This can be calculated using equation (12), so $\kappa \approx 0.34$.

$$\kappa n = a\zeta R + bX + c \tag{12}$$

In the second configuration, the number of common reference stations, ζ, is equal to zero and so, using equation (12), $\kappa \approx 0.17$.

The computation reduction with respect to the different groups is presented in Fig. 9. In the case where reference stations were utilized, the maximum reduction reached 57% when receivers were divided into 5 groups. It decreases when the number of group increased due to the overheads of the reference station when using more groups. In the case where no reference stations were used, the maximum reduction reaches 91.6% when receivers where divided into 16 groups with 2 receivers per groups.

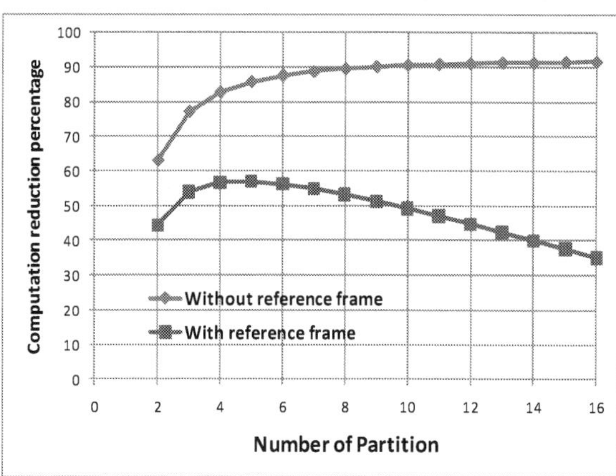

Fig. 9. Computation reduction for the Sumatra cGPS array using one level parallel processing

b.   Multilayer parallelism

For generalization, the multilayer parallel is studied with L layer and each layer includes power of p groups. It denotes that there are p power of L groups at level zero and each group at level j (1≤j≤L) receives data from p groups at the adjacent predecessor level j-1. For instance, p equals to two in Fig. 10.

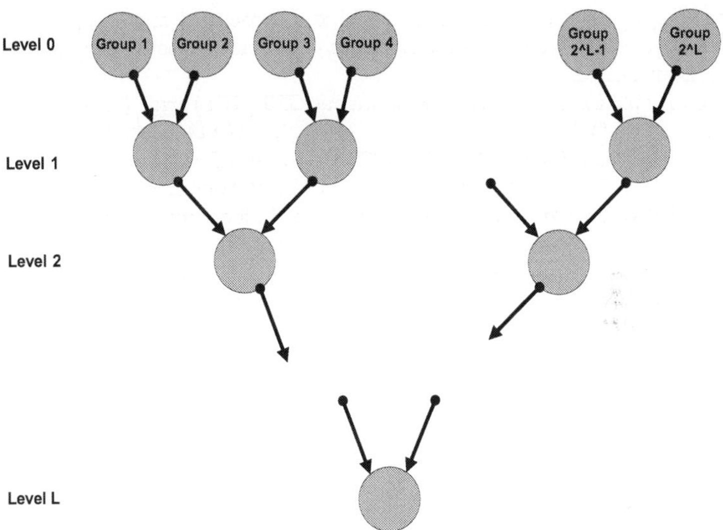

Fig. 10. Multilayer parallel processing with L layer with power of 2 groups. The processing tree will contain 2^L groups at level 0 and each group at level j (0<j≤L) is the combination of 2 node at level j – 1.

With the same assumption of common parameters and measurements with the one layer parallel method mentioned previously, the number of parameters is equal to the sum of the common parameters and private parameters of each group of receivers and number of measurements are equal to sum of the common measurements from common receivers and private measurements from the private receivers.

$$n_{0,i} = \kappa n + \frac{(1 - \kappa)n}{p^{L}} \quad and \quad m_{0,i} = \zeta m + \frac{(1 - \zeta)m}{p^{L}} \tag{13}$$

Therefore, the number of arithmetic operations of group i at level zero is

$$B_{0,i} \propto n_{0,i}^{2} m_{0,i} = (\kappa n + \frac{(1 - \kappa)n}{p^{L}})^{2}(\zeta m + \frac{(1 - \zeta)m}{p^{L}}) \tag{14}$$

So, the total computation burden for level zero which include p^{L} group equals to

$$B_{0} = \sum_{i=1}^{p^{L}} B_{0,i} \tag{15}$$

Furthermore, the computation burden for each group i at level j ($1\leq j \leq L$) is proportional to $n_{j,i}^2 m_{j,i}$, in which the number of parameter $n_{j,i}$ is equal to the sum of common parameters κn and the private parameters of p ancestor group at level j-1, each of which comprise of $\left((1-\kappa)n * p^{j-1}\right)/p^L$ private parameters. Therefore,

$$n_{j,i} = \kappa n + \frac{(1-\kappa)n}{p^L}p^j \tag{16}$$

In addition, the number of measurements at level j is equal to the summation of all estimated parameters of p ancestor at level j-1,

$$m_{j,i} = p(\kappa n + \frac{(1-\kappa)n}{p^L}p^{j-1}) = p\kappa n + \frac{(1-\kappa)n}{p^L}p^i \tag{17}$$

Therefore, the computation burden of each group i at level j equals to

$$B_{j,i} \propto (\kappa n + \frac{(1-\kappa)n}{p^L}p^j)^2(p\kappa n + \frac{(1-\kappa)n}{p^L}p^j) \tag{18}$$

The total computation burden for level j which include p^{L-j} groups is then derived as

$$B_j = \sum_{i=1}^{p^{L-j}} B_{j,i} \propto (\kappa n + \frac{(1-\kappa)n}{p^L}p^j)^2(p\kappa n + \frac{(1-\kappa)n}{p^L}p^j)p^{L-j} \tag{19}$$

The total computation burden of multiple parallel processing is equal to summation of computation of all level from level 0 to L as follows:

$$B = \sum_{j=1}^{L} B_j + B_0 \propto \sum_{j=1}^{L}(\kappa n + \frac{(1-\kappa)n}{p^L}p^j)^2(p\kappa n + \frac{(1-\kappa)n}{p^L}p^j)p^{L-j} +$$
$$(\frac{(1-\kappa)n}{p^L} + \kappa n)^2(1 + (p^L - 1)\varsigma)m \tag{20}$$

c.   Computation time

Assuming that the computation time is the dominant latency between processing groups at adjacent layer, the processing time of parallel GPS processing, in the worst case, is calculated by the summation of the maximum computation time at each layer at the critical computation path. The critical path for one layer and multilayer parallel processes is given in Fig. 11 and Fig. 12 respectively.

The computation time C is equal to number of arithmetic operation multiply by c, the computation time for each arithmetic operation. The equation for one layer and multilayer are therefore derived as follow:

$$C_{onelayer} = \left(n^2\left(1 + (J-1)\kappa\right)n + \left(\frac{(1+(J-1)\kappa)n}{J}\right)^2\frac{(1+(J-1)\varsigma)m}{J}\right) * c \tag{21}$$

5. Conclusion

A study using mesh networking for tectonic monitoring was presented. Mesh networks can be established between the GPS stations by means of long-range radios and data aggregation was performed to enable cluster-based compression. Using the actual data captured from the Sumatran cGPS array (SuGAr) in the evaluation and analysis, it was concluded that the proposed use of mesh networking not only reduces the number of costly satellite uplinks required, it also significantly reduces the total amount of data transferred through these links. Moreover, by making use of mesh networks between the GPS stations, parallel, distributed and hierarchical GPS processing methods can be made possible. By reducing the computation complexity, this proposed computational model allows the possible use of the spare computational power within the cGPS network such as from the routers and station controllers using the wireless mesh network connections between stations to transmit GPS data and perform collaborative GPS processing in a real-time fashion.

6. References

Ammon, C. J., Ji, C., Thio, H.-K., Robinson, D., Ni, S., Hjorleifsdottir, V., et al. (2005). Rupture Process of the 2004 Sumatra-Andaman Earthquake. Science, 308(5725), 1133-1139. doi: 10.1126/science.1112260

Gurtner, W., & Mader, G. (1990). Receiver Independent Exchange Format Version 2. GPS Bulletin, 3(3), 1-8.

Hatanaka, Y. (1996, 17-20 September). A RINEX Compression Format and Tools. Paper presented at the Proceedings of ION GPS-96.

Hudnut, K. W., Bock, Y., Galetzka, J. E., Webb, F. H., & W. H. Young. (2001). The Southern California Integrated GPS Network (SCIGN). 10th International Symposium on Crustal Deformation Measurement, 129-148.

Konca, A. O., Avouac, J.-P., Sladen, A., Meltzner, A. J., Sieh, K., Fang, P., et al. (2008). Partial rupture of a locked patch of the Sumatra megathrust during the 2007 earthquake sequence. [10.1038/nature07572]. Nature, 456(7222), 631-635. doi: http://www.nature.com/nature/journal/v456/n7222/suppinfo/nature07572_S1.html

Lay, T., Kanamori, H., Ammon, C. J., Nettles, M., Ward, S. N., Aster, R. C., et al. (2005). The Great Sumatra-Andaman Earthquake of 26 December 2004. Science, 308(5725), 1127-1133. doi: 10.1126/science.1112250

Miyazaki, S.-i. (1999). Construction of GSI's Nationwide GPS Array. Proceedings of the Joint Meeting of the U.S.-Japan Cooperative Program in Natural Resources Panel on Wind and Seismic Effects, 31, 518-528.

Patterson, N., Gledhill, K., & Chadwick, M. (2007). New Zealand National Seismograph Network Report for the Federation of Digital Seismograph Networks Meeting, 2007. Perugia, Italy: 2007 FDSN Meeting.

Segall, P., & Davis, J. L. (1997). GPS applications for geodynamics and earthquake studies. Annual Review of Earth and Planetary Sciences, 25, 301-336. doi: 10.1146/annurev.earth.25.1.301

Serpelloni, E., Casula, G., Galvani, A., Anzidei, M., & Baldi, P. (2006). Data analysis of permanent GPS networks in Italy and surrounding regions: application of a distributed processing approach. [Article]. Annals of Geophysics, 49(4-5), 897-928.

Sieh, K., Natawidjaja, D. H., Meltzner, A. J., Shen, C.-C., Cheng, H., Li, K.-S., et al. (2008). Earthquake Supercycles Inferred from Sea-Level Changes Recorded in the Corals of West Sumatra. Science, 322(5908), 1674-1678. doi: 10.1126/science.1163589

Tran, H.-H., & Wong, K.-J. (2009). Mesh Networking for Seismic Monitoring - The Sumatran cGPS Array Case Study. Paper presented at the Wireless Communications and Networking Conference, 2009. WCNC 2009. IEEE.

Yamagiwa, A., Hatanaka, Y., Yutsudo, T., & Miyahara, B. (2006). Real-time capability of GEONET system and its application to crust monitoring. Bulletin of the Geographical Survey Institute, 53.

Ziv, J., & Lempel, A. (1977). A Universal Algorithm for Sequential Data Compression. IEEE Transactions on Information Theory, 23(3), 337 - 343.

Zumberge, J., Heflin, M., Jefferson, D., Watkins, M., & Webb, F. (1997). Precise point positioning for the efficient and robust analysis of GPS data from large networks. J. Geophys. Res., 102(B3), 5005-5017.

Notations

R	number of receiver (GPS station)
X	number of transmitter (satellite)
n	total number of parameter have to estimate
m	total number of measurement
κ	share parameters percentage between groups
ζ	share measurement percentage between groups
B	computation burden
J	number of computation group
L	number of processing level
p	in multiple level processing method, group at level i receive data from p group at level i-1
$n_{j,i}$	number of parameter at level j and group i have to estimate
$m_{j,i}$	number of measurement at level j and group i
$B_{j,i}$	computation burden at group i of level j
B_j	total computation burden at level j

Bergano, E., Casola, G., Calleary, A., Ataidat, M., & Daint, F. (2002). Data analysis of permanent GPS networks in Italy and surrounding regions: application of a distributed processing approach. Annals of Geophysics, [illegible].

Shih, D. H., [illegible], Hsiao, [illegible], Chen, C.-S., Cheng, [illegible]. Particle Swarm [illegible] Influence in Market-Level Computers and [illegible]. [illegible]

Treddish & Wong, [illegible]. [illegible] Supporting a Remote Monitoring Physiol. [illegible] from [illegible] Area Network Wireless Cardiovascular and [illegible]. [illegible], IEEE.

Simpson, [illegible], & de Werd, [illegible], Da [illegible], E. (2008). Real time control of [illegible] sensor network for [illegible]. [illegible]

[illegible] (2008). [illegible] IEEE [illegible].